NATIONAL SECURITY CONSTITUTIONALISM IN THE COMMONWEALTH FIVE EYES STATES

This book examines the constitutional treatment of national security in the UK, Canada, Australia, and New Zealand.

These four states share their Commonwealth heritage and are members, alongside the USA, of the Five Eyes intelligence-sharing alliance. The book takes a comparative approach to the institutions through which, and tools with which, these four states seek to protect their national security against the threats of both terrorism and hostile state activity and how they have evolved over time. It identifies and examines the various specialised institutions, inside and outside of legislatures, which have grown up to oversee the exercise of public power for national security purposes while maintaining the required secrecy. It argues that the extent of the borrowing and sharing between these jurisdictions in the domain of national security, now and in the past, permits us to talk about a Commonwealth model of national security constitutionalism.

Volume 9 in Hart Studies in Security and Justice

Hart Studies in Security and Justice
Series editors: Liora Lazarus, Ben Saul and Natasa Mavronicola

This series pioneers the study of security and justice, whose controversial relationship has taken on particular urgency since the 'war on terror', and related phenomena such as targeted killing, preventive pre-trial detention and mass surveillance. It seeks to include all legal methods and approaches, cutting across traditional subjects such as constitutional and public law, human rights law, terrorism law, legal and political theory, international law and political science.

Recent titles in this series:

Surveillance, Privacy and Trans-Atlantic Relations
Edited by David Cole, Federico Fabbrini and Stephen Schulhofer

Parliament's Secret War
Veronika Fikfak and Hayley J Hooper

Permanent States of Emergency and the Rule of Law
Alan Greene

The National Security Constitution
Paul F Scott

The Constitutional Structure of Europe's Area of 'Freedom, Security and Justice' and the Right to Justification
Ester Herlin-Karnell

Security and Human Rights
Benjamin Goold and Liora Lazarus

Coercive Human Rights: Positive Duties to Mobilise the Criminal Law under the ECHR
Edited by Laurens Lavrysen and Natasa Mavronicola

The Offences Against the State Act 1939 at 80: A Model Counter-Terrorism Act?
Edited by Mark Coen

National Security Constitutionalism in the Commonwealth Five Eyes States

Paul F Scott

•HART•
OXFORD • LONDON • NEW YORK • NEW DELHI • SYDNEY

HART PUBLISHING

Bloomsbury Publishing Plc

Kemp House, Chawley Park, Cumnor Hill, Oxford, OX2 9PH, UK

1385 Broadway, New York, NY 10018, USA

29 Earlsfort Terrace, Dublin 2, Ireland

HART PUBLISHING, the Hart/Stag logo, BLOOMSBURY and the Diana logo are trademarks of Bloomsbury Publishing Plc

First published in Great Britain 2025

A catalogue record for this book is available from the British Library.

A catalogue record for this book is available from the Library of Congress.

Library of Congress Control Number: 2024946859

ISBN: HB: 978-1-50997-194-7
ePDF: 978-1-50997-196-1
ePub: 978-1-50997-195-4

Typeset by Compuscript Ltd, Shannon

ACKNOWLEDGEMENTS

This book was completed during a period of research leave from the University of Glasgow. Mark Bennett, Bernard Keenan, Daniella Lock, Micheál Ó Floinn and Alex Schwartz read and commented on one or more chapters: I am very grateful for their help and assistance, though any errors that remain are of course my own responsibility. Most of the thanks, however, go (as always) to Marta.

I have attempted to take account of developments up until the end of May 2024, though the scale and speed of change in this area of law has made that task difficult.

CONTENTS

Introduction

I. The Book and its Argument

All states seek to protect their (national) security, and their attempts to do so raise distinctive and important issues for scholars of constitutions. First, national security is considered to be amongst the highest goods the state might pursue – if not simply the highest – and so its pursuit justifies extraordinary capabilities, which might involve very significant interference with the liberties of the citizens of that state itself and, in particular, those of foreign states. Second, national security is a good that must be protected, at least in extremis, against threats emanating from anywhere and everywhere, and so states must be alert and responsive to the acts of people and bodies across the globe, and able and willing to act decisively outside of their own boundaries and those of their own legal jurisdiction. Third, and perhaps most significantly, much of what states and their agents do on this basis must take place in secret if it is not to be immediately futile, with obvious and important implications both for the ability of the press and public to become aware of their work, and their failings, as well as for the danger that their capabilities might come to be abused. As a result, the ordinary methods of scrutiny and accountability that operate within modern constitutional democracies will often prove to be inadequate in the domain of national security, and so must be supplemented or substituted with others that are adapted to that context. Against that background, this book considers the question of how four jurisdictions – Australia, Canada, New Zealand and the United Kingdom (UK) – linked, as we shall discuss below, by a number of important factors, seek to protect their national security, and the key constitutional issues that arise out of that pursuit.

The argument of the book is that there has emerged a model of national security constitutionalism that takes in the four Commonwealth states which are members of the 'Five Eyes' alliance. As those states set about constitutionalising the national security endeavour – granting to their security and intelligence agencies a clear legal basis and implementing processes and institutions to guard against the possibility that they might abuse their vast powers – they frequently borrowed from each other: borrowed rules, borrowed powers, borrowed the design of institutions, and sometimes borrowed even specific statutory language. That process has accelerated over time: in fact, it is self-reinforcing, as the constitutionalisation of national security in each jurisdiction, and the resulting mass of official and unofficial material discussing the relevant rules and practices, facilitates further such borrowing. In the contemporary world such borrowing has become the norm. Any reform within the domain of national security constitutionalism in one of the four Commonwealth Five Eyes states will usually now include and perhaps even begin from a consideration of how the relevant matter is handled in the other three jurisdictions. The reforming state will come under pressure to adopt the model considered most advanced, whether in terms of subjecting those security and intelligence agencies to fuller limitations or providing the most expansive or most demanding oversight of their activities. Declining to do so will therefore often require clear and specific justification, and will be criticised specifically by reference to the position in the other Commonwealth Five Eyes states. Increasingly often, then, individual states will simply choose to fall in line, knowing that it will be easier to resist criticism if they have adopted the model that prevails in their three counterparts. The result is that though there remains very significant divergence between the states, mostly as a result of historical and political contingencies that will likely never be overcome, there is an increasing convergence between them – one which goes far beyond what the shared underlying constitutional model and the specific functional logic of national security, alone or in combination, might compel. They therefore represent a distinctive and largely now self-contained ecosystem in which borrowing and sharing of innovations in the field of national security constitutionalism has become completely standard. The model that emerges from consideration thereof I call 'Commonwealth national security constitutionalism'.

The scope of the present work is therefore defined by a number of factors, which I will consider in turn in this introduction. Though each of these steps reflects an exercise of discretion that might be contested, it is hoped that what emerges is a coherent object of study, and a book that makes a useful contribution, as we shall consider in chapter 1, to the growing study of comparative constitutional law and comparative constitutionalism, by expanding it to an area of law and policy that has so far largely escaped its attention.

II. Constitutionalism

The concept of constitutionalism as a concept has been subject to an increasingly critical treatment in recent years, in response to what some take to be its imperialistic tendencies, or an unduly uncritical approach – verging, perhaps, on reverence – to the concept amongst public lawyers and (sections of) the political class. The truth or falsity of any claim about constitutionalism of course depends on the substance of its referent, with the term used in a range of different ways by different actors. Martin Loughlin, in a striking recent rejection of constitutionalism, paints it as an exceptionally thick idea, a 'discrete concept expressing a specific philosophy of governing,' which 'should not be conflated with more general themes revolving around constitutional government or constitutional democracy' because it involves not only a constitution, which establishes a 'system of fundamental law supervised by a judiciary charged with elaborating the requirements of public reason', but also various other assumptions about the role and status of a constitution: that it creates, most notably, a 'permanent governing framework' the content of which reflects a felt need 'to divide, channel, and constrain governmental powers for the purpose of safeguarding individual liberty' and assumes, via the judicial enforcement of fundamental norms, 'its true status as the authoritative expression of the regime's collective political identity'.[1]

Others take constitutionalism to refer to just one or two of the multiple aspects of the thick philosophy of governing that Loughlin identifies under the name of constitutionalism: in particular, the existence, within a given legal order, of higher-order rules against which the product of the 'ordinary' legislative process must be judged (and which, if found wanting, will be struck down in whole or part), and which themselves cannot be changed via that ordinary legislative process but only via some more demanding process (or, perhaps, not changed at all without tearing down or overthrowing the constitutional order to which they belong).[2] Acts done in violation of these higher-order rules are 'unconstitutional' and the actors seeking to do them are acting in a way they have no right to do, as the relevant judicial body, tasked with interpreting the constitutional document, would or should be willing to state. In this picture, 'constitutionalism' is the idea that 'government can and should be legally limited in its powers, and that its authority or legitimacy depends on its observing these limitations'.[3] The limits in question are, it would seems, those that cut across different institutions and the different powers they exercise, rather than those inherent in the grant of a power to do one thing, which is limited in the sense that it cannot be used to do some other thing. This is a standard to which we would expect all states with a codified, capital-C, Constitution to adhere to a greater or lesser degree, though of course the substance of the limits might take an essentially infinite range of forms. Most prominently, however, these limiting rules, which usually apply both to legislative and executive bodies, take the form of fundamental rights, usually negative in orientation, which prevent the other constitutional actors from interfering with the rights of individuals, either absolutely or where the extent of the interference would be disproportionate to whatever benefit might be achieved by carrying it out. These qualified norms, it is often alleged, possess a more open texture than do traditional legal norms, in particular those that emerge via the process of common law reasoning and adjudication, and require the reconciliation of incommensurable values, to the point

[1] M Loughlin, *Against Constitutionalism* (Harvard University Press, 2022) 6–8.

[2] For a consideration of the idea that some constitutional amendments are themselves 'unconstitutional' and so not permitted within the existing constitutional structure of a given state, see, eg, Y Roznai, *Unconstitutional Constitutional Amendments: The Limits of Amendment Powers* (Oxford University Press, 2017).

[3] W Waluchow and D Kyritsis, 'Constitutionalism', *Stanford Encyclopaedia of Philosophy* (18 May 2023).

that reasoning thereunder – answering, for example, the question of whether some interference with a protected interest is proportionate to the benefit achieved thereby – is not really legal analysis at all, and so should be reserved for those branches of the state that are democratically accountable.

Though these phenomena – higher-order law and fundamental rights enforced by the judiciary – are of course closely linked, amongst the jurisdictions under consideration here are several that demonstrate their severability. On one hand, higher-order, capital-C, Constitutions usually contain much beyond the Bills of Rights that are the source of much of the highest-profile litigation and, in turn, the greatest political controversy. The separation of powers – whether horizontal, as between the executive, legislature and judiciary, or vertical, as between the (possibly federal) centre and the relevant territorial subunits (states, or provinces, or whatever else) or both – will often also act as a limit upon the legislation of at least some constitutional entities. They might be policed by the courts asking themselves legal questions, some of which turn out to be just as incapable of determinate answer as those on which disputes in the context of modern human rights law usually turn. On the other hand, one might have, as certain of the Commonwealth Five Eyes states do, a 'Bill of Rights' that permits the courts to signal the incompatibility of other legislation with fundamental rights, while leaving it open to the legislature to make such incompatible laws and, if it desires, repeal the Bill of Rights itself. Here the effect that any counter-majoritarian (or even anti-democratic) effect is (formally, at least) rather more contingent than in those jurisdictions in which rights are founded on an instrument that is itself beyond the reach of the legislative process. Whether or not the latter arrangement is sufficiently obstructive of the executive and legislature to count as 'constitutionalism' in this limiting sense is of no great concern here. And we must be careful to remember here that we are dealing initially with limits that are legal in nature. All democratic states (and even, to some lesser and messier extent, those which are undemocratic) will also see the uses to which powers are put by public actors limited in various ways by the formal and informal elements of the political process. Even Dicey, whose name is still invoked as a shorthand for a commitment to the unlimited legislative competence of the Westminster Parliament, was in no doubt that such legal omnipotence was, even in the absence of anything like a perfect (or perhaps even passable) democracy, accompanied by very significant political limitations on how that competence might be deployed in practice.[4]

There is much to dislike about this notion of constitutionalism, thinner though it is than that rejected by Loughlin. Not the least of its difficulties is that it seems, in its rush to limit the state, to overlook the notion that the state must first act and in fact does act; that because the state is already always and everywhere acting, if often subtly and without fanfare, to uphold the existing

[4] AV Dicey, *Introduction to the Study of the Law of the Constitution*, 8th edn ([1885]; Liberty Fund,1982) 26–35.

distribution of private law rights and obligations, an insistence on first of all limiting its interventions is to disguise the role of the state, its laws and its coercive apparatus, in the existence of what might be myriad injustices and to insist, in effect, upon the perpetuation of those injustices by default. Here, I do not seek to limit my consideration to any such narrow notion of constitutionalism. Rather, by constitutionalism I mean here something much broader: the bodies by whom and the manner in which public power is exercised – its forms, legal and institutional – and the ways in which it is checked, both ex ante and ex post, within the constitutional order.[5] The primary reason for the use of the language of 'constitutionalism' rather than that of 'constitutional law' is therefore that I am concerned not only with legal rules that might be enforced by courts but also with rules that are not law and so might not be enforced, either by courts or, perhaps, at all. Indeed, some of the matters I discuss in this book have not at points in the past been directly governed by anything we might consider rules at all.

This means that I am concerned first of all with the relevant agencies of the state, and the powers they enjoy, whether found in statute or (as was perhaps the case historically) in the royal prerogative or somewhere else: the positive dimension, we might call it, of public power (or even 'positive constitutionalism')[6] in the domain of national security. In a democratic order, we must recall, the people are as likely to voice the demand that the state acts in certain ways, that it provide certain goods, as to demand that it does not act (a demand that, for the reason given above, is itself misleading). One of the goods that the electorate will inevitably demand from the state, rewarding its provision and punishing the failure to provide it, is security, as we have frequently seen in recent decades as political parties have sought to outbid each other as regards their willingness to take this or that step to protect the public against the threat, real or merely apprehended, of terrorism. One difficulty, of course, is the incentive this process might create to exaggerate or misstate the nature or extent of the threat, in which the mass media will also have an interest. The basic point nevertheless remains: if a democratic state did not possess bodies tasked with investigating and responding to threats

[5] What Wachlow and Kyritsis call a 'minimal sense' of the term, whereby 'a constitution consists of a set of norms (rules, principles or values) creating, structuring, and possibly defining the limits of, government power or authority': Wachlow and Kyritsis (n 3).

[6] See Nick Barber, arguing for an alternative account of constitutionalism than the negative one that was historically dominant: 'A richer account of the state, one that recognizes its role in advancing the well-being of its people, generates a richer account of constitutionalism. This positive model of constitutionalism acknowledges the need for constitutional structures to guard against abuses of power – it is not utopian – but is focused on creating a strong state able to work for the good of its people. Positive constitutionalism contains a range of principles – the separation of powers, state sovereignty, subsidiarity, and so forth – that help determine the institutional structure of the state and the constitutional interaction of these institutions.' NW Barber, *The Principles of Constitutionalism* (Oxford University Press, 2018) 19. This specific aspect of Barber's account is assessed in R Uitz, 'Barber's Pursuit of Positive Constitutionalism in The Principles of Constitutionalism: Towards Exposing Illiberal Constitutional Chicanery' (2021) 24 *Jerusalem Review of Legal Studies* 66.

to the security of the state and its people, it would quickly come under irresistible pressure to create them. The book considers, therefore – primarily in chapters 2 and 3 – what those bodies are: where they previously found, and find now, the source of their authority, as well as the way in which their mission is shaped by the instruments in question.

Only against this background – the state's being omnipresent in the form of its professed willingness to enforce private law rights and obligations; the further, more palpable, steps it takes being a response in part to political incentives within a given democratic order – does it make sense to turn to limits on what those bodies do. In that regard, I am concerned also with the different institutions that do not themselves exercise power for the purpose of protecting, in whatever particular form, the security of the state but which instead contribute to the process of ensuring accountability for that exercise, whether legal or political or – as I discuss in a later chapter – some combination of the two.[7] This, to make the point perhaps more crudely than might be desirable, is 'negative constitutionalism',[8] a part that is often treated as effectively the whole. Here, of course, some of the limiting instruments or actors are general to the constitutional order, contributing to the process of ensuring accountability for the way in which the state acts regardless of the specific domain in which it does so: the Bills of Rights whose existence I noted above generally apply to the relevant security bodies in the same way as they apply to other public actors. Others are special to particular domains: just as we have special institutions to pursue the protection of national security, what I call here in general terms the security and intelligence agencies (SIAs), we now frequently encounter in constitutional orders specialist bodies for carrying out oversight and review of the SIAs and their work. These latter bodies, though, have a heightened significance in the context of national security, given that the institutions possessing apparently general responsibility for ensuring accountability have often been denied (or simply disclaimed) responsibility for what goes on in that domain, being considered – by virtue of their form and processes – unsuited to the task of providing oversight therein. In particular, as we shall see at various points, the fact that the security enterprise occurs largely in secret, means (it has often been argued) that we cannot simply rely on the usual processes of political and legal accountability in relation thereto and so have been required to create specialist bodies that provide that

[7] See ch 5 of this volume.

[8] 'The common understanding of constitutionalism – the one most often found in scholarly writing and, so far as it exists, the popular understanding of the doctrine outside of academia – treats constitutionalism in negative terms: constitutionalism is equated with a demand for limited government.' Barber (n 6) 1. One implication of Barber's approach – contrasting what he takes to be a superior understanding with that which has historically dominated – is that the inferior understanding is put up front, a failing that exists in order to be corrected by the superior understanding that will follow. For that reason, I have sought to introduce the positive dimension of national security constitutionalism before turning to those institutional arrangements that give effect to its limiting (or 'negative') instincts.

accountability (or something like it) while respecting the overarching imperative of secrecy upon which the endeavour relies.

Two further points might be made in relation to the reliance upon the notion of '(national security) constitutionalism'. One is that, though the substantive focus of the work is the topic of national security, actions taken in pursuit thereof take place, as in any other area of policy, against the background of a broader constitutional structure that provides answers to all sorts of questions. Who makes law, and how? What is the relationship between the body or bodies that participate in the legislative process and those that give effect to the laws those bodies make? Does that distinction between the making and application of law, reflecting as it does the assumptions of a separation of powers model developed outside of the constitutional tradition to which the jurisdictions at issue belong, accurately represent how the relevant constitutions operate? What is the role of the courts, and how has that changed in recent decades, as human rights have become a dominant language of legal contestation? Though not all of them are considered directly in this work, the answers to these questions – and others like them – structure the operation of the national security enterprise in a fashion that a more direct, narrower focus upon the body of what we might call national security law risks obscuring. A second is that, as discussed further in chapter 2, the reliance on constitutionalism in place of constitutional law works perhaps to overcome the narrowness that has at times been evidenced by the comparative constitutional law literature, which is often focused not merely on courts but also on a small number of, potentially anomalous or otherwise unrepresentative, decisions of a small number of particularly prominent (or perhaps merely self-aggrandising) courts. For all of these reasons, 'constitutionalism' would seem to be – notwithstanding some of the baggage the term appears to have accumulated – the best term for delimiting the object of our study.

III. Five Eyes

A second key framing device of the book is the 'Five Eyes' intelligence-sharing alliance, the history of which has recently been written – though without any particular focus on the legal aspects – by Richard Kerbaj.[9] Kerbaj paints a picture of the alliance as caught between two states of being. On one hand, it is 'equivalent to a band of brothers and sisters drawn together by common values, language and cause'; on the other, it is 'a non-binding marriage of convenience riddled with

[9] R Kerbaj, *The Secret History of the Five Eyes: The Untold Story of the Shadowy International Spy Network* (Blink Publishing, 2022). For an older consideration of the alliance in the broader context of cooperation between the states that are party to it, including its secrecy and American dominance, see JT Richelson and D Ball, *The Ties That Bind: Intelligence Cooperation Between the UKUSA Countries* (Harper Collins, 1986) esp 4–8.

distrust, competing intelligence priorities, and a massive imbalance of power that predominantly favours the United States'.[10] There are, as the name suggests, five states that are party to the current version of what began as the UKUSA Agreement of 1946, which itself built upon prior wartime cooperation between the United States (US) and the UK, and which remains the paradigm of an intelligence-sharing agreement notwithstanding the vast geopolitical developments of the intervening period.

The text of the original Five Eyes Agreement, made available only in 2010,[11] shows that it was made between the State–Army–Navy Communication Intelligence Board ('representing the US State, Navy, and War Departments and all other US Communication Intelligence authorities which may function') and the London Signal Intelligence Board ('representing the Foreign Office, Admiralty, War Office, Air Ministry, and all other British Empire Communication Intelligence authorities which may function').[12] As this last formulation suggests, however, the matter was complicated by the fact that the authorities of the UK were also at this stage the authorities of an Empire still in the process of being dismantled, and for that reason a footnote clarified that, for the purposes of the Agreement, 'British Empire is understood to mean all British territory other than the Dominions'[13] – that is, those units that had previously been part of the British Empire but to which full self-government had been recognised, including not only three of current parties to the Five Eyes Agreement (Canada, Australia and New Zealand) but also, at that date, South Africa and (as far as the UK itself was concerned) Ireland.[14]

The parties to the 1946 Agreement agreed to the exchange 'of the products of the following operations relating to foreign communications': the collection of the traffic, the acquisition of communication documents and equipment, traffic analysis, cryptanalysis, decryption and translation, and, finally, 'acquisition of information regarding communication organizations, practices, procedures, and equipment'.[15] The restriction of the sharing to the product of operations relating to 'foreign communications' meant that the product of the purely domestic interception of communications – for, say, crime-fighting purposes – would not be shared,

[10] Kerbaj (n 9) xi.

[11] R Norton-Taylor, 'Not so secret: deal at the heart of UK-US intelligence' *The Guardian* (25 June 2010): 'Though its existence has long been known, the agreement, negotiated in London in March 1946, is only now being published, and for the first time officially acknowledged, after freedom of information requests in Britain and the US.'

[12] British–US Communications Intelligence Agreement ('UKUSA Agreement') (5 March 1946) [1].

[13] ibid fn 2.

[14] For a recent consideration of the phenomenon, see PC Oliver, '"Dominion status": History, framework and context' (2019) 17 *International Journal of Constitutional Law* 1173. Ireland's distinctive position is considered in L McDonagh, 'Losing Ireland, Losing the Empire: Dominion Status and the Irish Constitutions of 1922 and 1937' (2019) 17 *International Journal of Constitutional Law* 1192. The Ireland Act 1949 (UK) eventually recognised the reality of Ireland's status outside the Commonwealth.

[15] UKUSA Agreement (n 12) [3(a)].

but the category of 'foreign communications' was drawn broadly.[16] A foreign country for these purposes was any state – whether or not officially recognised by the states party to the Agreement – other than the US, the British Commonwealth of Nations and the British Empire.[17] Again, the liminal status of the UK – both a state in itself and the heart of broader configurations, themselves in a state of flux – complicated matters from the beginning. Exchange of the products of the various operations was to be 'unrestricted on all work undertaken', unless one party requested an exception and the other agreed; even then, the parties expressed an intention to keep exceptions to 'the absolute minimum'.[18] The sharing of information to which the parties committed went beyond the product of their operations to also include 'information regarding methods and techniques'.[19] Here too, exchange was to be unrestricted, though with a greater scope for exceptions recognised than in relation to the sharing of interception product itself. One party, it was agreed, might withhold information about methods and techniques where its 'special interests' required it to do so.[20] Even allowing for that exception, however, the obligations on the parties were remarkable in their intensity. When such 'special interests' required the withholding of information on methods and techniques, the party doing the withholding was nevertheless required to give a notification to the other party and to include within it 'a description of the information being withheld, sufficient in the opinion of the withholding party, to convey its significance'.[21] It seems improbable that an agreement of such breadth, whose requirements were so onerous, could have ever been agreed but for the shared experience of these two states in the context of the Second World War and the relationship of trust and cooperation that had developed between the UK and the US as a result.[22]

The UKUSA Agreement precluded cooperation with 'third parties' (again, notably, 'all individuals or authorities other than those of the United States, the British Empire, and the British Dominions') as regards communication intelligence, except under strict conditions: the existence of the Agreement itself was not to be revealed to any third party, any cooperation by one of the two parties to the Agreement with third parties required the agreement of the other such party, and the results of any cooperative action relating to communications intelligence

[16] 'Foreign communications' was defined to mean 'all communications of the government or of any military, air, or naval force, faction, party, department, agency, or bureau of a foreign country, or of any person or persons acting or purporting to act therefor' and included 'commercial communications of a foreign country which may contain information of military, political, or economic value'. ibid fn 3.

[17] ibid fn 3.

[18] ibid [3(b)].

[19] ibid [4].

[20] ibid [4(b)].

[21] ibid [4].

[22] What Churchill would call, in his 'iron curtain' speech, a year after the end of the war, a 'special relationship', and which is now often designated – sometimes still with a straight face, if a certain amount of optimism – with the definite article: see W Wallace and C Phillips, 'Reassessing the special relationship' (2009) 85 *International Affairs* 263.

were to be shared with that other party.[23] Special consideration was again given to the Dominions, which were for this purpose neither parties to the Agreement nor third parties. The UK was to inform the US of arrangements with agencies of Dominion states, and the US was to make no arrangements with those states – other than Canada – except 'through, or with the prior approval of' the UK, while arrangements with Canada could be made only after consulting the UK authorities.[24] Collaboration with Dominion agencies was conditional on those agencies' compliance with certain provisions of the Agreement.[25]

The UKUSA Agreement was signed on 5 March 1946. As befitting the doubly special status of Canada within it, it was extended to Canada a few years later,[26] and to New Zealand and Australia the following decade,[27] with the grouping becoming known in time, on the basis of its enlarged membership, as the 'Five Eyes' network, taking on its modern form as 'a secretive, English-speaking, global surveillance network of states'.[28] There has often been, predictably, a culture of considerable secrecy around the Agreement,[29] and its present content, as well has how it has (and has not) evolved in recent decades, while the sorts of developments discussed and analysed in this book were taking place, remains largely unknowable. What is clear, however, is that the Five Eyes Agreement is the most important intelligence-sharing agreement to which each of these states is party, and probably the most important such agreement in all of history. Now that the existence of the alliance is no longer hidden, tributes to its significance are frequent, and usually offered in strong terms. New Zealand's current national security strategy calls it, for example, 'an invaluable support to our understanding and ability to respond

[23] UKUSA Agreement (n 12) [5].

[24] ibid [6].

[25] ibid [6(e)].

[26] The underlying 'CANUSA' Agreement between Canada and the USA, which paved the way for Canadian entry into what became in time the Five Eyes Agreement, has been described as 'effectively a declaration of SIGINT sovereignty by Canada and an expression of a desire to be treated as an equal in a tripartite pact with the US and UK'. W Wark, 'The road to CANUSA: how Canadian signals intelligence won its independence and helped create the Five Eyes' (2020) 35 *Intelligence and National Security* 20, 22.

[27] C Pfluke, 'A history of the Five Eyes Alliance: Possibility for reform and additions' (2019) 38 *Comparative Strategy* 302, 302. John Ferris has suggested that New Zealand entered the Agreement 'as a matter of course, or courtesy, as an old Dominion'. J Ferris, *Behind the Enigma: The Authorised History of GCHQ, Britain's Secret Cyber-Intelligence Agency* (Bloomsbury, 2020) 376. These and similar claims have been contested, its being argued instead that 'New Zealand managed to navigate its way into Five Eyes by its integration into Allied intelligence systems and its leveraging of this involvement to obtain acceptance, formally in 1956, to the post-war UKUSA or Five Eyes arrangement'. J Battersby and R Ball, 'The Phantom Eye: New Zealand and the Five Eyes' (2023) 38 *Intelligence and National Security* 920, 931.

[28] Pfluke (n 27) 304.

[29] ibid: 'The alliance maintained extreme secrecy until 1999 when the head of Australia's DSD became the first person to openly admit their country's involvement in the global surveillance alliance and its main program, Echelon.'

to emerging and complex security issues'.[30] The UK's 'Integrated Review' (of security, defence, development and foreign policy) describes it as 'unique and highly valued'.[31] It exists within – though is severable from – a much broader culture of defence and security cooperation between these states, or various bilateral and multilateral configurations thereof.[32] While various claims have been made about the alliance – about the dangers associated with its asymmetry, given the dominance of the US,[33] the need for reform in light of shifting public opinion subsequent to the Snowden leaks of 2013, which demonstrated the scale of surveillance by the US National Security Agency,[34] or the desirability of expanding it to reflect evolving geopolitical challenges[35] – it seems inevitable that it will persist for time to come. And though there seems to be no reason to think that Five Eyes itself involves the harmonisation of, or other influence on, legal norms between member states, it seems clear – as discussed in chapter 7 – that there has been considerable convergence between the corpuses of national security law that exist within the Commonwealth Five Eyes states.

A. The Position of the United States

If, then, the key intelligence-sharing alliance was founded by the UK and the US, with the others joining only later, and the alliance is still undoubtedly dominated by the US,[36] why is the present work a study of national security constitutionalism in only four of the five Five Eyes states? Why, in particular, exclude the state

[30] New Zealand Government, *Secure Together: New Zealand's National Security Strategy 2023–2028* (2023) 18.

[31] HM Government, *Global Britain in a Competitive Age: The Integrated Review of Security, Defence, Development and Foreign Policy* (CP 403, 2021) 61.

[32] See, eg, the AUKUS 'enhanced trilateral security partnership' announced in 2021, under which the UK and the US committed to supporting Australia in acquiring nuclear-powered submarines, which contained what might well be understood to be a reference to Five Eyes: 'For more than 70 years, Australia, the United Kingdom, and the United States, have worked together, along with other important allies and partners, to protect our shared values and promote security and prosperity. Today, with the formation of AUKUS, we recommit ourselves to this vision.' Prime Minister of Australia, Prime Minister of the United Kingdom, and President of the United States of America, 'Joint Leaders Statement on Aukus' (16 September 2021).

[33] One author notes that 'as with all asymmetrical alliances, the Five Eyes network exposes junior partners to the hazard of being manipulated to make policy decisions at odds with their sovereign interests in favour of embracing assessments that reflect the dominant member's policy agenda', but concludes that there is little evidence to suggest that – with the possible exception of the Iraq War – Australia has made a significant foreign policy decision under the influence of US intelligence assessments. A O'Neil, 'Australia and the 'Five Eyes' Intelligence Network: the Perils of an Asymmetric Alliance' (2017) 71 *Australian Journal of International Affairs* 529, 540.

[34] PF Walsh and S Miller, 'Rethinking "Five Eyes" Security Intelligence Collection Policies and Practice Post Snowden' (2016) 31 *Intelligence and National Security* 345.

[35] See, eg, Pfluke (n 27).

[36] See the extract from Kerbaj in the text at n 10. Examples might be multiplied.

that is – all seem to agree – the most powerful member of the alliance, and indeed is central to global national security processes far beyond the confines of the Five Eyes alliance? A number of explanations might be offered. One is the purely practical one – the study of national security law and what I have called national security constitutionalism in the US has a longer and deeper history than in the other states under consideration. There is much more to say about the relevant phenomena in the US, but much less need, on my part at least, to say it. But this in turn is a function of a deeper and more consequential reason – the avowal and rationalisation of national security law and national security constitutionalism in the US has a longer history, with many of the key developments pre-dating by several decades their analogues in the other Five Eyes states. The reasons for this are partly historical, relating to the specific events that precipitated the relevant changes (which of course involve a considerable degree of happenstance), but they seem in some cases to reflect also the distinctiveness of the US constitutional order – in particular its presidential nature, which is liable to result in a greater antagonism between executive and legislature than is usually found in parliamentary systems, and its rejection of the royal prerogative in favour of a constitutional grant of the 'executive power'[37] – and the difficulty of employing in that context the same techniques as have been used elsewhere to keep the national security apparatus outside of the mainstream constitutional order. So, for example, the Central Intelligence Agency was established by the National Security Act of 1947,[38] earlier than any of its equivalents elsewhere in Five Eyes (one of which would have to wait more than 40 years for a statutory basis) were legislated for. While, as we shall see in chapter 6, (quasi-)parliamentary committees with responsibility for oversight of national security matters were first introduced into the Commonwealth Five Eyes states only in the 1986, and have existed in all four of those states for less than a decade, the US Senate Select Committee on Intelligence had been introduced in 1976. This is not, of course, to say that there were no attempts to maintain the secrecy, both factual and legal, of US intelligence activity – the National Security Agency, for example, which has primarily responsibility for signals intelligence in the US, was established in effect by a classified memo of 1952 but avowed only in 1974 – but rather that the techniques seem in many cases to have been distinctive, in light of a domestic political and, particularly, constitutional context very different from that encountered in the other four of the Five Eyes states.

Were we inclined to stretch this loose chain of causation back further, we might note that though the four of the Five Eyes other than the UK have historical links (to use, of course, a misleadingly neutral word) to it through its Empire, the links

[37] For a consideration of what is – and is not – captured by that language, see JD Mortenson, 'Article II Vests Executive Power, Not the Royal Prerogative' (2019) 119 *Columbia Law Review* 1169.

[38] See, eg, the enactment of the National Security Act of 1947 and, assessing it, D Stuart, *Creating the National Security State: A History of the Law That Transformed America* (Princeton University Press, 2008).

of three of those four with that Empire survived much longer than did those of the fourth. The United States of America was formed by the 13 British colonies that existed in the North American Atlantic in 1776, with the defeat of the UK in the American War of Independence in 1783 bringing to an end what is sometimes designated the 'First British Empire'.[39] The other three states, though self-governing Dominions before achieving formal independence in the course of the twentieth century, remained linked to the British Empire through the Commonwealth of Nations at the time of Five Eyes' founding, and indeed remain members thereof to the present day. From a constitutional point of view, the US, therefore, has much less in common with the UK than do the other Five Eyes states, having broken from the Empire far earlier than did they and only after having first taken up arms against it. Indeed, it had done so under the direct influence of a model of Enlightenment constitutionalism that never took hold in the Empire nor – at least in full – in those states whose constitutions grew, more organically, alongside and finally out of it. The Constitution of the United States of America is therefore the prototype – though not an archetype, and more often these days the subject of cautionary tales – of a constitutional order at odds with the model that still prevails in the UK and (to a greater or lesser degree) its various Commonwealth partners. There is much reason to think that at both the general level and specifically in the domain of national security, it has too little in common with the other members of Five Eyes to be worth analysing in conjunction with them. For these reasons, the present work does not seek to do so, focusing instead on the other four states, whose shared constitutional heritage is much more palpable, and which have, as a group, already been the subject of important scholarly attention in the modern turn to comparison in constitutional scholarship. I consider that shared position of New Zealand, Canada and Australia within the British Empire, and certain aspects of the process by which they came, in time and in stages, to extricate themselves from it, in chapter 2.

IV. Commonwealth Constitutionalism

The four states under consideration here – the UK, Canada, Australia and New Zealand – have, therefore, much more in common than simply being members of the Five Eyes alliance. Their constitutions each reflect to a greater or lesser degree what is often described as the Westminster system, or model, of government.[40]

[39] See, eg, AB Keith, *Constitutional History of The First British Empire* (Clarendon Press, 1930).

[40] For a discussion of the key features of the Westminster system see RAW Rhodes, J Wanna and P Weller, *Comparing Westminster* (Oxford University Press, 2009) esp chs 1 and 9. The authors claim (ibid 1) that Australia, New Zealand and Canada (along with South Africa) are polities that 'still regard themselves, in part, as variants of British parliamentary democracy, originating in Westminster, despite each having subsequently undergone substantial transformation'.

Though the Westminster model speaks most directly and most distinctively to the relationship between legislature and executive, it is linked to a set of ideas about the role of courts – what it is and what it is not – that are less settled, and so more contested, now than in the past. This section considers that model before turning to one aspect of the role of courts and the alleged existence of a 'new Commonwealth model' of constitutionalism that rethinks the contribution of both the courts and the legislature to the protection of rights within Commonwealth constitutional orders. The claim of this section is that these topics, though they attract the most attention from comparative constitutional lawyers, exclude those aspects of the constitutional order that are most significant from the point of view of the national security enterprise. The study of national security constitutionalism therefore involves the de-centring of courts, but without turning directly back to the other branches of the state in their most fundamental form. Rather, it calls upon us to consider the various institutions that have been introduced in order to remedy the inability, whether partial or total, of the three standard branches of the state in their ordinary functioning, to provide the sort of oversight of the national security endeavour that is now frequently demanded alongside the pursuit of that endeavour in the first place.

A. The Westminster Model

The Westminster model rests upon a parliamentary system of government, in which the executive is formed out of legislature and is required to retain its confidence. In three of the four states under consideration, the legislature is bicameral, with a directly elected lower chamber and an upper chamber that is populated in a range of ways and is generally secondary within the legislative process, limited by law or convention in its ability to block those initiatives supported by the primary chamber. The exception is New Zealand, in which there is a single chamber, the House of Representatives. The executive in Westminster states is headed by a Prime Minister (or equivalent), who is the head of government and separate from the head of state. In all four of the jurisdictions in question the head of state is a monarch – the same individual, now Charles III, who is the King of the United Kingdom, but also simultaneously the King of Canada, King of Australia and King of New Zealand. In each of these constitutional orders there remains considerable reliance upon prerogative powers, which as a matter of law belong to the Crown,[41] and which were in effect brought to (or imposed upon) these jurisdictions by the British Empire. In order to bridge the gap between this formal legal reality and the demands of a modern democracy, there is also, therefore, heavy reliance upon constitutional convention in order to circumscribe the exercise of

[41] On which, see ch 1.

powers by this Crown (in practice either the King or, in the states other than the UK, his Governor General),[42] with only small, and often contested, scope for the monarch or his representative to exercise them without or even against the advice of the government of the day.[43] One significance of this fact is that within this body of prerogative power has often been identified the power to act in pursuit of the defence of the realm or, as is now more frequently said, to protect national security. So, for example, Lord Diplock, in the *GCHQ* case in the UK, noted that there had

> survived into the present day a residue of miscellaneous fields of law in which the executive government retains decision-making powers that are not dependent upon any statutory authority … From matters so relatively minor as the grant of pardons to condemned criminals, of honours to the good and great, of corporate personality to deserving bodies of persons, and of bounty from moneys made available to the executive government by Parliament, they extend to matters so vital to the survival and welfare of the nation as the conduct of relations with foreign states and – what lies at the heart of the present case – the defence of the realm against potential enemies.[44]

The same general association of the prerogative and defence of the realm, or the prerogative and national security, is encountered over time and space, and appears to be or to have been (or been assumed to be) common to all of the Commonwealth Five Eyes states, albeit with significant variation as to when and why the question of the prerogative's existence and scope came to matter in practice. For that reason, it serves to note already at this stage that the association is a somewhat unsatisfactory one. The prerogative power is the power to the do certain acts – to appoint, say, a Prime Minister. But national security is not a particular act; it is an area of policy and, perhaps, a purpose for which particular acts might be done (as was the case in *GCHQ*). This is compounded by the shift from the language in law of defence of the realm – and its stronger military association – to that of national security. In the former case, it is conceivable that there are specific acts, with clear legal consequences, that one might attribute to the prerogative: to give orders to the armed forces, for example, or declare war. But national security seems to go beyond that, and what it might encompass by way of specific powers – the power to do what, exactly? – is unclear, and has not always been considered with the requisite care. We will return to this question at various points in this book.

[42] See on this issue B Galligan and S Brenton, 'Introduction' in B Galligan and S Brenton (eds), *Constitutional Conventions in Westminster Systems: Controversies, Changes and Challenges* (Cambridge University Press, 2015) 3, observing that there is 'a common conventional discourse across these countries deriving from the original British model and its adoption and retention as the dominion countries became equal Commonwealth countries and autonomous in their national government'.

[43] On the question of these 'reserve' powers, see A Twomey, *The Veiled Sceptre: Reserve Powers of Heads of State in Westminster Systems* (Cambridge University Press, 2018).

[44] *Council of Civil Service Unions v Minister for the Civil Service* [1985] AC 374, 410.

Another feature that is prominent within the Westminster model relates to the question of legislative competence – the ability of the relevant legislature, whatever its exact form, to make laws. That is, there are generally few, if any, limitations upon the competence of the relevant legislative body. In the UK, the Westminster Parliament is sovereign – it can make or unmake any law whatsoever – and appears to have seen off in recent years at least the most direct of the lurking threats to its sovereignty that had been present in the wider constitutional picture. The same is true of the New Zealand Parliament.[45] In relation to the Parliament of Canada and the Parliament of Australia, which are federal (or, in the Australian parlance, Commonwealth) institutions, the limits that have always existed relate in the first place to the division of power between the centre and the various sub-federal units recognised by the constitutional order as having a sphere of autonomy protected against federal encroachment,[46] with rights-based limits at best a secondary element of the constitutional settlement. For much of the twentieth century, therefore, these jurisdictions largely eschewed the rights-based limits on legislative competence characteristic of modern constitution-making, with courts therefore denied the prominence they have in resolving rights-based disputes in some (but by no means all) other constitutional orders. This has now changed in three of the four Commonwealth Five Eyes states: the Canadian constitution includes within it the Canadian Charter of Rights and Freedoms; New Zealand enacted a Bill of Rights Act (NZBORA) in 1990, and the UK a Human Rights Act (HRA) in 1998. In Australia, the absence of a (Commonwealth) Bill of Rights means that the range of rights explicitly protected against legislative encroachment is narrow,[47] with the short list augmented by an implied freedom of political communication identified by the High Court.[48] These three documents – the Canadian Charter, the NZBORA and the HRA (along with their sub-national equivalents in Australia, the Australian Capital Territory's Human Rights Act 2004 and Victoria's Charter of Human Rights and Responsibilities Act 2006) – have been argued to exemplify a 'new Commonwealth Model' of constitutionalism,[49] which is worth considering

[45] See the clarification and defence of the rule in the New Zealand context in J Goldsworthy, 'Is Parliament Sovereign?: Recent Challenges to the Doctrine of Parliamentary Sovereignty' (2005) 3 *New Zealand Journal of Public and International Law* 7.

[46] The Canadian constitution reserves certain topics to the exclusive jurisdiction of the provincial legislatures: Constitution Acts 1867 to 1982 (Canada), s 92; Section 51 of the Constitution of Australia lays down 'heads of power' in relation to which the Australian Parliament might make laws. For a helpful overview of the use of the language of parliamentary sovereignty in Australia and the reasons for which it is inapposite, see R Goss, 'What do Australians Talk About When They Talk About "Parliamentary Sovereignty"?' [2022] *Public Law* 55.

[47] The five usually identified as being explicitly protected by the Constitution are the rights to vote and to trial by jury, freedom of religion and prohibitions on acquisition of property on terms that are not 'just' and discrimination on the basis of state of residency.

[48] Originating in *Australian Capital Television Pty Ltd v Commonwealth* (1992) 177 CLR 106 and *Nationwide News Pty Ltd v Wills* (1992) 177 CLR 1.

[49] See, most fully, S Gardbaum, *The New Commonwealth Model of Constitutionalism* (Cambridge University Press, 2013).

in more detail specifically because it acts as the backdrop to the argument, made most fully in the concluding chapter of the present work, that there now exists something like an analogous model of Commonwealth national security constitutionalism.

B. The 'New Commonwealth Model' of Constitutionalism and its Limitations

The 'new Commonwealth model' of constitutionalism transcends (it is claimed) an older binary between systems in which legislatures are all-powerful, capable of interfering with the rights of individuals and groups, with the rights in question being for that reason not creatures of law but rather moral and political claims that may or may not succeed within the democratic process (such as it is), and those in which a Constitution places hard limits upon that legislative competence, with the courts tasked with interpreting those limits and having – for that reason, and at least in the short term – the crucial 'last word' on what the legislature, despite whatever democratic credentials it may possess, may or may not do. Against this, we are told by Stephen Gardbaum,[50] there has emerged in the Commonwealth a shared approach that introduces two key innovations.

On the one hand, there have been introduced into these legal orders Bills of Rights (whether or not under that specific name) that specify a set of rights, stated usually at a high level of generality, against which legislative proposals are to be tested within the process of enacting them into law, giving the legislature the ability to ensure that if and when it legislates incompatibly with those rights, it does so knowingly and willingly, and in a full understanding of what might be the implications of doing so. Those implications are the second distinctive feature of this approach. The 'new Commonwealth model' involves Bills of Rights that see courts charged with assessing legislation against the enacted rights in judicial or constitutional review proceedings, which do not, or do not necessarily, permit the courts to 'strike down' that legislation which does not comply with the rights as interpreted by the courts. Rather, paradigmatically, they might signal the existence of an incompatibility between legislation that has been made by the legislature and the rights earlier specified by it within the Bill of Rights, leaving open the question of how, or even if, the legislature should respond to that incompatibility. In doing so, it has been suggested that – rather than allowing one (type of) institution, legislature or court, to dominate the decision-making sphere – these approaches permit, or even require, a dialogue between different (types of) institutions.[51]

[50] ibid.

[51] A metaphor that originated in Canada – P Hogg and A Bushell, 'The Charter Dialogue Between Courts and Legislatures (Or Perhaps the Charter of Rights Isn't Such a Bad Thing After All)' (1997) 35 *Osgoode Hall Law Journal* 75 – but has been frequently applied elsewhere: see, eg, G Sigalet, G Webber and R Dixon, 'Introduction: The "What" and "Why" of Constitutional Dialogue' in G Sigalet, G Webber

The normative desirability of the new Commonwealth model has been called into question on a number of grounds, including that the dialogue it is claimed to support is illusory, and that in practice the model amounts to the same sort of judicial supremacy that it is supposed to avoid, with all the attendant consequences for the quality of democratic self-government. Particular instantiations of it are open to further criticisms: in the UK, for example, a distinctive feature is the relationship between the HRA 1998 and the European Convention on Human Rights. The injunction on the courts, in section 2 of the Act, to 'take into account' (inter alia) the judgments of the European Court of Human Rights has, for sound practical reasons, mostly seen the domestic courts hew very closely to those decisions. But those decisions are, many feel, insufficiently stable over time, with the 'living instrument' approach taken to the interpretation of the Convention by the Strasbourg Court meaning that its (open-textured) provisions have been interpreted in ways that would not have been foreseen, and might in some cases have been positively rejected, by those who originally agreed its terms. These innovations are (almost automatically) incorporated into the domestic legal regime, where they in turn destabilise established rules of public and private law. Though this might sound like a precursor to an argument for a purely domestic Bill of Rights, experience elsewhere suggests that the same pattern of unpredictable evolution might well emerge even in the absence of a practice of, in effect, following the jurisprudence of an international court. And though the Canadian 'notwithstanding clause', which permits the Parliament of Canadian and the provincial legislatures to override many of the protected rights (though only for a time-limited period), addresses some of the concerns about the democratic implications of the model – and has been mirrored elsewhere[52] – it does not, and does not seek to, exclude judicial oversight of legislative determinations altogether.

We might, though, accept the distinctiveness of the model, and nevertheless regret the limits of the lens it brings to the comparative study of constitutions. Dyzenhaus and Poole, for example, have treated Gardbaum's work as exemplary of the problem in comparative constitutional law of 'getting it too simple' (as opposed to 'getting it wrong', exemplified by 'the tendency to reduce or dilute law to such an extent that it dissolves into or is swallowed up by "politics" or "culture"'): 'What starts', they say, 'an attempt to escape the grip of the US-model of rights protection ends up replicating the US obsession with courts and the counter-majoritarian difficulty …',[53] because 'while analytically more subtle

and R Dixon (eds), *Constitutional Dialogue: Rights, Democracy, Institutions* (Cambridge University Press, 2019) 1, considering a range of examples of where the metaphor has been employed, or critiqued, in relation also to New Zealand, the UK and the relevant Australian jurisdictions. The fullest exploration of the idea of dialogue in this sense is offered, with primary reference to the UK, by Alison Young: AL Young, *Democratic Dialogue and the Constitution* (Oxford University Press, 2017).

[52] Charter of Human Rights and Responsibilities Act 2006 (Victoria), s 31.

[53] D Dyzenahus and T Poole, 'The Old Commonwealth Model of Constitutionalism' (2023) 1 *Comparative Constitutional Studies* 197.

and less overtly US-centric than many working in the field, Gardbaum accepts the same basic reference points – that what is most important in constitutional design and most worthy of comparative study is the way in which the apex court intersects with the legislature.'[54] That is, the new Commonwealth model remains focused upon the protection of rights, and the relationship between the courts and the political branches in that protection. It therefore might be thought first of all to overlook the positive aspects of constitutionalism – how the constitutional order permits the state to act, in what forms and for what ends – and, second and within the scope of the sort of negative constitutionalism with which it is most clearly concerned, to exclude from its consideration the issue of how much of that negative constitutionalism takes place outside of the relationship between the legislature and the courts. For present purposes, this includes the striking development of a variety of institutional forms that are distinctive within, perhaps even special to, the national security domain, to which we now turn.

[54] ibid 201.

1

Comparative National Security Constitutionalism

I. Introduction

The present book is a work of comparative national security constitutionalism, considering how the national security endeavour is pursued within the constitutional orders of the four Commonwealth Five Eyes states – the institutions charged with doing so, and the powers they possess, as well as the systems and institutions that have been developed in order to oversee that endeavour – and how these four states have influenced one another in the design and development of the relevant bodies of law. Its argument is that there exists a model of what I will call a Commonwealth of national security constitutionalism, characterised in the first place by a notable convergence upon a particular set of constitutional arrangements. Though some of this convergence is inevitable given the shared constitutional foundations of these states and the functional logic of national security, what we find when we consider them together appears to go far beyond what is logically inescapable: there has been, as we shall see, extensive borrowing and sharing between them, and the process of borrowing and sharing is accelerating over time.

This chapter considers the book's contribution within the context of the broader modern literature on comparative constitutional law and the methodologies employed within that literature. The argument of the chapter, in brief, is that comparative consideration of the national security context is particularly valuable because constitutional orders often deal with matters of national security via distinct and distinctive institutions, which are not encompassed by the standard institutional focus of comparative constitutional law. Given, that is, that not only is national security the responsibility of specialist, often secretive bodies – the security and intelligence agencies (SIAs) – but that oversight of the work of those SIAs is similarly carried out by specialist bodies, the study of national security constitutionalism takes us beyond the standard, generic division of constitutions into executive, legislature and judicial bodies. Though there are important challenges, including methodological, associated with the comparative study of national security constitutionalism (over and above those that apply to comparative constitutional law generally), the current work is, I suggest, able to evade the most serious of those by virtue of its closely defined scope and, in particular, its focus on a small number of closely related jurisdictions. This in turn has, of course, important implications for the breadth and depth of the lessons we might learn from the study of those jurisdictions. In particular, it limits our ability to generalise outwards from this work's conclusions about national security constitutionalism in the Commonwealth Five Eyes states to its equivalent in other constitutional orders, as well as to the wider world of constitutional law and practice.

II. The Turn to Comparison in Constitutional Law

In recent decades, there has been a very prominent turn to comparison in constitutional law, which has now crystallised in the existence of a well-defined and substantial body of literature, along with associated professional organisations, journals, international conferences and so on. This turn – probably the most important trend in the modern study of constitutions and constitutional law – has, it would seem, been driven by a number of factors. Some relate to changing patterns identifiable within constitutional law itself, such that the study of comparative constitutional law is to an extent a function of a logically prior turn to comparison by legal officials – in particular judges making decisions within so-called 'apex courts'.[1] We need not delve into the sociology of modern constitutionalism in detail, but the basic pattern is of interest. As liberal democracy, or some variant thereof, has taken hold in jurisdictions where it did not previously exist (or existed in purely formal terms), written constitutions and judicially enforced rights have been introduced or reintroduced into those jurisdictions, significantly increasing the number of jurisdictions whose basic outlines conform to the archetype of liberal constitutionalism.[2] Both the design of these (new or renewed) constitutional orders and their operation, including judicial interpretation thereof, have been clearly and repeatedly influenced by the design and operation of constitutional institutions (and in particular courts) from constitutional orders in which those phenomena have longer histories. This, in turn, has been promoted, no doubt, by the fact that often judges and constitutional scholars in these countries will have

[1] 'Apex courts' being preferred to 'supreme courts' because, one intervention suggests, 'it better captures the institutional position of a court at the top of the judicial hierarchy in a given jurisdiction and because many first-instance courts … are labelled supreme on the basis that they have inherent jurisdiction, and that word is liable to create misunderstandings'. P Daly, 'Introduction' in P Daly (ed), *Apex Courts and the Common Law* (University of Toronto Press, 2019) fn 1.

[2] 'In the wake of World War II, liberal constitutionalism emerged as a default design choice for political systems across Europe and North America. It then diffused more widely across the globe as a whole.' T Ginsburg, AZ Huq and M Versteeg, 'The Coming Demise of Liberal Constitutionalism?' (2018) 85 *University of Chicago Law Review* 239, 239. In this account, which charts the emergence of certain modern threats to liberal constitutionalism, the authors suggest it typically includes not only a written constitutional text protecting rights enforced by way of judicial review, but also (inter alia) 'a commitment to periodic democratic elections': ibid.

studied in, and been influenced by, certain key jurisdictions – in the Anglophone world, and almost certainly also in absolute terms, the US has often dominated. And so the turn towards comparative constitutional scholarship is to this extent a function of the fact that there is greater borrowing and influencing than there may have been in the past, where constitutional orders were treated at times as manifestations of an underlying and presumably distinctive national spirit, such that there was little that any one constitutional order might learn from any other. Constitutional designers and constitutional actors began to borrow from one another with greater frequency and greater alacrity, or at least in more visible fashions, and academics observed that borrowing and began to produce a literature that would in time come to facilitate further, perhaps more systematic and less ad hoc borrowing.

It is right and proper, of course, that lessons have been learned from those jurisdictions in which the sorts of arrangements being introduced for the first time have a longer history. In practice, however, this approach runs the risk of convergence on a model that is not necessarily suited to all jurisdictions, and which may in fact be (significantly?) inferior to other models that are available. In particular, the central position of the US Supreme Court within the American constitutional tradition has a potentially regressive effect on any constitutional system that takes that order as its model, and has contributed – it would seem – to an approach to comparative constitutional law that is at times too quick to acquiesce in or even endorse the excessive empowerment of courts and, more frequently and perhaps more insidiously, to focus upon the work of courts to the exclusion of other actors, with the effect of exaggerating their significance and heightening their prestige. As the phenomenon develops, however, there is no reason that such borrowing should be limited to a situation in which long-standing constitutional orders of the so-called 'Global North', with their esteemed judiciaries and linguistic privileges, exercise influence upon those of newer democracies, many of them in 'Global South': on a formal level, at least, there is no reason why the direction of influence cannot, at least on occasion, reverse. And so we can expect these patterns to continue to evolve: once the legitimacy of reliance upon the decisions of other jurisdictions' courts has become established, and the habit ingrained, it may be that it develops in unpredictable ways. And whether or not it does so, the use of foreign jurisprudence by courts deciding matters of constitutional law – in whatever direction, however methodologically (im)proper, and regardless of the particular end to which that jurisprudence is put – gives an obvious impetus and value to the (more) systematic study of constitutional law through a comparative lens.

Other factors driving the growth of comparative constitutional law would seem to be external to the constitutional orders being studied themselves. One is the fact that there is a globalised university system, with significant movement of staff and students around the world, but that system remains dominated by a small number of prestigious institutions in wealthy countries, which as a result have access to knowledge, and people, from across the globe. Students travel from their home jurisdictions to study at major research universities, and may find themselves considering the constitutional law of those home jurisdictions from the perspective of an increasingly globalised field of study. Academics research their 'home' country or region alongside others writing about different parts of the globe, many of them very far from home and exposed daily – or so one would hope – to knowledge of a range of distinctive ideas as to how public power is currently exercised, and how it should or could be otherwise. Given that those jurisdictions that are most prestigious, and linguistically dominant, are often common law jurisdictions, in which the central mode of legal education has historically involved considerable and sometimes perhaps excessive focus upon the decisions of appellate courts, by which common law doctrine evolved and was refined, this too potentially contributes to a mode of seeing the world of constitutional law in which the central actors are courts and the key reference points the decisions of those courts. While it may be difficult for a relative outsider to study constitutional law in its political and cultural context, or to navigate the work of a legislature with arcane and inhospitable procedures, and that produces vast and complex texts which might amend dozens of others such texts, it is very easy to find the latest major decision of an apex court and read it as a self-contained document. That the horizons of such a decision are so limited – that it brackets off much if not all of the wider social, cultural and historical context within which the dispute arises for determination – makes it simultaneously a useful and a potentially misleading tool for teaching. Moreover, it is much easier to produce research contrasting how apex courts have dealt with one specific issue (which might require reading as few as two judgments) than it is to compare and contrast how that matter is dealt with by a constitutional order as a whole.

Both inside and outside of the formal legal system, therefore, modern developments result in a new supply of comparative constitutional material, with the key trends mutually reinforcing: courts consider or draw upon the work of their counterparts elsewhere; academics begin to systematise the study of these issues; courts are confronted with a growing body of material upon which they might, if they choose, draw in future. New journals and new scholarly institutions focused upon the comparative study of constitutional law are, from this point of view, not merely supply-side factors but also, it would seem, important drivers of demand. Scholarly works on comparative constitutional law written in English can aspire to sales in a far larger market than will many domestic constitutional studies, possibly aimed at a small 'home' market and perhaps written in a language not spoken by those who dominate and so shape the field. English-language journals, as many of the leading comparative law journals are, can usually command a far greater readership than will those written in (one of) the language(s) of the 'home' jurisdiction. More broadly, there are the sorts of crucial incentives that push people to write on topics of 'international' or 'global' significance, allowing them to extend their influence into new spaces and, in some cases, to float across jurisdictions, participating in workshops, taking up fellowships and enjoying other markers of professional esteem. Formal and informal prestige, that is, is more easily acquired when one can show that one's audience is not a small community of domestic scholars but a far larger one, spread across the globe. Comparative constitutional law, we might suggest, has become prominent within the academy, but not always for reasons that relate solely to the inherent value of the exercise. It is important, for that reason and no doubt also for others, to be particularly clear about what we are doing when we engage in the comparative study of constitutional law, and why.

A. Purpose

As the literature on comparative constitutional law has grown, a meta-literature has emerged that seeks to clarify the purpose of the exercise – what it is that individual researchers, and perhaps the community of comparative constitutional lawyers as a whole, seek to achieve in engaging in such scholarship and teaching it to students. Within that, David Law, though writing from the perspective of pedagogy rather than research in the field, provides a useful account of the different reasons for which we might engage in comparison,[3] which we might then use in order to consider how we go about doing so. The first of these is 'instrumentalism', where we study other constitutions in order to learn from them, so that the specific topics that one chooses to study are those that 'lawyers and judges back home find important, while the countries you consider are those that face constitutional issues and challenges comparable to those in your own country'.[4] Another motive is tourism, the simple desire to encounter something that is not that with which one is familiar, though there is of course an important distinction between what we seek out and why we do so: tourism is likely to have as strong a normative bent as instrumentalism, even if the nature of the tourism means that the underlying impulse can often be left unstated or allowed to appear something other than it in fact is. We might not, that is, seek to understand how other jurisdictions deal with specific issues with a view to transplanting their approach back to our home jurisdiction, but our bare curiosity may nevertheless reflect a sense of dissatisfaction with approaches with which we have prior familiarity. A third reason is what Law calls 'immersion', that is, to seek to consider and eventually understand something that is different not as an object of difference, but rather as though one was in fact internal to it – to try, as he puts it, 'to learn to think like a Japanese lawyer, or a Dutch lawyer, or an Iranian lawyer'.[5] This – again, grounded in pedagogy – is significantly more ambitious than most of the literature on comparative constitutional law seeks to be. There is also 'abstraction', wherein we seek to generalise and categorise, sacrificing depth for breadth, and accepting the value of thinking

[3] DS Law, 'Introduction: Pedagogy and Conceptualization of the Field' in DS Law (ed), *Constitutionalism in Context* (Cambridge University Press, 2022).

[4] ibid 6.

[5] ibid 13.

about constitutionalism 'at a relatively high level of abstraction and, ideally, to see the forest for the trees'.[6] Finally, Law suggests, there is comparison as 'representation', which tries to encompass the whole while reducing its infinite complexity to a manageable set of jurisdictions and issues:

> The level of diversity is daunting: there are old states and new states, big states and small states, democratic states and autocratic states, liberal states and illiberal states, secular states and religious states, centralized and decentralized states, and so on. By focusing on a representative selection of topics and jurisdictions, however, it may be possible to gain a sense of how much constitutionalism varies throughout the world, and in what ways.[7]

Within this schema, therefore, I eschew any ambition to immersion. For the present work, it is, I would suggest, largely irrelevant, in that – as discussed in the Introduction as well as below – the choice of comparators reflects a sense that the various constitutional orders are not so different after all, and so there is increasingly little difference between thinking like a New Zealand or UK lawyer, at least in the field of national security and national security constitutionalism. It is therefore an underlying assumption of this project that there is no need for someone versed in one of the legal systems at issue to learn to think like a lawyer trained in one of the others: subject to certain caveats (the importance of which diminishes at the level of the constitution and in the specific area of national security), there is sufficient commonality between these systems that there is no requirement to do so. The shared assumptions and shared methods – to say nothing of the shared language – mean, I assume, that someone familiar with the legal system of one of the Commonwealth Five Eyes states is capable of navigating, with what must count as relative ease, the systems of the others. In fact, as we shall see in chapter 7, we are in many ways seeking to understand them as aspects of single whole, with the different jurisdictions' treatment of a range of particular matters now effectively variations on an increasingly well-defined theme. Nor, for similar reasons, is this an exercise in tourism. Again, the opposite would seem to be true: I am not seeking out the unfamiliar but rather the familiar, looking at jurisdictions that (I have assumed) resemble one another in their fundamentals for the sorts of commonalities and points of distinction in pursuit of national security that are significant specifically because of those underlying resemblances. Nor, though, am I seeking a representative consideration of the variety of approaches to questions of national security within individual constitutional orders: the four jurisdictions at issue are resolutely unrepresentative of the wider constitutional forms, and if they are representative of anything bigger – a point I leave open here – it is of the category of Commonwealth common law jurisdictions, within which they are (precisely because of their Five Eyes status) the most observed and the most developed as far as national security is concerned.

[6] ibid 15.
[7] ibid 17.

Though there is a degree of instrumentalism in my motivation, I am not seeking to solve some problem that has arisen: to say, for example, that its having been successfully done in some way in Canada, it might be done the same way in Australia or New Zealand. We shall discuss at various points in the book what the key drivers of past developments in Commonwealth national security constitutionalism have been; suffice it to say for now, future developments are unlikely to be meaningfully influenced by the observations of a rank outsider. Nevertheless, instrumentalism is a motive we shall encounter repeatedly in the present work, where those in one state who have sought to respond to some challenge – whether a distinctive one, which arises in specific circumstances at a specific point in time, or one that is, as many are, inherent to the project of protecting national security in the context of a liberal democracy – have turned in the past, and ever more frequently in the present, to the practices of other states, and especially the other Five Eyes states. So while my own motives are not instrumentalist, instrumentalism on the part of others has been in the past, and remains in the present, a major driver of the evolution of what I am calling here the Commonwealth model of national security constitutionalism.

What, then, I am seeking to do might be best understood as a form of abstraction: I am seeking to understand the key features of modern national security constitutionalism in the Commonwealth Five Eyes states, with a view to then understanding how and to what extent the contemporary picture reflects either or both the shared constitutional fundamentals of these jurisdictions and the demands of national security as a project of governance, and what cannot be explained by those factors but must be explained by something more. This, then, is a consciously limited ambition, which does not seek to offer lessons about constitutionalism, or even national security constitutionalism, more generally. To continue Law's metaphor, the present work is able, given the very strong and growing resemblances between the jurisdictions in this area, to marry – I hope – a degree of abstraction with an attention to detail, and so see the landscape as including both forest and trees simultaneously. Rather than generalising from a set of constitutional orders to make conceptual claims about constitutions and constitutionalism, in the field of national security or otherwise, I wish to demonstrate how these specific jurisdictions borrow and learn from each other. In particular, I want to show how they did so while national security law in its modern form did not yet exist, and how the mechanisms of borrowing and sharing evolved over the period in which national security was constitutionalised – given a legal basis and made subject to increased oversight. I will argue, on the basis of that consideration, that when we observe the four Commonwealth Five Eyes jurisdictions, we see, now, a number of variations upon a single model of Commonwealth national security constitutionalism. Though the differences between the jurisdictions remain significant, it seems clear that they are diminishing (and the relevant model therefore strengthening) and that they can, for a number of reasons, be expected to do so further in future. One of the key reasons is that the developments I describe in this work, many of which might be characterised as constitutionalisation, including the rationalisation and formalisation of the constitutional apparatus pertaining to national security, and the introduction and expansion of mechanisms of oversight and review, themselves work to facilitate further borrowing and sharing between jurisdictions.

B. Questions of Method

Closely related to the question of why we carry out scholarship on comparative constitutional law is that of how we do so. Though views vary as to the value of the explicit consideration of methodology,[8] it is clear that one prominent set of questions being asked in the contemporary literature relates to the different methodologies being employed therein, and the reasons for which they are employed.[9] Perhaps the key lesson of that body of literature is the need to pay attention to the question of method in connection with the aims of a particular piece of scholarly work.[10] What method should be employed will be determined, that is, by what one is trying to achieve, for certain things can only been achieved via certain methods. Conversely, the method adopted in any particular piece of work will limit what might be learned from the comparative enterprise. Here, we have been clear, the aim is not to make a descriptive claim about constitutions – in the round, or specifically in relation to their treatment of national security – generally. Nor is it to make claims about what causes constitutions to be one way rather than another. Rather, the aim is the more modest one of showing how a group of constitutions with a shared heritage, and which are bound together within a vital intelligence-sharing

[8] See, strikingly, M Tushnet, 'Saying and Doing in Comparative Constitutional Studies' (2016) 64 *American Journal of Comparative Law* 201 (reviewing R Hirschl, *Comparative Matters: The Renaissance of Comparative Constitutional Law* (Oxford University Press, 2014)): 'I am generally impatient with discussions of "method" or "theory" in comparative constitutional law … My general view is that people should simply get on with the job of doing what they regard as comparative constitutional research, and let others decide what is valuable in the product.'

[9] See the following contributions: R Hirschl, 'The Question of Case Selection in Comparative Constitutional Law' (2005) 53 *American Journal of Comparative Law* 125; M Tushnet, 'Some Reflections on Method in Comparative Constitutional Law' in S Choudhry (ed), *The Migration of Constitutional Ideas* (Cambridge University Press, 2006); VC Jackson, 'Methodological Challenges in Comparative Constitutional Law' (2010) 28 *Penn State International Law Review* 319; VC Jackson, 'Comparative Constitutional Law: Methodologies' in M Rosenfeld and A Sajó (eds), *The Oxford Handbook of Comparative Constitutional Law* (Oxford University Press, 2012); R Hirschl, 'From comparative constitutional law to comparative constitutional studies' (2013) 11 *International Journal of Constitutional Law* 1; Hirschl (n 8).

[10] As Hirschl puts it, including it amongst his proposed set of 'sensible guiding principles' for comparative constitutional lawyers, scholars should 'ensure that the research design and methods of comparison reflect the analytical aims or intellectual goals of specific studies, so that a rational, analytically adaptive connection exists between the research questions and the comparative methods used': Hirschl (n 8) 231. Tushnet sums up these principles by saying 'Do good work': Tushnet (n 8) 202.

alliance, have dealt with the issue of national security, how that approach has developed over time, how they have influenced one another in that regard and – finally – of considering what emerges out of a study that takes in all four rather than merely one or some of them.

In this sense, the work has of course a strong functionalist dimension,[11] which considers – as Hirschl puts it, describing the organisation of single-country encyclopaedic works – 'elements of the constitutional system being studied in terms of the function they fulfil'.[12] I have identified a particular area of policy – national security – that one might expect to find (and does find) pursued in all or almost all states, and am concerned with the question of how the different jurisdictions exercise the different constitutional functions associated with that area of policy: both instituting and empowering the bodies that seek to protect it and offering oversight of and accountability for how they do so. There is also, however, a notable historical dimension to this work, of a sort that would be absent in a purely functional consideration concerned only with how different jurisdictions dealt with national security – how they structured public power exercised for these ends and what oversight they provided for – in the here and now.[13] That is, the basic framing of the current project – which states it includes, and which it does not – reflects, it has been noted already, a strong assumption that these jurisdictions do not merely provide four different ways of answering the same questions we might compare and contrast in order to learn about the general position of national security within constitutional orders, whether actually-existing or not, or in order to determine how constitutional design causes policy or other outcomes. Rather, it starts from the belief that there are important commonalities between these four constitutional orders, reflected at least in part in the way in which each of the four addresses questions of national security, and that these commonalities result in part from a shared constitutional-imperial heritage, discussed in chapter 2. As I have suggested, by considering the manner in which the relevant powers, bodies and institutions within the national security enterprise have unfolded over time – from the time of empire through the period of self-government heading towards independence and the Cold War to the present day – we can learn about how that shared heritage has in the past shaped and continues in the present to shape a distinctive and shared approach to national security constitutionalism in the Commonwealth Five Eyes states.

A key methodological aspect of the present work, therefore, is what has been described as 'concept formation through multiple-descriptions', whereby

[11] See Jackson, *Methodologies* (n 9) 62–67, and F Bignami, 'Methodologies of Comparative Constitutional Law: Functional Approach' in R Grote, F Lachenmann and R Wolfrum (eds), *Max Planck Encyclopedia of Comparative Constitutional Law* (August 2021).

[12] Hirschl (n 8) 233.

[13] Jackson, *Methodologies* (n 9) 58–61.

the discussion of how particular issues are handled in a number of jurisdictions allows for the identification of novel legal strategies or hitherto unappreciated institutional forms.[14] That something is the same issue – that we are really, that is, examining the 'the same constitutional phenomena'[15] – is of course a crucial precondition for this exercise. To that end, it is perhaps important to note that because my attention is on an area of policy to which constitutional structures are a response, rather than assuming that certain constitutional institutions or mechanisms are necessarily each other's equivalent, some of the dangers of the assumption might be evaded. Nevertheless, the point draws attention to the possibility, perhaps greater outside of the specific context in which I am writing, that the same language of 'national security' (or its equivalent in other languages) might have varying referents, such that the institutions of the 'national security constitution' in each state are not as equivalent as one might initially assume. One influential example of this sort of work in fact relates to certain of the jurisdictions that are the object of the current study: the work of Stephen Gardbaum on the 'new Commonwealth model' of constitutionalism, which seeks to marry the two key impulses of constitutional democracies – self-government and constraint – in a fashion that escapes the binary between legislative supremacy (in which the legislature has the last word) and constitutional supremacy (in which the last word, unless and until it is amended, goes to the constitution as interpreted by the courts).[16] Instead, Gardbaum has argued by reference to Canada, the UK and New Zealand, these duelling impulses are reconciled within this new Commonwealth model of constitutionalism by a combination of two techniques: first of all, the mandatory review of proposed legislation for its compatibility with a specified set of fundamental rights; and, second, the review of legislation by courts on a 'weak-form' basis, where the result of a negative assessment is not, as is the case in 'strong-form' judicial review, the invalidation of the provisions in question but rather a declaration of that incompatibility, with the question of how (and indeed whether) the incompatibility is to be remedied left to that same legislature to answer.[17]

For now, what matters is how Gardbaum's work stands as an archetype of a particular approach: by describing how a number of linked jurisdictions have approached the same task – protecting rights against legislative encroachment – he is able to identify and describe a distinctive approach to doing so. The current

[14] Hirschl (n 8) 120. Hirschl notes (ibid 187) that value of the exercise but also its limitations as generally implemented: while we 'acquire a far more complex, nuanced, and sophisticated understanding of what, for example, solids or mammals are by studying the variance and commonality among exemplars within their respective categories', it is nevertheless the case that 'a key distinguishing mark of scientific inquiry is making valid inferences that go beyond the particular observations collected' and that comparative constitutional law scholarship has often failed to live up to this ideal.

[15] ibid 120.

[16] S Gardbaum, *The New Commonwealth Model of Constitutionalism* (Cambridge University Press, 2012).

[17] Gardbaum (n 16) 25–36.

work seeks to do something similar, though with appropriate modesty as to the nature and extent of its contribution. It seeks to map, that is, the ways in which the Commonwealth Five Eyes states approach the same task: that of pursuing national security and providing accountability for that pursuit while respecting the need for sensitive methods and actions to remain hidden from public view. That task has, I will suggest, seen a number of constitutional innovations introduced, variations of which can now be found in the four Commonwealth Five Eyes states. One of those – the 'hybrid institution', which cuts across traditional distinctions between legal and political institutions – I have described in earlier work,[18] and will consider in a broader context in chapter 5. Another is the parliamentary (or pseudo-, or quasi-parliamentary) committee, suitably modified so as to address the particularities of the national security context – a phenomenon that has already been identified and subjected to academic attention.[19] The point, however, is that these institutional forms emerge in the context of recurring policy imperatives and (of particular significance here) against the background of shared constitutional fundamentals, and so I seek to go further than merely describing them and noting their similarities, many of which might – in light of those two points – exist anyway. I also wish to show how these four states act as a distinct ecosystem, whereby not only do their constitutional arrangements pertaining to national security resemble one another, but we are also able to pinpoint moments at which and the mechanisms by which innovations and developments in one state are picked up by, or even directly transmitted to, the others. In this way I describe and assess what I take to be a model of national security constitutionalism that connects the Commonwealth Five Eyes states: one that is perhaps weaker or looser than the model described by Gardbaum but where the nature and extent of the borrowing and sharing between the four jurisdictions makes it reasonable to describe it as a model nonetheless. The paradox, however, is not hard to see. That is, I consider the Commonwealth Five Eyes states and describe a model of national security constitutionalism common (if not necessarily exclusive) to those states. It is hardly unthinkable that a consideration of a different grouping of states, whether or not overlapping, might have resulted in the description of a different model. What is observed, that is, will always be a function in part of what is studied, and what is studied cannot be justified by what is ultimately observed. We need, therefore, to break into that circle on some other basis – an instinct that makes us think that there is something to see before it is in fact seen; that what will be achieved through a study will be able to transcend the level of bare description. This is the question of 'case selection'.

[18] PF Scott, 'Hybrid Institutions in the National Security Constitution' (2019) 39 *Legal Studies* 432.

[19] See, eg, A Defty, 'From committees of parliamentarians to parliamentary committees: comparing intelligence oversight reform in Australia, Canada, New Zealand and the UK' (2020) 35 *Intelligence and National Security* 367.

C. Case Selection

The question of case selection – that is, which jurisdictions' constitutions will be studied[20] – is closely related to the question of what method will be used in order to study those jurisdictions. This is a question I have already addressed in the Introduction and so can deal with briefly here. The jurisdictions at issue are those of the Commonwealth states that are members of the Five Eyes intelligence-sharing alliance.[21] The exclusionary nature of these dual Five Eyes and Commonwealth framings – the privileging of these above all else in selecting these jurisdictions for consideration – means we need not concern ourselves with the specific, and perhaps rather futile, question of whether these constitutional orders are in some sense best suited to answer a particular research question. The logic of this selection does, though, suffice, I hope, to exclude the danger normally identified in this context: that of cherry-picking jurisdictions so as to influence and perhaps entirely to determine the conclusions at which one will then arrive.[22] The point here is not, then, so much to justify that choice, which to a considerable degree stands or falls quite apart from anything I might offer by way of justification (and which is perhaps, however irrationally, less in need of justification than would be the decision to focus on jurisdictions that are more linguistically or politically marginal), but rather, in keeping with the discussion of method, to be clear as to the limits of what we might learn from this project.

We cannot, that is, hope to learn anything universal about the question of how constitutions do or should deal with national security, or what the (general) implications are of addressing issues of national security in one way rather than another. The selected cases are too few and too similar to achieve such a thing. In particular, as we are considering only Commonwealth Five Eyes states and not any that do not sit within that grouping, we cannot hope to learn anything specific about how (non-)membership of that category affects the form taken by national security constitutionalism. What we can learn, and what seems valuable, is how a group of closely-related constitutional orders, linked by a shared constitutional and imperial heritage – including some that are highly influential, whether because they in some sense 'deserve' to be influential, or simply because they are over-represented in an unduly parochial scholarly literature – deal with the specific question of national security, and how they have in the past and continue in the present to borrow and share constitutional innovations between them. From there, we might learn something more about those constitutional orders that the existing literature, insufficiently attentive to a distinctive policy context

[20] See Hirschl, 'The Question of Case Selection' (n 9).

[21] The history of which is discussed briefly in the Introduction.

[22] '[T]oo many constitutional comparativists still adhere to a convenient "cherry picking" approach to case selection while overlooking (or being unaware of) basic methodological principles of controlled comparison and research design frequently drawn upon in the social sciences.' Hirschl, 'The Question of Case Selection' (n 9) 153.

that demands (and is conducive to) institutional innovation, misses. We might also learn something about modes of norm transfer, both within this constitutional grouping and, perhaps, beyond it – especially, but not solely, in the context of the broader vista of Commonwealth constitutionalism of which these states form an influential part but with which they are not by any means co-extensive. Both method and case selection constrain, in important ways, the questions a project might answer and the lessons it might offer.

III. The Comparative National Security Literature

I began this discussion by noting the turn to comparison in constitutional law. Though that turn is far and away the most important trend in contemporary constitutional scholarship, and though there is now a vast (if perhaps imbalanced, both geographically and in other ways[23]) literature on comparative constitutional law, there has been little work so far within this movement or trend on questions of constitutional law and practice as they apply to the specific domain of national security (or any close relation thereof – defence or military constitutionalism, for example). A large proportion of that which does exist – much of it relating, first, to the post-9/11 period and, second, to the longer arc of UN influence on the national security endeavour – relates to the law of counterterrorism specifically, to the exclusion of other threats to national security (including state threats).[24] A number of reasons for that suggest themselves. One is that the end of Cold War, during which these issues had a particular salience and many of the key constitutional moves were first made in the jurisdictions under consideration, pre-dated the comparative turn in constitutional law, to which the most important work on comparative national security law – Lustgarten and Leigh's *In from the Cold* – might in fact be understood as something of a forerunner.[25] Indeed, the origins

[23] Attempts to redress that imbalance – the existence of which no one seems to deny – have led to arguments for what has been described as a 'southern turn', reflecting the fact that (despite clear progress) 'the Global South still seems to punch under its weight in constitutional conversations. While it represents "most of the world" in terms of population and constitutions, it remains vastly under-represented in global constitutional debates, teaching materials, publications, and conferences.': P Dann, M Riegner and M Bönnemann, 'The Southern Turn in Comparative Constitutional Law' in P Dann, M Riegner and M Bönnemann (eds), *The Global South and Comparative Constitutional Law* (Oxford University Press, 2020) 1. And see also R Dixon, T Ginsburg and A Kassie Abebe (eds), *Comparative Constitutional Law in Africa* (Edward Elgar, 2022).

[24] See, eg, the following important contributions to the literature: K Lane Scheppele, 'The International Standardization of National Security Law' (2010) 4 *National Security Law and Policy* 437; K Roach, *The 9/11 Effect: Comparative Counter-Terrorism* (Cambridge University Press, 2011); K Roach (ed), *Comparative Counter-Terrorism Law* (Cambridge University Press, 2015); A Vedaschi and K Lane Scheppele (eds), *9/11 and the Rise of Global Anti-Terrorism Law: How the UN Security Council Rules the World* (Cambridge University Press, 2021).

[25] L Lustgarten and I Leigh, *In from the Cold: National Security and Parliamentary Democracy* (Oxford University Press, 1994). And see also, in the same period, from a primarily Australian perspective, HP Lee, PJ Hanks and V Morabito, *In the Name of National Security: The Legal Dimensions* (LBC Information Services, 1995).

of that turn have been traced by some to the period of apparent convergence on a model of liberal-democratic constitutionalism in the period following the end of the Cold War, when the self-proclaimed victors worked in tandem with global institutions to export their model of political organisation around the world.[26] It is striking that in the short gap between the end of the Cold War and the rise of comparison, we see work such as Lustgarten and Leigh's appear, because the process of rationalisation of UK national security law that stood at the heart of their work seems itself to have also been in part a function of the end of that Cold War. And even though the rise of the modern counter-terrorism apparatus, domestic and global, coincided with that turn to comparison, it has nevertheless tended to be at the margins of the comparative project, given that the comparative turn is focused often on central, structural questions of constitutionalism – the division of labour between courts and legislature, or the process by which constitutions might be amended – to which the law of counter-terrorism, like that of national security more broadly, speaks only indirectly. So, for example, the modern counter-terrorism apparatus that has grown up in and evolved rapidly in all of the jurisdictions under consideration may well implicate the sorts of major questions about the protection of rights within a constitutional order and/or the role of courts vis-à-vis legislature or executive that preoccupy many of the central thinkers in comparative constitutional law. It does not, however, do so alone but usually as one amongst a range of factors, the rest of which might in practice outrank it in significance.

Another factor that might explain the general absence of national security within the comparative literature, is that the comparative literature on any issue tends to build upon an underlying literature regarding the individual jurisdictions being compared. Comparative constitutional law, that is, rests upon – and no doubt in turn promotes – the study of the constitutional orders of individual jurisdictions. The historical prominence of American constitutional law within the field of comparative constitutional law is, one might therefore suggest, a function of the supply of writing on that topic as much as of demand for insights into it. The relevance of this point is that the study of national security law is inconsistently developed, with there being relatively little in some of the jurisdictions under consideration. We have already noted that in the US there is lots – in part, it would seem, because of the strong links that exist between national security law practitioners and academics teaching and researching national security law, with many of the latter having been at some stage also the former. In Canada too, now, there is a well-developed literature, including teaching materials, with the development

[26] See B Ackerman, 'The Rise of World Constitutionalism' (1997) 83 *Virginia Law Review* 771, in which Ackerman noted that American constitutional lawyers had been 'happy to cheer the fall of the Berlin Wall and to celebrate the rise of world constitutionalism with an orgy of junketeering to far-off places in need of legal lore', but that the growth of 'world constitutionalism' had 'not yet had the slightest impact on American constitutional thought'. Hirschl (n 8) 1, fn 1, suggests that this article 'may be considered an early field definer' of comparative constitutional law.

of that literature owing much to a small number of highly productive scholars.[27] In the UK, the national security law literature is growing but remains underdeveloped, with the first practitioner text in the topic only a few years old:[28] the major study already mentioned, by Lustgarten and Leigh, marked in large part the end of a body of work that had tracked the constitutionalisation of national security in the UK between the mid-1980s and mid-1990s, and which went into something of an abeyance thereafter. There is perhaps still at this point in time less of a literature on national security in Australia and, in particular, New Zealand, notwithstanding the major developments that have occurred in the latter in recent years[29] and the carrying out in the former of an official review of the relevant law, which seems to outrank in scale and ambition any that had ever before taken place in any of the Commonwealth Five Eyes states.[30] This speaks, perhaps, not so much to the existence of the raw material of national security law – in all cases, and in particular in Australia, there is nowadays no shortage of legislative material – but to the conception of it as a sub-discipline that brings together topics that are otherwise found in texts on international law, criminal law, constitutional law or even civil procedure. Neither the necessary expertise, nor perhaps the impetus to acquire it, is easy to come by.

Moving further down the causal chain, an important factor is that – though there is now (much) more national security law, both legislation and case law, than there once was – for a long time it would not have been clear what was being compared: what were the relevant legal materials. Even when different jurisdictions had moved beyond the era in which their SIAs were governed by (often unpublished) Orders in Council or informal 'directives', there were in some cases – into the 1990s or even 2000s – only a small number of, often rather laconic, statutes and, particularly significantly in common law systems, few cases in which these statutory materials were discussed or interpreted. Though it might be possible to offer an exegesis on the relevant statutes, doing so would require a considerable degree of speculation, given that the rules were often underspecified (and sometimes perhaps even actively misleading)[31] and, as noted further below, there was pervasive secrecy as

[27] C Forcese and L West, *National Security Law*, 2nd edn (Irwin Law Inc, 2020).

[28] R Ward and R Jones with C Stone (eds), *National Security Law, Procedure, and Practice* (Oxford University Press, 2021).

[29] The key development in question was the Intelligence and Security Act 2017 (New Zealand), enacting many of the recommendations made in M Cullen and P Reddy, *Intelligence and Security in a Free Society: Report of the First Independent Review of Intelligence and Security in New Zealand* (2016). For commentary, see D Rogers, 'Intelligence and Security Act 2017: A Preliminary Critique' [2018] *New Zealand Law Review* 65; and, on an official level, T Arnold and M Mahuika, *Taumaru: Protecting Aotearoa New Zealand as a Free, Open and Democratic Society, Review of the Intelligence and Security Act 2017* (Ministry of Justice, 2023).

[30] *Comprehensive Review of the Legal Framework of the National Intelligence Community* (2019), carried out on the recommendation of M L'Estrange and S Merchant, *2017 Independent Intelligence Review* (2017) [6.7]–[6.19].

[31] See the discussion of the UK situation in PF Scott, 'New Labour's Secret National Security Constitution' in M Gordon and A Tucker (eds), *The New Labour Constitution: Twenty Years On* (Hart Publishing, 2021).

to the factual matrix to which any legislative provision might apply. Some early academic contributions read – very reasonably – like a series of guesses as to what statutory provisions, on which no detailed elaboration or justification had been offered at the time of their enactment, might mean in practice. Only insiders could know for sure, and they were not inclined to indulge curious outsiders. In place of the range of materials that might be the basis of an academic consideration of national security law, what there was instead was an at times rather arbitrary and disconnected set of cases touching on national security without being directly about it: comments from this or that judge made in some context or other, from which it was often felt necessary to generalise widely (and maybe even wildly) in order to understand the broader legal position, such as it was, regarding national security. For a long time, that is, the law was not systematic, was not amenable to systematisation and so was naturally difficult to compare systematically.

Another obvious reason for the arrested development of a literature on national security law in many jurisdictions is the pervasive secrecy associated with the endeavour. Constitutional law happens – almost by definition must happen – largely in public, and in modern times operates so as to ensure that much, though by no means all, political activity also happens in public: perhaps the key exception, relevant to all of the jurisdictions under consideration, is the interaction between domestic governments and the monarch or his or her representative, where secrecy is considered (with no little irony) to be a necessary condition of maintaining political neutrality. National security law has not always been created in the open, having relied (and to an uncertain degree continuing to rely) both on prerogative powers, which have no authoritative legal formulation and are often subject to considerable uncertainty, or legal rules or their close equivalent which are in fact secret. These might include, for example, internal directives of some status or other, which are used in place of statutes, and so leave no mark on the public record, notwithstanding that they ultimately frame what does or does not happen in much the same way a statute would, and are for that reason not liable to be discussed or debated by scholars, or even (in the context of significant factual secrecy) being pronounced upon by courts.

A classic example of this phenomenon is the Maxwell-Fyfe Directive by which the UK's MI5 was 'governed' in the years prior to its being given a legislative basis in the late 1980s, which was promulgated in 1952 but the contents of which were only revealed a decade later in Lord Denning's report on the Profumo Affair.[32] Equivalents elsewhere, as discussed in chapter 2, in many cases similarly entered the public domain only belatedly and often only in part. Though the situation is now much better in each of the Commonwealth Five Eyes states – where most of the relevant bodies now not only have a statutory basis, as discussed in chapter 3, but have one that is clear and (apparently) comprehensive – it is easy to see how this legal secrecy has inhibited the carrying out of comparative scholarship on

[32] Lord Denning, *Lord Denning's Report* (Cmnd 2152, 1963).

national security law. If one does not know what law there is, what is it one should be comparing? Moreover, if one virtue of legal scholarship (and comparative legal scholarship in particular) is to inform the process of making and remaking the relevant rules – whether by political or judicial bodies – the incentive to produce such scholarship about national security issues, where the executive may not tell you it is making or remaking rules, and where it does so admit is likely to be more than usually unreceptive to views as to what their substance should be, is much weaker. There is, therefore, reason to think that scholarship on national security law might be not just difficult but also, in part, futile.

But legal secrecy is in large part a mere adjunct of an underlying factual secrecy, which persists even where the tide of legal transparency can be held back no longer, and a statutory basis is given to the SIAs of a state and their intrusive capacities. Even, that is, where there is statute, it is not as though the use of the powers possessed by the SIAs are necessarily well known – intercept evidence is often suppressed, and much else about the methods of the SIAs, to say nothing of particular operations carried out by them, has always been and remains to this day entirely secret. They were in many cases excluded – de facto or de jure – from the supervision of the courts, and so there is little to be found about the SIAs and their deeds in the record of the bodies that produce much of the documentation on which legal scholarship draws most heavily, and with which constitutional lawyers are most familiar. Intelligence work is not discussed in detail in legislatures – not in terms of specific operations, of course, but often not even in terms of capabilities. Quite apart from any internal culture of secrecy that doubtless existed and still exists, strict legal regimes punish disclosure of sensitive material and mean that even though they enjoy a greater public profile than in the past, much about the work of these bodies remains unknown.

Historically, exceptions to this secrecy generally arose in the context of scandal, where wrongdoing was suspected or alleged with sufficient plausibility to justify some sort of a (relatively) public inquiry or Royal Commission or similar. In several jurisdictions, these sorts of events have been a key driver not only for the evolution of the law of national security but also, more fundamentally, for allowing outsiders to understand what institutions existed, what (sorts of) work they were doing and on what (if any) legal basis. Key examples, alongside the Denning Report already noted in the UK, include the two Royal Commissions under Justice Hope – one in the 1970s and one in the 1980s – in Australia,[33] the Mackenzie Commission and McDonald Commission in Canada,[34] and the report by the Chief Ombudsman

[33] A number of reports were published by each of the two Hope Commissions. Those that might be considered the primary reports are Royal Commission on Intelligence and Security, *Third Report: Abridged Findings and Recommendations*, No 92/1977 (1977) and Royal Commission on Australia's Security Intelligence Agencies, *General Report*, Parliamentary Paper No 231/1985 (1984).

[34] Royal Commission on Security, *Report of the Royal Commission on Security (Abridged)* (1969) and Commission of Inquiry Concerning Certain Activities of the Royal Canadian Mounted Police, *First Report: Security and Information*, (October 1979); *Second Report: Volume 1 – Freedom and Security under the Law* (1981); *Second Report: Volume 2 – Freedom and Security under the Law* (1981);

Guy Powles in New Zealand.[35] But though these reviews and reports generally went beyond the specific incidents that had prompted their institution, providing insight into the SIAs, their legal frameworks and their work that was not otherwise available, they were in some cases either hamstrung by limited terms of reference and/or had their outputs subject to (considerable) redaction (or simply left partly unpublished), which means that they were at times more limited in their ability to shed light on the work of the SIAs, and in turn of more limited value for the purposes of scholarship, than they might have been. In the absence of more reliable information, myth and rumour dominated: the field of intelligence studies, though now very well developed, was for a long time hampered by the prominence of popular, often highly sensationalised, accounts that did not evidence (perhaps because they could not have evidenced) their most important claims and which at times ended up obscuring rather than clarifying matters, getting in the way of a sober consideration of issues the importance of which has been proved beyond doubt by the passage of time.

While, eventually, specialist bodies were formed, inside or on the margins of the legislature, in order to provide the sort of political oversight that legislatures, in their entirety, could not, these bodies (discussed in chapter 6) of course do not, by definition, provide a perfect substitute for the disclosure and open debate of issues on the floor of the relevant chamber. Membership is still often subject to executive control, evidence is (usually) taken behind closed doors and reports are redacted. Though several are now permitted access to information about operational matters, that information must usually remain hidden from public view. Courts in many cases remain on the sidelines: no one who might be affect by potentially unlawful activity of the SIAs can litigate what they do not know has happened or is happening, while state parties, however hostile to one another, do not tend to bring their disputes about the propriety of others' intelligence-gathering activities to court. Though there is nevertheless, for a variety of reasons, more litigation about national security matters now than in the past, there are also a range of doctrines which operate so as prevent the courts from inquiring into what has happened and its legal implications. Even in the context of such doctrines, the legislatures in various jurisdictions have responded by providing for a degree of secrecy that the common law constitutional tradition traditionally abjured. And so even though much more is published than in the past, the executive often has a veto of some sort over it, and there is as a result significant redaction, which limits the possibilities of a sustained scholarship of national security law. The temptation to simply throw one's hands up can be strong.

Third Report: Certain R.C.M.P. Activities and the Question of Governmental Knowledge (1981). Before McDonald there were R Taschereau and RL Kellock, *Report of the Royal Commission to Investigate the Facts Relating to and the Circumstances Surrounding the Communication, by Public Officials and Other Persons in Positions of Trust of Secret and Confidential Information to Agents of a Foreign Power* (1946) and Royal Commission on Security, *Report of the Royal Commission on Security (Abridged)* (1969).

[35] G Powles, *Security Intelligence Service: Report by Chief Ombudsman* (1976).

In the absence of a consistently strong tradition of writing on national security law (whether or not under that name) in many jurisdictions, it is perhaps unsurprising that little has emerged by way of comparative national security law, or comparative national security constitutionalism, at least within the context of the modern turn to comparison that has become the dominant approach to the study of constitutions in recent years. Here, I seek to change that, though in a consciously and deliberately limited way. As already noted, the jurisdictional scope of the present work, justified on the basis of two of the clear connections that exist between these jurisdictions and how they pursue their national security goals, means that it cannot hope to offer strong conclusions about national security constitutionalism as a general phenomenon. Though the constitutions of other states formerly within the British Empire – some Commonwealth Realms, some Commonwealth Republics and some outside of the Commonwealth entirely – are of course in many cases influenced by it in constitutional terms, and perhaps also in terms of their national security rules and structures, few or none share with those under discussion the same strong links in the field of foreign policy and, in particular, intelligence as exist between the members of Five Eyes.

IV. The Virtues of Comparative National Security Constitutionalism

Even if it has not been widely carried out in recent times, there are, it would seem, a number of major virtues to bringing the comparative method to bear upon the issue of national security constitutionalism. Here I identify a few of those, and consider them in relation to the specific comparative project being undertaken in this work. One is that, as we have already noted, the issue of national security is well suited to a functionalist approach to comparison. While not all states are also nations, it seems highly likely that all constitutions create institutions that seek to protect something we might understand as 'national security' – the protection of that state, its territory, and its people and their property against threats from within and those posed by other states. Whether they use that term, therefore, all states except perhaps the very smallest will seek to protect their national security in some fashion. Comparative national security law is valuable because there will in almost all cases be something to study, and what there is will likely shed interesting light upon the underlying constitutional structures.

A second virtue of the application of this method here is that it takes us beyond what has usually been studied within comparative constitutional law and, in particular, beyond (and indeed away from) courts. A major criticism of the turn to comparison is that it has in the past tended to focus on the work of courts, in two senses. One is that it looks at what courts do, comparing the decisions of apex courts in different jurisdictions on analogous issues so as to draw conclusions about those courts and the constitutional orders of which they form part. The other is that it looks, specifically, at what courts do with the jurisprudence of other courts: what use they do and do not make of 'foreign' jurisprudence, and what that use reveals about patterns of influence and, perhaps, ideologies of constitutionalism. A number of reasons for this might be suggested. In many of the most influential jurisdictions, the common law method means that court cases are the bread and butter, as it were, of the scholar, such that reading and commenting upon case law can provide the core of an academic career. A judgment is largely self-contained, meaning that one can write about it with confidence without needing to read much, if anything, other than the judgment itself. The language of a judgment is (usually?) richer than that of a statute, and judgments have theoretical underpinnings that can be reconstructed, explored and unpacked at length. A judgment might be summarised, whereas the breadth and detail of many modern statutes means that justice can be done to their content and likely effect only via extensive, perhaps tedious, description of that statute, including copious quotation of its language. And though the correctness or attractiveness of an interpretation of a judgment might be contested, it is unlikely to be objectively 'wrong' in the way that exegesis on a statutory text is capable of being. This is particularly true as cases become longer and more sophisticated – a single decision by a major apex court can give rise to a vast literature of critiques and defences, which will grow and evolve as the decision and commentary on it are integrated into existing doctrinal and theoretical disputes. The attractions for the comparativist are obvious.

But despite the impression that such an approach may give, constitutions are not composed solely of what goes on in courts – indeed, a range of actors, from a variety of political perspectives, have sought in recent decades to argue for, and to implement, the reduction of the prominence of courts and their work within these and other constitutional orders. To understand a constitutional order as it exists involves considering also (at least) the work of the executive in its myriad forms (both core political executive and the range of bodies around it, as well as, in turn, the broad administrative state at the heart of which it sits) and the legislative bodies that empower those executive bodies to pursue the myriad tasks that in a modern democracy are expected, if not demanded, of the state. Why constitutional lawyers might at times be slower to seek to study these bodies is again in many ways obvious. They produce a much larger range of documentation than do courts, much of it of ambiguous relevance, and (in the case of the executive) that which is most significant does not enter the public domain, at least in the short term. Their processes are messier and more complex than those of courts, and they operate according to rationalities that are not only much less disciplined than those of courts (at least on their surface) but are not always even reasonable. The decision of a legislative body to legislate for one rule rather than another, that is, cannot be understood simply by reading a legislative text, or even the associated debate. Instead, an attempt to make sense of it might spiral out in time and space, taking into account a range of official and unofficial materials – consultation documents, explanatory notes, briefing documents – the study of which might ultimately work not to explain that decision but rather to highlight the apparently arbitrary nature of certain decision-making. Nor is there any doctrine of precedent by which conflicting or ambiguous statements of different executive actors might be reconciled and systematised. What is meaningful (dicta?) and what is politicking (obiter?) – and whether that distinction even makes sense in the domain of politics rather than law – is unclear. And so a focus on the courts, with their rules of precedent and distinctive (technocratic) rationality, makes a considerable degree of practical and professional sense, even if it results in an unbalanced, and perhaps actively misleading, picture of what constitutions are and what goes on within them.

This danger – a court-centric approach that neglects where much the real constitutional action in fact takes place – is less likely to manifest itself in the context of national security law, for a number of reasons, some of them already hinted at. One, though much truer of the past than the present, is that in the national security context the courts say less, and say it less assertively or authoritatively, than they do elsewhere. That is, courts have in the past often pronounced on matters of national security primarily in order to state that such matters are either not within their purview at all or are subject to a much less intensive level of scrutiny than are other matters. A number of modern trends – not least the presence of the Bills of Rights discussed in the Introduction – make such an approach less common, and indeed states have responded to those trends by seeking to have more judicial decision-making subject to rules of secrecy of a sort that were unnecessary when there were ample legal obstacles to a claim based on sensitive national security issues. More important, however, for present purposes, is that in the national security domain there has been a striking degree of institutional innovation, designed at least in part to counteract the weaknesses in this area not only of judicial but also of parliamentary oversight. And so while it is still possible to consider national security constitutionalism exclusively as it emerges out of the decisions of courts, such an approach is now hopelessly partial, missing out – to repeat the phrase used above – on where the real action is: the reports of independent oversight institutions, parliamentary or quasi-parliamentary bodies, and the sorts of ad hoc bodies that historically did the bulk of the oversight work in this sphere and which continue to be convened when the circumstances are thought, for reasons good or bad, to demand it.

V. Conclusion

The purpose of this chapter was to locate the current work within the context of modern turn to comparison in the study of constitutional law, which necessitated a brief overview of the ways in which, as well as some brief speculations as to the reasons for which, that turn took place and has developed as it has so far. The literature that has emerged out of that turn has given rise not only to much important consideration of constitutions, but also to a body of work that seeks to offer clarity as to the methodological aspects of the study of constitutions. We have discussed certain key ideas of these methodological contributions, and their lessons for the present work. The key such lesson, it is suggested, is the need for a conscious appreciation of the link between the methodology that is employed in a given piece of work and what it is that one aims to achieve from that particular study – as well, we might add, as the link between methods and the limit of what one can hope to learn. Here, my work is primarily within a functionalist scheme: I am looking at how a group of constitutional orders deal with a set of interlinked problems within their constitutional order – the problems of seeking to protect national security while ensuring that the apparatus put in place in order to do so, which for clear practical reasons is unsuited to oversight by the institutions and bodies of the 'ordinary' constitution, does not become a source of arbitrary or oppressive power. But the methodological literature also places considerable emphasis on the question of case selection: which jurisdictions are we 'comparing' and according to which principles do we select them? In the present work the issue of case selection is effectively pre-ordained: the four jurisdictions under consideration are those Commonwealth states that are members of the Five Eyes intelligence-sharing alliance. This has certain clear advantages: that three of these states emerged out of the Empire built by the fourth means, as we shall see in chapter 2, that a functionalist consideration can also be an historical one, showing not only how different constitutions address the same issue but also how their approaches to doing so have evolved over time. It also means, however, that we must be conscious of the limits of what might be learned from the work that follows. I start, in chapter 2, by considering the manner in which the security and intelligence agencies of the Commonwealth Five Eyes states were (and were not) regulated during the Cold War period.

2

Imperial Origins and Cold War Connections

I. Introduction

In the Introduction to this book, I noted, both in discussing the original Five Eyes Agreement and in seeking to justify the framing of the book (and in particular its limitation to only four of the Five Eyes states), the imperial context of that original Agreement. When it was signed, the British Empire was given a special status, as were the self-governing Dominions that existed at that time, amongst which were numbered three states that would soon become signatories to the Agreement in their own right: Australia, Canada and New Zealand. Against that background, this chapter explores the imperial origins of the modern national security enterprise in the Commonwealth Five Eyes states, which – as noted – share not only a constitutional tradition, but also a common law heritage, which means that judicial decision-making in each continues at times to draw upon that of the other states. The chapter's argument is that this imperial context is evidenced not only by the shared constitutional traditions of the Four Eyes states, but also by the specific fashion in which they came, during the Cold War, to develop institutions for protecting their national security. To understand the modern frameworks of national security constitutionalism, and how they came to be, requires an understanding of the way in which equivalent matters were addressed within the British Empire and how they were impacted by the transition from Empire to Commonwealth. As we shall see, the picture that emerges is one in which, though there are certain commonalities that result from the shared constitutional heritage of these states and the common task being pursued, we can see the direct transfer of norms between these jurisdictions, often at the behest of the former imperial power, the UK, itself.

II. 'Defence of the Realm' and the Fragmentation of the Realm

In the common law tradition, the dominant concept in this area of policy was for many centuries that of 'Defence of the Realm'.[1] So, for example, in the *Case*

[1] As used by, eg, W Blackstone, *Commentaries on the Laws of England*, vol I, 408: 'The military state includes the whole of the soldiery, or such persons as are peculiarly appointed among the rest of the

of Saltpetre (1606), it was said by the various judges called upon to consider the question of the King's prerogative in taking saltpetre in order to make gunpowder that, 'when enemies come against the realm to the sea-coast, it is lawful to come upon my land adjoining to the same coast, to make trenches or bulwarks for the defence of the realm, for every subject hath benefit by it' and so 'by the common law, every man may come upon my land for the defence of the realm'.[2] In the UK, where it originated, that language has now been taken over by the dual concepts – distinct, though not always clearly distinguished[3] – of 'defence' and 'national security'.[4] In the *GCHQ* case of the mid-1980s on the reviewability of the prerogative powers,[5] Lord Diplock – who would know better than most judges[6] – said that those powers extended 'to matters so vital to the survival and welfare of the nation as the conduct of relations with foreign states and – what lies at the heart of the present case – the defence of the realm against potential enemies'. He continued by noting that under the influence 'the phraseology used in the European Convention on Human Rights 1953 … to which the United Kingdom is a party', it had by now 'become usual in statutes to refer to the latter as "national security"',[7] though that term can also be found (in the context of the phrase 'the interests of national security') in enactments that pre-date the drafting of the European Convention on Human Rights (ECHR),[8] and seems to have been used with a degree of regularity in other parts of the Empire before it had become dominant in the UK itself.[9]

people for the safeguard and defence of the realm.'; and CM Clode, *The Military Forces of the Crown: Their Administration and Government*, vol 1 (John Murray, 1869) 1: 'The Primary object for which the Military forces of the Crown are retained in arms is the Defence of the Realm.'

2 *The Case of the King's Prerogative in Saltpetre* (1606) 77 ER 1294, 1295. The first appearance of the formulation in the English Reports seems to be in *R v The Earl of Northumberland* (1568) 75 ER 472 ('*The Case of Mines*'), relating to Queen Elizabeth's claim to a mine found on the land of the Earl of Northumberland. It was argued for the Queen that the monarch is required to protect her subjects, for which she requires an army, and that for an army she requires treasure: '[T]herefore inasmuch as God has created mines within this realm, as a natural provision of treasure for the defence of the realm, it is reasonable that he who has the government and care of the people, whom he cannot defend without treasure, should have the treasure wherewith to defend them; so that the law has for necessity's sake appropriated the mines of gold and silver to the King.'

3 See, eg, Freedom of Information Act 2000 (UK), ss 24, 26 and 27.

4 Older cases use the two formulations in what would appear to be an interchangeable fashion: see *Chandler v DPP* [1964] AC 763. Though nothing in particular turns on the point, it was said in a key UK national security case in the early 2000s that '[n]ational security and defence of the realm may cover the same ground though I tend to think that the latter is capable of a wider meaning': see *Secretary of State for the Home Department v Rehman* [2001] UKHL 47 [18].

5 *Council of Civil Service Unions v Minister for the Civil Service* [1985] AC 374 ('*GCHQ*').

6 Lord Diplock, who later became a trusted figure to be called upon when the government of the day required an independent consideration of sensitive issues, had worked with the 'Security Executive' during the Second World War: see PF Scott, 'Judicial Biography in the National Security Constitution: Lord Diplock and a "Rather Silly Little Secret Racket"' (2024) 87 *Moden Law Review* 624.

7 *GCHQ* (n 5) 410.

8 See, eg, Transport Act 1947, s 4(7).

9 See, eg, *Marconi's Wireless Telegraph Co Ltd v Commonwealth (No 2)* [1913] HCA 19, in which Justice Isaacs of the High Court of Australia said that the question is 'whether the political branch of the government is entitled to guard wholly, effectively, and in its complete integrity, a political secret with which it has been entrusted, and with it the national security and welfare which, to that extent, are in its exclusive charge'. This pre-dates the influential use of the term in *The Zamora* [1916] 2 AC 77.

Strikingly – for example – the Australian legislation making provision related to the Second World War was entitled the National Security Act 1939. In most cases, however, the key purpose of any discussion of the concept was not to define it but rather to assert – time and again – the priority of the executive, and the minimal role of the court, in determining what it did, and did not, require. That 'defence', though it survives as a legal concept, has been largely shorn of the reference to 'the realm' that was once its constant companion, would seem to be a function of the same processes of dismantling the British Empire that meant that Australia, Canada and New Zealand could be, as Dominions of the British Empire, given a special status within the original UKUSA Agreement and yet, shortly thereafter, become signatories to the Agreement's successors in their own right.

A. The Unity of the Realm

The British Empire, which at its height covered a quarter of the world's land, was as a matter of law a single entity. It was, that is, one realm with one Crown, which united the various independent states – England, Scotland, Ireland – which were brought together as one, United, Kingdom as well as the (lower-case 'd') dominions of the Crown that made up that one Kingdom's global Empire. The UK's constitution was an imperial constitution.[10] This legal unity also made sense of the singular object in the phrase 'defence of the realm'. That realm was also considered by those ruling it to be subject, in its entirety, to the authority of the UK Parliament (which was in this sense an Imperial Parliament), though the point was often contested in particular circumstances,[11] so that – for example – disputes about the authority of the Parliament over the 13 American colonies had precipitated the American Revolution and the end of the first British Empire.[12] When individual colonies were granted self-government within the British Empire – such as Canada by the British North America Act 1867, now renamed in that jurisdiction the Constitution Act, or the Commonwealth of Australia Constitution Act 1900 (formulated so as to potentially apply also to New Zealand if it chose to join the Commonwealth), both of which permitted the relevant bodies to legislate on matters relating to

[10] For a restatement of that truth, see C Kirkby, 'The Making of Empire' in P Cane and H Kumarasingham (eds), *The Cambridge Constitutional History of the United Kingdom*, vol II: *The Changing Constitution* (Cambridge University Press, 2023).

[11] See, considering some of these controversies beyond the most famous, American, one, RL Schuyler, *Parliament and the British Empire: Some Constitutional Controversies Concerning Imperial Legislative Jurisdiction* (Columbia University Press, 1929).

[12] The Stamp Act 1765, which imposed taxes on the American colonies, was repealed the following year as a result of widespread protest, but the Imperial Parliament responded with the American Colonies Act (or Declaratory Act) 1766, which reasserted its own unlimited right to legislate for the American colonies, which 'have been, are, and of right ought to be, subordinate unto, and dependent upon the imperial crown and parliament of Great Britain'.

defence[13] – the Imperial Parliament retained its supremacy over them, and the laws of their domestic legislative bodies were invalid if in conflict with those of that Imperial Parliament.[14] The Colonial Laws Validity Act 1865 provided that Acts of 'Colonial Legislatures' were not to be invalid on the ground of 'Repugnancy to the Law of England' but reaffirmed that they were 'void and inoperative' to the extent of any incompatibility with an Act of the Imperial Parliament extending to that colony.[15] Unity therefore implied, in fact, colonial subordination – the interests of the individual colony could be, as a matter of constitutional law, subordinated to those of the Empire as a whole, which in reality were closely identified with those of the UK itself, which was much more than a mere *primus inter pares*,[16] and which alone elected representatives to that Parliament.

B. The Balfour Declaration and the Fragmentation of the Realm

In the inter-war period, the unity of the Empire had begun to come under pressure, and the Empire itself began to give way to a 'Commonwealth of Nations', distinguished most importantly by the voluntary nature of each state's belonging thereto[17] and which in time would open up even to states that were no longer realms nor even formerly part of the British Empire. At the 1926 Imperial Conference, attended by seven of the King's Prime Ministers from across the Empire, the participants had rejected the notion of instituting a constitution for the British Empire, whose 'widely scattered parts have very different characteristics, very different histories, and are at very different stages of evolution' and which 'defies classification and bears no real resemblance to any other political organisation which now exists or has ever yet been tried'.[18] Instead, the Conference sought

[13] The Constitution Act 1867 (Canada), s 91(7) places within the exclusive jurisdiction of the federal Parliament the following matters, 'Militia, Military and Naval Service, and Defence'. The Commonwealth of Australia Constitution Act 1901 (Australia), s 51(vi) permits the Commonwealth Parliament to make laws with respect to 'the naval and military defence of the Commonwealth and of the several States'. Though this was at times interpreted as being limited to defence against external enemies, modern case law – drawing on historic English practice – disclaims any such limitation. See *Thomas v Mowbray* [2007] HCA 33, in which it was said (at [140]) that there was 'a long history in English law before the adoption of the Constitution which concerned defence of the realm against threats posed internally as well as by invasion from abroad by force of arms'.

[14] See the discussion in DB Swinfen, *Imperial Control of Colonial Legislation, 1813–65: A Study of British Policy Towards Colonial Legislative Powers* (Oxford University Press, 1970).

[15] Colonial Laws Validity Act 1865 (UK), ss 2 and 3.

[16] This remains the case for those Overseas Territories that are, alongside the UK, part of the still-existing, single, unified realm: *R (Bancoult) v Secretary of State for Foreign and Commonwealth Affairs* [2009] 1 AC 453.

[17] WP Hall, *Empire to Commonwealth: Thirty Years of British Imperial History* (Jonathan Cape, 1929). For a critical consideration of the contemporary Commonwealth, see P Murphy, *The Empire's New Clothes: The Myth of the Commonwealth* (Hurst Publishers, 2018).

[18] HM Government, *Imperial Conference, 1926 – Summary of Proceedings* (Cmd 2768, 1926) 14.

to recognise – in a manner that had already been done, occasionally but less fully, with the term 'Dominion' having first been used in 1907 – the special status of the self-governing Dominions, in the form of the 'Balfour Declaration', whereby the UK and those Dominions were said to be 'autonomous Communities within the British Empire, equal in status, in no way subordinate one to another in any aspect of their domestic or external affairs, though united by a common allegiance to the Crown, and freely associated as members of the British Commonwealth of Nations'.[19]

This new position was given effect by the Statute of Westminster 1931. Where the Colonial Laws Validity Act 1865 had clarified the priority of laws of the Imperial Parliament at Westminster over 'colonial laws', the Statute of Westminster provided that this supremacy did not apply to 'any law made after the commencement of this Act by the Parliament of a Dominion',[20] defined originally to mean Canada, Australia, New Zealand, the Union of South Africa, the Irish Free State and (at a point before it had entered into Confederation with Canada) Newfoundland.[21] From now on, new laws made by Dominion parliaments would be capable of amending law made in the past or future by the UK Parliament for their jurisdiction, and would be valid even if incompatible with that imperial law. Though not yet wholly subtracted from the jurisdiction of the Imperial Parliament, the Dominions gained a veto over its exercise of that jurisdiction in their regard: no new Act of Parliament of the UK that was passed after the commencement of the Statute of Westminster was to 'extend, or be deemed to extend, to a Dominion as part of the law of that Dominion, unless it is expressly declared in that Act that that Dominion has requested, and consented to, the enactment thereof'.[22] The Imperial Parliament had voluntarily imposed upon itself a limitation as to how it might exercise its previously unbounded legislative competence. Though it might yet purport to throw off this new restraint, the Statute of Westminster was recognising a new reality rather than creating it, and so it seemed clear that if – for example – the Parliament at Westminster had sought to legislate in even explicit contradiction to the new consent requirement, the courts of the various Dominions would not have given effect to the product of those attempts.[23]

[19] See HD Hall, 'The genesis of the Balfour declaration of 1926' (1962) 1 *Journal of Commonwealth & Comparative Politics* 169.

[20] Statute of Westminster 1931 (UK), s 2(2).

[21] ibid, s 1.

[22] ibid, s 4.

[23] It was this possibility that was the subject of Lord Sankey's famous remark that it was 'doubtless true that the power of the Imperial Parliament to pass on its own initiative any legislation that it thought fit extending to Canada remains in theory unimpaired: indeed, the Imperial Parliament could, as a matter of abstract law, repeal or disregard s 4 of the Statute [of Westminster]. But that is theory and has no relation to realities.' *British Coal Corporation v The King* [1935] AC 500, 520. The need to account for this reality was the basis of William Wade's argument that parliamentary sovereignty was not (as Ivor Jennings had claimed) a legal rule, which Parliament itself might amend, but rather the 'ultimate political fact' on which the system of legislation in the UK was based: HWR Wade, 'The Basis of Legal Sovereignty' (1955) 13 *Cambridge Law Journal 172.*

The effect of these developments on the legal position of the Crown, rather than that of Parliament, was not addressed in explicit terms at the time, and it was only much later that a clear account of the position was given. Representative groups of Indigenous Canadians – fearing that their interests would not be protected by the Bill that became the Canada Act 1982, by which the Canadian constitution was finally 'patriated', bringing to an end the right of the Westminster Parliament to legislate for Canada – sought a declaration from the English courts that obligations entered into by the Crown with what are described in the judgment as 'Indian peoples of Canada' remained binding upon 'Her Majesty in right of Her Government in the United Kingdom'.[24] The Court of Appeal rejected this claim, Lord Denning noting that the 'single and indivisible' nature of the Crown had altered, though not by statute but rather through 'constitutional usage and practice',[25] including the Imperial Conference's statement of the implications of the equality of states asserted by the Balfour Declaration for the position of the Governors-General of the Dominions. The implication of that fact, the Conference had agreed, was that the Governor-General of a Dominion

> is the representative of the Crown, holding in all essential respects the same position in relation to the administration of public affairs in the Dominion as is held by His Majesty the King in Great Britain, and that he is not the representative or agent of His Majesty's Government in Great Britain or of any Department of that Government.[26]

Lord Denning spelled out the consequences of this in clear terms: 'Thenceforward the Crown was no longer single and indivisible. It was separate and divisible for each self-governing dominion or province or territory.'[27] The approach taken has not usually been, though, to talk about – say – the Crown of Canada, distinct from the Crown of the United Kingdom, but rather to the Crown 'in right of Canada', with the reality of fragmentation thus recognised within a weakened assertion of ongoing unity. Alongside the question of whether it remains subject to the legislative competence of the Westminster Parliament, this is a key part of what distinguishes a colony of the UK (now an 'Overseas Territory')[28] from an independent state within the Commonwealth of Nations. Though the former may have legislative institutions and a considerable degree of self-government within the confines of its constitution (made, usually, by Order in Council), there is no Crown in right of the British Indian Ocean Territory, or Crown in right of Bermuda. Rather, the Overseas Territories remain part of the indivisible realm with an undivided Crown. Where it seems now clear that the Crown in right of the United Kingdom is entitled to put the interests of that realm as a whole

[24] *R v Foreign Secretary, ex parte Indian Association of Alberta* [1982] QB 892. See also *R v Secretary of State for the Home Department, ex parte Bhurosah* [1968] 1 QB 266; and A Twomey, 'Responsible Government and the Divisibility of the Crown' [2008] *Public Law* 742.

[25] *Ex parte Indian Association of Alberta* (n 24) 916.

[26] HM Government (n 18) 16.

[27] *Ex parte Indian Association of Alberta* (n 24) 917.

[28] British Overseas Territories Act 2002 (UK), s 1; and British Nationality Act 1981 (UK), sch 6.

(or, indeed, some particular part of it) over those of the Overseas Territories in relation to which it is exercising powers, this does not apply where the Crown acts in right of some independent state of which the monarch remains the head of state. For present purposes there are two key points to be made. One is that, whether or not it was seen in these terms at the time, it would no longer make sense to talk of 'defence of the realm' as though a single entity encompassed the whole of what had until recently been the British Empire. There were now multiple, self-governing realms, and with them the possibility of divergent, and even conflicting, approaches to questions of defence and security. The other is that this dynamic was by no means new: the Empire had been wrestling with the problems of imperial defence and imperial defence cooperation for decades beforehand.

Defence had been one of the primary topics of discussion and debate within the series of 'Colonial' and (later) 'Imperial' conferences that took place between 1887 and 1937 – at one of which, as we have seen, the Balfour Declaration was made – with the conferences' substance reflecting the shifting configuration of the Empire. Until shortly after the Second World War, there existed a Committee of Imperial Defence,[29] a successor to the Cabinet Defence Committee.[30] During the First World War, however, there was a far greater involvement from the Dominions in the project of imperial defence in the form of the Imperial War Cabinet.[31] This grew, said Lloyd George, 'not by design, but out of the necessities of the war', and its essence was that

> the responsible heads of the Governments of the Empire, with those Ministers who are specially entrusted with the conduct of Imperial Policy should meet together at regular intervals to confer about foreign policy and matters connected therewith, and come to decisions in regard to them which, subject to the control of their own Parliaments, they will then generally execute.[32]

The Committee of Imperial Defence continued in existence after the Great War, with the Joint Intelligence Committee (JIC), which persists to the current day within the Cabinet Office, established as a subcommittee thereof in 1936.[33] Though originally purely military in nature, the JIC came after a few years to incorporate also the civilian intelligence agencies,[34] creating a continuity between old

[29] On which see most fully FA Johnson, *Defence by Committee: The British Committee of Imperial Defence, 1885–1959* (Oxford University Press, 1960).

[30] 'The Cabinet Defence Committee established in 1895 had no clear relationship with either the Cabinet or the service ministries, let alone the Empire, and proved, in the words of Balfour's Private Secretary, Jack Sandars, 'an absolutely useless body': P Catterall, 'How Imperial was the Committee of Imperial Defence?' (Political Studies Association, 1998). See also Johnson (n 29) 40–41.

[31] See, playing down the novelty of the arrangements, AB Keith, 'The Imperial War Cabinet and the Dominions' (1918) 38 *Canadian Law Times* 695.

[32] HC Deb 17 May 1917, vol 93, cols 1790–92.

[33] MS Goodman, *The Official History of the Joint Intelligence Committee*, vol I: *From the Approach of the Second World War to the Suez Crisis* (Routledge, 2015).

[34] MS Goodman, 'Learning to Walk: The origins of the UK's Joint Intelligence Committee' (2008) 21 *International Journal of Intelligence and CounterIntelligence* 40, 50.

questions of imperial defence and modern ones of the SIAs of the Commonwealth states and their cooperation. And after the Second World War, the Committee of Imperial Defence shed most of its imperial livery,[35] becoming simply the Defence Committee.[36]

III. National Security Constitutionalism in the Shadow of Empire

Against the background of the developments that had taken place between the two world wars, the post-war period saw the strengthening of domestic constitutional arrangements within the various Dominions, though reflecting and in some cases limited by their ongoing membership of the Commonwealth of Nations, and by the desire on the part of the UK and others to retain the formal legal unity of an Empire that (future developments would make clear) had been irrecoverably undermined by the changes recognised in the Balfour declaration and their logical consequences. A key example of these tensions – with obvious implications for security – is the manner in which the question of citizenship was dealt with: the formal unity was preserved by the creation of a single legal category with two names – 'British subject' and 'Commonwealth citizen' – which was, however, subdivided into the distinct categories of 'Citizen of the United Kingdom and Colonies' (the residual British Empire) and citizens of the independent Commonwealth states (the Dominions).[37] What seems another such example, though not for the most part evident on the legal record, might be found in the moves made, in this same period, to implement a domestic national security apparatus in Canada, Australia and New Zealand. In the years following the war, the Commonwealth Five Eyes states began to rationalise and at times formalise their security and intelligence agencies, distinct from those of the British Empire in which they had hitherto participated. In this section I consider the processes by which they did so and the legal position that emerged and evolved in the period beginning with the end of the Second World War and ending, roughly, with the dissolution of the Soviet Union. What, I suggest, appears at first sight

[35] Discussed by Johnson (n 29) 306–07. See HM Government, *Central Organisation for Defence* (Cmd 6923, 1946) [20], proposing a new Defence Committee, under the Chairmanship of the Prime Minister, which would 'take over the functions of the old Committee of Imperial Defence' and 'be responsible to the Cabinet both for the review of current strategy and for co-ordinating departmental action in preparation for war'.

[36] A change that was itself much criticised: see, eg, Lord Hankey, HL Deb 16 October 1946, vol 143 cols 305–06: 'My second criticism is the change of title from Committee of Imperial Defence to Defence Committee. That is a black blot on the White Paper, and on the fine Empire record of the Party in office … It destroys a living monument to Lord Balfour, our greatest Empire statesman, who founded the Committee as a focus of Empire co-operation, and watched over its destinies for nearly thirty years.'

[37] See British Nationality Act 1948 (UK) and the discussion in R Hansen, 'The Politics of Citizenship in 1940s Britain: The British Nationality Act' (1999) 10 *Twentieth Century British History* 67.

an example of the desire on the part of independent states for domestic (national security) constitutionalism in the post-war period, largely in the form of what I have called 'positive constitutionalism', was in fact to a considerable extent driven by the UK – the former colonial power – itself.

A. The United Kingdom

The UK's Security Service (MI5) has existed since 1909 – originally as the Secret Service Bureau,[38] encompassing what would later become MI6 – and performed important work in both the world wars.[39] It was initially part of the defence forces of the realm, with the two founding members of the Bureau, Mansfield Cumming and Vernon Kell, a Royal Navy Commander and Army captain respectively.[40] Cumming would become in time the first head of MI6; Kell of MI5. In the period between the wars, on the Service's 25th anniversary, it was claimed by its Deputy Head that '[o]ur Security Service is more than national; it is Imperial':

> We have official agencies cooperating with us, under the direct instructions of the Dominions and Colonial Offices and the supervision of local Governors, and their chiefs of police, for enforcing security laws in every British Community overseas.[41]

Historians have queried exactly how realistic an appraisal of the situation this in fact was, with the official historian of the Security Service calling the claim 'essentially aspirational',[42] though it no doubt captures the reality that in this period there could be no strict division, in law or in practice, between the security of the UK and that of its Empire, which was thus internal rather than external. The division of responsibility between the bodies reflected that fact: the Empire was the responsibility of MI5, with MI6 assigned responsibility for countries outside of it as part of a set of 1931 reforms that saw the Security Service moved out of the War Office,[43] beginning its transition to its modern status as a civilian rather than military agency. Though of course the point was not mentioned in any contemporary discussion of imperial defence, this meant that the Security

[38] C Andrew, *The Defence of the Realm: The Authorized History of MI5* (Allen Lane, 2009), introduction: 'The Origins of the Secret Service Bureau'.

[39] ibid sections A and C.

[40] ibid 3.

[41] Quoted ibid 138.

[42] On the basis that '[w]ith less than a hundred staff (only a quarter of whom were officers), the Service was simply too small to provide security supervision and guidance for an empire which covered a quarter of the globe': ibid.

[43] ibid 130: 'The Security Service ceased to be a section of the War Office and acquired an enhanced but ill-defined status within Whitehall as an interdepartmental intelligence service working for the Home, Foreign, Dominion and Colonial Offices, the service departments, the Committee of Imperial Defence, the Attorney General, the Director of Public Prosecutions and chief officers of police at home and throughout the Empire.'

Service was inaugurated and grew up within the institutional schema described in section II – indeed, the original creation of the Secret Service Bureau took place at the recommendation of a sub-committee of the Committee of Imperial Defence.[44]

The governance of MI5 was rethought in the aftermath of the Second World War. In 1944, the Foreign Secretary Anthony Eden commissioned a report by Sir Findlater Stewart, which was completed the following year.[45] The report was released, in redacted form, in 2013, and offers some insight into certain elements of the Service's work. MI5 existed, Stewart said, solely 'for the purposes of the Defence of the Realm' and only within the Empire: 'M.I.5 should continue to be responsible for obtaining "counter intelligence" in the Empire by the means used in the past. But the acquisition of intelligence, including counter-intelligence, by secret means elsewhere, must remain a matter for S.I.S.'[46] That is, the division between inside and outside remained not that between the UK and the rest of the world, but that between the British Empire and the world beyond it. Despite, it has been noted, 'showing some concern for civil liberties and constitutional propriety, [Stewart] showed no concern for the most fundamental of all questions of legality',[47] and so – as is the case also with a number of later considerations – his report does not contain a clear explanation of the Service's legal basis, a point to which I will return. The functions identified for the Service by Stewart were very closely tied to the task of addressing the work of the Communist Party of Great Britain:

> In MI5's view, close study of the Communist Party in this country and its membership is justified on two counts, (a) apart from remnants of extreme Right Wing movements and such people as the Anarchists and the IRA, most of the persons concerned with the promotion of political aims by unconstitutional methods are members of the Communist Party, and (b) many of its members are exposed to, and some succumb to, pressure to engage in espionage on behalf of international Communism, and, at one remove, the Soviet Union.[48]

Stewart was also, and notably considering later developments elsewhere, concerned with the question of ministerial responsibility for the Service ('The Service should have a responsible Ministerial head. He should be the Prime Minister'),[49] with the burden to be lessened by the fact that there was to be no operational responsibility on the part of the Prime Minister.[50] Reflecting the

[44] ibid 3.

[45] K Ewing, J Mahoney and A Moretta, *MI5, the Cold War, and the Rule of Law* (Oxford University Press, 2020) ch 2. And see also DWB Lomas, '"... the Defence of the Realm and Nothing Else": Sir Findlater Stewart, Labour Ministers and the Security Service' (2015) 30 *Intelligence and National Security* 793.

[46] K Jeffrey, *MI6: The history of the Secret Intelligence Service, 1909–1949* (Bloomsbury, 2010) 620.

[47] Ewing, Mahoney and Moretta (n 45) 21.

[48] Quoted ibid 21–22.

[49] Quoted ibid 29.

[50] ibid.

ongoing transition of MI5 from its military to its modern civilian status, however, Stewart's account was queried shortly afterwards by Sir Norman Brooke, who said that he had 'exaggerated the "defence" aspects of the Security Service':

> In practice the Security Service has little to do with those aspects of the 'defence of the realm' with which the Minister of Defence is concerned … In practice the functions of the Security Service are much more closely allied to those of the Home Office, which has the ultimate constitutional responsibility for 'defending the realm' against subversive activities and for preserving law and order.[51]

The responsibility of the Service to the Prime Minister was the arrangement implemented by the so-called 'Attlee Directive', the drafting of which followed Stewart's report. This Directive gave the following as the description of the mission of MI5, mirroring Stewart's account in most of its aspects, and included language that would resonate – in the UK and elsewhere – for decades to come:

> Its task is the Defence of the Realm as a whole, from external and internal dangers arising from attempts at espionage and sabotage, or from actions of persons and organisations, whether directed from within or without the country, which may be judged to be subversive of the security of the State. In consultation with the Colonial Office you will be responsible for similar work in Colonial and other British territories overseas.[52]

Daniel Lomas has noted that – specifically as a result of MI5's overseas links, to which we turn below – this Directive became something of a 'Nicene Creed' for the broader intelligence community in the Commonwealth,[53] with not only its scope but also its specific language proving exceptionally influential elsewhere. Recent work has shown that there was in fact a series of supplementary directives, which added to and clarified certain elements of the framework within which the Service operated. Perhaps the most important Directive, however, if only due to the period of time for which it was in place, was the Maxwell-Fyfe Directive,[54] named for the Home Secretary who issued it in 1952. The Directive was made public a little over a decade later in the report by Lord Denning arising out of the 'Profumo affair',[55] where the eponymous Profumo – the Secretary of State for War – had been having an affair with a young model who was also involved with a Soviet Naval attaché. Though this Directive, unlike its predecessors, does not make anything of the point, the Service retained in this period a very significant role in relation to Britain's past and present possessions, including what had been the Dominions, with Christopher Andrew noting that 'During

[51] Quoted in *Lord Denning's Report* (Cmnd 2152, 1963) [237].

[52] Quoted in Ewing, Mahoney and Moretta (n 45) 35.

[53] DWB Lomas, *Intelligence, security and the Attlee governments, 1945–51: An uneasy relationship?* (Manchester University Press, 2016) 225–26.

[54] See Ewing, Mahoney and Moretta (n 45) 40–45.

[55] For the Directive, see *Lord Denning's Report* (n 51) [238].

the quarter-century after the Second World War, its officers and many other staff could expect to spend a quarter to a third of their careers in the Empire and Commonwealth.'[56] As more and more colonies gained independence and became members of the Commonwealth, 'the continued presence of [an MI5 security liaison officer] became a significant, though usually undisclosed, part of the transfer of power'.[57]

The Maxwell-Fyfe Directive was the governing instrument of the Service until almost the end of the Cold War, being supplanted by the enactment of the Security Service Act 1989,[58] and though its specific language may have been less influential than was that of its predecessor, it too captures a number of themes that remain prominent not only in the UK but also in the other Commonwealth Five Eyes states. It is a curious document, addressed directly to the Director-General of the Service, who will – it tells him – be responsible to the Home Secretary personally, with access directly to the Prime Minister on appropriate occasions.[59] Even here, however, it was clear that the role of the Home Secretary was, as Stewart had suggested, a limited one: both the Director-General and the staff of the Service were to maintain 'the well-established convention whereby Ministers do not concern themselves with the detailed information which may be obtained by the Security Service in particular cases, but are furnished with such information. only as may be necessary for the determination of any issue on which guidance is sought'.[60] The task of the Service, the Directive sets out, was 'the Defence of the Realm as a whole, from external and internal dangers arising from attempts at espionage and sabotage, or from actions of persons and organisations whether directed from within or without the country, which may be judged to be subversive to the State'. The Director-General was enjoined to take 'special care' to ensure that the Service's work was strictly limited to what was necessary for that task, and – reflecting a concern that is evident in the UK and elsewhere to this day – it was noted in particular that it was essential that it should be 'kept absolutely free from any political bias or influence and nothing should be done that might lend colour to any suggestion that it is concerned with the interests of any particular section of the community'.[61]

The Directive, though, was not, and did not purport to be, law: the European Commission of Human Rights, in an application made to it by Patricia Hewitt and Harriet Harman in the mid-1980s that became part of the motive for the enactment of the 1989 Act, noted that it was 'not claimed by the Government that it has the force of law or that its contents constitute legally enforceable rules

[56] Andrew (n 38) ix.
[57] ibid 442.
[58] For contemporary legal commentary on which see I Leigh and L Lustgarten, 'The Security Service Act 1989' (1989) 52 *Modern Law Review* 801.
[59] *Lord Denning's Report* (n 51) [238].
[60] ibid [238].
[61] ibid.

concerning the operation of the Security Service'.[62] Nor was any mention made in it of any particular (legal) powers the Service might possess. When Lord Denning considered the position of the Service in his Profumo Report, he made a striking claim in this regard, which is in considerable tension with later invocations of the prerogative in relation to the Service. Having observed that the Security Service was 'not established by Statute nor is it recognised by Common Law', he continued:

> The members of the Service are, in the eye of the law, ordinary citizens with no powers greater than anyone else, they have no, special powers of arrest such as the police have. No special powers of search are given to them. They cannot enter premises without the consent of the householder, even though they may suspect a spy is there. If a spy is fleeing the country, they cannot tap him on the shoulder and say he is not to go. They have, in short, no executive powers. They have managed very well without them.[63]

If the Security Service did not, as Denning claimed and is consistent with the absence of any reference to what he describes as 'executive powers' in the Maxwell-Fyfe Directive, possess any powers then there is no need to concern ourselves with the source of those (absent) powers. It has often been claimed, however, including in recent years, that the Security Service was in fact empowered under the prerogative.[64] Strikingly, this claim was not made in circumstances in which it might have been significant, including within the same Hewitt and Harman litigation, and Denning himself makes no mention of the prerogative. When MI5 was eventually given a statutory basis by the Security Service Act 1989,[65] in the final years of the Cold War, the statute in question was short and bare, containing a single (albeit broad) legal power, in the form of a provision stating that 'No entry on or interference with property shall be unlawful if it is authorised by a warrant issued by the Secretary of State under this section.'[66] MI5 was, though, one of the bodies capable of availing themselves of the power to intercept communications introduced a few years earlier, even if that statute – the Interception of Communications Act 1985 – did not name it. Given the differential development not only of the positive elements of national security constitutionalism but also its negative elements, one issue prominent within debates on what became the 1989 Act was its failure to provide for parliamentary oversight of MI5, of a sort for which by that point other Commonwealth Five Eyes jurisdictions had begun

[62] *Hewitt and Harman v United Kingdom* (1992) 14 EHRR 657 [40].

[63] *Lord Denning's Report* (n 51) [273(1)].

[64] See *Privacy International v Secretary of State for Foreign and Commonwealth Affairs* [2021] EWCA Civ 330 (the 'third direction' case), and the discussions of it in R Craig and G Phillipson, 'Protecting National Security by Breaking the Law? Prerogative, Statute and the Powers of MI5' (2022) 85 *Modern Law Review* 1274; and PF Scott, 'Authorising Crime: The Covert Human Intelligence Sources (Criminal Conduct) Act 2021' (2022) 85 *Modern Law Review* 1218.

[65] On the circumstances of which see Andrew (n 38) 766–68, noting that the staff of the Service were convinced of the desirability of legislation and that it was Ministers who required convincing.

[66] Security Service Act 1989 (UK) (as enacted), s 3.

to provide,[67] a criticism that – it seems likely – would not have been made had the Bill been introduced 20 or even 10 years earlier.

That is the picture as far as MI5 was concerned, with a formal, unambiguous legal basis arriving only at the tail end of the Cold War. However incomplete the picture is, and however unedifying, it is considerably fuller than that which can be offered in relation to either of MI5's counterparts, the Secret Intelligence Service (MI6) and the Government Communications Headquarters (GCHQ).[68] In neither case was there any statutory authority until the enactment of the Intelligence Services Act 1994, and the avowal of the two bodies came later than did that of MI5. Though there may have been some equivalent, or even many equivalents, of the Maxwell-Fyfe Directive and its predecessors, the existence of such a thing – to say nothing of its content – has never entered the public domain. What, then, were their legal status and legal basis in the period before 1994? By analogy with the claim that has been made in relation to MI5 (and leaving aside for the moment the problems with that claim), we might be tempted to say that the legal basis was the royal prerogative: either that of the defending the realm, or that of keeping the Queen's peace, which was recognised by a court for the first time exactly in the period that pressure was growing to give to the UK's SIAs a statutory basis.[69] The same problem applies, however: loose invocations of the prerogative tell us nothing about what specific powers these bodies had, nor about what they might have done with no or weak legal basis, even if the extent to which their work took place outside of the jurisdiction may have meant these questions arose less frequently and less urgently than they did in relation to MI5. We shall return in chapter 3 to the modern legal framework of the UK's SIAs, having first considered how, in the post-war period, the UK in effect exported to the Dominions the model of the Security Service as the key element of what has been described elsewhere as a broader 'British intelligence culture'.[70]

B. Australia

The Australian Security Intelligence Organisation (ASIO) was formed in 1949,[71] founded upon a Directive by the Prime Minister to Geoffrey Reed, a

[67] See, eg, the Second Reading debate on the Bill in the House of Commons: HC Deb 15 December 1988, vol 143, cols 1104–79.

[68] See, generally, K Jeffrey, *MI6: The history of the Secret Intelligence Service, 1909–1949* (Bloomsbury, 2010); and J Ferris, *Behind the Enigma: The Authorised History of GCHQ, Britain's Secret Cyber-Intelligence Agency* (Bloomsbury, 2020).

[69] *R v Secretary of State for the Home Department, ex parte Northumbria Police Authority* [1989] 1 QB 26.

[70] Lomas (n 53), citing P Murphy, 'Exporting a British Intelligence Culture: The British Intelligence Community and Decolonisation, 1945–60' (Political Studies Association, 2004).

[71] The history of ASIO has been written in considerable detail: see D Horner, *The Spy Catchers: The Official History of ASIO, 1949–1963* (Allen & Unwin, 2014); J Blaxland, *The Protest Years: The Official History of ASIO, 1963–1975* (Allen & Unwin, 2015); J Blaxland, *The Secret Cold War: The Official History of ASIO, 1976–1989* (Allen & Unwin, 2016). I use here the modern spelling – with an 's' rather than a 'z' – of ASIO's name, except where quoting statutes that employ the latter.

Justice of the South Australian Supreme Court, who was the Organisation's first Director-General.[72] The Organisation was in effect the successor to a counter-espionage Bureau originally formed in Australia in 1916 specifically at the request of MI5, and the first head of which, though he reported to the Australian Prime Minister, 'appears' – it has been said – 'to have believed that his main responsibility was to the head of Britain's MI5'.[73] The setting up of ASIO as a permanent organisation was again specifically urged by MI5, which desired improved security for Australia following US discoveries – via the 'Venona' programme, involving the interception and decryption of almost 3,000 messages between Soviet spies in the US and their handlers in the USSR[74] – regarding the extent of Soviet intelligence-gathering in the country. Two senior MI5 officers, Roger Hollis (later its Director-General) and Robert Hemblys-Scales, visited Australia in 1948 with 'two closely connected tasks: to encourage and assist Australia to establish a more effective security organisation; and to investigate the [Soviet] espionage ring'.[75] Amongst the reasons that have been identified for the establishment of ASIO, even in the context of significant civil-liberties concerns, were not only revelations about the extent of Soviet espionage but also 'the importance of security in the context of Australia's role in the British Commonwealth and Empire'.[76] Hollis returned to Australia in 1949 'to provide the Australian Government with advice on the establishment of the new security organisation, including its charter, responsibilities, organisational structure and senior appointments'.[77] And so not only was the fact of ASIO's establishment very heavily influenced by MI5 – so too was the specific design of the organisation. The 'Directive for the Establishment and Maintenance of a Security Service',[78] it has been claimed, was 'couched in language which was very similar to the Maxwell-Fyfe directive in the United Kingdom';[79] though it of course pre-dates the Maxwell-Fyfe Directive, it was issued subsequent to that Directive's post-war predecessors, discussed in section III.A, and so in fact the language was that of the Attlee rather than Maxwell-Fyfe Directive. The 1949 Directive stipulated that ASIO was 'part of the Defence Forces of the Commonwealth and save as herein expressed has no

[72] Reed had been chairman of the South Australian National Security Advisory Committee and had undertaken 'a number of security-related inquiries' on behalf of the Commonwealth Authorities. On being appointed to head ASIO, 'Reed faced a difficult and politically delicate task. He set about his job in a dedicated and methodical manner, his integrity and bipartisan approach winning him the early confidence of his political masters.' R Stevenson, 'Reed, Sir Geoffrey Sandford (1892–1970)' *Australian Dictionary of Biography*, vol 16 (Melbourne University Press, 2002).

[73] Horner (n 71) 15.

[74] On which see JE Haynes and H Klehr, *Venona: Decoding Soviet Espionage in America* (Yale University Press, 1999).

[75] Horner (n 71) 71.

[76] ibid 78.

[77] ibid 91.

[78] The text of the Directive can be found in Royal Commission on Intelligence and Security, *Fourth Report – Vol 2*, Parliamentary Paper No 249/1977 (1977), Appendix 4-A.

[79] HP Lee, 'The Australian Security Intelligence Organisation – New Mechanisms for Accountability' (1989) 38 *ICLQ* 890, 896.

concern with the enforcement of the criminal law' and provided – in language taken almost directly from the UK, though with 'Commonwealth' substituted to reflect the distinctive constitutional context – that its task was 'the defence of the Commonwealth from external and internal dangers arising from attempts at espionage and sabotage, or from actions of persons and organisations, whether directed from within or without the country, which may be judged to be subversive of the security of the Commonwealth'.[80] Given its direct origins within the UK and that country's own attempts to clarify the role of its Security Service in the post-War world, we might think of this instrument as an early indication of the emergence of a sort of Commonwealth national security constitutionalism that, as we shall see in later chapters, persists to this day.

The 1949 Directive was superseded the following year, upon appointment as the new Director-General of Charles Spry, who had previously served in the British Army, by a 'Charter of the Australian Security Intelligence Organisation',[81] which tweaked and added to the language of its predecessor in a number of ways.[82] ASIO took statutory form in 1956,[83] following the report of the Royal Commission on Espionage,[84] with the other components of the Australian Intelligence Community remaining non-statutory until into the new millennium. The establishment of the Royal Commission (the unfolding of which was watched, very closely, by MI5)[85] was a response to the so-called 'Petrov Affair', relating to a KGB officer who defected to Australia in 1954, and in doing so revealed the extent of Soviet espionage in the country.[86] Given this context, the bulk of the Commission's report relates to factual issues about the work of the Soviet Ministry of Internal Affairs, which directed espionage abroad during the relevant period, with little concern for the legal position of ASIO or its activities. Nevertheless, it has been said, the Royal Commission was a 'turning point' for ASIO:

> Before the defection, ASIO was a shadowy organisation. Its name had never actually been secret … but in public statements it was generally described simply as the 'Security Service'. Now the name ASIO became widely known. During the royal commission hearings, ASIO officers … gave evidence publicly. Other ASIO officers were present in the courtroom and were seen conversing with the commission's counsel. The proceedings were covered widely, and sometimes sensationally, in the press …[87]

ASIO emerged from the report as 'an efficient, reputable and useful government service',[88] but the heightened attention it attracted prompted a reconsideration of

[80] Quoted ibid 896.
[81] For the text of the Directive, see Commission on Intelligence and Security (n 78), Appendix 4-B.
[82] See the discussion in Lee (n 79) 897–98.
[83] Australian Security Intelligence Organisation Act 1956 (Australia).
[84] See *Royal Commission on Espionage*, Report (1955).
[85] Horner (n 71) ch 14.
[86] For an overview, see ibid chs 13 and 14. A classic, though outdated, account of the Affair is given in R Manne, *The Petrov Affair: Politics and Espionage* (Pergamon Books, 1987).
[87] Horner (n 71) 349.
[88] ibid 376.

its legal basis, with Spry himself requesting that a statute be put in place,[89] something that would not be done in the UK for several decades, and so 'In seeking to have ASIO underpinned by legislation, Spry was moving away from his British parent.'[90] The primary reason for giving ASIO a statutory basis, it was said when the Bill was introduced into Parliament, was that 'this course will give the officers of the service contractual rights as against the Commonwealth … and will protect them from the otherwise possible exercise of the Crown's right to terminate at pleasure the services of officers who do not serve in pursuance of statutes'.[91] On the surface, that is, the key driver of this important step in the constitutionalisation of national security was not – say – civil liberties, but rather employment rights. It was also observed, however, and in an apparently secondary fashion, that

> attacks made on our own security service in the course of the Royal Commission on Espionage in Australia have convinced the Government that it is necessary for the protection, and therefore also for the efficiency, of the security service to take a similar step in Australia [to that taken in the US], and to give the service statutory authority and protection.[92]

This claim is a striking one, and might be connected with one historian's assessment that the Bill's intention was 'not to make ASIO more accountable, but to make it less vulnerable to dismantling by a possible … Labor Government',[93] indicating perhaps that the concern with employment rights was not about the position of individuals but about the persistence of the organisation as a whole. The Bill, the Prime Minister emphasised on introducing it, did not 'make any changes in the constitution, organization, or functions of the Australian Security Intelligence Organization'.[94] Notably, in light of points made in section III.A about the question of ministerial responsibility for MI5, the position as regards ministerial responsibility for ASIO was consciously left unspecified by the Bill:

> The bill makes no attempt to specify the manner in which, or the degree to which, ministerial authority should be exercised in relation to the service. It is clearly impossible, and in any event undesirable, for a Minister to exercise in this field the same degree of supervision and authority that he exercises in his own department. The proper course, in the Government's view, is to make the Director-General responsible for the due control of his service, and to allow the measure of authority of the responsible Minister to be worked out as in the past, by convention and in the light of the circumstances of the time.[95]

[89] ibid 387–9.
[90] ibid 390.
[91] House of Representatives Hansard (Australia) no 43, 1746 (24 October 1956).
[92] ibid.
[93] F Cain, *The Australian Security Intelligence Organization: An Unofficial History* (Frank Cass, 1994) 252.
[94] House of Representatives Hansard (Australia) no 43, 1746 (24 October 1956).
[95] ibid.

The 1956 Act is significant in many ways, including its status as the first statute governing a security and intelligence agency in the Commonwealth Five Eyes states, and its palpable influence in New Zealand, discussed in section III.C. It provided first of all that ASIO ('being the Organization established in pursuance of a directive given by the Prime Minister on the sixteenth day of March, One thousand nine hundred and forty-nine') was to continue in existence.[96] Three functions were identified for that Organisation: to 'obtain, correlate and evaluate intelligence relevant to security'; to 'advise Ministers, where the Director-General is satisfied that it is necessary or desirable to do so, in respect of matters relevant to security'; and to cooperate with other bodies, whether of the Commonwealth, the Australian States or other countries, in performing its functions.[97] It was not, this original legislation provided, a function of ASIO to 'to carry out or enforce measures for security within a Department of State or authority of the Commonwealth'.[98] The Organisation was 'under the control' of its Director-General,[99] and in keeping with the remarks quoted above, no provision was made for ministerial direction or control of its activities. The only operative concept to which the Act gave a definition was that of 'security', defined to mean 'the protection of the Commonwealth and the Territories of the Commonwealth from acts of espionage, sabotage or subversion, whether directed from, or intended to be committed, within the Commonwealth or not'.[100] No specific legal powers, of any sort, were provided to ASIO by the statute in order to assist it in carrying out these functions, though a statute of 1960, enacted against the backdrop of the UK's Birkett Report and again apparently supported by MI5,[101] introduced statutory powers for the interception of communications.[102] Another statute, of 1976, later made special provision for the possibility of appointing a judge as Director-General of ASIO,[103] permitting the appointment of Justice (Albert) Edward Woodward as its head.[104] Throughout this period, links with the other Commonwealth Five Eyes states were strong. MI5, with which ASIO had its 'closest international relationship', had maintained a liaison officer in Australia until 1965, and re-established the position in 1973,[105] with a historian of ASIO

[96] Australian Security Intelligence Organisation Act 1956 (Australia), s 4(1).

[97] ibid, s 5(1).

[98] ibid, s 5(2).

[99] ibid, s 4(2).

[100] ibid, s 2.

[101] Horner (n 71) 393: 'Spry continued to build his case for appropriate legislation … In October 1959 Spry sent Menzies a paper analysing the UK privy councillors' report. Later that month, the Director-General of MI5, Roger Hollis, visited Australia and met Menzies, Spry, Barwick and Bailey. In January 1960 Spry wrote to Menzies that Hollis had stated it would be "impossible to conduct counter espionage without this facility".' The Report in question is Committee of Privy Councillors appointed to inquire into the interception of Communications, *Report* (Cmnd 283, 1956–57).

[102] Telephonic Communications (Interception) Act 1960 (Australia).

[103] Australian Security Intelligence Organization Act 1976 (Australia) ('ASIO Act 1976').

[104] F Cain, 'Australian Intelligence Organisations and the Law: A Brief History' (2004) 27 *UNSW Law Journal* 296, 308.

[105] Blaxland, *Protest Years* (n 71) 271–72.

quoting its external liaison coordinator as saying, in 1975, that a 'very close and long standing "family" relationship exists between the two services'.[106] ASIO in this period also maintained predictably close relations with the New Zealand Security Intelligence Service (NZSIS) and the Royal Canadian Mounted Police (RCMP).[107] Along with the American CIA, these four bodies met on a sporadic basis in the context of a forum, established in 1964, known as 'CAZAB' on the basis of the countries (Canada, Australia, New Zealand, America and Britain) that made it up, and focused – as might have been expected – on the issue of Soviet penetration of Western institutions.[108]

The next major reform to the law governing ASIO was carried out by an Act of 1979, enacted in the first place to give effect to the recommendations of the Royal Commission on Intelligence and Security under Justice Robert Hope of the New South Wales Court of Appeal.[109] This Royal Commission – the first of two under Justice Hope[110] – was instituted following a period of tension between ASIO and the Australian Labor Party, during which the Attorney-General Lionel Murphy had ordered a 'raid' on ASIO offices and a 'dossier' produced by ASIO on Deputy Prime Minister Jim Cairns was leaked.[111] ASIO's political neutrality and indeed competence had – for these reasons and others – been widely called into question. The statute, which repealed its predecessors and became the new basis for the Organisation,[112] was enacted contemporaneously with a new statute providing for the interception of telecommunications.[113] Though the basic functions of the Organisation were largely unchanged – to collect intelligence for security purposes, to communicate it for security purposes, and to advise Ministers on security – 'security' was now defined much more expansively, to mean not only 'the protection of, and of the people of, the Commonwealth and the several States and Territories' from one of five threats – espionage, sabotage, subversion, active measures of foreign intervention and terrorism – whether the threat or activity in question was 'directed from, or committed within, Australia or not', but also now 'the carrying out of Australia's responsibilities to any foreign

[106] ibid 439.

[107] ibid 273–75.

[108] ibid 276–78.

[109] See, in particular, Royal Commission on Intelligence and Security, *Fourth Report – Vol 1*, Parliamentary Paper No 248/1977 (1977). The recommended amendments to the ASIO Act 1976 are at [747]–[771]. At [27] et seq, Justice Hope considers, somewhat inconclusively, the constitutional basis of ASIO, noting that it was established 'by administrative action'. Though there are 'various heads of [legislative] power upon which the Commonwealth can draw in order to support ASIO's existence', the question of the relevant source of executive power seems, in Hope's telling, much less clear.

[110] See P Edwards, *Law, Politics and Intelligence: A life of Robert Hope* (NewSouth Publishing, 2020) chs 9 and 10. Edwards suggests that 'On the bench Hope demonstrated a concern to reach judgements that represented justice as well as being legally sound. He brought the same pragmatic liberalism to his work on public policy, seeking the right balance between propriety and effectiveness.'

[111] Blaxland, *Protest Years* (n 71) 373 and 330–37.

[112] Australian Security Intelligence Organization Act 1979 (Australia).

[113] Telecommunications (Interception and Access) Act 1979 (Australia).

country in relation to' any of those five things.[114] 'Subversion' – a central concern of the SIAs in this period – was given a detailed, and limited, definition where domestic in nature or directed against Australia rather being of 'foreign origin' or directed against a foreign government,[115] subversion of these latter type being left undefined and therefore no doubt understood more broadly. One element of the definition of domestic subversion is striking: amongst the activities to be regarded as subversion were 'activities directed to promoting violence or hatred between different groups of persons in the Australian community so as to endanger the peace, order or good government of the Commonwealth'.[116] It remained the case under the 1979 Act that ASIO was 'under the control' of its Director-General. Now, however, the gap left by the original enactment on the topic of ministerial responsibility had been filled, reflecting a recommendation made by Hope that the ambiguity of the statute be removed, as both the relevant Minister and the Director-General 'must be free from doubt as to whether the Minister can give lawful directions'.[117] It was therefore provided explicitly that the Director-General was subject, in performing his functions, to the 'general directions' of the relevant Minister.[118] On three specific issues, it was provided that the Minister was not empowered to override the opinion of the Director-General, effectively communicating of course that on other issues he was so empowered. These three specific points included questions about whether the criteria for the lawful collection or communication of intelligence relating to a given person were met, and the opinion of the Director-General regarding 'the nature of the advice that should be given by the Organization to a Minister, Department or authority of the Commonwealth'.[119] Another novelty was the powers conferred upon ASIO for the first time by the 1979 Act, including search warrants and authorisations for the use of listening devices, with the context of these powers' introduction discussed in chapter 4.

A second Royal Commission, again under Justice Hope, took place in the subsequent decade,[120] inquiring into the Australian SIAs generally but also into the implementation of decisions made following the first Hope Commission. The context here included the 'Combe-Ivanov' affair, in which former Australian Labor Party politician David Combe had been targeted and possibly compromised by Soviet diplomat Valery Ivanov, resulting in the latter's expulsion. A number of

[114] Australian Security Intelligence Organization Act 1979 (Australia), s 4.

[115] ibid, s 5.

[116] ibid, s 5(1)(c).

[117] Royal Commission (n 109) [345]. As to how that ambiguity should be resolved, Hope observed (at [352]) that 'it seems to me that, in general terms, the Director-General must be subject to proper directions by the Minister, and that the Minister should be responsible, "in a general way", to Parliament for the organization and its activities' but identified three exceptions, which are reflected in the subsequent statutory amendments.

[118] Australian Security Intelligence Organization Act 1979 (Australia), s 8(2).

[119] ibid.

[120] See Edwards (n 110) ch 15.

reports were published by the Commission in the year leading up to December 1984.[121] In one of them Hope noted that 'one of the greatest changes' that he had found relating to ASIO since his first inquiry was 'in the degree of its concern for compliance with the requirements of the law and of propriety':

> ASIO has been concerned to ensure that its operations and actions are within its charter, the Australian Security Intelligence Organization Act 1979 …, since that Act came into force, whether in relation to the collection or communication of intelligence or to advice to Ministers and Commonwealth authorities. It has been substantially successful in achieving that goal. The exceptions have been cases such as the inadvertent continuance of the interception of a telephone for a day after the warrant had expired and compliance with formalities such as delegations and like matters. Mistakes have been made, some bad and unprofessional, but all within the terms of the charter. This stands in contrast with some things that happened in ASIO's earlier period.[122]

Further changes were nevertheless made following the completion of this second Royal Commission, including reform to the rules regarding the relationship between the Director-General and the Minister introduced in 1979,[123] one of which allowed the Director-General to require the Minister to put directions in writing. Alongside these reforms, reflecting the same tendency towards ministerial control that Hope had endorsed as part of his first Royal Commission, a new provision permitted the Minister to give to the Director-General, in writing, 'guidelines to be observed in the performance by the Organization of its functions or the exercise of its powers'.[124] This discretionary power was accompanied by an obligation to give such guidelines relating to the performance of that part of ASIO's functions relating to 'politically motivated violence'.[125] In both cases, a copy of the guidelines was to be given to the Leader of the Opposition and the Inspector-General of Intelligence and Security (created by the same enactment, and considered in chapter 5); so too was a copy to be laid before Parliament (subject to a public interest exception) and the newly created Parliamentary Joint Committee on the Australian Security Intelligence Organization (unless the Minister considered it inappropriate to do so).[126] Growing ministerial control was accompanied, therefore, by increased (but nevertheless limited) political oversight of that control.

For the Australian Secret Intelligence Service (ASIS), the legal position during the Cold War can be stated more briefly. ASIS was formed in 1952 by

[121] See, primarily, Royal Commission on Australia's Security Intelligence Agencies, *General Report*, Parliamentary Paper No 231/1985 (1985).

[122] ibid [2.5].

[123] Australian Security Intelligence Organization Amendment Act 1986 (Australia), s 5 (amending s 8 of the 1979 Act).

[124] ibid, s 6 (inserting a new s 8A into the 1979 Act).

[125] Australian Security Intelligence Organization Act 1979 (Australia), s 8A (as inserted by the 1986 Act).

[126] ibid.

a decision of the Federal Executive Council – coming into the world 'at a time when fear and suspicion gripped Western governments and their intelligence agencies'[127] – and given a Charter in 1954, which identified its functions as being 'to obtain and distribute secret intelligence, and to plan for and conduct special operations as may be required'.[128] Again, it was 'closely modelled on its United Kingdom counterpart'.[129] It existed, in its first few years, it has been claimed, 'essentially as a nucleus, with officers being trained in Britain and then attached to [MI6] field stations abroad'.[130] That existence, however, was not made public until 1972, and ASIS was not avowed by the Government until 1977 (again on the recommendation of the first Hope Commission), in a statement in which it was said that the 'main function of ASIS is to obtain, by such means and subject to such conditions as are prescribed by the Government, foreign intelligence for the purpose of the protection or promotion of Australia or its interests'.[131] It did not, though, gain a statutory basis at that time, or for several decades thereafter, despite Hope's having recommended that one be given to it.[132] Its position was addressed again by the second Hope Royal Commission – that on 'Australia's Security and Intelligence Agencies' – in the period following the so-called 'Sheraton Hotel Incident', in which ASIS trainees were tasked with carrying out a rescue of a 'hostage' from the Sheraton Hotel in Melbourne in a staged scenario and ended up threatening members of the public with weapons.[133] Hope noted pointedly therein that ASIS was required to comply with Australian law: 'it has no special exemption, as the High Court has recently emphasised'.[134]

The third body with which we are concerned in the present work, the Defence Signals Bureau, was created earlier, in 1947, again by an executive order. The first Hope Commission produced a report on the Bureau – whose name was subject to frequent amendment – but, like that on ASIS, this was not made public at the time.[135] In the House of Representatives, in the same statement in which ASIS was avowed, the Prime Minister was willing to say only that the Bureau was 'concerned with radio, radar and other electronic emissions from the standpoint both of

[127] B Toohey and W Pinwill, *Oyster: The Story of the Australian Secret Intelligence Service* (Heinemann, 1989) 32.

[128] Quoted in Commission of Inquiry into the Australian Secret Intelligence Service, *Report on the Australian Secret Intelligence Service – Public Edition* (1995) [1.1].

[129] ibid [1.2].

[130] Toohey and Pinwill (n 127) 34.

[131] House of Representatives Hansard (Australia) no 43, 2238–39 (25 October 1977).

[132] See the consideration of the point in Commission of Inquiry (n 128), ch 3.

[133] Royal Commission on Australia's Security and Intelligence Agencies, *Report on the Sheraton Hotel Incident* (February 1984), Parliamentary Paper No 1/1984 (1984). The facts of the incident are described at [1.5]–[1.7].

[134] Royal Commission on Australia's Security and Intelligence Agencies (n 121) [2.14].

[135] See the discussion of some of the Royal Commission's observations on the DSD and its dual lack of independence – from the Defence Department and within the UKUSA regime – in J Blaxland and C Birgin, *Revealing Secrets: An unofficial history of Australian Signals intelligence & the advent of cyber* (NewSouth Publishing, 2023) 268–72.

the information and the intelligence that they can provide and of the security of our own Government communications and electronic emissions'.[136] Though the name of the body was to be changed to the Defence Signals Directorate (DSD) (in recognition of the 'enhanced status that the Royal Commission recommends should be accorded' to it), it was said also at that point that 'this Government will not provide further information about DSD, nor confirm or deny speculation or assertion about it'.[137] In the context of the second Royal Commission, Justice Hope claimed that DSD had 'less occasion to be affected by questions of legality or propriety' than did ASIO, and that he had 'no doubt' that it complied with its legal obligations.[138] Both ASIS and the DSD were eventually given a statutory basis only much later, with the enactment of the Intelligence Services Act 2001, discussed in chapter 3.

Picking up the theme introduced in the discussion of the UK position, it is striking that little attention seems to have been paid, at any point, to the role (if any) of the prerogative in this picture, perhaps because ASIO was given a statutory basis at such a relatively early stage in the Cold War, and given intrusive and investigatory powers, of a clear enough basis and substance, rather earlier than was the case in the UK. The question of what – if any – role was played by the prerogative, and what might follow from that point, was never therefore a very urgent one, demanding a clear answer. It is notable, however, that in 1984, Justice Hope – reconsidering in the context of his second Royal Commission issues he had worked on a decade earlier in the context of his first – observed that in 1974, ASIO 'had little legislation, governmental guidance or direction as to what it should or should not do. A lot of what it did was based on implied powers, or on the vague support of the prerogative.'[139] And so the prerogative seems indeed to have been part of the picture, if not an element that was ever called upon to do much justificatory work. If that is true, however, then the mootness of that particular question – ASIO's relationship to the prerogative – implies simultaneously the urgency of the question of the prerogative's role in the work of ASIS and (what is now) the DSD, where statutory underpinnings were put in place only much later. And yet that question seems to have been similarly neglected. One can find, in Australia as elsewhere, various comments regarding the centrality of the prerogative to the national security enterprise, but specifics are much harder to come by, and it appears unlikely that their absence is a function of some impotence on the part of these other two legs of the national security stool in Australia. More likely, at least some of their work – to whose value Hope repeatedly attested – was a mixture of the doubtfully legal, the openly illegal and the extra-territorial, protected against findings to that effect only by the secrecy associated with it. In this too, it seems fair to

[136] House of Representatives Hansard (Australia) no 43, 2239 (25 October 1977).
[137] ibid.
[138] Royal Commission on Australia's Security and Intelligence Agencies (n 121) [2.17].
[139] ibid [2.3].

conclude, the Australian SIAs were following in the footsteps of their UK counterparts on which, we have seen, they were clearly and directly modelled. One might reasonably conclude that a key feature of the model of Commonwealth national security constitutionalism that emerged in the course of the Cold War was a weak, or at least secondary, concern for questions of law – especially as regards activities undertaken outside the jurisdiction.

C. New Zealand

The New Zealand Security Service (as it was at first known, under the influence of MI5) was founded in 1956,[140] there having been before then a short-lived body known as the Security Intelligence Bureau operating for a period during the Second World War.[141] As with Australia, there had been concerted efforts by the British, in the aftermath of the war, to convince the New Zealand Government to set up an equivalent of MI5, with that body's head, Percy Stilltoe, visiting New Zealand on that mission in 1948.[142] When, in the aftermath of Australia's 'Petrov Affair', and in the context of suggestions of Soviet penetration also of the New Zealand authorities, the New Zealand Government bowed to the inevitable and set up the Security Service, Stilltoe's replacement cabled MI5's congratulations.[143] One reason for MI5's enthusiasm seems to have been a fear the New Zealand might have acted as 'something of a clearing house for spies who could get hold of secrets more easily [there] than elsewhere',[144] a fear that continues to be expressed in the present day in relation to the contemporary objects of anxiety in the field of national security. The founding of the Service was done via an (unpublished) Order in Council. It was, again, explicitly modelled on MI5 in the UK,[145] and was designed 'as a civilian, specialist body without executive powers and with a strictly advisory role'.[146] Its first head, Brigadier Bill Gilbert, was invited to spend time with MI5 in London before taking up the post, where – it has been claimed – the Maxwell-Fyfe Directive made a 'great impression' on him,[147] with the Service as

[140] GR Weller, 'Change and Development in the New Zealand Security and Intelligence Services' (2001) 21 *Journal of Conflict Studies* 1.

[141] FLW Wood, *The New Zealand People at War: Political and External Affairs* (New Zealand Department of Internal Affairs, 1958) 160–62; and A Gillespie, 'The Security Intelligence Agencies in New Zealand: evolution, challenges and progress' (2021) 36 *Intelligence and National Security* 676.

[142] M Parker, *The SIS* (The Dunmore Press, 1979) ch 1. Parker indicates that a fear of excessive British involvement was part of the reason the efforts failed, quoting (ibid 20) a source who told him that 'the Australian Security Intelligence Organisation at this time was being run by the British'.

[143] ibid 25.

[144] HW Orsman, 'Security Issues' (September 1966) *Comment* 1, 2, quoted in BR Hancock, 'The New Zealand Security Intelligence Service' (1973) 2 *Auckland University Law Review* 1, 1.

[145] Hancock (n 144) 1.

[146] *Submissions to the Statutes Revision Committee by the New Zealand Security Service on the New Zealand Security Service Bill 1969*, 1, quoted in Hancock (n 144) 1.

[147] Parker (n 142) 41.

a result of this visit taking some of its initial staff from MI5 in London and the British colonies.[148]

The Service was given a formal basis, under a slightly modified name, by the New Zealand Security Intelligence Service Act at the end of the following decade, by a statute that – when originally introduced as a Bill – was 'virtually identical with the Australian Security Intelligence Organisation Act 1956',[149] indicating the extent to which the New Zealand model was not taken directly from the British example but rather mediated by that of Australia. As it was put by the Prime Minister, Keith Holyoake, on introducing the Bill that became the New Zealand Security Intelligence Service Act 1969:

> We have studied practices in other countries, particularly Commonwealth countries, and as a result it has been decided to follow fairly closely the pattern of the Australian Security Organisation Act. The Australians call it an organisation, we call it a service. Our information is that this has worked very well in Australia in conditions very similar to but not exactly the same as those in New Zealand. The Bill therefore follows the Australian Act closely except in relation to matters that have special significance in New Zealand.[150]

This illustrates neatly one point we shall pick up in chapter 7: the constitutionalisation of national security in one state – here, Australia, which gave ASIO a statutory basis for contingent domestic political motives – facilitates the borrowing of norms by other jurisdictions – here, New Zealand, which was able to consider that statutory basis and largely adopt it for itself. One change that was made to that Bill before it became law was to make clear the fact of ministerial responsibility for the Service,[151] which, as noted, had been deliberately excluded from the Australian legislation. A major criticism of the Bill in its original form was the failure to define 'subversion';[152] submissions from the Director of the Service at the time of its enactment relied on the definition offered by Lord Denning in his report on the Profumo affair, which the Director called 'penetrating and authoritative',[153] though the definition eventually included in the legislation was broader than that, encompassing 'attempting, inciting, counselling, advocating, or encouraging' one of two things: either the 'overthrow by force

[148] ibid 45.

[149] Hancock (n 144) 2. And see Parker (n 142) 140–41, giving credit for the provision of a statutory basis not to the government of the day but rather to the leader of the Labour Party (and later Prime Minister), Norman Kirk.

[150] House of Representatives Hansard (NZ) vol 360, 34 (16 May 1969).

[151] Hancock (n 144) 3–4: 'The minister responsible for civil intelligence organisations in New Zealand has always been the Prime Minister and there is no reason to expect that this practice will change. This is a sound practice in that security matters are brought to the highest level of government but it must be recognised that, consequently, ministerial discretion can only be in the broadest terms.'

[152] See Parker (n 142) 132–33, claiming that when the Statutes Revision Committee examining the Bill sought out existing legislative definitions of 'subversion', they could not find a single one in the Western world.

[153] *Address to the Statutes Revision Committee by the Director of Security* (1 July 1969), 1, quoted in Hancock (n 144) 7.

of the Government of New Zealand' or the 'undermining by unlawful means of the authority of the State in New Zealand'.[154]

The 1969 Act continued the Service in existence, declaring it to be the same organisation as had been instituted in 1956.[155] Its functions – subject, in its final form 'to the control of the Minister' – were threefold: to 'obtain, correlate, and evaluate intelligence relevant to security, and to communicate any such intelligence to such persons, and in such manner, as the Director considers to be in the interests of security'; to 'advise Ministers of the Crown, where the Director is satisfied that it is necessary or desirable to do so, in respect of matters relevant to security, so far as those matters relate to Departments or branches of the State Services of which they are in charge'; and to 'co-operate as far as practicable and necessary with such State Services and other public authorities in New Zealand and abroad as are capable of assisting the Security Intelligence Service in the performance of its functions'.[156] Security was, therefore, the central concept defining the Service's work, and was defined in this first governing statute to mean 'the protection of New Zealand from acts of espionage, sabotage, and subversion, whether or not it is directed from or intended to be committed within New Zealand'.[157] The rest of the statute had two main concerns: the employment status and conditions of the Service's officers,[158] which as we have seen had been identified as a key motive for the introduction of the Australian legislation; and the work of an actor known as Commissioner for Security Appeals, who was to investigate complaints against the Service,[159] and who might be seen as the forerunner of the sorts of oversight actors discussed in chapter 5.

A number of changes to the regime introduced in 1969 were made in 1977, responding in part to a report carried out by the Chief Ombudsman, Sir Guy Powles,[160] by a statute that was 'a source of controversy, at its peak unusually heated for the New Zealand political climate'.[161] The report by Powles was prompted by the 'Sutch Affair', relating to the trial under the Official Secrets Act of a former Secretary General in New Zealand's United Nations office, during which it was alleged

> that his investigation and arrest had been made without properly informing the responsible minister, the Prime Minister, that officers of the Security Intelligence Service perjured themselves at the trial, and that Dr Sutch was 'framed' as a result of collusion between the SIS and the KGB.[162]

[154] New Zealand Security Intelligence Service Act 1969 (NZ), s 2.
[155] ibid, s 3.
[156] ibid, s 4.
[157] ibid, s 2.
[158] ibid, ss 6–11.
[159] ibid, ss 14–24.
[160] G Powles, *Security Intelligence Service: Report by Chief Ombudsman*, Appendix to the Journals of the New Zealand House of Representatives (1976).
[161] G Crowder, 'The Security Intelligence Service Amendment Act 1977 and the State Power to Intercept Communications' (1978) 9 *Victoria University Wellington Law Review* 145, 145.
[162] Weller (n 140).

The purpose of the Powles review (it was claimed by Powles himself) was 'to ensure that the functions of the Service were in conformity with both the needs of our country and the character of our society, and our democratic form of government'.[163] Powles visited Australia to discuss matters relating to his inquiry with Justice Hope, who was then carrying out one Royal Commission on security matters there and would carry out another the following decade.[164] And the Service itself, when called upon to respond to the question of the extent to which a security service was needed in New Zealand at all, pointed to the report of a Canadian Royal Commission of 1969,[165] indicating that whether or not outsiders were engaged in comparison, the SIAs themselves were alert to developments elsewhere. That the New Zealand arrangements were modelled on British practice was noted again and again, with Powles quoting, in his discussion on subversion, the famous passage from Lord Denning's Profumo report, whereby the SIAs

> are not to be used so as to pry into any man's private conduct, or business affairs: or even into his political opinions, except in so far as they are subversive, that is, they would contemplate the overthrow of the government by unlawful means.[166]

This, said Powles, 'is how we understand matters in New Zealand':

> I have no doubt that it is the worry that the Service is going beyond the defence of the realm to inquire into political opinions and activities that have nothing to do with overthrowing the Government by unlawful means that is the major reason for public anxiety about the Service. In this connection I do not feel it profitable to embark on any semantic discussion of the difference between 'overthrowing' as used by Lord Denning and 'undermining' as used in our Statute.[167]

A reliance on British practice seemed in a few contexts to have been, however, somewhat misleading. So, for example, the Director of Security was taken to have suggested, at certain points, possible 'qualifications' to the principle of ministerial responsibility for the NZSIS, based in part on 'Lord Denning's endorsement of the British Service's decision not to pass to Ministers information concerning the moral misbehaviour of a Minister', as well as the contents of the Maxwell-Fyfe Directive. This was given short shrift by Powles:

> I believe that the Director and the Service, while purporting to rely on the English practice have, in fact, misunderstood it. A reading of the Maxwell Fyfe and Denning pronouncements … shows that in the United Kingdom the Director (General) is personally responsible to the Home Secretary, but may approach the Prime Minister, to whom he is not responsible in the ordinary way. In New Zealand, where there has been no Minister having responsibilities for the Service analogous to those of the Home

[163] Powles (n 160) 1.

[164] ibid 16. Powles also noted (ibid 15) that, even allowing for the greater scope and complexity of the Australian inquiry, it enjoyed far greater resources than his own, which had been 'conducted somewhat on a shoestring'.

[165] ibid 18–19.

[166] Quoted ibid 29.

[167] ibid 29.

> Secretary, the Prime Minister has had a dual role – Minister in Charge of the Service, and Prime Minister – and it is not right to model the New Zealand Service's relation to the New Zealand Prime Minister on the United Kingdom Service's relation to the United Kingdom Prime Minister. The relationship in New Zealand must be akin to that between the United Kingdom Service and the Home Secretary, which, according to information received, involves close and regular consultation.[168]

Powles, as discussed in chapter 4, was similarly dismissive of attempts to analogise from the UK legal position regarding the interception of communication so as to justify that practice in New Zealand.[169]

A number of important changes resulted from this report and the legislation that followed. Some relate to oversight of the Service, and are discussed in chapter 5.[170] Others, discussed in chapter 4, involved the introduction of an explicit regime for the interception of communications.[171] Amongst those relevant to the general framework within which the NZSIS was to operate was the insertion into the definition of 'security' of a reference to terrorism as something against which New Zealand was to be protected. The definition given to 'terrorism' was 'planning, threatening, using, or attempting to use violence to coerce, deter, or intimidate' either the 'lawful authority of the State in New Zealand' or the 'community throughout New Zealand or in any area in New Zealand for the purpose of furthering any political aim'.[172] The functions of the Service were now to include informing the (recently introduced) New Zealand Intelligence Council – 'a committee of the Permanent Heads of the relevant government departments chaired by the Permanent Head of the Prime Minister's Department', the reform of which Powles had recommended[173] – of 'any new area of potential espionage, sabotage, terrorism, or subversion in respect of which the Director has considered it necessary to institute surveillance'.[174] The provision stating that it was no function of the New Zealand SIS 'to enforce measures for security' was augmented by one providing that it was similarly not its function to 'institute surveillance of any person or class of persons by reason only of his or their involvement in lawful protest or dissent in respect of any matter affecting the Constitution, laws, or Government of New Zealand'.[175] Though three statutes made changes (some of them significant) to the NZSIS legislation in the late 1990s,[176] this basic picture, and in particular

[168] ibid 54.

[169] ibid 57–61.

[170] New Zealand Security Intelligence Service Amendment Act 1977 (NZ), ss 9–14.

[171] ibid, s 4, inserting a new s 4A into the 1969 Act. For a contemporary assessment of this element of the statute, see Crowder (n 161), focusing in particular on the question of whether there was a power to intercept communications prior to the statute's enactment, and criticising the statute for 'covering only a comparatively small part of a much greater problem that is left mostly unsolved'.

[172] New Zealand Security Intelligence Service Amendment Act 1977 (NZ), s 2(1).

[173] Weller (n 140).

[174] New Zealand Security Intelligence Service Amendment Act 1977 (NZ), s 3.

[175] ibid, s 3(2).

[176] New Zealand Security Intelligence Service Amendment Act 1996 (NZ); New Zealand Security Intelligence Service Amendment Act 1999 (NZ); and New Zealand Security Intelligence Service Amendment Act (No 2) 1999 (NZ).

the absence of a legislative basis for the other of the main New Zealand SIAs, the Government Communications Security Bureau – which had been created in 1977[177] – was left largely in place into the new millennium. That picture was, we might recall, very much influenced by the British position – again, sometimes as the result of direct and deliberate efforts by MI5 – though mediated in important ways by the distinctive example of Australia and its early decision to give ASIO a statutory basis. Thus far, therefore, what we have considered is best understood not as three stories of the independent development of security and intelligence agencies but rather as a single tale that unfolded across multiple parts of what had once been the British Empire and was by this point the (British) Commonwealth of Nations.

D. Canada

In Canada, domestic intelligence and security were the responsibility of the RCMP for most of the twentieth century,[178] with a series of institutions within the RCMP being given special responsibility for security matters in the post-war period, before the creation of the Canadian Security Intelligence Service (CSIS) in the 1980s.[179] Immediately after the Second World War a Royal Commission on Espionage, similar in origin and scope to that which would later be carried out in Australia, considered the issue of Soviet espionage in Canada.[180] As with the Australian analogue, the Commission was concerned with factual questions rather than the legal framework of national security. Its report, though, it has been claimed, found 'an international audience far beyond anything previously attained' by a Canadian government publication, for if 'the Soviets had been spying on Canada, it could be assumed that they were doing the same to other wartime allies'.[181] A 1969 Royal Commission (the 'Mackenzie Commission') considered some of the issues that had arisen, or which were to arise, elsewhere,

[177] Its creation was promoted by the head of its predecessor, the New Zealand Combined Signals Organisation, which itself 'had been created in 1955 as the very small and restricted arm of the UKUSA network.' Weller (n 140).

[178] See GS Kealey, *Spying on Canadians: The Royal Canadian Mounted Police Security Service and the Origins of the Long Cold War* (University of Toronto Press, 2017) esp chs 4–6.

[179] See the account of the historical development in Commission of Inquiry Concerning Certain Activities of the Royal Canadian Mounted Police, *Second Report – Volume 1: Freedom and Security Under the Law* (August 1981), pt 2, ch II.

[180] R Taschereau and RL Kellock, *The Report of the Royal Commission Appointed under Order in Council P.C. 411 of February 5, 1946 to Investigate the Facts Relating to and the Circumstances Surrounding the Communication, by Public Officials and Other Persons in Positions of Trust of Secret and Confidential Information to Agents of a Foreign Power* (1946). For discussion, see D Clément, 'The Royal Commission on Espionage and the Spy Trials of 1946–9: A Case Study in Parliamentary Supremacy' (2000) 11 *Journal of the Canadian Historical Association* 151.

[181] R Whitaker and G Marcuse, *Cold War Canada: The Making of a National Insecurity State, 1945–1957* (University of Toronto Press, 1996) 81.

noting that the RCMP had assumed a security role 'because, as the existing federal police force, it was at that time the natural federal instrument in this area' but that there was 'no explicit statutory authority for the security role' played by it.[182] Alongside the vague and implicit statutory authority that might – with some reach – be identified, authority (of sorts) for the RCMP's security and intelligence functions was 'contained in certain instructions and directives issued by the Government, which in effect authorize the RCMP to conduct the investigations necessary for a security screening programme'.[183]

The Commission showed itself to be more concerned with questions of policy-making and coordination than with the rather fundamental legal questions raised by the position it described. It nevertheless argued for the creation of a new, civilian security service in Canada, rejecting arguments against doing so which included the threat that a new civilian agency would be penetrated by hostile intelligence services.[184] The Commission's approach to the question of how that new service should relate to the executive is of interest, for it captures more directly than do other considerations from this period the possibility that it was excessive, rather than inadequate, executive control that was the danger. It said:

> Although the Service must remain part of the executive arm of government and must be generally responsive to the orders of the government, arrangements must be made to provide the Head of the Service with some independence; especially in circumstances in which he may feel that orders (to provide information, for example) may be inappropriate.[185]

In the event, however, the proposed change was not made at that stage: 'the reaction of RCMP senior officers to this recommendation was one of shock and disbelief' and the RCMP immediately began to push back against it.[186] What was done instead was to begin to set up a civilian security service within, rather than outside of, the RCMP.[187] Even here, however, progress was slow as a result of transparent RCMP hostility to the project.[188] It is perhaps significant that the position of the SIAs in other jurisdictions does not loom large in the Mackenzie Commission's report, notwithstanding that by this point in time ASIO had been given a statutory basis in Australia.

[182] Royal Commission on Security, *Report (Abridged)* (1969) [38].
[183] ibid [41].
[184] ibid [59].
[185] ibid [63].
[186] Commission of Inquiry Concerning Certain Activities of the Royal Canadian Mounted Police, *Second Report – Volume 2: Freedom and Security Under the Law* (1981) 671–72.
[187] 'It is therefore the government's intention … to ensure that the Directorate of Security and Intelligence will grow and develop as a distinct and identifiable element within the basic structure of the force, and will be more responsive, in its composition and character, to the national security requirements described by the commissioners … The security service, under the Commissioner of the RCMP, will be increasingly separate in structure and civilian in nature.' Quoted in Commission of Inquiry, *Second Report – Volume 2* (n 186) 672.
[188] ibid 673–74.

A further Royal Commission – the McDonald Commission – was established less than a decade later, prompted by reports of unlawful activities by the RCMP in the context, in particular, of its targeting of the Quebec nationalist movement. The second of the Commission's three reports provides a detailed catalogue of 'activities engaged in by members of the RCMP which might be described as institutionalized wrongdoings' – practices carried out by the RCMP that were not 'not authorized or provided for by law', including

> improper acts of a deceitful character, surreptitious entries, electronic surveillance, mail checks, access to and use of confidential information, countering, physical surveillance, violation of the law by undercover operatives, interrogation of suspects and acts beyond the Security Service mandate.[189]

Against the background of impropriety of such striking breadth and depth, the Commission offered a detailed blueprint for the establishment of a discrete security service, including the threats with which it should concern itself, the methods it should use in the collection of intelligence and the powers it should possess. Where the Mackenzie Commission, making the same basic proposal, had shown little interest in practice elsewhere, the McDonald Commission – with the benefit of a little more than a decade of developments, amongst them the enactment and then amendment of the New Zealand Security Intelligence Service Act in New Zealand – noted that its research had 'taken us to several countries to learn about the organization and governing patterns of the security intelligence function. We have visited the United States, the United Kingdom, Australia and New Zealand.'[190] Though on the central question – whether there should be introduced a security body separate from the ordinary police – it noted the examples of the other states, all of which but the US possessed such an arrangement, 'do not settle the question one way or the other', the Commission stated that in recommending that such a body be introduced, it took comfort from 'the fact that variations of the solution we are proposing for Canada have proved to be practicable in other countries'.[191] On a number of other issues, in particular relating to the relationship between the leadership of this new body and the government of the day, the Commission made extensive reference to the position under the legislation by then in place in both Australia and New Zealand.[192] Most notably, perhaps, it suggested that – subject to the ability of the Director-General to go directly to the Minister, or the Prime Minister – the Director-General should be responsible to the senior civil servant in the department, who 'would have the right to give direction to the Director-General on all matters':

> Our purpose in recommending this structure is to counterbalance what would otherwise be the tremendous power in the hands of the Director General, given his control

[189] Commission of Inquiry, *Second Report – Volume 1* (n 179) 3.
[190] Commission of Inquiry, *Second Report – Volume 2* (n 186) 766.
[191] ibid 766.
[192] ibid 698–705.

> of a secret agency, the special method of approval of his appointment, and his tenure of office for a term of years.[193]

The effect of all of this is that the statute eventually enacted to implement the McDonald Commission's recommendations – the Canadian Security Intelligence Service Act (CSIS Act), enacted in 1984 – is distinctive in that it was establishing a new institution rather than continuing one that previously existed on some other, weaker legal basis. Offering background to the Bill, the Solicitor General deployed the sort of comparative rhetoric that is now a feature of so much of what is now done in the national security context, saying that 'the proposed legislation before us today represents a major turning point for Canada's security intelligence system':

> We are asking Parliament to provide, for the first time in Canada's history, a legal framework more comprehensive, and more detailed, than that of any other security system in the world. Every other country leaves a large part of their security system wholly within the prerogative of government. With [this Bill] we have tried to reduce that element to an absolute minimum.[194]

The Act put in place a Director for CSIS, who was to have 'control and management' of the Service but – contrary to the McDonald recommendation – under the 'direction' of the Minister (in this case the Solicitor General).[195] Directions could be in writing, in which case a copy thereof was to be supplied to the Security Intelligence Review Committee (SIRC) that was provided for by the Act.[196] A number of functions were identified for CSIS by the new statute. The first of these, the only one couched in mandatory terms, was that CSIS was obliged to

> collect, by investigation or otherwise, to the extent that it is strictly necessary, and analyse and retain information and intelligence respecting activities that may on reasonable grounds be suspected of constituting threats to the security of Canada and, in relation thereto, shall report to and advise the Government of Canada.[197]

Other functions, all of them discretionary, included the provision of security assessments and the advising of Ministers.[198] At the request of the relevant

[193] ibid 702. The Commission did not want, based on past experience, the Director-General to report directly to the Minister: 'All the evidence before us leads inescapably to the conclusion that Ministers, although willing to exercise control over the RCMP Security Service, were unable to do so because they had no effective means of finding out what the Security Service was doing. In most cases members of the Security Service would no doubt have been willing to provide the Minister with whatever information he requested, although we have referred to cases earlier in this Report where members were less than forthcoming, and, in certain instances, intentionally misled the Minister – but the real difficulty is that the Minister has not known enough about the Security Service to know what questions to ask.'

[194] House of Commons Debates (Canada) 32nd Parliament, 2nd Session, vol 2, 1271 (10 February 1984).

[195] CSIS Act, RSC, 1985, c C-23 (Canada), s 6(1).

[196] ibid, s 6(2).

[197] ibid, s 12.

[198] ibid, ss 13 and 14.

Minister, and with the consent of the Solicitor General, CSIS was also empowered to collect information or intelligence 'relating to the capabilities, intentions or activities' of foreign states (or a group thereof) or persons who were neither Canadian citizens, nor permanent residents, nor Canadian corporations.[199] 'Threats to the security of Canada' was therefore the central organising concept of CSIS's work from its inception, and was defined originally to encompass four phenomena. First, espionage or sabotage against Canada or otherwise detrimental to its interests. Second, 'foreign influenced activities' that were within or relating to Canada and detrimental to its interests and either clandestine, deceptive or involved a threat to 'any person'. Third, what was in effect terrorism, though that term was not used. Fourth, what is effectively subversion, though again the term is not used: 'activities directed toward undermining by covert unlawful acts, or directed toward or intended ultimately to lead to the destruction or overthrow by violence of, the constitutionally established system of government in Canada'.[200] Two oversight bodies, discussed in chapter 5, were also created: an Inspector General and the SIRC.[201] A contemporary commentator effectively endorsed the comparative claims made for the Act by its promoters, suggesting that it gave to CSIS 'a comprehensive mandate framed in legislation that, despite its occasional defects, represents a significant advance on anything that can be pointed to in the same field in other Western democracies', which might be used in turn to argue for similar in the UK,[202] now the only one of the Commonwealth Five Eyes states in which none of the SIAs possessed a statutory basis.

The founding of the Communications Branch of the National Research Council of Canada (CBNRC), later the Communications Security Establishment (CSE), took place in 1946.[203] The CBNRC was formed, via a secret Order in Council,[204] out of the merger of two organisations that had operated in this sphere during the course of the war – one (the 'Examination Unit') that was civilian in nature and other (the 'Joint Discrimination Unit') that was military. A major exposé of (largely American) spying that was broadcast by the Canadian public broadcaster CBC in 1974, revealed for the first time details of the CBNRC and its work.[205] The following year it was transferred to the Canadian Department of National Defence and renamed the 'Communications Security Establishment',[206] but it would not

[199] ibid, s 16.

[200] ibid, s 2.

[201] ibid, ss 30 and 34.

[202] JLlJ Edwards, 'The Canadian Security Intelligence Act 1984-a Canadian appraisal' (1985) 5 *Oxford Journal of Legal Studies* 143, 144.

[203] KF Jensen, *Cautious Beginnings: Canadian Foreign Intelligence, 1939–51* (University of British Columbia Press, 2008) 135. And see Communications Security Establishment, 'Our Story' (nd).

[204] 'The order-in-council … did not state the purpose of the organization, but only that a wartime activity "of great value" should be continued on a postwar basis.' Jensen (n 203) 134–35.

[205] CBC, 'The Fifth-Estate – the Espionage Establishment' (9 January 1974).

[206] M Rudner, 'Canada's Communications Security Establishment from Cold War to Globalization' (2001) 16 *Intelligence & National Security* 97, 99.

be until 2001 that its work was acknowledged and framed by statute.[207] Before then, it appears to have been accepted that whatever legal basis the CSE had was to be found in the prerogative, though what that might have meant in practice is not clear. That this was to at least some extent undesirable was occasionally noted: a 1990 report by a Special Committee on the Review of the CSIS Act and the Security Offences Act noted that the CSE 'clearly has the capacity to invade the privacy of Canadians in a variety of ways' yet was not subject to the usual processes of accountability:

> It was established by Order in Council, not by statute, and to all intents and purposes is unaccountable. While the Committee understands that this agency must be shrouded in secrecy to some degree, it believes that Canadians should be in a position to understand what the organization does and should not have to wonder whether their rights and freedoms have been infringed. The Committee has evidence that both the [RCMP] and the [CSIS] have asked the CSE for assistance. As such, the Committee believes that the Communications Security Establishment should have a statutory mandate that provides for review and oversight mechanisms for the agency.[208]

Though the focus here is on safeguards, the question of whether the prerogative was in fact capable of providing a suitable legal base for the CSE and its work must have also been a live one. And, as with other jurisdictions, the question retains a significance in Canada, even in the era in which the SIAs enjoy clear statutory authority, given that the ability of the prerogative to ground the intelligence-gathering work of the Canadian Armed Forces has been contested in recent years.[209]

IV. Themes of Cold War National Security Constitutionalism

There are, of course, significant variations in the various security and intelligence bodies that were created in the Commonwealth Five Eyes states between the end of the Second World War and the end of the Cold War, as there are in the manner and the timing of their creation. The specific decisions to give a particular body a statutory basis, as well as the form they were given by the legislation in question, reflect

[207] Anti-terrorism Act, SC 2001, c 41 (Canada).

[208] Special Committee on the Review of the CSIS Act and the Security Offences Act, *In Flux But Not in Crisis* (1990), 152–53. In response the Government noted, amongst other things, that 'arrangements have been put in place to ensure that CSE responds to the government's foreign intelligence requirements in a manner that is lawful, effective and sensitive to changes in international relationships'. Cited in P Rosen, 'The Communications Security Establishment – Canada's Most Secret Intelligence Agency', Library of Parliament, Research Branch (1993).

[209] See National Security and Intelligence Committee of Parliamentarians, *Annual Report 2018* (2019) ch 4. And see P Lagassé, 'Defence intelligence and the Crown prerogative in Canada' (2021) 64 *Canadian Public Administration* 539; and L West, 'The perilous prerogative: An argument for legislating defence intelligence in Canada' (2022) 65 *Canadian Public Administration* 585.

in many cases happenstance in domestic affairs: as is usually the case in this area of policy, law-making was largely reactive. It depended to a considerable extent on the coming to light of unlawful or otherwise suspect behaviour by the SIAs, so that some sort of external scrutiny was carried out. It depended also on what were the specific recommendations that resulted from that exceptional scrutiny, as well as the overall political context, which determined if and how those recommendations were or were not implemented. None of this was preordained. Nevertheless, the pictures painted above of the development of the SIAs in the Commonwealth Five Eyes states demonstrate a range of important similarities. Some of these, no doubt, reflect little more than the common nature of the task these bodies were being introduced in order to carry out, as well as the shared constitutional heritage of the states introducing them, which had worked closely together in military affairs and intelligence even after they had ceased to be part of one, imperial body, but some – we have noted at various points – reflect more directly moments of explicit borrowing and sharing between them.

A. The Influence of MI5 and Imperial Domination

A first theme, already prefigured in the discussions of the Australian and New Zealand experience, is that there appears to have been very explicit modelling of domestic intelligence and security bodies in other states on the UK's MI5, which has at various times been identified as the model for its equivalent in each of the other three states. But this is not simply a case of anglophone allies choosing to draw on the model that came most easily to hand. Rather, we have noted, there seems to have been a concerted effort on the part of MI5 itself – acting, one might presume, with the support, even if only implicit, of the UK Government – to have equivalents to itself set up elsewhere in the Commonwealth, with which it could cooperate and which it seems, at least in the early years, to have often dominated. MI5, of course, had operated throughout the Empire and the Commonwealth that in part replaced it. And so, the UK, the imperial power, continued to assert itself over its former Dominions via the mechanism of its intelligence apparatus. Once these bodies existed, there came a demand – amongst those who knew of their existence, sometimes including (we have seen) the bodies themselves – for a more solid legal basis than they had previously possessed. That demand reflected a range of considerations: sometimes it was about limiting their mandate, sometimes merely giving the existing tasking a democratic mandate, and in the Australian case in particular its seems to have reflected a fear that without a statutory basis the long-term persistence of the key security body was not guaranteed. And whatever their content, and however perfunctory early examples were, statutes are publicly available documents. Not only could they be read (interpreted, speculated upon) by the public, but they were available as a model to those in other jurisdictions, who wished to give to their own SIAs a statutory basis, or who simply wanted to argue for this to be done. And so it is unsurprising that the Australian statute of 1956 acted as the template for its New Zealand counterpart a decade later. From there on, the patterns of influence seem to become in the short term weaker, reflecting a range of contingencies, including when and where the SIAs of each state would break into public consciousness and how, and by whom, their legal position would be investigated. Strikingly, in light of its early efforts at encouraging the creation of domestic security bodies across the Commonwealth, the UK's MI5 was the last of these domestic security bodies to obtain a statutory footing, doing so only at the tail end of the Cold War. Later on, as we shall see, this process of constitutionalisation sets the scene for yet further borrowing and sharing.

There is less obvious resemblance between the other bodies of these states, with the number of such bodies and division of powers between them more varied. On one hand, this might be thought surprising: given the nature of the Five Eyes partnership, focused upon the sharing of the product of signals intelligence in particular, the relevant bodies from each state would have, one would have thought, more frequent and more intensive interactions than would the domestic security bodies, whose interactions were no doubt important but perhaps less systematised. On the other hand, it is not clear, in relation to these foreign intelligence bodies, what it is that one might have borrowed. MI5 had the Attlee Directive and the Maxwell-Fyfe Directive, but no equivalent (that we know of) for MI6 or GCHQ. The other Commonwealth Five Eyes states were not prompted to give their own equivalents (where they had one) a statutory footing until much later, perhaps because foreign intelligence bodies were less subject to politicisation than their domestic security counterparts and so less liable to be swept away with a change of government, or perhaps because these bodies were (and are) more secretive, more sensitive than their domestic counterparts and, in so far as they operated abroad, the question of their domestic legal position was neither here nor there. Though there is considerable contingency (and path dependency) evident in the history of the relevant bodies, one other factor that may have influenced this picture is the point insisted upon by Findlater Stewart immediately after the Second World War: that 'MI5 should continue to be responsible for obtaining "counter intelligence" in the Empire by the means used in the past. But the acquisition of intelligence, including counter-intelligence, by secret means elsewhere, must remain a matter for SIS.'[210] The past work of MI5 there, that is, linked the Dominions in a way that the work of MI6 did not.

B. The Cold War Mission of the SIAs

A particular point of commonality between the different regimes is to be found in the responsibilities given to SIAs, starting from the UK's Attlee Directive, which provided that MI5's task was 'the Defence of the Realm as a whole, from external

[210] Jeffrey (n 46) 620.

and internal dangers arising from attempts at espionage and sabotage, or from actions of persons and organisations, whether directed from within or without the country, which may be judged to be subversive of the security of the State', language that found its way – albeit at times with modifications – not only into the better-known Maxwell-Fyfe Directive, but also into the legal instruments governing ASIO and the NZSIS. The former's task was (originally) defined in large part by reference to security, defined to mean 'the protection of the Commonwealth and the Territories of the Commonwealth from acts of espionage, sabotage or subversion, whether directed from, or intended to be committed, within the Commonwealth or not'.[211] Subversion was not further defined. The latter gave a similar definition to security, but added a definition of 'subversion', which was to mean 'attempting, inciting, counselling, advocating, or encouraging' either '[t]he overthrow by force of the Government of New Zealand' or '[t]he undermining by unlawful means of the authority of the State in New Zealand'.[212] Though the word 'subversion' was not used, CSIS's task was also defined in part by reference to a related concept when it was first created, alongside the typical references to espionage and sabotage.

This concern with espionage and subversion reflects the Cold War context of the SIAs and their creation, and in particular the fact that the primary threat to which they were oriented was that posed by hostile states – the USSR and its allies. A number of points might be made about this. One is that the distinction between subversion and the legitimate operation of the democratic process is not always easy to draw, and in each state, therefore, the inclusion of the language of subversion within the relevant instrument and debates as to implications of its presence there were perhaps the defining theme of political debates around the SIAs and their mandates in this period. Perhaps the best statement of the difficulties associated with it, evidencing its potentially dangerous breadth, comes from the Mackenzie Commission report in Canada, which noted that it had not been able to find a 'satisfactory simple' definition of the term:

> [T]he range of activities that may in some circumstances constitute subversion seems to us to be very wide indeed: overt pressures, clandestine influence, the calculated creation of fear, doubt and despondency, physical sabotage or even assassination – all such activities can be considered subversive in certain circumstances. Subversive activities need not be instigated by foreign governments or ideological organizations; they need not necessarily be conspiratorial or violent; they are not always illegal. Again fine lines must be drawn. Overt lobbying or propaganda campaigns aimed at effecting constitutional or other changes are part of the democratic process; they can however be subversive if their avowed objectives and apparent methods are cloaks for undemocratic intentions and activities. Political or economic pressures from domestic or foreign sources may be subversive, particularly when they have secret or concealed facets, or when they include attempts to influence government policies by the recruitment or

[211] Australian Security Intelligence Organization Act 1956 (Australia), s 2.
[212] New Zealand Security Intelligence Service Act 1969 (NZ), s 2.

alienation of those within the government service or by the infiltration of supporters into the service.[213]

Another is that this was not a purely theoretical debate: it is clear that the SIAs in the various Commonwealth Five Eyes states at times took (as a result of their focus on subversion and the Communist threat more specifically) actions that were or might have been seen as illegitimate in a constitutional democracy. This was both the background to a number of the reports or investigations discussed in section III, and the impetus for the inclusion, within many of the resulting statutes, of provisions designed to exclude partisan interventions by the SIAs (discussed further in chapter 3). Another point, however, is that this element of the SIAs' work seems to have been diminished by the end of the Cold War and the rise, a decade later, of international terrorism as the most prominent and politically salient threat to (national) security. As we discuss in chapter 7, the return to prominence of what are now sometimes called 'state threats' might in this sense be understood as a return to the historically normal position – the context, that is, within which the SIAs were first created, formalised and rationalised – a fact that potentially has implications for the apparatus of 'negative constitutionalism' that has grown up around them in recent decades.

C. Informality and Prerogative

Another central theme is that which we have encountered repeatedly in our treatment of the different SIAs in each jurisdiction: a hesitation to give the bodies a clear legal basis, and a reliance – in the absence of such a basis – on instruments of uncertain legal significance. As a consideration of the different contexts has shown, the idea that the SIAs might be founded on the prerogative that had been exported to (or even imposed on) the colonies by the UK was occasionally expressed, but explicit reliance upon the prerogative by the authorities was rare. There is good reason for that: even if the bodies in question were in some sense founded on the prerogative in the specific form of their original Orders in Council (where one existed), it is not clear that the prerogative did give them, or could have given them, any particular intrusive or investigatory capabilities. The prerogative was at various points referenced in the specific context of the interception of communications,

[213] Royal Commission (n 182) [6]–[7]. See also the discussion of the concept in Australia's Royal Commission on Intelligence and Security (n 109) [55]–[83], starting from the observation that it 'is difficult to define but is nonetheless a very real, and may be a very dangerous, form of activity'. Hope revisited the issue (at even greater length) in his second Royal Commission: Royal Commission on Australia's Security Intelligence Agencies, *Report on the Australian Security Intelligence Organization*, Parliamentary Paper No 232/1985 (1985), ch 4, concluding that 'activities relating to the overthrow of the constitutional system of government which it is proper for ASIO to investigate should be defined by reference to violence'. The use of 'subversion' in the UK through the Cold War period is considered, along with its political implications, by L Lustgarten and I Leigh, *In from the Cold: National Security and Parliamentary Democracy* (Oxford University Press, 1994) 395–405.

but the Birkett Committee in the UK, which considered the matter in the 1950s, had not relied on it to justify such activities, and – as discussed in chapter 4 – it seems usually to have been agreed that whatever (weak) case might have been made for doing so in the UK did not apply elsewhere. It is particularly striking that in many cases, references to the prerogative become more frequent and more confident after statutory authority is in place: when the stakes are lower, because any illegality now belongs to the past rather than the present, it is easier to make a legal claim that might turn out to be wrong or the consequences of which are nevertheless uncertain. We need not rehearse the point any further, but it is important to note the obvious connection between this fact, the apparent reliance on the prerogative instead of statute, and the fact that these were all states that were once part (in the UK's case, rather more than that) of the British Empire. The reliance on the prerogative to gloss over inconvenient legal gaps, even if largely rhetorical, has long been a feature of Commonwealth national security constitutionalism, and might by definition be distinctive to it.

D. Secrecy

Standing behind this reluctance to legislate, and consequent (contestable) reliance on the prerogative, was the (felt) imperative of secrecy that obtained in this field. For much of this period, the security and intelligence bodies were kept largely if not entirely secret: not just the details of their operations, but also at various times and in various places the very fact of their existence. But that desire to maintain secrecy to such an extent also meant that the legal instruments of the pre-statutory era could not be publicised: to publish the Directive or Charter that creates or governs one of the SIAs is to admit that it exists. Giving some security and intelligence body or other a statutory basis – as happened in all cases eventually – therefore meant, if nothing else, admitting that the body in question existed there was such a body, though there was in some cases a significant gap between the avowal and the move to a statutory footing, while of course the existence of a body can be known with reasonable, sometimes even total, confidence even before formal avowal takes place. This question of secrecy would seem to be connected to the different patterns of avowal and legislation that applied to domestic security and foreign intelligence bodies: for a number of reasons, the latter were seen as some combination of more sensitive and less politically salient, and so avowed later and so legislated for later.

Even assuming that the desire for secrecy was a reasonable one in the constitutional and (geo)political context of the time, certain costs accrued. The legal instruments relied upon in the absence of statute were weak, of uncertain status and – from the point of view of the security endeavour itself – wholly incapable of giving to the SIAs in clear and unambiguous terms the powers they might have wanted or needed. The desire to maintain factual secrecy implied in turn a degree of legal secrecy that impacted not only upon the rule of law, in the form of a lack of clear legal norms governing the SIAs and their work, but also upon the effectiveness of the SIAs in pursuing the ends to which such secrecy purported to contribute. There is, in retrospect, an argument that the strategy chosen was the wrong one. If any observer would have been confident that the various states possessed domestic and foreign intelligence agencies, and participated to at least some degree in the collection of (at least) signals intelligence, it is not clear that the cost of admitting the existence of the relevant agencies and publishing their missions – always defined in broad terms, and always likely to have been politically acceptable to mainstream opinion in the states in question – outweighed the benefits, whether legal, political or practical, of admitting they existed and giving them a clear statutory basis much earlier than was in fact done.[214] Though they might do much without any legal authority whatsoever (whether because it has no legal effect, or because it takes place outside of the jurisdiction and so is a breach only of somebody else's rules), and though they might find legal authority in other places, it seems inevitable that security and intelligence agencies will eventually want to do things that they can only (lawfully) do if a statute is enacted to permit them to do so. This last qualification is important – a willingness to engage in pervasive illegality will help postpone the moment at which the introduction of a statutory basis is felt necessary. It is therefore not surprising that the proximate cause of many of the relevant statutory interventions in the Cold War period was some scandal or other that demonstrated either or both that a body existed and was acting in a way that was not – or not only – politically indefensible but rather outright unlawful.

E. (The Absence of) Democratic Oversight

The legal position of the SIAs had implications for the political configuration that were obvious but no less important for that. Where there was no statutory authority, there was no direct democratic legitimacy for their work and the powers they possessed. Nor, when there was pervasive secrecy, was there any possibility of meaningful democratic oversight of those bodies, even after the fact. Courts were (largely) shut out of the process, if only via obscurity (one cannot legally challenge actions one does not know are taking place, carried out by bodies one does not know exist); legislatures were given little or no insight into the national security domain (and often liked it that way); and the modern phenomenon of independent actors providing oversight, which might have made up for some of the many limits of orthodox legal and political scrutiny, emerged only partially and often belatedly. This position might be – and, we shall see, at least sometimes was – justified by reference to the fact of executive responsibility for the work of the SIAs

[214] See, in this regard, RJ Aldrich, *GCHQ: The Uncensored Story of Britain's Most Secret Intelligence Agency* (Harper Collins, 2011) 483–85, discussing the legislation that gave the UK's GCHQ a statutory basis in 1994, and the way it disappointed those who 'presumed that more regulation would mean more restrictions': 'Being "legit" often meant that the agencies could carry out even more operations.'

(and the national security endeavour more broadly) with which the courts and the legislature had no right to interfere. As we have seen, however, there was in many cases a lack of clear executive responsibility for the SIAs, with members of governments limited in their ability to give directions to the SIAs and the SIAs not obliged to inform them of their work and sometimes claiming the right to actively withhold information from their political masters. The issue of whether the SIAs were complying even with the loose instruments that constituted their pre-statutory mandates was therefore, in effect, often left up the SIAs themselves. Seen in that light, it is perhaps unsurprising that important examples of incompetence and outright illegality are identifiable across time and space. As we shall see in future chapters, many of the key developments of the late- or post-Cold War period have either the aim or the direct or indirect effect of increasing the fact, or at least the possibility, of democratic accountability for the SIAs and their work. In chapter 7, we consider the question of whether that aspect of the project of constitutionalising the national security enterprise in the Commonwealth Five Eyes states – a project that started with the giving to the domestic security bodies of a legislative base – can survive the turn back to state threats rather than terrorism as the central focus of that enterprise.

V. Conclusion

This book is focused on what I call the Commonwealth model of national security constitutionalism. We noted in the Introduction to this book the dominant focus, under the heading of constitutionalism, on the notion of limitation; of preventing or discouraging, through legal and political means, the state and its various limbs from acting in excessive or arbitrary fashions – sometimes from acting at all. And indeed, it is in relation to limits – human rights norms, new mechanisms of parliamentary or hybrid oversight and review – that much of the novelty in national security constitutionalism in recent decades is to be identified: we consider these issues in chapters 5 and 6. During the period of the Cold War itself, however, it was the positive dimension that (eventually) predominated: the creation and then (later) the formalisation of the SIAs in each jurisdiction, with defined missions and relationships to other parts of the constitutional order beginning to be clarified and at times evolving to meet changing security needs and changing political expectations. Though this project was by no means complete at the end of the Cold War, the developments described and analysed in this chapter are a necessary precondition for the more obvious and more prominent project of constitutionalisation that has been the dominant aspect of national security constitutionalism in the last 20 or 30 years. And, crucially, just like that more recent project, the development of national security constitutionalism during the Cold War period reflected, though loosely and imperfectly, movement towards a common model. Though the fact, never mind the specific mechanisms, of causal influence during this period is often difficult to evidence, there are points at which both are clearly documented, as when emissaries from MI5 travelled to Australia and New Zealand to convince the governments of each state to introduce a domestic security service specifically on the model of MI5 itself, and when New Zealand transposed into its own system an Australian statute of only a few years earlier. Later, as greater divergence came about, the influence appears to have worked more broadly, and in a variety of directions, with the process of constitutionalisation itself facilitating further such borrowing and sharing by bringing out into the open much that would once have remained secret, on which other states might then draw.

3

The Modern National Security Apparatus

I. Introduction

In this chapter, against the background of the tale of introduction and evolution told in chapter 2, I consider the modern national security apparatus in the Commonwealth Five Eyes states. The bodies in question (the SIAs) were, we saw there, shaped by the Cold War context, even when in some form or other their creation preceded that period, and many of their initial similarities can be attributed to the deliberate export of the British model to its former Dominions in the period after the Second World War. The focus of this chapter, therefore, is the post-Cold War period, in which the relevant bodies have by no means stood still but have become more recognisably modern and more stable: though they continue to evolve, and are occasionally transformed, this is the era in which such changes happen almost entirely in the open via the making of legislation, which is debated and scrutinised within the ordinary political process rather than via, for example, unpublished 'directives' or secret Orders in Council. What were once bare, minimalist statutory frameworks have in many cases bulked out to reflect the changing political and legal context. This process was accelerated, most notably, by the 'global war on terror', in the context of which new powers in the domain of national security were created and as a result of which there was, even where the basic institutional formation of the national security apparatus was relatively stable, frequent and often contested legislative intervention. Though there remains considerable secrecy as to operations and methods, the legal framework of the security and intelligence agencies in each of the Commonwealth Five Eyes states is, therefore, no longer marked by the same obscurity that it was for much of the Cold War, with clear and significant implications for their democratic credentials.

As is the case elsewhere in this book, the purpose of the chapter is not to give an exhaustive account of the agencies and their missions as they have developed in the period since the fall of the Berlin Wall. I pick out key details about their status and mandate, and key moments from their modern history, in order to identify points of similarity and contrast, and to demonstrate – in particular – the patterns of mutual influence that are discernible only when the SIAs of the four Commonwealth Five Eyes states are considered together. In particular, I seek to show that the patterns of influence identified in chapter 2 have not disappeared but have instead been transformed, in two ways. On one hand, the influence has a multi-directional nature that was not the case in the early years of the Cold War, when the UK dominated the field and sought to shape, in a direct fashion, the SIAs elsewhere in the Commonwealth. On the other hand, the methods of influence appear to be more subtle than was previously the case, often operating without the taking of any direct action by agents of the state(s) in question. Moreover, as we have already observed, the process is self-reinforcing: the constitutionalism of the SIAs in this period, and the associated transparency as to the legal position, makes possible increased borrowing and sharing, now often at the initiative of the recipient party. Given, however, that these changes do not take place in a vacuum but are strongly influenced by (and, perhaps to a lesser extent, also shape) the wider constitutional context of the jurisdictions in question, I first consider briefly certain key issues relating to that context, and in particular questions of how human rights are (and are not) protected nationally and internationally. The consideration of the contemporary SIAs that is offered in this chapter is followed, in chapter 4, by discussion of certain issues and themes relating to the intrusive and investigatory powers afforded to those SIAs by the modern legislative regimes.

II. The Changing Context

A. The Threat Matrix

Geopolitically, the four Commonwealth Five Eyes states are of course distinct in a range of important ways. The UK is geographically, if not always spiritually, part of Europe, and so is affected by threats to it even if it did not, even while still a member of the European Union, participate in the full panoply of responses to those threats. Australia and New Zealand are within the Asia-Pacific region and so far more directly affected than is the UK, in particular, by the 'rise' of China. Canada has also been, it would appear, targeted by China in recent years and is, by virtue of its location, more directly affected, for better and worse, by its dominant neighbour, the United States of America. Notwithstanding these important differences, reflected in the specific factual matrix upon which questions of national security law play out in each jurisdiction, all four of the states we are considering here have a range of important features in common, contemporary and historical, some of which were canvassed in the Introduction to this book. All were part of the geopolitical 'West' during the Cold War, and we have seen that it was often Soviet espionage – actual or merely apprehended – that drove the introduction of many of the SIAs, shaped their missions and prompted their evolution over the course of the Cold War. Though it generally – for reasons on which we have speculated – left less of a mark upon the public record, it is certain that the posture of each of these four states was not merely defensive, seeking to protect the state and its secrets against those who might seek to steal them. They also collected signals and other intelligence relating to the Soviets and their activities at home and abroad, and no doubt engaged in espionage within the Soviet Union. These activities may not have had, and may not have needed, a clear legal basis, but they will of course have had a part to play in influencing the development of the SIAs over that period.

With the end of the Cold War, the drivers and direction of legal evolution become less certain. As we shall discuss in section III.B, the UK's MI5, in the middle of the 1990s, took on new responsibilities related to the fight against 'ordinary' crime.[1] Contemporaneously, a statute gave the NZSIS analogous powers, and introduced into the definition of 'security' in New Zealand a new reference to 'the making of a contribution to New Zealand's international well-being or economic wellbeing'.[2] One concern of an Australian enactment of this period was to replace the word 'Organization' with its variant 'Organisation' in ASIO's name.[3] This period of uncertainty, even drift, was brought to an end with the 9/11 attacks of 2001, which gave new impetus to the project of modernising, rationalising and in many cases expanding the corpus of national security law, albeit now with the primary focus upon the threat of terrorism rather than that of hostile state threats, and under the coordinating influence, in many cases, of the United Nations.[4] Sometimes the reforms to the general frameworks of SIAs prompted by or undertaken during the 'war on terror' were minor in comparison with those of the Cold War era, but in many cases, including where the SIAs had not already been given a statutory basis before 2001, they were much more significant. How these states' understanding of the threat of terrorism evolved over the decades that followed is a complex story, with the focus eventually turning – after the emergence and decline of the so-called 'Islamic State' – to the phenomenon of 'foreign fighters': those who had left their home state to participate in conflicts in Iraq or Syria, and who would, by virtue of their ideological commitments and experiences abroad, pose a threat to that home state if and when they managed to return there.[5]

[1] Security Service Act 1996 (UK).

[2] New Zealand Security Intelligence Service Amendment Act 1996 (NZ), s 2(3), inserting a new definition into s 2 of the New Zealand Security Intelligence Service Act 1969 (NZ), and s 6, inserting a new s 4c into the 1969 Act, which would permit the Director of NZSIS, 'for the purpose of preventing or detecting serious crime in New Zealand or in any other country', to 'retain any information that comes into the possession of the Security Intelligence Service and … communicate any such information to members of the New Zealand Police or to such other persons, and in such manner, as the Director thinks fit'. Though not all SIAs have an explicit role in relation to (serious) crime, it is clear that some forms of criminal activity – of which terrorism and sabotage are obvious examples – will necessarily be caught by the language of 'national security'.

[3] Australian Security Intelligence Organisation Legislation Amendment Act 1999 (Australia), sch 3.

[4] On which, see F de Londras, *The Practice and Problems of Transnational Counter-Terrorism* (Cambridge University Press, 2022) esp chs 1 and 2; and A Vedaschi and K Lane Scheppele (eds), *9/11 and the Rise of Global Anti-Terrorism Law: How the UN Security Council Rules the World* (Cambridge University Press, 2021).

[5] On various aspects of the phenomenon, see F Capone, C Paulussen and R Mignot-Mahdavi (eds), *Returning Foreign Fighters: Responses, Legal Challenges and Ways Forward* (Springer, 2023).

Though the legal system of each of the four states continues to grapple with that issue of 'foreign fighters' and other of their citizens who were involved, in some capacity or other and often blamelessly (as with those children born in refugee camps in Syria), the collapse of the Islamic State means that the legal regimes put in place when the phenomenon was at its most prominent are unlikely to be augmented significantly in the short term. History strongly suggests, however, that when the threat of terrorism does resurge in the future then, no matter its specific form, the existing body of counter-terrorism law will be deemed insufficient or otherwise inadequate to respond to the exigencies of the moment. The temptation to respond in legislation, and the political demand to be seen to take the matter seriously, will compel action, whether truly necessary or not. Nevertheless, this context – the apparent vacuum left by the fall of the Soviet Union before the rise of international terrorism as the most prominent threat to national security – appears to have influenced the development of the SIAs, and in particular the accountability landscape as it grew up and was reformed in the post-Cold War context. One question, therefore, to which we shall turn in the chapter 7, is whether the apparent reversal of this trend in the 2020s, with a renewed focus on the threat to national security posed by hostile states, can and will be accommodated within oversight structures that were either brought into being or took on their modern form at a time when the key national security threat was considered – by both, it appears, the public and their elected representatives – to be that of international terrorism.

B. Fundamental Rights

Regardless of the extent to which the changing threat matrix is reflected in the legal frameworks currently applicable to the SIAs in each of the Commonwealth Five Eyes states, it seems clear that there is another change to the context that exercises an important influence on the design of those SIAs (discussed in this chapter) and, especially, their powers (discussed in chapter 4). I noted in the Introduction and in chapter 2 some of the constitutional context within which the SIAs first emerged in the Commonwealth Five Eyes states, and in particular the so-called 'Westminster model' that is common to all of those states and that, I suggested, influenced certain elements of the Commonwealth model of national security constitutionalism in the Cold War period: the reliance on the prerogative and associated secrecy, the exclusive responsibility of the executive and the weak political oversight of the SIAs. A point on which less stress was laid, but which again seems common to all of these jurisdictions, was the limited role of the courts in reviewing and pronouncing upon the lawfulness of the actions of the SIAs. Some of this, as was noted, was a simple function of the secrecy that surrounded not only the work of the SIAs, but also their very existence. One cannot, that is, easily challenge in court the lawfulness of actions one does not know were taken by a body the existence of which the government has never avowed. Some of the absence of the courts from the scene, however, was a function of a belief on the part of those courts themselves, echoes of which can be found in each of the four states, that responsibility for national security (under that or another name) belonged largely or exclusively to the executive, such that decisions the executive made in that sphere could not be reviewed or gainsaid by those courts, either to the same extent as would be the case for an act or decision in another area of policy or, sometimes, at all.

Against that background, it seems clear that one other influence upon the modern national security settlements in the Commonwealth Five Eyes states is the changing human rights regimes, with three of the four states now possessing some form of national-level Bill of Rights, which – along with State-level equivalents in Australia – make up the so-called 'new Commonwealth model' of rights protection to which reference was made in the Introduction.[6] Following an earlier attempt to protect human rights through federal legislation via the Canadian Bill of Rights of 1960 – limited in its effect because it did not apply to provincial legislation[7] – the Canadian Charter of Rights and Freedoms was included in the Constitution Act, 1982 as part of the patriation of the Canadian constitution.[8] The Charter guarantees a range of rights that are said to be subject only to 'such reasonable limits prescribed by law as can be demonstrably justified in a free and democratic society'.[9] Being within the Constitution, it is part of the 'supreme law' of Canada, any law that is inconsistent with which 'is, to the extent of the inconsistency, of no force or effect',[10] though the 'notwithstanding clause' in section 33 of the Charter permits a (time-limited) override of a set of the rights protected by it where the relevant legislature states explicitly that it is its intention to do so. Against this background, the CSIS Act of 1984 – enacted in the years following the introduction of the Charter – now provides first of all that all measures the Service would take to reduce threats to Canada must comply with the Charter's requirements (which, we are reminded, is 'part of the supreme law of Canada'), while using it as a trigger for a requirement of judicial authorisation, so that any such measures that reduce or limit one of the rights or freedoms protected by the Charter may be taken only where authorised by a judicial warrant.[11] A warrant

[6] S Gardbaum, *The New Commonwealth Model of Constitutionalism* (Cambridge University Press, 2013).

[7] By s 5(3) of the statute, the operative provisions were to be construed 'as extending only to matters coming within the legislative authority of the Parliament of Canada'. See B Laskin, 'Canada's Bill of Rights: A Dilemma for the Courts?' (1962) 11 *International and Comparative Law Quarterly* 519. For a discussion of the model of rights protection offered by the Bill of Rights, see DB Fowler, 'The Canadian Bill of Rights – A Compromise between Parliamentary and Judicial Supremacy' (1973) 21 *American Journal of Comparative Law* 712.

[8] By the Canada Act 1982 (UK), which enacted for Canada the Constitution Act, 1982 of which the Charter forms part. Edward McWhinney called it 'a flawed, certainly incomplete exercise that left undisturbed the main institutions and processes of Canadian Government': E McWhinney, 'The Constitutional Patriation Project, 1980–82' (1984) 32 *American Journal of Comparative Law* 241.

[9] Canadian Charter of Rights and Freedoms, Part 1 of the Constitution Act, 1982 (Canada), s 1.

[10] Constitution Act, 1982 (Canada), s 52(1).

[11] CSIS Act (1984) (Canada), s 12.1(3.1) and (3.2).

may be given only where the judge is satisfied that the measures in question comply with the Charter.[12] The Charter also acts as a limitation – discussed in chapter 4 – upon the ability of CSIS to commit or authorise others to commit criminal offences.[13] Often, however, the impact of these rules appears to be limited by the fact that the Charter does not, or does not always, apply to CSIS's activities outside of Canada.[14]

Though the Canadian Charter is a forerunner here, the statute that has been most influential elsewhere would seem to be the New Zealand Bill of Rights Act (NZBORA) 1990, an ordinary statute with, in the context of a sovereign legislature, no special constitutional status and that is not subject to any special amendment procedure.[15] The NZBORA again affirms a range of rights, and provides that the rights in question 'may be subject only to such reasonable limits prescribed by law as can be demonstrably justified in a free and democratic society'.[16] And, in line with the absence of a formal distinction between constitutional and ordinary law in the New Zealand legal order, the NZBORA does not contain a strike-down power, with the effect that courts may not hold 'any provision of the enactment to be impliedly repealed or revoked, or to be in any way invalid or ineffective' or '[d]ecline to apply any provision of the enactment' because of its incompatibility with the rights protected by the Act.[17] It does, though, introduce an interpretive obligation, whereby courts, in interpreting statutes, are obliged to prefer a meaning that is consistent with the Bill of Rights, where available, over one that is inconsistent.[18] The Bill of Rights applies generally to acts done by the three branches of the New Zealand state (as well as those bodies performing legally imposed public powers, functions and duties).[19] One of the purposes of the Intelligence and Security Act 2017, moreover, by which was implemented a major reform of the New Zealand security apparatus, is – that Act tells us – to 'protect New Zealand as a free, open, and democratic society' by 'ensuring that the functions of the intelligence and security agencies are performed', inter alia, 'in accordance with New Zealand law and all human rights obligations recognised by New Zealand law'.[20] Obligations to so act are placed by the 2017 Act on the SIAs generally,

[12] ibid, s 12.1(3.3).
[13] ibid, s 20.1(22).
[14] For discussion of the point and an argument in favour of an alternative approach, see L West, '"Within or outside Canada": The Charter's application to the extraterritorial activities of the Canadian Security Intelligence Service' (2023) 73 *University of Toronto Law Journal* 1.
[15] For accounts of the origins of the NZBORA, see KJ Keith, 'Concerning Change: The Adoption and Implementation of the New Zealand Bill of Rights Act 1990' (2000) 31 *Victoria University Wellington Law Review* 721; and D Erdos, 'Aversive constitutionalism in the Westminster world: The genesis of the New Zealand Bill of Rights Act (1990)' (2007) 5 *International Journal of Constitutional Law* 343 (contesting the application to the New Zealand case of, amongst other things, Ran Hirschl's 'hegemonic preservation' thesis).
[16] NZBORA 1990 (NZ), s 5.
[17] ibid, s 4.
[18] ibid, s 6.
[19] ibid, s 3.
[20] Intelligence and Security Act 2017 (NZ), s 3(c)(i).

and on their Directors-General specifically, these latter being required to 'take all reasonable steps to ensure that … any co-operation with foreign jurisdictions and international organisations in the performance of any of the agency's functions is in accordance with New Zealand law and all human rights obligations recognised by New Zealand law'.[21]

The UK's HRA 1998 is far closer to the New Zealand model than it is to that found in Canada. It includes, under section 3 of the Act, an interpretive obligation whereby, '[s]o far as it is possible to do so', courts must 'read and give effect' to legislation (both primary and secondary) in a manner compatible with the protected rights. It does not include a strike-down power, with legislation that is not capable of a rights-compatible interpretation instead being subject to a (discretionary) declaration of its incompatibility with those same rights.[22] The rights in question were copied or transposed into the domestic legal order from the ECHR, with a view to making it possible to enforce one's rights under that instrument without a slow and costly trip to the Strasbourg Court.[23] Nowadays, though – unlike in other jurisdictions – there is no specific reference made to either the HRA 1998 or the Convention within the statutes that establish and govern the SIAs; they, like other public authorities, may not act incompatibly with the rights protected by the Act unless, in effect, they are obliged to do so by primary legislation. The requirements of the HRA 1998 do, though, feature as one of a number of considerations that public authorities might take into account when deciding whether and how to make use of a range of powers under the primary piece of legislation providing for their investigatory powers.[24] Even before then, however, the fact that the UK was a party to the ECHR had exercised a significant influence on the law in this area. Though arguments in favour of placing MI5 (the first of the UK's SIAs in relation to which this was done) on a statutory footing had long circulated, the proximate cause of the decision to do so, via the Security Service Act 1989, appears to have been litigation brought in Strasbourg arguing – successfully – that MI5's activities were not 'in accordance with the law' as required by the Convention.[25] The dual domestic and international nature of the regime of human rights protection in the UK – overlapping and interacting rather than wholly separate – continues to be a driver of the law in the more general domain of national security. Nevertheless,

[21] ibid, s 18(b).

[22] HRA 1998 (UK), s 4.

[23] Home Secretary, *Rights Brought Home: The Human Rights Bill* (Cm 3782, 1997).

[24] Investigatory Powers Act 2016 (UK), s 2(4)(d).

[25] See *Hewitt and Harman v United Kingdom* (1992) 14 EHRR 657 [40]: 'The Commission notes that the activities of the Security Service are governed by a Directive of the Home Secretary to the Director-General of the Security Service dated 24 September 1952. Although the Directive is published, it is not claimed by the Government that it has the force of law or that its contents constitute legally enforceable rules concerning the operation of the Security Service. Nor does the Directive provide a framework which indicates with the requisite degree of certainty the scope and manner of the exercise of discretion by the authorities in the carrying out of secret surveillance activities.'

because jurisdiction under the ECHR (and so the HRA 1998) is primarily territorial, and so usually determined by the physical location of the person claiming to enjoy rights against those agencies, it will often be the case that the actions of – say – MI6 do not engage the Convention because of where they are undertaken.

Of the four states under discussion, only Australia is without a modern Bill of Rights at Commonwealth level – though a small number of rights are protected against the Commonwealth by the Australian Constitution, while a number of Australian States have enacted legislative Bills of Rights – with obvious implications for the sorts of legal challenges that might be brought against the work of Australia's security and intelligence agencies. But though it lacks one aspect of the 'new Commonwealth model' of human rights protection, Australia does conform to the other key aspect thereof: a Parliamentary Joint Committee on Human Rights, which examines proposed legislation for human rights compatibility, has existed since 2012.[26]

The result of all of this is that there are important, and overarching, limits upon the ability of the SIAs in the majority of the Commonwealth Five Eyes states to act, the introduction of which has to a considerable extent coincided with the shift in focus within those states from the threat posed by hostile states to that posed by (international) terrorism. Those limits can be, and at times have been, enforced against the SIAs by the courts; and if all is operating as it should, they will have influenced the activities and operations of the SIAs even where the possibility of enforcement has been remote or negligible.

III. The SIAs of the Commonwealth Five Eyes States

In this section, I consider the modern form of the SIAs in Canada, the UK, Australia and New Zealand, including their legal status, the concepts that define and limit their mission, and their relationship to other organs of state, before then going on to consider first of all how those key concepts vary as between the four (sets of) SIAs and then certain themes that recur in multiple jurisdictions. As with chapter 2, the temporal scope of this chapter is not set in stone: though our key concern is with the period since the end of the Cold War through to the present day, some of the SIAs continue to take a form originally given to them before the end of the Cold War, albeit often with important modifications in the 1990s and through into the era of the 'war on terror'.

[26] For an overview of the first decade of its work, see C Fletcher and A Coles, 'Reflections on the 10th anniversary of the Parliamentary Joint Committee on Human Rights' *Senate Lecture Series* (August 2022). The work of the Committee, amongst others, in relation to counter-terrorism law-making specifically, is discussed in S Moulds, *Committees of Influence: Parliamentary Rights Scrutiny and Counter-Terrorism Lawmaking in Australia* (Springer, 2020) esp ch 3.

A. Canada

We have noted that when CSIS was created in the mid-1980s – just a few years after the 'patriation' of the Canadian constitution and the introduction of the Charter of Rights and Freedoms – it took over from the RCMP, which previously possessed responsibility for intelligence matters and which retains responsibility for national security in the form of the investigation of criminal acts. The CSIS Act, which first created CSIS, remains the governing law to this day, and identifies its mission largely via the concept of 'threats to the security of Canada', defined as follows:

> (a) espionage or sabotage that is against Canada or is detrimental to the interests of Canada or activities directed toward or in support of such espionage or sabotage,
> (b) foreign influenced activities within or relating to Canada that are detrimental to the interests of Canada and are clandestine or deceptive or involve a threat to any person,
> (c) activities within or relating to Canada directed toward or in support of the threat or use of acts of serious violence against persons or property for the purpose of achieving a political, religious or ideological objective within Canada or a foreign state, and
> (d) activities directed toward undermining by covert unlawful acts, or directed toward or intended ultimately to lead to the destruction or overthrow by violence of, the constitutionally established system of government in Canada …[27]

We might agree with the view that the four categories of threat are 'broad and vague, and thus capable of expansive definition',[28] though the statute further provides (and has always provided) that the concept of threats to the security of Canada does not encompass 'lawful advocacy, protest or dissent' unless carried out in conjunction with one of the four specified (sets of) activities.[29] We also noted that Canada, unlike the UK and Australia, does not possess a separate foreign intelligence organisation. Moreover, CSIS's task of collecting foreign – rather than security – intelligence is, by virtue of the statute, currently geographically limited: CSIS may only assist the Minister of National Defence or the Minister of Foreign Affairs to do so 'within Canada'.[30] This restriction, which has been the subject of significant judicial attention,[31] has long been questioned, however,[32] particularly in light of the limitation (discussed below) that prevents the Communications Security Establishment from targeting persons within Canada. In late 2023, the possibility of removing it was floated, its being noted that the combination of these rules creates a 'foreign intelligence gap', the closing of which 'is critical to supporting the Government of Canada in managing Canada's foreign relations

[27] CSIS Act (1984) (Canada), s 2.
[28] C Forcese and L West, *National Security Law*, 2nd edn (Irwin Law Inc, 2020) 96–97.
[29] CSIS Act (1984) (Canada), s 2.
[30] ibid, s 16.1.
[31] *Re Canadian Security Intelligence Service Act* 2021 FCA 165.
[32] Forcese and West (n 28) 102–4.

and national defence by understanding the capabilities, intentions or activities of foreign states or foreign individuals, who may be involved in foreign interference activities'.[33] That is, the turn (back) to state threats – discussed in chapter 7 – may prompt the amendment of a rule that was tolerable while the national security enterprise was focused largely on terrorism.

The CSIS Act now also provides that if there are 'reasonable grounds to believe that a particular activity constitutes a threat to the security of Canada, the Service may take measures, within or outside Canada, to reduce the threat'[34] – what are known as 'threat reduction measures'. This formulation, notable in particular both for taking CSIS beyond its original intelligence-gathering mandate and for its explicit reference to the right of CSIS to take measures outside of Canada (something previously absent), was introduced by the Anti-terrorism Act 2015, an omnibus bill that responded to the perceived deficiencies of Canadian law in the wake of a number of domestic terrorist incidents.[35] The power is subject to a number of caveats, both procedural and substantive, with these reframed and augmented by the National Security Act, 2017. One in the former category is that CSIS is required ('as appropriate') to consult with other departments and agencies of the federal Government as to whether 'they are in a position to reduce the threat'.[36] One that is substantive is that the measures CSIS takes to reduce threats to the security of Canada are required to be

> reasonable and proportional in the circumstances, having regard to the nature of the threat, the nature of the measures, the reasonable availability of other means to reduce the threat and the reasonably foreseeable effects on third parties, including on their right to privacy.[37]

All measures taken by CSIS must, as noted in section III.B, comply with the Charter of Rights and Freedoms[38] (where it applies)[39] – measures interfering with which are permitted only where authorised by a judicial warrant – and though

[33] Public Safety Canada, *Enhancing measures to counter foreign interference: Whether to amend the Canadian Security Intelligence Service Act* (2023).

[34] CSIS Act (1984) (Canada), s 12.1(1).

[35] For a detailed consideration, see C Forcese and K Roach, *False Security: The Radicalization of Canadian Anti-Terrorism* (Irwin Law, 2015). Forcese and Roach consider the amendment to the CSIS Act, ibid 247–68. And see M Nesbitt, 'Bill C-59 and CSIS's "New" Powers to Disrupt Terrorist Threats: Holding the Charter-Limiting Regime to (Constitutional) Account' (2019) 57 *Alberta Law Review* 233.

[36] CSIS Act (1984) (Canada), s 12.1(3).

[37] ibid, s 12.1(2).

[38] Nesbitt notes that '[o]f course the *Charter* is part of the Constitution, the supreme law; and of course all government agencies must comply with it; saying so is merely reiterating the most fundamental law operating at all times in Canada', and so the provision in question should be read 'less as a substantive legal clause, for it is hard to describe precisely what substantive purpose the clause might serve other than, one supposes, a slightly randomly placed reminder of how Canada's laws generally work': Nesbitt (n 35) 247.

[39] See West (n 14) for a discussion of the very significant practical gaps left by this rule. West noted (ibid 3) that, likely for this reason, several years after the introduction of these measures, 'CSIS has never sought judicial authorization to conduct a [threat reduction measure].'

the Service is permitted to take action that would otherwise be unlawful where authorised by warrant, there are certain actions it may not take in any circumstances, including causing ('intentionally or by criminal negligence') death or bodily harm, wilfully attempting to pervert the course of justice, violating the 'sexual integrity of an individual', or torturing or subjecting a person to cruel, inhuman or degrading treatment.[40] The Act also provides that CSIS may provide security assessments to government departments[41] and – with the approval of the responsible Minister – provincial governments, provincial police forces, foreign states or their institutions, and to international organisations.[42]

A Director, who is appointed by the Government in Council, heads CSIS. The Director may be appointed for a term of up to five years, and may be reappointed on more than one occasion, but may hold office only up to a maximum of 10 years.[43] The Director, 'under the direction' of the Minister of Public Safety and Emergency Preparedness, has the 'control and management' of the Service and all connected matters.[44] The Director of CSIS is obliged to report to the Minister at least every 12 months, or more frequently if the Minister requires it, with respect to 'the Service's operational activities' during the relevant period, with such reports again to be supplied to the National Security and Intelligence Review Agency (NSIRA).[45] Certain requirements are put in place regarding the content of the reports: they must include, for example, details of measures taken in respect of each of the elements of the definition of 'threats to the security of Canada', as well as details of the number of warrants sought (and refused) regarding measures to reduce threats to the security of Canada.[46] The Director is required to consult with the Deputy Minister of Public Safety and Emergency Preparedness (a civil servant) regarding any matter in respect of which the directions given by the Minister require him or her to do so, as well as regarding 'the general operational policies of the Service'.[47]

Canada's foreign signals intelligence agency, the CSE, is now governed by the Communications Security Establishment Act,[48] having first been given a legislative basis by the Anti-Terrorism Act of 2001, Canada's primary legislative response to the 9/11 attacks of that year.[49] The relevant Act now provides that the CSE is 'the national signals intelligence agency for foreign intelligence and the technical authority for cybersecurity and information assurance', and that this mandate has

[40] CSIS Act (1984) (Canada), s 12.2(1). See the discussion in ch 4.
[41] ibid, s 13(1).
[42] ibid, s 13(2).
[43] ibid, s 4.
[44] ibid, s 6(1).
[45] ibid, s 6(4).
[46] ibid, s 6(5).
[47] ibid, s 7.
[48] Communications Security Establishment Act, SC 2019, c 13, s 76 (Canada).
[49] See, discussing the other elements of that Act and calling the legislation as a whole a 'massive undertaking', K Roach, 'Canada's New Anti-Terrorism Law' [2002] *Singapore Journal of Legal Studies* 122.

five elements (up from an original three): foreign intelligence; cybersecurity and information assurance; defensive cyber operations; active cyber operations; and technical and operational assistance.[50] Each of these elements is further elaborated, so that – for example – the foreign intelligence aspect is that the CSE is

> to acquire, covertly or otherwise, information from or through the global information infrastructure, including by engaging or interacting with foreign entities located outside Canada or by using any other method of acquiring information, and to use, analyse and disseminate the information for the purpose of providing foreign intelligence, in accordance with the Government of Canada's intelligence priorities.[51]

The active cyber operations element is to

> carry out activities on or through the global information infrastructure to degrade, disrupt, influence, respond to or interfere with the capabilities, intentions or activities of a foreign individual, state, organization or terrorist group as they relate to international affairs, defence or security.[52]

The Minister for National Defence (or another Minister so designated) is 'responsible' for the CSE,[53] but the Governor in Council must appoint a Chief, who may hold the post for up to five years in the first instance, and whose term may be renewed (only once) for a further term of five years.[54] As with CSIS, the Chief of the CSE, 'under the direction of the Minister', has management and control of the Establishment,[55] but the Minister may issue written directions to the Chief 'respecting the performance of the Chief's duties and functions'.[56] The CSE is subject to a number of limitations on how it pursues the various aspects of its mandate, the most sweeping of which is that those of its activities directed at anything other than the technical and operational assistance aspect of its mandate (in pursuit of which it will be limited by the rules applicable to the body it is assisting) 'must not be directed at a Canadian or at any person in Canada and must not infringe the Canadian Charter of Rights and Freedoms'.[57] This, though, is in turn subject to a rule that permits, amongst other things, the 'acquiring, using, analysing, retaining or disclosing [of] publicly available information'.[58] Other restrictions are procedural and prevent the CSE from carrying out aspects of its mandate in a fashion that contravenes other Acts of Parliament or in a way that involves – to use the example of the foreign intelligence aspect – 'the acquisition by the Establishment of information from or through the global information infrastructure that interferes with the reasonable expectation of privacy

[50] Communications Security Establishment Act (2019) (Canada), s 15(2).
[51] ibid, s 16.
[52] ibid, s 19.
[53] ibid, s 6.
[54] ibid, ss 8(1) and (2).
[55] ibid, s 9(1).
[56] ibid, s 11(1).
[57] ibid, s 22(1).
[58] ibid, s 23.

of a Canadian or a person in Canada' without a warrant permitting it to do so.[59] A number of different types of authorisation might be given to the CSE, aligning with different aspects of its mandate, and some of which – those that meet the criterion of acquiring information from the 'global information infrastructure' in a way that interferes with the reasonable expectation of Canadians or persons in Canada – require (except in cases of emergency) not merely ministerial authorisation but also the approval of an Intelligence Commissioner.[60] As discussed in chapter 4, therefore, the overarching mandate of the CSE is cut down in order to avoid excessive interference with the rights of certain persons, with the category of persons who enjoy additional protection defined by a mixture of citizenship and geography.

B. United Kingdom

The UK's MI5, we have already observed, was given a statutory basis in 1989, at the tail end of the Cold War, with the enactment in question – the Security Service Act – providing for its continuance 'under the authority of the Secretary of State'.[61] The Act to this day provides first of all that the function – the singular is used – of the Service is

> the protection of national security and, in particular, its protection against threats from espionage, terrorism and sabotage, from the activities of agents of foreign powers and from actions intended to overthrow or undermine parliamentary democracy by political, industrial or violent means.[62]

'National security' is therefore illustrated rather than defined, and only indirectly; it is something that is threatened by espionage and so on, as well (it would appear) as by various other phenomena not identified by name. One set of questions stands out from the definition: what it means to undermine (rather than overthrow) parliamentary democracy, and in particular what it means to do so via 'political means'. And are such actions inherently a threat to national security with which MI5 might legitimately concern itself, or only some subset of them? The focus on 'parliamentary democracy' rather than democracy per se is itself intriguing: this appears to be the only appearance of the term on the statute books of the UK.

[59] ibid, s 22(3).

[60] ibid, s 26(1); and Intelligence Commissioner Act, SC 2019, c 13, s 50 (Canada), s 13.

[61] Security Service Act 1989 (UK), s 1(1). See, for a contemporary assessment, I Leigh and L Lustgarten, 'The Security Service Act 1989' (1989) 52 *Modern Law Review* 801, who suggest that the statute was '[u]nexpected in its introduction, unaccompanied by any White Paper or other supporting reasoned document, unclear in its underlying rationale, uncertain in its constitutional impact'. Zellick noted that the Bill was enacted within five months of introduction 'without a single amendment: Not so much as a word or comma had been altered.' G Zellick, 'Spies, Sub Spies, Subversives, Terrorists and the British Government: Free Speech and Other Casualties' (1989–90) 31 *William and Mary Law Review* 773, 791–92.

[62] Security Service Act 1989 (UK), s 1(2).

And how might one 'undermine' parliamentary democracy via industrial means? Long before the 1989 Act came into being, the Security Service appears to have taken a greater interest than was justified in the operation of British trade unions,[63] and the presence of this language in the Act would seem to risk leaving open the door to the continuation of such activity. Though this first function is identified with the definite article, as 'the' function of MI5 rather than 'a' function, the Act immediately thereafter provides for another, again using the definite article: it 'shall also be the function of the Service', it says, 'to safeguard the economic well-being of the United Kingdom against threats posed by the actions or intentions of persons outside the British Islands'.[64] This is a defensive mandate – unlike that of MI6 in relation to economic well-being – and would seem to work to exclude interference with domestic trade unions, unless of course, and as was frequently alleged in the past, those unions were working with or manipulated by foreign actors. We return in section IV.C to the question of what exactly 'economic well-being', a formulation that has proved influential elsewhere, might encompass. A further function was added to the 1989 Act in 1996,[65] and in its current form provides that it shall 'also be the function of the Service to act in support of the activities of police forces, the National Crime Agency and other law enforcement agencies in the prevention and detection of serious crime',[66] indicating a limited role for MI5 in relation to criminal activity that is not relevant to national security.

What the status of these functions is has been called into question in recent years. In the so-called 'third direction' litigation, the Court of Appeal – siding with the majority in a divided Investigatory Powers Tribunal[67] – rejected the claim that the statement of MI5's functions was a purely limiting one, holding that in fact it continued in force legal powers that previously existed, though without explicitly saying so:

> [S]ince the Security Service's functions could not be achieved without its having the necessary powers, it follows by necessary implication, in our view, that the 1989 Act is confirming the continuance of the powers which the Security Service previously had, in order to fulfil the functions now specified in [the Act]. The functions of the Security Service being similar to those before the 1989 Act, by necessary implication the powers to carry out those functions continued and remained the same.[68]

[63] See, eg, K Ewing, J Mahoney and A Moretta, *MI5, the Cold War, and the Rule of Law* (Oxford University Press, 2020) ch 12.

[64] Security Service Act 1989 (UK), s 1(3).

[65] Security Service Act 1996 (UK). See M Hunt and P Duffy, 'Goodbye *Entick v Carrington*: The Security Service Act 1996' [1997] *European Human Rights Law Review* 11.

[66] Security Service Act 1989 (UK), s 1(4).

[67] *Privacy International v Secretary of State for Foreign and Commonwealth Affairs* [2019] UKIPTrib IPT/17/186/CH. For discussion, see PF Scott, 'Authorising Crime: The Covert Human Intelligence Sources (Criminal Conduct) Act 2021' (2022) 85 *Modern Law Review* 1218.

[68] *Privacy International v Secretary of State for Foreign and Commonwealth Affairs* [2021] EWCA Civ 330 [65].

This seems unconvincing both in terms of principle and as a matter of simple statutory interpretation, but it is, unless and until revisited by the UK Supreme Court, the law. What specific legal powers this might confer on the Security Service beyond that identified by the Court of Appeal – the power to authorise participation in criminality by its 'agents' (as opposed to its employees), now in practice eclipsed by more specific statutory authority[69] – is nevertheless left uncertain. The Service is headed by a Director-General whom the Secretary of State appoints, and who is responsible for the efficiency of the Service and for ensuring certain matters. These include, first of all, that arrangements are in place to ensure that the Service does not acquire information except 'so far as necessary for the proper discharge of its functions', nor disclose information except for that purpose or those relating to crime.[70] Another duty is to ensure that 'the Service does not take any action to further the interests of any political party'.[71] The Director-General, the 1989 Act provides, 'shall make an annual report on the work of the Service to the Prime Minister and the Secretary of State and may at any time report to either of them on any matter relating to its work'.[72] As we shall see in section V.A, the question of the relationship between the political executive and the Security Service is therefore left – at least compared to other jurisdictions – under-specified.

The Secret Intelligence Service, MI6, was given a statutory basis in 1994, along with GCHQ, the UK's signals intelligence body.[73] The functions of MI6 are 'to obtain and provide information relating to the actions or intentions of persons outside the British Islands' and 'to perform other tasks relating to the actions or intentions of such persons'.[74] These functions might be exercised only on the trifecta of grounds that has become standard in the UK law of national security: 'in the interests of national security, with particular reference to the defence and foreign policies of Her Majesty's Government in the United Kingdom', 'in the interests of the economic well-being of the United Kingdom' or 'in support of the prevention or detection of serious crime'.[75] The modification of the reference to 'national security' here – which applies also to GCHQ – is of interest, in that it would seem to acknowledge that an objectively identified understanding of national security and the relative priority of different issues under that heading might not align entirely with the position of the government of the day (or, perhaps, that at least so far as foreign intelligence is concerned, the former does not exist), and permits the government to guide – within the broad concept of

[69] See the discussion of which in Scott (n 67) 1237–43.
[70] Security Service Act 1989 (UK), s 2(2)(a).
[71] ibid, s 2(2)(b).
[72] ibid, s 2(4).
[73] Intelligence Services Act 1994 (UK). See J Wadham, 'The Intelligence Services Act 1994' (1994) 57 *Modern Law Review* 916.
[74] Intelligence Services Act 1994 (UK), s 1(1).
[75] ibid, s 1(2).

national security and, it seems, only indirectly – the work of MI6. The reference to economic well-being is also notable: unlike the inclusion of the phrase in the 1989 Act, which offers MI5 a purely defensive mandate, the 1994 Act seems (it has been noted) to allow MI6 (and indeed GCHQ) 'to act positively in promoting the Country's economic well-being, as distinct from merely protecting it'.[76] The UK's GCHQ may also exercise its functions only on those same grounds (though it may exercise them in the interests of economic well-being only 'in relation to the actions or intentions of persons outside the British Islands', a qualification that does not apply to MI6).[77] It has two sets of functions. The first, as amended, is to 'monitor, make use of or interfere with electromagnetic, acoustic and other emissions and any equipment producing such emissions and to obtain and provide information derived from or related to such emissions or equipment and from encrypted material'.[78] The second is to provide 'advice and assistance about (i) languages, including terminology used for technical matters, and (ii) cryptography and other matters relating to the protection of information and other material' to certain (categories of) public actor and, 'in such cases as it considers appropriate, to other organisations or persons, or to the general public, in the United Kingdom or elsewhere'.[79] Both MI6 and GCHQ are under the authority of the Secretary of State (in practice the Foreign Secretary); both are headed by an individual (the Chief of the Intelligence Service in the case of MI6, and the Director of GCHQ) who is responsible for their efficiency and subject to similar obligations as is the Director-General of MI5 regarding the acquisition and disclosure of information.

C. Australia

The primary present-day functions of ASIO, as laid out in the same statute of 1979 enacted subsequent to the first Hope Royal Commission and discussed in chapter 2, are to 'obtain, correlate and evaluate intelligence relevant to security', to communicate that intelligence for purposes relevant to security and to advise Ministers accordingly.[80] 'Security' is defined to mean – in the first instance,

> the protection of, and of the people of, the Commonwealth and the several States and Territories from
>
> (i) espionage;
> (ii) sabotage;
> (iii) politically motivated violence;

[76] Interception of Communications Commissioner, *Report of the Commissioner for 1998* (Cm 4364, 1999) [16].
[77] Intelligence Services Act 1994 (UK), s 3(2).
[78] ibid, s 3(1)(a).
[79] ibid, s 3(1)(b).
[80] Australian Security Intelligence Organisation Act 1979 (Australia) ('ASIO Act 1979'), s 17(1).

(iv) promotion of communal violence;
(v) attacks on Australia's defence system; or
(vi) acts of foreign interference;

whether directed from, or committed within, Australia or not ...[81]

Of those activities, perhaps the most interesting is (iv) above, 'promotion of communal violence' being defined to mean 'activities that are directed to promoting violence between different groups of persons in the Australian community so as to endanger the peace, order or good government of the Commonwealth'.[82] The promotion of 'communal violence' with which ASIO is concerned includes, therefore, that carried out within Australia itself by domestic actors: there is no limitation to situations in which it is foreign powers or their proxies who are promoting the violence in question. 'Security' also includes 'the protection of Australia's territorial and border integrity from serious threats' and 'the carrying out of Australia's responsibilities to any foreign country' in relation to any of the other aspects of security.[83] It is not, however, a function of ASIO 'to carry out or enforce measures for security within an authority of the Commonwealth'.[84] ASIO is headed by a Director-General of Security, appointed by the Governor-General on the recommendation of the Prime Minister (following consultation with the Leader of the Opposition).[85]

The other Australian SIAs with which we are concerned – ASIS and the Australian Signals Directorate (ASD) – were both given a statutory basis by the Intelligence Services Act 2001, the origins of which go back to an inquiry carried out into ASIS in the mid-1990s.[86] That Commission of Inquiry had been prompted – or so it was claimed – by 'the perception of the Government that there was a normative case for periodic root and branch review of secret organisations', which (as the public report of the Commission put it, with something like a straight face) 'fortuitously coincided' with the culmination of a long-standing campaign by former ASIS officers to have allegations of wrongdoing by it taken seriously.[87] Writing at a point when the UK had recently enacted legislation for MI6 and GCHQ, the Commission concluded that 'legislation to continue ASIS in

[81] ibid, s 4.
[82] ibid, s 4.
[83] ibid, s 4.
[84] ibid, s 17(2).
[85] ibid, s 7.
[86] Parliament of Australia, House of Representatives, *Intelligence Services Bill 2001 – Explanatory Memorandum* (2001): 'The Intelligence Services Bill had its genesis in the recommendations of the judicial inquiry into the Australian Secret Intelligence Service ... which reported to Government on 31 March 1995.' The report in question is Commission of Inquiry into the Australian Secret Intelligence Service, *Report on the Australian Secret Intelligence Service – Public Edition* (1995).
[87] Commission of Inquiry into the Australian Secret Intelligence Service (n 86) [10]. Cain connects these events to the end of the Cold War: F Cain, 'Australian Intelligence Organisations and the Law: A Brief History' (2004) 27 *UNSW Law Journal* 296, 309–10.

existence and to provide authority for its activities is desirable in principle and will be of benefit in practice':

> ASIS carries out important functions in the national interest. Its operations are usually sensitive and potentially controversial. It is no longer appropriate that the formal conferral of authority for the exercise of these functions should be the exclusive province of the executive arm of government. The existence of ASIS should be endorsed by Parliament and the scope and limits of its functions defined by legislation. International comparisons demonstrate how widely this principle is now accepted in parliamentary democracies.[88]

Reflecting these international comparisons – made easier, we have noted, by the existence of primary legislation – a draft bill produced by the Commission therefore drew not only on the ASIO Act 1979 but also on the UK's recently-enacted Intelligence Services Act,[89] but legislation was not introduced to give effect to its recommendations for many years thereafter.

The functions of ASIS are, like those of MI6,[90] external and include the following: 'to obtain, in accordance with the Government's requirements, intelligence about the capabilities, intentions or activities of people or organisations outside Australia'; 'to communicate, in accordance with the Government's requirements, such intelligence'; 'to conduct counter-intelligence activities'; 'to liaise with intelligence or security services, or other authorities, of other countries'; and to undertake such other activities as the responsible Minister directs relating to the capabilities, intentions or activities of people or organisations outside Australia.[91] Again, the Director-General is appointed by the Governor-General on the recommendation of the Prime Minister, who must consult with the Leader of the Opposition before making a recommendation.[92] Appointment is for a term of up to five years, which is renewable.[93] The Act provides that ASIS is under the control of the Director-General, but also that the Director-General, 'under the Minister', is responsible for managing ASIS and must 'advise the Minister in matters relating to ASIS'.[94]

The 2001 Act also gave the ASD a statutory basis for the first time, originally under the name Defence Signals Directorate.[95] The ASD's functions are many, but – again reflecting an external orientation – the key ones are 'to obtain

[88] Commission of Inquiry into the Australian Secret Intelligence Service (n 86) [3.29].
[89] ibid [3.39].
[90] The arrangements in Australia, it has been claimed, are 'most similar to the United Kingdom where, while the distinction is not legislated, foreign and security intelligence are separated in practice. Indeed, the separation is considered essential for reasons of clarity in respect of functions, responsibilities and accountability.' *Comprehensive Review of the Legal Framework of the National Intelligence Community*, Volume 1: *Recommendations and Executive Summary; Foundations and Principles; Control, Coordination and Cooperation* (2019), [3.33].
[91] Intelligence Services Act 2001 (Australia), s 6.
[92] ibid, s 17.
[93] ibid, s 20.
[94] ibid, s 18.
[95] ibid, s 27A.

intelligence about the capabilities, intentions or activities of people or organisations outside Australia'; to 'prevent and disrupt, by electronic or similar means, cybercrime undertaken by people or organisations outside Australia'; and to provide to State and Commonwealth authorities assistance in relation to 'cryptography, and communication and computer technologies'.[96] There is again a Director-General of the ASD, who is appointed by the same process as the other Directors-General. Again, the Act provides both that the ASD is under the control of the Director-General, and that the Director-General 'under the Minister' is responsible for managing the ASD and 'must advise the Minister in matters relating to ASD'.[97]

As part of the Comprehensive Review of the legislative framework governing the Australian intelligence community carried out in the late 2010s, there was considered the question of whether it might be desirable to consolidate these legal regimes into a single Act governing most or all of the relevant bodies – not just ASIO, ASIS and the ASD, but also, for example, the Australian Geospatial-Intelligence Organisation. The review's terms of reference framed this point as asking 'whether Australia should adopt a common legislative framework, as has been done in the United Kingdom and New Zealand', but as the review itself noted the first part of these comparisons is misleading.[98] The legislative framework of the UK's SIAs is not comprehensive in the sense of a single statute that applies to all three of MI5, MI6 and GCHQ, and though such a statute might be introduced without difficulty, given the modest scope of the Security Service Act 1989 and Intelligence Services Act 1994, the task of bringing all of the powers and immunities of these bodies together in a single piece of legislation would be a more significant task – one that, as the Comprehensive Review observed in relation to Australia, where the legislation is longer, messier and more scattered, would be almost guaranteed to be disproportionate to the benefits that might be achieved:

> It would be unlikely that the intended benefits of streamlining and simplifying [National Intelligence Community – NIC] legislation could be achieved due to the diversity of NIC agency functions – from intelligence to law enforcement, regulatory and policy – and the need to maintain differences in powers, immunities and authorising frameworks … [R]eform of this scale would cost over $200 million and take up to 10 years to complete. This would be an impractical and disproportionate undertaking for no substantial gain. In our view, the significant costs and risks of moving to a single, consolidated Act clearly outweigh the limited potential benefits.[99]

Of the four Commonwealth Five Eyes states, therefore, it remains the case that only New Zealand has a single statute setting out, in one place, the SIAs that exist, their missions, their governance and their powers.

[96] ibid, s 7.
[97] ibid, s 27C.
[98] *Comprehensive Review*, Volume 1 (n 90) [3.20].
[99] ibid [3.21].

D. New Zealand

New Zealand, like Canada, has two primary SIAs, rather than the three in Australia and the UK: the NZSIS and the Government Communications Security Bureau (GCSB), both now finding their legal basis in the Intelligence and Security Act 2017,[100] enacted following a recommendation that the previous framework be replaced with a single Act that 'would give a comprehensive and much clearer view of the Agencies' functions and powers, and the checks and balances that apply to the operation of their powers'.[101] The context of that review, it was said, was in part

> increasing concern about the privacy of New Zealanders, the Agencies' compliance with the law and the prospect of widespread data collection, particularly in the wake of Edward Snowden's information leaks and controversies such as the GCSB's involvement in the events leading up to Kim Dotcom's arrest.[102]

The Snowden leaks are well known; the Dotcom affair involved the interception of the communications of Kim Dotcom, a German-Finnish national whose extradition from New Zealand to the US was sought on the basis of various charges relating to the website Megaupload, of which Mr Dotcom was CEO. The GCSB intercepted those communications under the mistaken belief that he was not a New Zealand resident. He in fact was, and the interception was therefore unlawful, prompting both an apology from New Zealand's Prime Minister and a report that demonstrated systemic problems within GCSB.[103]

The 2017 Act that eventually resulted from this process established the two SIAs separately, its being stated therein that the NZSIS 'specialises in human intelligence activities' and that the GCSB 'specialises in signals intelligence and information assurance and cybersecurity activities'.[104] Their principal objectives, however, are common to both of them: these are 'the protection of New Zealand's national security'; 'the international relations and well-being of New Zealand'; and 'the economic well-being of New Zealand'.[105] Contrary to the

[100] The background to that Act includes, in particular, M Cullen and P Reddy, *Intelligence and Security in a Free Society: Report of the First Independent Review of Intelligence and Security in New Zealand* (2016) and, before that, R Kitteridge, *Review of Compliance at the Government Communications Security Bureau* (2013). The Act is discussed in its immediate context by D Rogers, 'Intelligence and Security Act 2017: A Preliminary Critique' [2018] *New Zealand Law Review* 657; and in longer perspective in A Gillespie and C Breen, 'The Security Intelligence Agencies in New Zealand: evolution, challenges and progress' (2021) 36 *Intelligence and National Security* 676.

[101] Cullen and Reddy (n 100) [4.14].

[102] ibid [1.1]–[1.3].

[103] Kitteridge (n 100). And see D Rogers, 'Extraditing Kim Dotcom: a case for reforming New Zealand's intelligence community?' (2015) *10 Kōtuitui: New Zealand Journal of Social Sciences Online* 46. Strikingly, in light of what followed, Rogers concluded (ibid 55) that 'The prospects of an immediate transformation of New Zealand's intelligence community … remain dim.'

[104] Intelligence and Security Act 2017 (NZ), ss 7 and 8.

[105] ibid, s 9.

recommendation of the review that was its direct progenitor,[106] no further definition is provided in the Act of either 'security' or 'national security'. The effect of this approach – no definition of security, and the grant to the SIAs of objectives that sit alongside rather than within that of protecting national security – was, it has been argued, that of 'radically expand[ing] the operating environment for the NZSIS and the GCSB, which is now limited only by the elasticity of these vaguely worded objectives'.[107] Their statutory functions, which are again common to both of the New Zealand SIAs, include collecting and analysing intelligence 'in accordance with the New Zealand Government's priorities' – allowing for an indirect control by the executive of their work – and providing both the intelligence collected and any analysis of it to either the responsible Minister, the Chief Executive of the Department of the Prime Minister and Cabinet, or any person or class of persons authorised by the Minister to receive them.[108] Another function is that of providing 'protective security services, advice, and assistance', relating to things such as personnel security, information security and physical security, to public authorities (whether in New Zealand or not) or other persons, or classes of persons, authorised by the relevant Minister to receive such things.[109] A further function is to cooperate – not only with each other but also with the New Zealand Police and the country's Defence Force – and to provide 'advice and assistance to the New Zealand Police and the New Zealand Defence Force for the purpose of facilitating the performance or exercise of the functions, duties, or powers of those public authorities'.[110] The final function provided for by the 2017 Act itself involves the New Zealand SIAs in working with others to respond to imminent threats to the life and safety of, in the first place, people in New Zealand or New Zealand citizens or permanent residents overseas.[111] What is only implied in some contexts, and indeed in others has been abandoned, is here made explicit: the functions of the New Zealand agencies do not, with limited if no doubt significant exceptions, include enforcing measures for national security.[112]

A series of general duties apply to the agencies, each of which, when performing its functions, must act, the 2017 Act, provides, 'in accordance with New Zealand law and all human rights obligations recognised by New Zealand law', 'in the performance of its operational functions, independently and impartially', 'with integrity and professionalism' and, perhaps most interestingly given the absence of any equivalent in the other jurisdictions at issue, 'in a manner that facilitates effective democratic oversight'.[113] Each agency has a Director-General,

[106] Cullen and Reddy (n 100) [5.78]–[5.85].
[107] Rogers (n 100) 675.
[108] Intelligence and Security Act 2017 (NZ), s 10.
[109] ibid, s 11.
[110] ibid, s 13.
[111] ibid, s 14.
[112] ibid, s 16.
[113] ibid, s 17.

and the Directors-General are themselves under certain notable duties, some of which implicate issues that have also arisen elsewhere. They must, that is, take 'all reasonable steps' to ensure that, first, the activities of the agency are 'limited to those that are relevant to the performance of its functions', 'kept free from any influence or consideration that is not relevant to the performance of its functions' and 'politically neutral' and, second, and as noted in section II.B, that 'any co-operation with foreign jurisdictions and international organisations in the performance of any of the agency's functions is in accordance with New Zealand law and all human rights obligations recognised by New Zealand law'.[114] A final, striking, obligation of the Director-General of a New Zealand SIA is to 'regularly consult' the Leader of the Opposition for the purpose of keeping him or her 'informed about matters relating to the agency's functions'.[115] Though it is common in the states under consideration for the government of the day to be obliged to consult the Leader of the Opposition (or equivalent within the relevant institutional arrangements) on certain matters within the broader constellation of national security institutions, this sort of ongoing direct access to the head of the SIAs (which had also been included in previous regimes) is remarkable, and might be taken to indicate, in this context at least, a degree of constitutional maturity in the New Zealand context that is not always evidenced elsewhere. Notably, perhaps, the review leading up to the 2017 Act argued for the inclusion of a rule like this on the specific basis that it was in the interests of the SIAs themselves.[116] It must also be beneficial to the wider democratic culture, though, working to at least some degree to counter any suspicion that the SIAs might be, or become, too close to the government of the day.

IV. Key Concepts of the Modern SIAs

In this section I consider the key concepts that are used, in law, to define the mandates of the SIAs in the Commonwealth Five Eyes states at present. These have evolved over time, as part of the processes discussed in chapter 2, and the overall effect has been to drift away from the original model of Commonwealth national security constitutionalism that emerged in the decades following the Second World War, as the MI5 model – and the concepts that framed it – was exported, often in a very direct manner, to what had been, in the earlier part of the century, the UK's Dominions. Though commonalities remain, many of those commonalities would appear to be a function not so much of the shared origins of the various SIAs – now somewhat faded into history – as their shared function, centred on the concept of (national) security. There are, though, a number of particularly striking

[114] ibid, s 18.
[115] ibid, s 20.
[116] Cullen and Reddy (n 100) [4.21]: 'We think it is in the interests of the Agencies to keep the Leader of the Opposition up to date.'

examples of where a development in the framing of the SIAs in one state has been picked up elsewhere, indicating that the borrowing and sharing identified in chapter 2 persists beyond the Cold War.

A. Security

The concept of security stands, as it must by definition always do, at the centre of the enterprise undertaken by the SIAs in each of the Commonwealth Five Eyes states. It does though occur in a range of different formulations, the distinctions between which may or may not be particularly significant in practice. One is that in some cases we encounter the language of 'national security', while in others the preference is for 'the security of [state]', this latter perhaps avoiding awkward questions about what the nation in question is. Whatever form is preferred, we can assume that the language is capable of encompassing (at the very least) responding to or countering both of the key threats identified in relation to the Cold War period and thereafter: hostile states and terrorism. We see this, for example, in the UK, which employs a general, holistic concept of national security to define the work of the SIAs, specifying particular threats against which it is to be defended in the case of MI5 ('threats from espionage, terrorism and sabotage, from the activities of agents of foreign powers and from actions intended to overthrow or undermine parliamentary democracy by political, industrial or violent means'),[117] as well as particular issues to which reference is to be made in conceptualising it ('the defence and foreign policies of Her Majesty's Government in the United Kingdom') in the context of MI6 and GCHQ.[118] The effect of this approach must be that there is much that might be legitimately dealt with by each of these SIAs without being specifically named in the relevant enactments. There is no attempt, either in legislation or in case law, to define the matter exhaustively, and the European Commission of Human Rights long ago rejected the claim that the absence of such a definition in the relevant legislation meant that any interference carried out by MI5 was not 'in accordance with the law': 'Many laws,' it said, 'which by their subject-matter require to be flexible, are inevitably couched in terms which are to a greater or lesser extent vague and whose interpretation and application are questions of practice.'[119]

In New Zealand, the SIAs have as one (the first) of their 'principal objectives' the 'protection of New Zealand's national security',[120] with – again – no further definition of the point, though the statement of the overall purpose of the Act suggests that establishing the SIAs and having them protect national security is one of a number of ways in which it aims to 'protect New Zealand as a free,

[117] Security Service Act 1989 (UK), s 1(2).
[118] Intelligence Services Act 1994 (UK), ss 1(2)(a) and 3(2)(a).
[119] *Esbester v United Kingdom* (1994) 18 EHRR CD72.
[120] Intelligence and Security Act 2017 (NZ), s 9(a).

open, and democratic society', which may offer some guidance as to how national security is and is not to be interpreted in particular contexts. Moreover, the availability of one type of intelligence warrant is defined by reference to certain harms, an approach that might – it was argued during the passage of the 2017 Act – work to counteract the absence of an exhaustive definition.[121] Rogers has noted that the Independent Review of Intelligence and Security that preceded the 2017 Act proposed that national security be defined by reference to a list of exhaustive harms against which it was to be protected, but that officials identified a number of difficulties with the proposed definition, including that there would be '[a] lack of clarity around the scope of the definition (meaning that it would not be clear what types of activities would be covered and what would not)', as well as '[c]oncerns that an attempt to define national security would interact with other legislation and conceptions of national security across government'.[122] The approach that was therefore rejected is broadly that taken in Australia, where the ASIO Act 1979 defines security in the first place with reference to things against which 'the Commonwealth and the several States and Territories' and their people are to be protected.[123] In Canada, the concept of security is again not defined directly, with the mission of CSIS framed instead by the concept of threats to that security, which, as we have seen, are identified exhaustively but nevertheless broadly.[124] Though these distinctions, and in particular the contrast between the open-ended UK approach and the attempt, elsewhere, to provide an exhaustive lists of things against which national security is to be protected, are striking, the basic thrust of this issue is in large part, as we have noted, dictated by the underlying logic of the security endeavour as understood in the modern world: a security and intelligence agency that did not, that is, seek to protect against, say, terrorism, would not be a security and intelligence agency. Though in other times and other places this may not be or have been the case, it appears to be baked into the security endeavour as understood within this project. What is more interesting, therefore, is what the SIAs are tasked with doing beyond this self-justifying project of security: what other ends or concepts, that is, are given in law a status equivalent or even comparable to this central good.

B. International Relations

Two questions that arise via a consideration of the different SIAs and their missions is whether and how the notion of international relations enters into their

[121] Rogers (n 100) 675.

[122] Office of the Minister for National Security and Intelligence, Office of the Minister Responsible for the GCSB and Office of the Minister in Charge of the NZSIS, *Intelligence and Security in a Free Society: Report of the first Independent Review of Intelligence and Security in New Zealand – Paper Four: Institutional reform of the agencies, appointment of judicial commissioners and general administrative matters* (nd), quoted in Rogers (n 100) 674.

[123] ASIO Act 1979 (Australia), s 4.

[124] CSIS Act (1984) (Canada), s 2.

mandates. In some cases, as we have seen, the notion is identified explicitly as an aspect of the security of the state. So, for example, the recommendation of the review that preceded the enactment of New Zealand's Intelligence and Security Act 2017, that 'national security' be defined so as to include protection against 'unlawful acts, or acts of foreign interference, that may cause serious damage to New Zealand's economic security or international relations',[125] was, we have already seen, rejected, but – in accordance with a separate recommendation[126] – the Act identifies, as the second 'principal objective' to which the New Zealand SIAs are to contribute, 'the international relations and well-being of New Zealand'.[127] What exactly might be at stake in this formulation, and in particular the latter element, is hard to discern – none of these terms is defined further, and though 'well-being' is a long-standing element of New Zealand national security law, it was previously used in the context of 'international well-being' rather than in its now, apparently stand-alone, form. The approach taken therefore constitutes the international relations of New Zealand as something distinct from its national security, even if, as has been claimed, in many situations 'New Zealand's international relations and well-being, economic well-being and national security are inextricably linked, or at least have a significant degree of overlap.'[128] This approach makes sense to the extent it evades the difficulty drawing an artificial line between those parts of international relations that do relate to national security and those (if any) that do not.

In the UK, where 'international relations' is not identified by name as one of the aims or objectives of any of the SIAs, the courts have nevertheless accepted that actions harmful to the UK's international relations can be indirectly harmful to its national security, thereby bringing much – though presumably not all – of the former topic within the province of the latter.[129] Elsewhere, a similar logic might be taken to apply: so, for example, 'threats to the security of Canada' in the CSIS Act is defined so as to include certain activities – sabotage, for one – not only where it is 'against' Canada but also where it is detrimental to Canada's interests,[130] which might well include where it harms the international relations of Canada. In Australia, the question of international relations is not incorporated into the task of ASIO by name, but 'security' is defined to include the carrying out of Australia's responsibilities to any foreign country in relation to the matters against which the SIAs are to protect Australia and its people, and so 'security' in effect would seem to include security-related international relations. ASIS and the ASD are to perform their functions only, the governing statute provides, in the

[125] Cullen and Reddy (n 100), recommendation 40.
[126] ibid, recommendation 30.
[127] Intelligence and Security Act 2017 (NZ), s 9.
[128] T Arnold and M Mahuika, *Taumaru: Protecting Aotearoa New Zealand as a free, open and democratic society* (2023) [1.15].
[129] *Secretary of State for the Home Department v Rehman* [2001] UKHL 47. And see the discussion in PF Scott, *The National Security Constitution* (Hart Publishing, 2018) 281–86.
[130] CSIS Act (1984) (Canada), s 2.

interests of certain goods – one of them 'Australia's foreign relations' and 'only to the extent that those matters are affected by the capabilities, intentions or activities of people or organisations outside Australia'.[131] The broad effect would seem to be that of recognising in law what history (and perhaps logic) makes plain: that the national security enterprise is not one in which states are self-contained units, with each acting autonomously and with regard only to themselves. Rather, they exist within a complex eco-system of interaction and cooperation, such that the security interests of the 'home' state might be advanced by protecting or promoting its relationships with other states. None of these provisions, we might note, names specific foreign countries, leaving it in effect to the government of the day to determine which are the states relations with which are to be prioritised by the SIAs. In practice, however, these provisions are no doubt the basis of particular concern for relationships with certain foreign states rather than others, including those that are fellow members of Five Eyes.

C. Economic Issues

The questions regarding whether and when the SIAs of each state can act in pursuit of economic aims are particularly interesting ones. They allow for an unusually clear tracing of the patterns of influence that exist in this area, but which are often difficult to discern clearly where the concern is with (national) security, the language of which one would expect to encounter in each of the statutes framing the work of the SIAs even if they had developed entirely without reference to each other.[132] The idea that this is a legitimate basis of SIA activity appears to originate in the UK, where it entered the legal system under the influence of the ECHR, which gave the impetus to the original statute providing for the interception of communications through the decision in *Malone v United Kingdom*.[133] It was necessary, therefore, to put in place a statutory regime for the interception of communication that was capable of meeting the requirements of Article 8 ECHR, which provides that everyone has the right to 'respect for his private and family life, his home and his correspondence'. Article 8(2), which sets out in broad terms the circumstances in which the right might be interfered with without violating the Convention, identifies a number of 'legitimate aims' in pursuit of which such interferences may take place.[134] Though the statute put in place in response to *Malone*, the Interception of Communications Act 1985, did not transpose into domestic law all of those legitimate aims as

[131] Intelligence Services Act 2001 (Australia), s 11(1).

[132] I have made a number of the points in this paragraph previously: see PF Scott, '"Economic Well-Being' in National Security Law and Practice' (2022) 33 *King's Law Journal* 358.

[133] *Malone v United Kingdom* (1984) 7 EHRR 14.

[134] For some sense of the background to its inclusion therein, see Scott (n 132) 360–61.

grounds upon which a warrant for the interception of communications might be granted, it did include that such a warrant may be granted where necessary 'for the purpose of safeguarding the economic well-being of the United Kingdom',[135] with the language of 'economic well-being' mirroring that used in Article 8(2) ECHR itself.

The same language of 'economic well-being' was then used to help define the mandates of the UK SIAs when they were formalised by the Security Service Act 1989 and the Intelligence Services Act 1994, albeit in ways that are subtly different. For example, it became one of the functions of MI5 to 'safeguard the economic well-being of the United Kingdom against threats posed by the actions or intentions of persons outside the British Islands'.[136] MI6's functions, on the other, are stated by the 1994 Act to be exercisable only on limited grounds, one of which is 'in the interests of the economic well-being of the United Kingdom'.[137] For GCHQ, the ground in question is more limited, being 'in the interests of the economic well-being of the United Kingdom in relation to the actions or intentions of persons outside the British Islands'.[138] This appears to create a distinction between acting negatively, as it were, to protect economic well-being against threats, and being able to act positively so as to promote the UK's economic well-being,[139] though what is in fact at stake in that distinction is difficult to know without a clearer sense of what 'economic well-being' might in fact mean. That is, although the formulation is a recurring feature of UK national security law to this day, there remains a significant lack of clarity as to what the practical significance is of its continued inclusion – a continuation of a criticism that has been levelled at the formulation ever since it was first introduced into the legal order.[140] The Constitution Committee of the House of Lords has for that reason suggested that the concept and its role within national security law be reviewed by the Intelligence and Security Committee (ISC):[141] that Committee's first consideration of the point, early in its existence, was not published.[142] What does seem clear, however, is that regardless of how it might originally have been intended by those who chose to include

[135] Interception of Communications Act 1985 (UK), s 2(2)(c).

[136] Security Service Act 1989 (UK), s 1(3).

[137] Intelligence Services Act 1994 (UK), s 1(2)(b).

[138] ibid, s 2(2)(b).

[139] See the discussion in Interception of Communication Commissioner (n 76).

[140] 'Will it be used, for example, for the surveillance of communications by currency dealers as the level of the pound is a matter of economic well-being? Will it be used for the surveillance of international trade union links in connection with, say, the miners' strike? It could be used for partisan political purposes disguised as the national interest.' HC Deb 7 February 1985, vol 72, col 1119 (Gerald Kaufman).

[141] House of Lords Constitution Committee, *Covert Human Intelligence Sources (Criminal Conduct) Bill* (HL 2019–21, 174) [9].

[142] The Committee made an unpublished special report to the Prime Minister on the question in 1996 and later summarised its conclusion as being that 'intelligence work in support of economic well-being is an important, valuable and, on the evidence we have taken, properly conducted area of the Agencies' activities': Intelligence and Security Committee, *Annual Report 1996* (Cm 3574, 1997) [34].

it in the 1985 Act and those who followed them in retaining it in the corpus of UK national security law, under the Convention the formulation denotes a broad concept, denoting – it would seem – something like the economic health of the state generally.[143] Perhaps for that reason, in recent enactments it is used in a more limited fashion, so that the most intrusive powers enjoyed by the SIAs can be made use of for the purposes of protecting the UK's economic well-being only where one of the other grounds also applies.[144]

But the same language – the same, specific, 'economic well-being' formulation – shows up in the bodies of national security law of other Commonwealth Five Eyes states, notwithstanding that they, of course, are not signatories to the ECHR and so have no special need to align themselves, the work of their SIAs and the availability of their various intrusive powers with the requirement of Article 8 ECHR. In contemporary Australian law, for example, it is provided that the functions of the relevant agencies – including ASIS and the ASD – are only to be performed 'in the interests of Australia's national security, Australia's foreign relations or Australia's national economic well-being and only to the extent that those matters are affected by the capabilities, intentions or activities of people or organisations outside Australia'.[145] This limitation to external actors can, as noted, also be found in places within the UK legal framework; the language of 'national' economic well-being in the Australian context would seem at first glance to exclude acting specifically in the interests of one of the sub-national constitutional units: the States and Territories that make up the Commonwealth of Australia. This formulation was not in the 1979 Act as enacted, and was only later introduced in reference to the circumstances in which certain intrusive powers – all of them relating to its foreign intelligence function – might be used by ASIO. The 2001 Act that gave ASIS and the ASD a statutory basis appears to have been the first to include the language in relation to the role of the Australian SIAs, though the documents relating to the Bill that became that Act suggest that little attention was paid to the inclusion of the language.[146] The report on ASIS that was the background to the 2001 Act did not consider this issue directly, but it did endorse ASIS's proposal for a public information campaign focused on the publication of a booklet giving information about ASIS and its work, which could – the authors suggested – 'give examples of ASIS operations, suitably sanitised, to illustrate the benefit of ASIS's work to Australia's national security and economy'.[147]

[143] See Scott (n 132) 361–64 and the materials discussed there.

[144] See, eg, Investigatory Powers Act 2016 (UK), s 138 (outlining the conditions for the grant of a bulk interception warrant), and the discussion in Scott (n 132) 370–71.

[145] Intelligence Services Act 2001 (Australia), s 11(1).

[146] See, eg, Joint Select Committee on the Intelligence Service, *An advisory report on the Intelligence Services Bill 2001, the Intelligence Services (Consequential Provisions) Bill 2001 and certain parts of Cybercrime Bill 2001* (2001) [2.32]–[2.51], where attention was focused primarily on the role of ASIS and the DSD in relation to intelligence relating to 'serious crime'.

[147] Commission of Inquiry into the Australian Secret Intelligence Service (n 86) [15.73].

A similar story might be told in relation to New Zealand: under the Intelligence and Security Act 2017, one of the three principal objectives of the New Zealand SIAs is to contribute to 'the economic well-being of New Zealand'.[148] Neither this language nor any analogue was found in the 1969 Act that first gave that body a legislative basis. It was introduced into the country only decades later by New Zealand Security Intelligence Service Amendment Act 1996, enacted at the point at which the process of giving to the UK SIAs a statutory basis had only recently finished and in the period between the Cold War and the rise of international terrorism, in which the role of the SIAs was being reconsidered in many states. That statute inserted into the 1969 Act a new definition of 'security', which was now to mean 'the making of a contribution to New Zealand's international well-being or economic well-being; and the protection of New Zealand from acts of espionage, sabotage, terrorism, and subversion, whether or not they are directed from or intended to be committed within New Zealand'.[149] A journalist suggested at the time that the inclusion gave the impression that 'economic intelligence is primarily just a convenient argument used by the intelligence organisations to justify their existence and budgets in the post-Cold War era',[150] just as it has frequently been suggested that MI5's new crime-fighting role (also given to it in 1996) was an attempt to justify its funding after the Cold War. Concerns about the implications of the language's introduction into law were heightened by an incident – just days after the enactment of the 1996 Act – in which NZSIS targeted the home of a spokesman for an organisation opposed to free trade.[151] One consequence of the resulting litigation was the enactment of the New Zealand Security Intelligence Service Amendment Act (No 2) 1999, which altered once again the definition of 'security' in the 1969 Act,

[148] Intelligence and Security Act 2017 (NZ), s 9.

[149] See New Zealand Security Intelligence Service Amendment Act 1996 (NZ), s 2(3). It was said by the Prime Minister of the day that the intention of amending the definition was 'to enable the New Zealand Security Intelligence Service to function more effectively in the more complex security environment with which we are faced in the post-cold war period. Issues such as weapons proliferation, threats to sensitive proprietary and strategic information and technology, and international organised crime involving drug trafficking and money-laundering, all have an international reach with the potential to affect New Zealand.' House of Representatives Hansard (NZ) vol 556 (19 June 1996). The formulation originally proposed was replaced at the recommendation of the Committee that examined the Bill: 'We accept the extended definition of security with the use of the word "ensuring" has been interpreted in some submissions as giving the Service the sole responsibility for achieving New Zealand's international and economic well-being. This is not the intention. The function of the Service is contributory and we recommend that the definition of security be amended accordingly.' Committee on the Intelligence and Security Agencies Bill, *Intelligence and Security Agencies Bill* (1996), x.

[150] N Hager, *Secret Power: New Zealand's Role in the International Spy Network* (Craig Potton, 1996), quoted in GR Weller, 'Change and Development in the New Zealand Security and Intelligence Services' (2001) 21 *Journal of Conflict Studies* 1.

[151] Weller (n 150). See *Choudry v Attorney-General* [1999] 2 NZLR 582 and *Choudry v Attorney-General* [1999] 3 NZLR 399, discussed in A Sandberg, 'Keeping a Watch on Big Brother: The SIS and the Court of Appeal' (2000–2003) 9 *Auckland University Law Review* 257.

so limiting the relevance of economic well-being: now 'security' would include (amongst other things) the 'identification of foreign capabilities, intentions, or activities within or relating to New Zealand that impact on New Zealand's international well-being or economic well-being' and the protection of New Zealand from activities 'within or relating to' the country that impacted 'adversely on New Zealand's international well-being or economic well-being'. And when the GCSB was given a statutory form in 2003, it was stated in the relevant Act that the Bureau's objective was, in part, to 'contribute to the national security of New Zealand' by providing foreign intelligence that the Government required 'to protect and advance … New Zealand's international well-being or economic well-being', its being clarified that 'the interests of New Zealand's international well-being or economic well-being are relevant only to the extent that they are affected by the actions or intentions of foreign organisations or foreign persons'.[152] This was broadened out by a statute of 2013, which provided simply that the GCSB's objective, 'in performing its functions', was to contribute to one of three things, one of which was 'the economic well-being of New Zealand'.[153]

The Review that preceded and framed the reforms made by the Intelligence and Security Act 2017 recommended that the GCSB should be able to contribute to the objective of advancing NZ's economic well-being, but that both NZSIS and the GCSB 'should only be able to carry out activities for the wider purposes of contributing to or advancing New Zealand's economic or international well-being where those activities target foreign persons and organisations',[154] making the sort of distinction we discuss further in chapter 4. At the same time, however, the definition of 'security' recommended (but which did not eventually become law) included protecting against 'unlawful acts, or acts of foreign interference, that may cause serious damage to New Zealand's economic security or international relations'.[155] This would be dually limited: economic security rather than economic well-being, and protecting against damage thereto rather than seeking to promote it, recalling the distinction between the roles of MI5 and MI6 in relation to economic well-being. 'While we consider the Agencies also have a legitimate role in *advancing* New Zealand's economic and international interests in order to compete globally,' the reviewers said, 'consideration must be given to the importance of the information to be collected relative to the potential impact

[152] Government Communications Security Bureau Act 2003 (NZ), s 7(2).

[153] Government Communications Security Bureau Act 2013 (NZ), s 7, inserting a new s 7 in the Government Communications Security Bureau Act 2003 (NZ).

[154] Cullen and Reddy (n 100) [5.64]. 'In general, we do not consider it to be appropriate for New Zealanders to be the subject of the Agencies' intrusive powers for the broader purposes of advancing New Zealand's economic and international interests. Such an approach would be inconsistent with New Zealand's status as a free and democratic country and would entail an unjustifiable intrusion on New Zealanders' privacy and liberty. We note that the UK and Australia take a similar approach of limiting targeting of citizens, permanent residents or (in the case of the UK) persons inside the country to situations where there are national security implications.'

[155] ibid, recommendation 40.

on individual rights in collecting it.'[156] This is the background to the 2017 Act's inclusion of economic well-being as one of the principal objectives to which the New Zealand SIAs are to contribute,[157] and the position whereby warrants on economic well-being grounds (like international relations grounds) can target New Zealand persons only where those persons are acting on behalf of foreign or terrorist entities.[158]

It seems in relation both to Australia and New Zealand, therefore, highly unlikely that the introduction of the language of economic well-being in relation to the SIAs, as well as the specific formulation used, was not ultimately influenced by its inclusion within the statutory mandates of the UK's SIAs, which – we have noted – in turn originates in the ECHR. It is therefore perhaps the best example of what I have called Commonwealth national security constitutionalism in the modern frameworks of the Commonwealth Five Eyes states, in that it cannot be explained in purely functional terms: it does not, that is, seem to be inherent in the logic of the national security endeavour that the work of the SIAs would also encompass 'economic well-being' or something analogous, nor that that specific formulation would be used. More important, though, than the specific language and its origins is the acceptance of the principle that defending or protecting economic well-being is a legitimate role for the SIAs to play – not merely as an aspect of national security but as a separate aim with a broadly equivalent stature. The employment of the formulation or an equivalent does not, as things stand, appear to have made it to Canada, but the experience of the other Commonwealth Five Eyes states suggests that if and when the mandates of the Canadian SIAs are revisited, a key question will be what – if any – explicit role they should have in relation to economic matters.

V. Thematic Questions in the Governance of the Modern SIAs

Having laid out the general organisation of the SIAs in each of the four jurisdictions, and some of the key concepts that define their mandates, I turn here to consider certain themes that arise in relation to the modern SIAs in some or all of the Commonwealth Five Eyes states that are of particular constitutional interest or significance: their relationship to the political executive; the desire to protect against political partiality; and their implications for rights of free speech and protest.

156 ibid [5.81] (original emphasis).
157 Intelligence and Security Act 2017 (NZ), s 9(c).
158 ibid, s 59.

A. The SIAs and the Political Executive

In chapter 7, I consider the question of the relationship between the national security enterprise and democracy. The reason for addressing that question is that the general position in the states under discussion has usually been that the enterprise in question was insulated against meaningful democratic control. Rather than being directed with any great specificity by the legislature, national security is solely the concern of the executive. Though the executive is – in Westminster systems – directly accountable to the (relevant chamber of the) legislature, the accountability of the SIAs to the legislature for their work in the domain of national security was therefore at best indirect. The legislature's role in relation to these bodies was solely – and to a great degree remains – that of empowering the work of these bodies, and establishing the broad legal guidelines within which they were required to operate, with which the executive would then concern itself on an ongoing basis. But this point is normally framed negatively, in terms of what the legislature could not know or not do. It also serves to consider it from the point of view of the executive and to ask what is – and, again, what should be – the nature of the executive's ongoing concern with the SIAs. Within, that is, the scope of the bounds set for those SIAs by legislation – usually framed, for obvious reasons, in discretionary rather than mandatory terms – what is the ability of the executive of the day to shape or even direct the work of the SIAs? As prefigured by our discussion of this point in chapter 2, the regimes in place in the Commonwealth Five Eyes states offer rather different answers to that question in the modern era.

The basic outlines of the dilemma might be appreciated. On one hand, the national security endeavour is – or at least so the executive frequently tells the courts, and the courts often accept – one requiring expertise: expertise about the nature of threats, expertise as to whence they originate, expertise as to the relative priority that should be given to each, and expertise as to how they should be combatted. Though we might question the extent to which this is true, we can accept the point for the sake of argument. Though some of that expertise might be found in the relevant political actors – those responsible for internal security, say – it will rest more obviously and more fully within the professionalised and permanent security and intelligence agencies. We should, therefore, permit those bodies to operate as they see fit within the boundaries laid down for them by the legislature, on the understanding that it is open to them to make the case to the government of the day if they regard that legislative framework as giving them insufficient powers to do what they feel necessary to keep the country safe, or indeed as permitting actions that should not be tolerated for one reason or another. On the other hand, this emphasis on expertise runs up, in a manner familiar within the modern state, against the question of democratic accountability, which is also frequently, and correctly, cited to courts as a basis for offering appropriate respect to the decision-making of the political executive in domains including that of national security. Decisions have to be made, priorities have to be determined, and if these turn out to have been poor decisions or misplaced priorities, it is not the leadership of the SIAs that will be called upon to justify them to the legislature and the public at large: it is likely to be the government of the day. Regardless of where blame might properly lie as a matter of causality, it is the political actors, who as we have noted will often bid for public support in the language of security, that will bear the brunt of public anger.

Against that background, there is a genuine difficulty in determining the extent to which the executive should have any role in setting the operational priorities of the SIAs. If they do enjoy such a role, there is a risk of the making of decisions about what those priorities should be that is out of step with an objective assessment of the danger, on the basis of what is most politically salient. In extreme but by no means unthinkable cases, an ability to direct the operational priorities of the SIAs will run the risk of effectively deploying them in a fashion more concerned with political advantage than the security of the state: perhaps even deploying them against political rivals. Such politicisation has been the basis of numerous scandals in the past, in a number of the jurisdictions in question, and indeed has been one of the major drivers of their legal evolution. If the executive, by contrast, enjoys no power to direct, in however loose or indirect a fashion, the operational priorities of the SIAs, then it ends up having to pay a political price for decisions and actions that it not only did not influence but in fact could not have influenced. In practice, therefore, the executive is often given a level of operational influence that falls short of direct instructional authority and is often negative (permitting it, in effect, to block the SIAs from acting in a certain way) rather than positive (allowing it to direct their attention to this or that issue) in nature. The former is most often the case in relation to specific exercises of intrusive powers, where the general need for executive approval (discussed in chapter 4) creates an effective veto over their use, which might be exercised on grounds that are not limited to the view that the criteria for granting a warrant (or authorisation, or so on) are not met, and so might in practice be exercised on what are effectively policy or political grounds.

Variation is more apparent once we turn from negative to positive intervention by the executive. The law in the various jurisdictions differs in the extent to which it permits the government of the day to set policy or even direct operations, though in most cases it reflects a distinction between security intelligence (where there is less or no possibility of ministerial direction) and foreign intelligence (where there is often more). Sometimes the executive's powers are limited to specific topics. So, for example, the New Zealand Intelligence and Security Act 2017, which overhauled the regime in New Zealand, provides for what are known as 'ministerial policy statements'.[159] The Minister responsible for each

[159] In New Zealand, since 2014, the portfolios of Minister Responsible for the GCSB and Minister in Charge of the NZSIS are both held by one Minister, so far always the Attorney-General, while the Prime

of the SIAs must make such a statement about certain matters specified in that Act.[160] These include, amongst other things, the questions of 'conducting surveillance in a public place' and 'obtaining and using publicly available information'.[161] A second set of obligations, to make policy statements regarding 'co-operating with an overseas public authority', 'providing advice and assistance to an overseas public authority' and 'sharing intelligence with an overseas public authority', are distinguished by a requirement to provide copies of the statement(s) to the ISC.[162] They must include details of the applicable procedure, 'the protections that need to be in place in relation to the matter (if any)' and 'the restrictions in relation to the matter (if any)'.[163] Though, as these stipulations suggest, these mandatory statements are mostly about the use of specific powers or the carrying out a specific type of act, the statute permits the Minister responsible for one of the agencies, if he or she considers it 'necessary or desirable', to issue policy statements 'that provide guidance to the intelligence and security agency in relation to any other matter'.[164] And though these policy statements are not binding upon the SIAs, it is nevertheless the case that, when 'making any decision or taking any action', the Director-General of the body and its employees must 'have regard to' any policy statement relevant to that decision or action.[165] We see, for example, that in relation to the example given above – the conducting of surveillance in a public place – the current policy statement is a detailed document that identifies a number of principles that 'constitute a framework for good decision making and must be taken into account by GCSB and NZSIS when planning and conducting surveillance in a public place'[166] (some of them reflecting the underlying law, but others seeming to go beyond that), as well as matters that should be reflected within internal policies and procedures (including, for example, that employees may participate in such surveillance only if they have been appropriately trained)[167] and the procedures that should apply to the authorisation of such procedures.[168] These are in many ways impressive documents, which offer a level of safeguards not found in the legal text, but they risk – as is often the case where non-legal rules and norms are layered on top of their legal

Minister is the Minister for National Security and Intelligence and 'has responsibility for the overall direction, policy and oversight of the broad national security and intelligence sector': see Cullen and Reddy (n 100) [3.55]–[3.58]; and Arnold and Mahuika (n 128) [3.5].

[160] Matters, it has been said, that are 'significant because they cover activities that are lawful (and therefore do not need a warrant) but that may involve elements of deception or intrusion and other areas where ministerial guidance was considered appropriate': Arnold and Mahuika (n 128) [4.15].

[161] Intelligence and Security Act 2017 (NZ), s 206.

[162] ibid, s 207.

[163] ibid, s 210.

[164] ibid, s 208.

[165] ibid, s 209.

[166] Minister Responsible for the Government Communications Security Bureau and Minister Responsible for the New Zealand Security Intelligence Service, *Ministerial Policy Statement – Conducting Surveillance in a Public Place* (1 March 2022).

[167] ibid [36].

[168] ibid [44].

counterparts – muddying the waters as to what is lawful and what is not; what is obligatory and what is merely desirable. They do not, most importantly, permit Ministers to direct the day-to-day activities of the SIAs.

In Australia, as discussed in chapter 2, the position is very different, and the SIAs are subject to what is sometimes described, bluntly, as 'ministerial control'.[169] Though the ASIO Act 1979 now provides that ASIO is 'under the control' of its Director-General, it states that he or she in turn is subject to the directions of the Minister (which the Director-General can require the Minister to put in writing) in the performance of his or her functions under the Act.[170] There are, though, limits on the ability of the Minister to override the Director-General: the Minister cannot override the Director-General 'concerning the nature of the advice that should be given by the Organisation', while the Minister can only override the opinion of the Director-General as to whether the collection of intelligence about a particular individual 'would, or would not, be justified by reason of its relevance to security' or whether the communication of intelligence concerning a particular individual 'would be for a purpose relevant to security' if he or she provides written reasons for doing so.[171] That is, the statute recognises the special expertise of the Director-General in matters of security, and though it permits that special expertise to give way, in certain cases, to the opinion of a democratically accountable figure, it includes safeguards that, or at least so one would hope, diminish the possibility that the override power of the Minister will be abused. This therefore largely accords with Justice Hope's recommendation that the provision as introduced be amended to recognise that 'the Minister's power over ASIO is ultimately paramount'.[172] Moreover, as a result of another provision first introduced in 1986, also following a recommendation of the second Hope Royal Commission,[173] the Minister may – following consultation with the Attorney-General and in writing – give guidelines that are to be observed in 'the performance by the Organisation of its functions or the exercise of its powers'.[174] In each case, the guidelines are to be given to the Leader of the Opposition and the Inspector-General of Intelligence and Security (IGIS), and, unless the Minister considers it to be inappropriate (for what reasons is not specified), also to the Committee on Intelligence

[169] See generally, *Comprehensive Review*, Volume 1 (n 90) ch 14, including (ibid [14.13]) the claim that 'Ministerial control of intelligence agencies is important to uphold principles of ministerial responsibility and accountability. However, ministerial control also needs to be balanced with the statutory independence of agencies and need for intelligence agencies to be neutral and above politics …'.

[170] ASIO Act 1979 (Australia), ss 8(1)–(3).

[171] ibid, ss 8(4) and (5).

[172] 'I have concluded that it is appropriate that this be so; that the elected office-holder accountable for ASIO and its activities to Parliament and the public should in the end be able to determine – and assume responsibility for – activities pertaining to the security of Australia.' Royal Commission on Australia's Security Intelligence Agencies, *Report on the Australian Security Intelligence Organization* (1984) [16.47].

[173] ibid [16.51]–[16.53].

[174] ASIO Act 1979 (Australia), ss 8A(1) and (1A). See the discussion in HP Lee, PJ Hanks and V Morabito, *In the Name of National Security: The Legal Dimensions* (LBC Information Services, 1995) 46–47.

and Security.[175] Though guidelines made under one or the other of these powers must be laid before Parliament, they can be redacted on broad grounds.[176] New guidelines were issued under this provision in 2020, replacing a set which had been in place since 2007.[177]

The degree of ministerial control over ASIS would seem to be even greater than applies to ASIO:[178] one of ASIS's functions is to undertake, in relation to the 'capabilities, intentions or activities of people or organisations outside Australia', both 'such activities of a general or specific nature as the responsible Minister directs' and 'activities included in such a class or classes of activity or activities as the responsible Minister directs'.[179] Any directions of this sort that are given must be in writing and may be given only if the Minister is satisfied, inter alia, that 'there are satisfactory arrangements in place to ensure that, in carrying out the direction, nothing will be done beyond what is necessary having regard to the purposes for which the direction is given' and that 'there are satisfactory arrangements in place to ensure that the nature and consequences of acts done in carrying out the direction will be reasonable having regard to the purposes for which the direction is given'.[180] On top of this, the responsible Minister may give written directions to be observed by ASIS or the ASD in the performance of their respective functions,[181] with a copy of these directions (like others) to be given to the IGIS.[182] This level of ministerial power over the SIAs – or at least its formalisation in clear statutory rules – is unusual, and it might be feared that the various political controls on how it is exercised do not suffice to exclude the dangers identified above.

It was noted in section III.A that in Canada, the Director of CSIS, 'under the direction of the Minister', has the control and management of the Service. The Minister may, as part of that role – having been advised by the Deputy Minister, a senior official – give written directions to the Director, but there is no obligation to do so, and the directions shall – it is provided – 'be deemed not to be statutory instruments'.[183] This example of explicitly leaving open the possibility

[175] ASIO 1979 (Australia), ss 8A(5) and (6).

[176] ibid, s 8A(4).

[177] P Dutton, *Minister's Guidelines in relation to the performance by the Australian Security Intelligence Organisation of its functions and the exercise of its powers* (2020). For a detailed critique, see G Carne, 'Guiding Light or Opaque Filter?: The Minister's Guidelines for the Australian Security Intelligence Organisation in Performing its Functions and Exercising its Powers as Relevant to Security' (2022) 43 *Adelaide Law Review* 814.

[178] 'In theory, a minister has been accountable to the Parliament for ASIS at all times since its establishment. Until the late 1970s, however, this was meaningless in practice because of the absence of authoritative information on the Service and a government policy (accepted by the Parliament) of refusing to comment on matters relating to intelligence and security.' Commission of Inquiry into the Australian Secret Intelligence Service (n 86) [5.7].

[179] Intelligence Services Act 2001 (Australia), s 6(1)(e).

[180] ibid, ss 6(2) and (3).

[181] ibid, s 8(2)(a).

[182] Inspector-General of Intelligence and Security Act 1986 (Australia), s 32B(2)

[183] CSIS Act (1984) (Canada), s 6(2).

of ministerial direction was relied upon by the second Hope Royal Commission in Australia in declining to recommend, as Justice Hope put it, that the ASIO Director-General's opinion be treated 'in the same way as the quasi-judicial pronouncements of certain statutory bodies which are put beyond ministerial intervention'.[184] Where written directions are given, however, a copy must be provided to the NSIRA, which replaced the SIRC in 2019,[185] political controls again being leveraged to discourage possible abuse of the legal power. The Chief of the CSE, again 'under the direction of the Minister', has the management and control of the Establishment,[186] and the Minister may issue written directions 'respecting the performance of the Chief's duties and functions'.[187] The NSIRA must produce annual reports on both CSIS and the CSE, which are required to include consideration not only of the SIAs' compliance with the law, but also their compliance with any applicable ministerial directions.[188] A number of such directions have been issued, with one of general significance setting out the Minister's 'expectations of the Service with regard to accountability',[189] and so resembling the New Zealand ministerial policy statements discussed above, and one of the most recent setting out more specifically the Minister's expectations in regard to CSIS's response to 'threats to the security of Canada directed at Parliament and parliamentarians'.[190]

At the other end of the spectrum from Australia, in the UK there appears to be very little formal scope for the executive to exercise a direct day-to-day influence on the work of the SIAs. The Security Service Act 1989, for example, provides that MI5 exists 'under the authority of the Secretary of State'[191] but also that its operations are 'under the control of a Director-General appointed by the Secretary of State'.[192] The position of MI6 and GCHQ is the same, and in each case the head of the relevant body must make an annual report to the Prime Minister and the Secretary of State on the work of the body in question, and may, in addition, make to either of them, at any time, a report on 'any matter relating to its work'.[193] These statutes therefore, it has been said, 'did little more than to put onto the

[184] Royal Commission on Australia's Security Intelligence Agencies (n 172) [16.48].
[185] CSIS Act (1984) (Canada), s 6(2). See the discussion in ch 5.
[186] Communications Security Establishment Act (2019) (Canada), s 9(1).
[187] ibid, s 11(1).
[188] National Security and Intelligence Review Agency Act, SC 2019, c 13, s 2 (Canada), ss 32(2)(a) and 33(2)(a).
[189] Minister of Public Safety, 'Ministerial Direction to the Canadian Security Intelligence Service: Accountability' (10 September 2019). Though much of what is contained in the 'principles of accountability' set out in the Direction simply restates the need for compliance with the law, one of those principles notes that CSIS 'has a duty to inform the Minister of any such matter as is relevant to enable the Minister to fulfill the Minister's accountabilities as outlined in the CSIS Act'.
[190] Minister of Public Safety, 'Ministerial Direction on Threats to the Security of Canada Directed at Parliament and Parliamentarians' (16 May 2023).
[191] Security Service Act 1989 (UK), s 1(1).
[192] ibid, s 2(1).
[193] ibid, s 2(4); and Intelligence Services Act 1994 (UK), ss 2(4) and 4(4).

statute books the light touch approach which had hitherto characterised executive oversight of the UK agencies':

> The legislation sets out in some detail the role of those appointed to lead the intelligence and security agencies but says relatively little about the role of ministers. Aside from appointing the heads of the agencies and providing approval for some activities … the legislation places very little responsibility on ministers to oversee the working of the agencies.[194]

This of course does not exclude an informal influence, the existence and operation of which it would not be possible to evidence. The key route for general executive influence of the work of the SIAs would therefore appear to come from the inclusion, noted elsewhere, in the statement of the functions of MI6 and GCHQ that they are to be exercised only in pursuit of certain ends, one of which is 'the interests of national security', with – the statute continues in each case – 'particular reference to the defence and foreign policies of Her Majesty's Government in the United Kingdom'.[195] In this way the policies of the Government filter through, indirectly but no doubt in many cases decisively, into the mandates of the foreign intelligence bodies. No such reference to governmental policy is found in the statutory mandate of MI5. Andrew Defty has therefore argued that, 'while there have been innovations in other areas of intelligence oversight in the UK … the role of ministers has changed little since the days when they provided the only form of democratic oversight'.[196] Though this may, as Defty notes, have suited and still suits both Ministers and SIAs, the examples of the other Commonwealth Five Eyes states shows that there is considerable divergence between them on this point, and it may be that the time will come that the UK Government seeks, on that basis, greater (formal) control than the current legislative framework seems to permit, whether in the form of written Directions (which might be scrutinised and even published if appropriate) or even of a more direct and ongoing control of a sort that has historically been absent in the UK. As with other points we have considered – and will consider in chapter 7 – it may be that the current position, found in statutes of 1989 and 1994, reflects a post-Cold War understanding of the nature of the national security task; an understanding that more recent developments may put under pressure.

B. The Threat of Political Partiality

Against the background of variation in the extent to which, and means by which, the executive may influence or even direct (some of) the work of the SIAs, the

[194] A Defty, '"Familiar but not intimate": executive oversight of the UK intelligence and security agencies' (2022) 37 *Intelligence and National Security* 57, 61.
[195] Intelligence Services Act 1994 (UK), ss 1(2)(a) and 3(2)(a).
[196] Defty (n 194) 68.

regimes governing the SIAs in the Commonwealth Five Eyes states mostly attempt to write into law related protection against what we might think of in broad terms as the politicisation of the SIAs. These provisions no doubt reflect both generalised concerns about the implications for the political process of giving over to the SIAs highly intrusive powers that are open to abuse, but also the fact that there are various examples, across time and across jurisdictions, of allegations of political interference by the SIAs – though in light of the discussion in section V.A, it serves to note that many of these examples seem to involve action taken by the SIAs autonomously, rather than at the behest of some political party or faction or other. Though the basic endeavour is common to a number of jurisdictions, the approach taken varies, including in ways that appear potentially significant. Some of the provisions in question take the form of specific references to acting for or against political parties; others by emphasising that the SIAs are to act only for their specific functions and nothing else.

In the UK, for example, the Director-General of MI5 must ensure that the Service acquires and discloses information only for limited purposes, including the proper discharge of its functions and (in relation to the disclosure of information) certain crime-fighting purposes. But the Director, the 1989 Act provides, must also ensure that 'the Service does not take any action to further the interests of any political party'.[197] This restates, in plainer language, the thrust of the injunction contained in the Maxwell-Fyfe Directive that 'the Security Service should be kept absolutely free from any political bias or influence and nothing should be done that might lend colour to any suggestion that it is concerned with the interests of any particular section of the community, or with any other matter than the Defence of the Realm as a whole'.[198] The history of the Service, and allegations (whether or not well-grounded) of its political bias, would seem to be the background to this provision, but its framing is striking: there is no parallel obligation to ensure that the Service does not take action to harm the interests of any political party, something that at least in some circumstances might be done without furthering the interests of any other party. Nor is there any reference to, or possibility of catching, any other sort of political grouping. Though an equivalent rule about obtaining and disclosing information applies to the heads of MI6 and GCHQ, the rule regarding political intervention applicable to these two bodies differs. Where the Director-General of MI5 is subject to a duty to ensure that no action is taken by it to 'further the interests of any political party', the equivalent in respect of the heads of MI6 and GCHQ limits the scope of that duty via the specification of 'any *United Kingdom* political party'.[199] Given the external orientation of these two bodies, this is of course no coincidence, and it is not particularly difficult to see that in certain circumstances the national

[197] Security Service Act 1989 (UK), 2(2)(b).
[198] Quoted in *Lord Denning's Report* (Cmnd 2152, 1963) [238].
[199] Intelligence Services Act 1994 (UK), ss 2(2)(b) and 4(2)(b) (emphasis added).

security of the UK or (say) its economic well-being might be served by furthering the interests of some political party in another polity (whether or not, in practice, any efforts are made to do so).

Provisions elsewhere perform an analogous function in distinct forms. In Australia, for example, the Director-General of ASIO is to take, the governing Act provides, 'all reasonable steps' to ensure both that 'the work of the Organisation is limited to what is necessary for the purposes of the discharge of its functions' and, moreover, that 'the Organisation is kept free from any influences or considerations not relevant to its functions and nothing is done that might lend colour to any suggestion that it is concerned to further or protect the interests of any particular section of the community, or with any matters other than the discharge of its functions'.[200] The contrast between this 'special responsibility' (the term used in the heading of the relevant section of the Act) and the rule that applies in relation to the Director-General of MI5 is of interest: that applicable to ASIO is (being taken from the original ASIO Charter, itself drawing on a predecessor of the Maxwell-Fyfe Directive)[201] rather mealy-mouthed, containing no specific reference to what one would have thought was the primary danger (party political interference) and instead including language – 'any particular section of the community' – whose referent is unclear. The lack of specificity might be thought either to reflect, or perhaps to be particularly unfortunate in the context of, the regime of 'ministerial control' described above. The other Australian SIAs at issue are made subject to a rule whereby their functions – which are to be performed 'only in the interests of Australia's national security, Australia's foreign relations or Australia's national economic well-being and only to the extent that those matters are affected by the capabilities, intentions or activities of people or organisations outside Australia' – do not include 'undertaking any activity for the purpose of furthering the interests of an Australian political party or other Australian political organisation'.[202] This mirrors the UK position, whereby the foreign intelligence agencies might lawfully take action to further the interests of political parties that are not Australian, and – perhaps – might even be compatible with a position where those bodies act to hinder the interests of an Australian political party if the other conditions for those bodies acting are met.

In New Zealand, the Directors of the SIAs must take 'all reasonable steps' to ensure that, first, the activities of each agency are 'limited to those that are relevant to the performance of its functions', 'kept free from any influence or consideration

[200] ASIO Act 1979 (Australia), s 20.

[201] 'It is essential that the security service should be absolutely free from any political bias or influence, and nothing should be done that might lend colour to any suggestion that it is concerned with the interests of any particular community, or with any matters other than those that influence the Commonwealth. You will impress on your staff that they have no connection whatever with any matters of a party political character and that you must be scrupulous to avoid any action which could be so construed.' Article 6 of ASIO's founding Charter, quoted in *Comprehensive Review*, Volume 1 (n 90) [6.24].

[202] Intelligence Services Act 2001 (Australia), s 11(2A).

that is not relevant to the performance of its functions' and 'politically neutral'.[203] This is glossed within the 2017 Act itself with the example that 'the activities are not carried out for the purpose of promoting or harming the interests of any political party or candidate', with no explicit (though perhaps an implied) limitation to New Zealand parties or candidates. Though the second of these duties would – one would expect – logically require the third, it is for perhaps obvious reasons given separate recognition. The inclusion of both 'promoting' and 'harming' works in particular to draw attention the absence of the latter (or similar) in the frameworks applicable elsewhere. The language of political neutrality is interesting, though, in that it seems to potentially encompass more than the sort of neutrality as to parties that is found in its equivalents elsewhere, but without offering a clear sense of what that something more might be. No generalised rules regarding political neutrality appear to exist in the relevant Canadian legislation, even though it, like that in Australia, seems to allow for a degree of more direct executive control of the SIAs. One question that occurs is what these duties and limitations – aimed at protecting the political neutrality of the SIAs – might mean for attempts, which appear increasingly common, by foreign states to interfere with the political and electoral processes of the Commonwealth Five Eyes states, as well as the work of the SIAs of those states to resist such interference?

C. Rights of Free Speech and of Protest

A related, though distinct, feature of some of the relevant frameworks seeks – at the level of the general functions of the SIAs rather than the specific powers afforded them – to exclude the possibility that they will operate so as to limit or undermine rights of, in particular, free speech or protest. Here, that is, the danger they are accepted as potentially posing is not primarily to those operating within the formal political process – the party or parties of government and its or their rivals – but rather to those who might contribute to the wider, informal political discourse, including as engaged in by private actors. The relevant protections are not always legally operative, doing little or perhaps even nothing that is not already done by the generalised regimes of human rights protection to which many of the SIAs are now subject (and which are, as noted, incorporated into some of the SIAs' legal frameworks), and yet for reasons of clarity or (perhaps) public relations, it was felt necessary to place protection for the relevant rights on the face of the statutes that govern these bodies. In Canada, for example, we are told that the concept of 'threats to the security of Canada' does not encompass 'lawful advocacy, protest or dissent', unless carried out in conjunction with one of those phenomena that constitute such a threat.[204] It has been noted, however, that the language of 'carried

[203] Intelligence and Security Act 2017 (NZ), s 18(a).
[204] CSIS Act (1984) (Canada), s 2.

on in conjunction with' is ambiguous, and may as a result 'exclude a broad swath of otherwise legitimate activity from the exemption, and thereby authorize CSIS investigations of these activities'.[205] In Australia, where there is no Bill of Rights at the Commonwealth level, and so the danger that the work of the SIAs might limit individual rights (understood as much as a moral or political concept as a legal one) is a more live one, the ASIO Act 1979 provides – in a provision first inserted in 1986,[206] and reflecting what Justice Hope took to be the original intention behind the political neutrality provision – that it

> shall not limit the right of persons to engage in lawful advocacy, protest or dissent and the exercise of that right shall not, by itself, be regarded as prejudicial to security, and the functions of the Organisation shall be construed accordingly.[207]

The language shared with the Canadian provision enacted two years before the insertion into the 1979 Act – 'lawful advocacy, protest or dissent' – reflects the consideration by Hope of the Canadian legislation,[208] though of course the caveat of lawfulness means that the protection of advocacy is more apparent than real, or at least any protection that is offered is offered by some limit, necessarily found elsewhere, on what advocacy might be rendered unlawful. In both cases, no equivalent protection appears to be written into the missions of the other SIAs: CSE in Canada, and ASIS and the ASD in Australia.

The New Zealand equivalent, such as it is, applies to all of the SIAs, and provides:

> The exercise by any person in New Zealand or any class of persons in New Zealand of their right to freedom of expression under the law (including the right to advocate, protest, or dissent) does not of itself justify an intelligence and security agency taking any action in respect of that person or class of persons.[209]

As with the other jurisdictions, however, it is not clear that this adds anything of significance to the underlying rules about when the SIAs are entitled to act – though lawful speech (etc) does not justify their doing so, the fact that rights of protest are being exercised does not stop them from acting when the conditions for doing so are met. Moreover, the reference to 'taking any action' may – it has been suggested – leave open the possibility of data collection and analysis by the New Zealand SIAs that nevertheless has a chilling effect.[210] Also notable is the geographic focus of the rule, such that the exercise of the right to freedom of expression by persons outside of New Zealand can (in and of itself) in principle justify the SIAs' taking action in respect of those persons, including where the

[205] Forcese and West (n 28) 97.

[206] By the Australian Security Intelligence Organization Amendment Act 1986 (Australia).

[207] ASIO Act 1979 (Australia), s 17A.

[208] Royal Commission on Australia's Security Intelligence Agencies (n 172) [4.81]–[4.84].

[209] Intelligence and Security Act 2017 (NZ), s 19. This is the spiritual successor of a provision first inserted into the 1969 Act by the New Zealand Security Intelligence Service Amendment Act 1977 (NZ), and in turn replaced by the New Zealand Security Intelligence Service Amendment Act 1999 (NZ).

[210] Arnold and Mahuika (n 128) [5.87].

person in question is, say, a New Zealand citizen or permanent resident. Finally, as in other states, the right to freedom of expression is a qualified one, and the limits imposed on the New Zealand SIAs must be understood in that context. In recommending that the provision be retained, the reviewers of the 2017 Act noted that in light of the qualified nature of the right of freedom of expression, 'the Agencies are, in our view, entitled to make an assessment that some types of expression in particular circumstances justify their interest, although they should adopt a cautious approach':

> We therefore consider that there will be circumstances where the Agencies may legitimately investigate situations where, for example, violent extremist views are being expressed without, in doing so, breaching [the restriction]. We acknowledge, however, that that the issue is difficult and requires careful judgment by the Agencies.[211]

Overall, therefore, these provisions seem primarily to aim to reassure those who might be concerned about the possibility of illiberal acts on the parts of the SIAs. It is though by no means clear that those who might be so concerned are likely to have those concerns assuaged by this sort of, what is often, in effect, legislative tautology. No such special reference to protest or speech rights is found in the UK. Nevertheless, given that the fact that the SIAs are public authorities for the purpose of section 6 of the HRA 1998 means that they will not be able to act in a way that gives rise to a disproportionate interference with the rights of free expression or assembly of those within the UK's jurisdiction, any such reference would be of significant benefit (if at all) only to those outside of the UK's jurisdiction.

VI. Conclusion

In each of the four jurisdictions, a statutory framework for the SIAs is now in place, and we might anticipate that these frameworks will remain generally stable even as the powers of the bodies in question, discussed in chapter 4, continue to evolve to reflect – at least – changing threat models and technological developments. What is striking is how modest some of these frameworks are: the number of operative provisions is generally small, and these provisions mostly straightforward, with particular complexity entering the picture only in those cases in which the statutes in question seek to answer questions about, say, the employment status of those who work for the SIAs and how they are or are not impacted by general rules applicable to other parts of the public service. We saw in chapter 2 that there was reasonably clear evidence of borrowing and influencing in the period in which the SIAs were coming out of the shadows – or in from the cold, if one prefers.[212] As the SIAs have matured, they have moved a certain

[211] ibid [5.106].

[212] L Lustgarten and I Leigh, *In from the Cold: National Security and Parliamentary Democracy* (Oxford University Press, 1994).

distance away from these shared roots, and there are, as we have seen, a number of important differences between them and their organisation and missions. Some of this would seem to reflect historical happenstance and some of it the subtle divergences in constitutional culture that have taken place in the different Commonwealth Five Eyes states, with different tolerance of legal transparency and different levels of enthusiasm for putting matters on the face of the governing statutes. And some of it must be simply a matter of timing rather than anything more consequential – when and why the relevant bodies were first given statutory basis and whether or not something has happened since then to prompt a reform or reappraisal. The core of (national) security, however, remains common to each, as it must do so given their common function, which shapes their current forms and limits the possible extent of any divergence, particularly against the background of a shared constitutional model or heritage. Nevertheless, at the margins of the modern national security enterprise – the spread of the language of 'economic well-being' is a good, but by no means the only, example – we find clear evidence for the existence of a model of Commonwealth national security constitutionalism that brings together the four Commonwealth Five Eyes states, both constituted by and developed within a process of borrowing and sharing that takes place between them. In later chapters, as we turn from positive to negative constitutionalism – from the powers of the SIAs to the mechanisms by which oversight of them and their work is carried out – we shall see even more, and more fundamental, examples of this phenomenon in action.

4

Powers, Sources, Safeguards

I. Introduction

We have considered in earlier chapters the manner in which the SIAs in the Commonwealth Eyes states were first constituted, often secretly and without particularly robust legal bases, and later reformed to greater or lesser degrees so as to take on their current, (mostly) rational and legally transparent form. Against that background of the creation and evolution – in general terms, the constitutionalisation – of those SIAs, this chapter considers some of the legal powers they now possess, and how those powers have grown and evolved over time. The focus of the chapter is largely, but not exclusively, on powers that are investigatory in nature – permitting the acquisition of information via surveillance or other surreptitious means – and those that are special to the SIAs, not being shared (at least in their entirety) by the 'ordinary' policing authorities, with their focus on 'ordinary' criminality. The intention of the chapter is not to offer a general overview of those powers in the fashion of a textbook but rather to pick out themes to be found in those powers, to identify patterns that exist, and in turn any exceptions to or anomalies within those patterns, so as to consider what might be learned from those.

Amongst the specific (sets of) powers considered are those relating to the interception of communications – the modern instantiation of what was once, and still includes, the power to intercept mail or tap telephones. These actions had, it was often claimed, some origins in the royal prerogative, which we have considered in chapter 2, and so one important aspect of the relevant powers in the Commonwealth Five Eyes is the story of the different moments at which, and reasons for which, the prerogative came to be recognised as an insufficient basis for what the SIAs desired to do as regards different modes of communication. A modern approach to these powers must also account for variants thereof that are 'bulk' in nature, taking advantage of modern technological developments so as to intercept communications in large quantities, including (and this is crucial) those of persons who are of no interest to the SIAs. Another category of powers considered here is those the SIAs enjoy in relation to the masses of data the modern technological environment makes available to them as well as to private actors, and the regulation of which varies quite significantly between the jurisdictions at issue as a result of differences in the background regulation of the use of data generally. Many of these powers work as specific and limited exceptions to rules of criminal law that apply to the SIAs as much as to any other party. Finally, therefore, powers that lack this limited and specific nature are considered: those, that is, that grant the SIAs a broad, sometimes unlimited, power to commit crimes, or to permit others to do so.

One pattern that emerges from this consideration, though not a surprising one, is the notable enlargement of the capacities of the SIAs over time, with powers of postal and telegraphic interception now accompanied by a range of others that may be more intrusive, whether in terms of the level of interference with the liberties of the person who is the target of their exercise or the number of persons who might be impacted by that exercise, than those available historically. In particular, the modern technological environment has made available to the SIAs a quantity of data and the ability to query that data that was historically inconceivable, and the law in the Commonwealth Five Eyes states has not always managed to keep up with this development. Amongst the other themes considered in this chapter is the question of place and status: the states under consideration differ in terms of where and how they draw the lines marking the availability of their most intrusive powers or the application of heightened safeguards; whether, that is, they draw the line in purely geographic terms or whether, instead, they make the question of citizenship (or some analogue, such as permanent residence) the crucial question – with citizens therefore enjoying heightened protection regardless of where they find themselves in the world – or whether other factors play a role. A further issue, with which I close the chapter, is the question of safeguards. That is, one important trend in these jurisdictions has been the introduction of new and more restrictive safeguards relating to the use of intrusive powers. One, often described as the 'double-lock', is of particular interest, for its migration from one jurisdiction to another exemplifies certain important themes about national security constitutionalism in these states, how it has evolved over time, and the relationship between these four constitutional orders and their treatment of national security – a theme that I pick up in chapter 7.

II. Interception

A. The Early Development of the Law

The archetypal power of the SIAs is that to intercept communications: in the past, postal communications; later telegraphic communications; now, all manner of both analogue and digital communications. As elsewhere, the origins of modern Canada, Australia and New Zealand within the British Empire oblige us to look to the UK for the historical law governing, and practices relating to, interception. There, the practice of postal interception was usually, if not invariably, legislated for indirectly, with enactments relating to the postal service prohibiting the interference with mail but excepting from that prohibition any interference that took place in accordance with a warrant from the Secretary of State – that is, authorisation invariably came from the executive rather than outside of it.[1] This pattern was continued into legislation relating to telegraphy, including the statute that granted the Postmaster General a monopoly over the operation of telegram systems, which in turn was treated as applying also to modern telephony.[2] That this state of affairs was inadequate was demonstrated by the attempt in 1957, by the Birkett Committee – which had been convened to address the question of interception following a scandal in which a barrister had been barred from practice after transcripts of intercepted conversations between him and a client had been handed over to the Bar Council – to explain what was the legal position at that point in time. '[T]he state of the law might fairly be expressed', it said, in the following way:

> (a) The power to intercept letters has been exercised from the earliest times, and has been recognised in successive Acts of Parliament.
> (b) This power extends to telegrams.
> (c) It is difficult to resist the view that if there is a lawful power to intercept communications in the form of letter and telegrams, then it is wide enough to cover telephone communications as well.[3]

That legal position, uncertain – perhaps absurd – as it was, survived challenged in the English courts in *Malone*,[4] on the basis that the interception of telephone calls involved (at that time) no interference with any right protected by private or public law, demonstrating the limits of the logic of the great case of *Entick v Carrington*, whereby interferences with such rights require positive legal authority.[5] When challenged at the European Court of Human Rights at Strasbourg, however, this position was held to be contrary to Article 8 ECHR: in the absence of a clear legal basis for the interception of communications, the very obvious interference with the right to respect for private and family life that such interception involved was not, in the language of the Convention, 'in accordance with the law'.[6] This decision, of course, could have no (direct) relevance to the other Commonwealth Five Eyes states, but the wider question of the English legal position certainly did.

The basic logic of *Malone* – that at common law it was only necessary for the state to have authority to carry out activities that were otherwise contrary to law in some way – also seems to have been embraced, both before and after that case, in the other jurisdictions at issue here: what varied, if anything, was whether or not the interception of communications, whether postal or telephonic, was in a

[1] See, eg, Post Office (Revenues) Act 1710 (UK), s 40.

[2] See the discussion in PF Scott, 'The First Interception Provision: Section 4 of the Official Secrets Act 1920' (2022) 43 *Journal of Legal History* 352, 357–62.

[3] Committee of Privy Councillors appointed to inquire into the interception of Communications, *Report* (Cmnd 283, 1956–57) [51].

[4] *Malone v Metropolitan Police Commissioner* [1979] Ch 344.

[5] *Entick v Carrington* (1765) 19 Howell's State Trials 1029.

[6] *Malone v United Kingdom* (1984) 7 EHRR 14.

given place, at a given moment, contrary to law. So, for instance, the McDonald Commission in Canada observed in the early 1980s that the intelligence section of the RCMP used 'used "wire supervision" (the interception of telephone calls) for the first time in the late 1930s as a means of gathering information about suspected subversive organizations', which it could do because there was 'no statute making such a technique a crime at that time'.[7] This logic in fact persists to the present day, though usually now in reference to actions that the SIAs in the Commonwealth Five Eyes states might wish to undertake other than interception. A major review of the New Zealand legal framework, for example, includes the observation that the legislation then in force covered only a small portion of the activities of the NZSIS: 'In reality, the NZSIS undertakes a much wider range of activities that are not referenced in the legislation or subject to any legislative authorisation regime. They are currently done on the basis that they do not involve any unlawful activity.'[8] Similarly, as we shall see in section IV, the introduction of a 'special intelligence operations' regime in Australia was justified in large part on the basis that the expansion of the criminal law, and in particular rules as to secondary liability, made unlawful actions that ASIO had previously been able to undertake without legislative permission. Any consideration of the capabilities of the SIAs in the Commonwealth Five Eyes jurisdictions therefore must be attentive not only to the question of what those bodies are explicitly permitted to do by legislation, but also to that of what the legal background permits them to do without positive legal authority.[9] Public law, private law, criminal law, the law of privacy or data protection, and human rights law might all be relevant to this exercise, which can as a result be exceptionally complex.

All of the modern law of interception in the UK follows from the decision of the European Court of Human Rights in *Malone v United Kingdom*. Before it was given, however, the claim had occasionally been made that the interception of communications (in whatever form) might have some sort of basis in the royal prerogative. It is important to understand how unconvincing that claim was even at the height of its plausibility. The Birkett Report, on which later considerations across the globe placed reliance, noted that the claim had not been sustained by leading nineteenth-century considerations of the point,[10] and discussed various forms that it might take without endorsing any of them.[11] When the matter of interception was litigated in the High Court, the prerogative was not relied upon,

[7] Commission of Inquiry Concerning Certain Activities of the Royal Canadian Mounted Police, *Second Report – Volume 2: Freedom and Security Under the Law* (1981) 60.

[8] M Cullen and P Reddy, *Intelligence and Security in a Free Society: Report of the First Independent Review of Intelligence and Security in New Zealand* (2016) [6.16].

[9] Forcese and West, for example, note in their consideration of CSIS's requirement to acquire warrants for extraterritorial activity that the matter is complicated by the fact that neither the Canadian Charter nor the Criminal Code generally applies outside Canada, making 'the usual barometers signalling that CSIS needs a warrant inapplicable in extraterritorial investigations'. C Forcese and L West, *National Security Law*, 2nd edn (Irwin Law Inc, 2020) 422–23.

[10] Report of the Committee of Privy Councillors (n 3) [19]–[26].

[11] ibid [19]–[29].

the judgment making that point in terms that capture the looseness of many of its invocations in this context (and, indeed, in the national security context more broadly):[12] 'although the royal prerogative was mentioned from time to time,' said Megarry VC, 'no claim was made that there was any prerogative power to tap telephones, and so I need say nothing of that'.[13] Nor did the prerogative feature in the subsequent decision of the European Court of Human Rights. The significance of its invocation, however, derives from the fact that the prerogative was exported to the colonies – including those that later enjoyed Dominion status – by the UK in its imperial phase, and it was occasionally suggested that, alongside the established prerogative powers, there was transmitted to these jurisdictions as part of this process a power to intercept communications.[14] The Powles report in New Zealand addressed this possibility, noting that the legal basis of interception in England was uncertain – 'it may be based upon prerogative powers, common law rights, usage, implication from statutory provision or absence of legal prohibition' – but that in New Zealand the prerogative could 'afford no basis to authorise interception of postal communications in New Zealand, at least in times of peace'.[15] In New Zealand at that time, there was 'no legal basis for the interception by postal authorities of letters, telegrams, and telephone conversations in times of peace other than for the purpose of protecting postal facilities and communications and of ensuring the operation of adequate and efficient postal services'.[16] Noting that at that point in time, of the Commonwealth Five Eyes states only Canada possessed comprehensive legislation on the topic, Powles argued for the introduction of a similarly comprehensive provision permitting the interception of communications, to add to what was then a power (of contested scope)[17] to intercept postal communications.[18]

The Canadian legislation in question was the Protection of Privacy Act, which had amended the Official Secrets Act in the early 1970s so as to, first, prohibit the interception of communications, including by the Crown, and then to make the usual exception for those doing so in accordance with an authorisation. Before then the position applicable to Canada seems to have been similar to that described

[12] A point made by K Ewing, J Mahoney and A Moretta, *MI5, the Cold War, and the Rule of Law* (Oxford University Press, 2020) 20.

[13] *Malone v Metropolitan Police Commissioner* [1979] Ch 344, 356.

[14] As it was put by one writer in New Zealand, 'there appears to be no reason why a prerogative power to intercept, if it existed in England, cannot be exercised in New Zealand. When the Crown came to New Zealand the prerogative travelled with it.' G Crowder, 'The Security Intelligence Service Amendment Act 1977 and the State Power to Intercept Communications' (1978) 9 *Victoria University Wellington Law Review* 145, 147.

[15] G Powles, *Security Intelligence Service: Report by Chief Ombudsman* (1976), [16]. See the discussion in Crowder (n 14) 146–50.

[16] Powles (n 15) [16].

[17] 'I should note, however, that the view that the statutory authority must be used [only] for the purpose of protecting postal authorities and communications and ensuring the operation of adequate and efficient postal services has not been accepted by at least one of our Postmasters-Generals': ibid.

[18] ibid.

by Birkett in England, with the Mackenzie Commission in 1969 endorsing some of the conclusion of the Birkett Report and noting that legislation prohibiting interception was on the horizon:

> We think it important that any such legislation should contain a clause or clauses exempting interception operations for security purposes from the provisions of the statute. We think it reasonable however that arrangements should exist for the control of such operations. In the case of telephone interception, we think this control should be ministerial rather than judicial, since ministers are more readily aware of the full details of the cases brought to their attention, are in better position to understand the special requirements of security, and could maintain more centralized control of the complete range of wiretapping operations.[19]

The resulting legislation did exactly that, with the relevant form of authorisation able to be given by the Solicitor General of Canada (again, a member of the executive, though one with legal expertise) if he was satisfied 'by evidence on oath that such interception or seizure is necessary for the prevention or detection of subversive activity directed against Canada or detrimental to the security of Canada or is necessary for the purpose of gathering foreign intelligence information essential to the security of Canada'.[20] Unlike those given under provisions simultaneously inserted into the Criminal Code, authorisations of this type were not subject to judicial approval.[21] Powers to intercept communications were then given to CSIS when it was created in the mid-1980s,[22] though with important differences.

Following Powles' report, New Zealand followed suit, with the New Zealand Security Intelligence Service Amendment Act 1977 inserting into the 1969 Act, which gave the Service its statutory basis, a power of interception. The new provision permitted the granting, again by the Minister alone, of a warrant for the interception of 'any communication not otherwise lawfully obtainable by the person making the interception' if he or she was satisfied that a number of conditions were met. Amongst those was that the interception was necessary for either 'the detection of activities prejudicial to security' or 'the purpose of gathering foreign intelligence information essential to security', and that the value

[19] Royal Commission on Security, *Report (Abridged)* (1969) [291]–[292]. For further consideration of the (shaky) legal basis of interception in Canada, see Commission of Inquiry (n 7) 158–61.

[20] Protection of Privacy Act (Canada) (1974), s 6, inserting new provisions into the Official Secrets Act (Canada) (1939). For a critique of the weakness of these provisions, see N MacDonald, 'Electronic Surveillance in Crime Detection: An Analysis of Canadian Wiretapping Law' (1987) 10 *Dalhousie Law Journal* 141, 148–50. A range of legal and policy issues arising under s 16 were considered by Commission of Inquiry (n 7) 178–97.

[21] Compare, for instance, the provisions inserted by the Protection of Privacy Act (Canada) (1974), s 2, into the Criminal Code (Canada).

[22] CSIS Act (Canada) (1984) (as enacted), ss 21–28. For discussion, see JLlJ Edwards, 'The Canadian Security Intelligence Act 1984 – a Canadian appraisal' (1985) 5 *Oxford Journal of Legal Studies* 143, 149–50. The practice of CSIS interception under this regime is discussed in L Lustgarten and I Leigh, *In from the Cold: National Security and Parliamentary Democracy* (Oxford University Press, 1994) 80–84.

of the information it was sought to obtain was 'such as to justify the particular interception'.[23]

In Australia too, the possibility that the prerogative could found practices of interception (in this case postal interception) was mentioned by Justice Hope, who, writing at a time when legislative provision had already been made for the interception of telephonic communications in the jurisdiction, observed the claim – cited to the Birkett Report – that 'has been expressed that the Crown has a right, said to be part of the prerogative, to open and inspect mail'. Hope though denied the relevance of this to the jurisdiction of which he was writing:

> Whether or not this view is correct in England, I do not think that it is correct in Australia. In this country, particularly having regard to the federal organization of power, the question whether the Crown in right of the Commonwealth has a right to open mail would appear to depend upon the provisions of the relevant statutes.[24]

At that point in time, he suggested, 'ASIO cannot safely act on the basis that it has power to open mail, or can be authorized by the Australian Postal Commission to do so, or to inspect mail covers', but it should, Hope said, have such powers, and so he recommended legislation 'giving ASIO powers in respect of mail [that] should be in terms similar to those relating to the interception of telephonic communication'.[25]

The body of legislation referred to by Hope had started with the Telephonic Communications (Interception) Act 1960 – frequently amended over time – which prohibited interception generally but excepted that done in pursuance of a warrant, which might be given by the Attorney-General (on request of the Director-General of Security) where satisfied that the telephone was being or was likely to be used either by 'a person engaged in, or reasonably suspected by the Director-General of Security of being engaged in, or of being likely to engage in, activities prejudicial to the security of the Commonwealth' or for 'for purposes prejudicial to the security of the Commonwealth', and also that 'the interception by the Organization of communications passing to, from or over the telephone service will, or is likely to, assist the Organization in carrying out its function of obtaining intelligence relevant to the security of the Commonwealth'.[26] Here too, telephone interception had been taking place even prior to the institution of a clear legislative framework, and latterly without even ministerial approval: 'Initially,' it was later noted, 'telephone interception was verbally approved by

[23] New Zealand Security Intelligence Service Amendment Act 1977 (NZ), ss 4 and 5. For discussion, see Crowder (n 14).

[24] Royal Commission on Intelligence and Security, *Fourth Report – Volume II* (1978), 161.

[25] ibid 165.

[26] Telephonic Communications (Interception) Act 1960 (Australia). See AWLeP Darvall and DMcL Emmerson, 'Eavesdropping: Four Legal Aspects' (1962) 3 *Melbourne University Law Review* 364. At this stage there were no exceptions to the prohibition of interception for that carried out for law-enforcement purposes. For discussion of the extent of the use of this power and its successor, see HP Lee, PJ Hanks and V Morabito, *In the Name of National Security: The Legal Dimensions* (LBC Information Services, 1995) 54–55.

the Prime Minister without written approval', but '[i]n 1951, the Prime Minister delegated the power to approve telephone interception to the Director-General of Security', with the Director-General able to 'authorise the monitoring of telephones provided there was evidence "that the person concerned is engaged [in] or is reasonably suspected of subversive sabotage or espionage activity"'.[27] The powers of postal interception that Hope had recommended were then included in the ASIO Act 1979,[28] along with powers relating to the use of 'listening devices'.[29] In both cases, warrants were to be granted by Ministers. At this stage, therefore, three of the four Commonwealth Five Eyes states had a clear legal basis for interception, with any particular act of interception in all cases requiring only executive approval.

When, then, the UK legislated, following the judgment of the European Court of Human Rights in *Malone*, to provide explicitly for interception of communications – both postal and telephonic – it was (as with the granting to its security intelligence body of a statutory basis) the last of the Commonwealth Five Eyes states to take that step.[30] As with its counterparts elsewhere, the Interception of Communications Act 1985 proceeded by making it an offence to intercept communications in the course of their transmission, subject to an exception where the interception was authorised by a warrant. The power to grant warrants in the 1985 Act was exercisable by the Secretary of State:[31] the executive, rather than the judiciary, was (at least originally) entrusted with decision-making authority over this most intrusive of powers. In all jurisdictions, however, the law has evolved (and expanded) substantially over time, reflecting a range of considerations – perhaps above all else the way in which a changing technical environment makes possible the interception of communications on a scale that would have been unthinkable when these powers were first introduced.

B. The Modern Law of Interception

In the UK, different investigatory powers are provided for separately, rather than (as is sometimes the case elsewhere) there existing a general power in exercise of which one might carry out a range of different actions, of which interception is only one. The governing law (the Investigatory Powers Act 2016) makes distinct provision for what are described as 'targeted' and 'bulk' variants of certain powers,

[27] *Comprehensive Review of the Legal Framework of the National Intelligence Community*, Volume 2: *Authorisations, Immunities and Electronic Surveillance* (2019) [18.5] (references omitted).

[28] ASIO Act 1979 (Australia), s 27.

[29] ibid s 26.

[30] For the position before 1985, see Ewing, Mahoney and Moretta (n 12) ch 5; and Scott (n 2). The 1985 Act was preceded by a White Paper: Home Office, *The Interception of Communications in the United Kingdom* (Cmnd 9438, 1985).

[31] For a contemporary assessment, see I Cameron, 'Telephone Tapping and the Interception of Communications Act 1985' (1986) 37 *Northern Ireland Legal Quarterly* 126.

amongst them the power to intercept communications.[32] Warrants for targeted interception, which can take place at the behest not only of the SIAs but also various policing bodies, can be granted where necessary and proportionate on one of the following grounds: the interests of national security, for the purpose of preventing or detecting serious crime, or in the interests of the economic well-being of the UK so far as those interests are also relevant to the interests of national security.[33] This third ground – economic well-being, discussed in chapter 3 – is limited not only by the need for the interests to be relevant to the interests of national security, but also by the fact that the information it is considered necessary to obtain 'is information relating to the acts or intentions of persons outside the British Islands'.[34] The reference to 'targeted' warrants should not be allowed to mislead, however: it is not a requirement of a targeted warrant that it identify a specific individual whose communications (as sender or recipient) are to be intercepted, or a specific set of premises. Rather, a targeted interception warrant may, the statute provides, relate to 'a group of persons who share a common purpose or who carry on, or may carry on, a particular activity', or 'more than one person or organisation, or more than one set of premises, where the conduct authorised or required by the warrant is for the purposes of a single investigation or operation'.[35] This is what has been described – though the term is not used in any UK statute – as a 'thematic' or 'class' warrant,[36] and means that the question of both necessity and proportionality need not be assessed at the level of each individual but that the intercepting authorities possess an important but largely invisible discretion as to who belongs to the group of persons who share the common purpose used to determine the boundaries of a warrant: an implication that was central to the common law's historic suspicion of so-called 'general warrants',[37] and which – we shall see below – has seen class warrants rejected elsewhere. These warrants are granted in the first place by the Secretary of State but, as with most contemporary investigatory powers in the UK, come (except in cases of urgency) into force only where the decision to issue them has been approved by a Judicial Commissioner.[38] We discuss this so-called 'double-lock' further in section VI.

[32] Investigatory Powers Act 2016 (UK), pt 2, ch 1 and pt 6, ch 1. See the discussion in PF Scott, *The National Security Constitution* (Hart Publishing, 2018) 79–85.

[33] Investigatory Powers Act 2016 (UK), ss 19 and 20.

[34] ibid, s 20(4).

[35] ibid, s 17(2).

[36] For discussion of this distinction and its significance, see PF Scott, 'General Warrants, Thematic Warrants, Bulk Warrants: Property Interference for National Security Purposes' (2017) 68 *Northern Ireland Legal Quarterly* 99. The phenomenon goes back to the 1985 Act, which defined 'person' as 'any organisation and any association or combination of persons': Interception of Communications Act 1985 (UK), s 10(1).

[37] See A Tomkins and P Scott (eds), *Entick v Carrington: 250 Years of the Rule of Law* (Hart Publishing, 2015) and esp T Hickman, 'Revisiting Entick v Carrington: Seditious Libel and State Security Laws in Eighteenth-Century England' ibid 43.

[38] Investigatory Powers Act 2016 (UK), s 19(1)(d).

Bulk interception warrants, including those for the bulk interception of communications, do not need to be targeted at specific persons, and so can (in accordance with their 'bulk' nature) be used to intercept the communications of people who are not, and could never conceivably be, of specific interest to the SIAs. Reflecting this difference, bulk warrants are available to a more limited set of actors (only the SIAs) on a more limited set of grounds (either national security alone or national security in conjunction with one of the other grounds), and must in the first place be aimed at 'overseas-related' communications, being those that are either sent to or received by persons outside the British Islands.[39] Though the SIAs are in effect indemnified against the interception of non-overseas-related communications if it is necessary to intercept them in order to do what the warrant authorises,[40] there are limits on what might be done with the material acquired via bulk interception. Most importantly, it cannot be searched using factors 'referable' to a person known to be in the British Islands – the regime, that is, employs a geographic distinction – in order to select communications for examination (and so avoid the need to demonstrate the necessity and proportionality of intercepting that particular person's communications).[41] If the SIAs wish to search bulk material for that reason, they require a targeted examination warrant, given out on the same grounds as a targeted interception warrant.[42] This scheme has so far been held to be compatible with the ECHR, in light not only of the specific limitations to which the various powers of interception are subject, but also the broader landscape of oversight and review that surrounds those and other investigatory powers,[43] some aspects of which are discussed in later chapters. Predictably, many more targeted warrants are issued than bulk warrants: 4,574 of the former and 30 of the latter were issued in 2022, with 74 targeted examination warrants issued in order to permit searches of bulk intercept material that would otherwise be prohibited.[44]

By comparison with this complex scheme, the modern statutory framework in New Zealand is very bare. The Intelligence and Security Act 2017 provides for two types of intelligence warrants (described simply as 'Type 1' and 'Type 2' warrants) that permit the carrying out of certain otherwise unlawful activities, with the type to be used in any specific case determined by the status of those who are to be targeted by it – a point discussed in section V. It suffices for now to note that a Type 1 warrant is necessary if a New Zealand SIA proposes to collect information about, or do anything in relation to, either a person who is a New Zealand citizen or permanent resident, or a class of persons that includes

[39] ibid, s 136.
[40] ibid, s 136(5)(a).
[41] ibid, ss 152(3)(a) and (4).
[42] ibid, s 152(3)(d).
[43] *R (National Council for Civil Liberties) v Secretary of State for the Home Department* [2023] EWCA Civ 926.
[44] Investigatory Powers Commissioner, *Annual Report of the Investigatory Powers Commissioner 2022* (HC 2023-24, 364) table 19.2.

such a person.[45] These Type 1 warrants are subject to greater safeguards than are their Type 2 equivalent. They must be issued by the Minister and a Commissioner of Intelligence Warrants, both of whom must be satisfied that the relevant conditions are met; Type 2 warrants need be issued only by the Minister.[46] There are two varieties of Type 1 warrant. One relates to national security and – broadly – involves assessing, or protecting against, certain specific harms, including (for example) terrorism or violent extremism, sabotage or proliferation of weapons of mass destruction. The harms also include, however, 'espionage or other foreign intelligence activity' that is 'directed at a New Zealand interest', 'carried out by a person who is a New Zealand citizen or permanent resident of New Zealand', or 'occurs in New Zealand'.[47] It does not, therefore, encompass foreign intelligence activity outside of New Zealand or carried out inside New Zealand by those who are neither citizens nor permanent residents of the country. The second variety of Type 1 warrant permits the SIAs to carry out an activity that will contribute either to the 'international relations and well-being of New Zealand' or 'the economic well-being of New Zealand', and requires that a person (or person within a class of persons) in respect of whom the activity is to be carried out is, in effect, a foreign agent.[48] A Type 2 warrant may be issued where the authorising Minister is satisfied that its issuing will permit an SIA to carry out an activity that is either 'necessary to contribute to the protection of national security' or, alternatively, will contribute to either the international relations and well-being of New Zealand or the economic well-being of New Zealand.[49] It must also be the case that the activity in question is not in respect of a person or class of persons whose involvement would make the seeking of a Type 1 warrant necessary.[50] Notably, however, there appears to be a degree of disagreement amongst relevant bodies as to whether or not a Type 1 warrant is needed for the incidental collection of New Zealanders' communications under a Type 2 warrant, and if so on what standard: when such incidental collection is likely, or merely possible, or so on.[51] The substance of this disagreement is perhaps less important than is what it confirms: that incidental collection might result from the lawful interception of communications.

Finally, in New Zealand, intelligence warrants – of whatever type – can be authorised on a 'class' basis: the 2017 Act requires merely that they specify 'the person or class of persons (if any) in respect of whom the otherwise unlawful

[45] Intelligence and Security Act 2017 (NZ), s 53.
[46] ibid, ss 57 and 60.
[47] ibid, s 58.
[48] ibid, s 59.
[49] ibid, s 60.
[50] ibid, s 60(3)(b).
[51] T Arnold and M Mahuika, *Taumaru: Protecting Aotearoa New Zealand as a Free, Open and Democratic Society* (2023), [7.36]. And see also Inspector-General of Intelligence and Security, *Warrants issued under the Intelligence and Security Act 2017* (2018) [136]–[142]; and Inspector-General of Intelligence and Security, *Warrants issued under the Intelligence and Security Act 2017–2019 update* (2019) [20]–[24].

activity is being carried out'.[52] Such 'class' or 'thematic' warrants,[53] in which specific individuals are not identified but a class of persons is, were previously only available to the GCSB, and only in respect of interception.[54] In an early consideration of warrants under the 2017 Act, the IGIS expressed concern about the precision with which the relevant classes were being defined, arguing that it must be 'tolerably clear who will fall within the class and who will not' as the

> necessity and proportionality of proposed activities against a class of targets cannot be analysed properly if the definition of the class is abstract and imprecise, or essentially subjective; nor is it possible to articulate or envisage the full range of privacy interests engaged.[55]

These points have been reaffirmed in relation to specific class warrants issued to the NZSIS, in which – the Inspector-General said – the targeted classes 'were too broad and required too subjective of an assessment to justify the prior authorisation of the most intrusive powers against individuals who may fall within the target classes', giving the Service 'too wide a discretion to operate without any external scrutiny of the case against any particular target'.[56] They did not, therefore, meet the statutory requirements of necessity and proportionality. But alongside the legal issues was an important point of policy: the IGIS expressed the view that even where a class warrant can lawfully be issued, 'there should be a preference for individual warrants, all other things being equal, as this provides for better oversight of the Service's activities, greater protection of individual rights and a greater safeguard against agency overreach'.[57]

What sort of activities might be authorised under the warrant is laid out only very briefly in statute, but includes 'intercepting any private communications or classes of private communications' alongside a range of other activities, including the conduct of surveillance, search and seizure, and the use of human intelligence,[58]

[52] Intelligence and Security Act 2017 (NZ), s 66(e). The reviewers recommended the inclusion of provision for what were described as 'purpose-based' warrants, which would 'specify the type of information sought and the operational purposes for which it is required rather than identifying a particular person, premise or thing as the target' (Cullen and Reddy (n 8) [6.57]), but though the Bill originally made provision for such warrants, this was removed during the legislative process.

[53] Confirming the principle, other activities that might be authorised include 'conducting surveillance in respect of 1 or more' of the categories of 'persons or classes of persons', 'places or classes of places' and 'things or classes of things': Intelligence and Security Act 2017 (NZ), s 67(1)(a).

[54] It was suggested that this caused problems: 'For example, the NZSIS may be aware that a foreign delegation is travelling to New Zealand with intelligence agents as part of the group, but they may not know the identity of the intelligence agents until they are on their way to, or have arrived in, the country. Under the current scheme, the NZSIS could not obtain a warrant in advance to target those people on arrival.' Cullen and Reddy (n 8) [6.15].

[55] Inspector-General of Intelligence and Security, *Warrants issued under the Intelligence and Security Act 2017* (n 51) [109]. And see also ibid [143]–[148] on the question of what level of certainty is required that a person is a member of the defined class.

[56] Inspector-General of Intelligence and Security, *Review of NZSIS counter-terrorism and violent-extremism class warrants – Public Report* (2024) 1.

[57] ibid 1. See also Inspector-General of Intelligence and Security, *Annual Report 2022–2023* (2023) 5–6.

[58] Intelligence and Security Act 2017 (NZ), s 67.

and so this scheme includes the SIAs' power to intercept communications. In giving effect to an intelligence warrant, both the NZSIS and the GCSB might do a range of things in order to give effect to that warrant, including for example, install and use an 'interception device' (being 'any electronic, mechanical, electromagnetic, optical, or electro-optical instrument, apparatus, equipment, or other device that is used or is capable of being used to intercept communications'),[59] and may also 'do any other act that is reasonable in the circumstances and reasonably required to achieve the purposes for which the warrant was issued'.[60]

Though it has only been in place for a short period, the distinction between Type 1 and Type 2 warrants has already come under pressure, in part because of the uncertainty noted above as to incidental collection of New Zealanders' information under a Type 2 warrant. In their review of the 2017 Act, Arnold and Mahuika recommended the abolition of the distinction, noting that

> the Agencies commonly obtain 'partner' warrants – Type 1 and Type 2 warrants together – which means that the distinction is effectively meaningless. It creates unnecessary work for the Agencies and for those who issue warrants for no purpose. We therefore do not believe there is merit in retaining this distinction.[61]

Their proposal was, in effect, one for levelling up: making all warrants subject to the additional requirements currently applicable only to Type 1 warrants, and so increasing the level of protection enjoyed by non-New Zealanders to that currently enjoyed by New Zealanders (both citizens and permanent residents).[62] A range of further, generic criteria – including the proportionality of the proposed activity to the purpose for which it is to be carried out – apply to all intelligence warrants, whether of Type 1 or Type 2.[63] Finally, reflecting the possibility of incidental interception noted above, the 2017 Act requires destruction of 'unauthorised information' (including 'information unintentionally obtained' that is outside the scope of an authorisation),[64] though the specific import of that provision has been disputed.[65] Information that has, in the alternative, been incidentally obtained, may be retained only for the purpose of passing it on to certain bodies or categories thereof, for one of a number of specified purposes. The bodies in question include, notably, 'any public authority (whether in New Zealand or overseas) that the Director-General considers should receive the information', and the grounds include 'identifying, preventing, or responding to threats or potential threats to the security or defence of New Zealand or any other country'.[66] Material incidentally obtained via lawful interception in accordance

[59] ibid, ss 68(1)(b)(iii) and 47.
[60] ibid, s 68(1)(l).
[61] Arnold and Mahuika (n 51) [7.31].
[62] ibid [7.32].
[63] Intelligence and Security Act 2017 (NZ), s 61.
[64] ibid, s 102.
[65] Arnold and Mahuika (n 51) [8.21]–[8.27].
[66] Intelligence and Security Act 2017 (NZ), s 104.

with a warrant could therefore be retained for communication to, for example, a Five Eyes partner for national security purposes.

In Canada, CSIS can be granted a warrant permitting it to

> intercept any communication or obtain any information, record, document or thing and, for that purpose,
>
> (a) to enter any place or open or obtain access to any thing;
> (b) to search for, remove or return, or examine, take extracts from or make copies of or record in any other manner the information, record, document or thing; or
> (c) to install, maintain or remove any thing.[67]

A warrant must specify, amongst other things, 'the type of communication authorized to be intercepted' and 'the identity of the person, if known, whose communication is to be intercepted'.[68] This sounds like what I have called above 'targeted interception', though the 'if known' caveat may work to undermine to some extent the requirement of specificity.[69] The grounds for the making of an application are that the requesting party (in the first place the Director of CSIS) believes that the warrant is required to permit CSIS to investigate (whether inside or outside of Canada)[70] threats to the security of Canada or otherwise to perform its statutory functions.[71] Warrants of this sort are ultimately granted not by the Minister – whose approval for the making of an application is however required – but by a judge,[72] a point discussed in section VI of this chapter. Within the application for a warrant, CSIS may request that it be permitted to retain information collected incidentally in the execution of a warrant as a dataset,[73] and it is now therefore the case that one of the things that must be specified within a warrant is, 'when it is anticipated that information would be incidentally collected in the execution of a warrant, the grounds on which the retention of the information by the Service is likely to assist it' in the performance of certain of its duties or functions.[74]

[67] CSIS Act (1984) (Canada), s 21(3). Reporting suggests that only a few dozen such warrants are sought and issued each year: National Security and Intelligence Review Agency, *2022 Annual Report* (2023) 8.

[68] CSIS Act (1984) (Canada), s 21(2).

[69] In *Application for warrants pursuant to s 21 of the Canadian Security Intelligence Service Act, Re* (19 September 1997), the Federal Court was called upon to rule upon the proposed inclusion in a warrant of a clause the effect of which, McGillis J said, would be to 'vest in a Service employee the discretion to apply the terms of the warrant against a person, without a judge ever scrutinizing the evidence to determine whether intrusive powers ought to be used against that individual'. This was rejected as an unlawful delegation of the judicial function under the CSIS Act.

[70] This language was inserted by the Protection of Canada from Terrorists Act, SC 2015, c 9 (Canada) to reverse, in effect, the decision of the Federal Court in *Canadian Security Intelligence Service Act, Re* 2008 FC 301. Also inserted was s 21(3.1), which provides that '[w]ithout regard to any other law, including that of any foreign state, a judge may, in a warrant issued under subsection (3), authorize activities outside Canada to enable the Service to investigate a threat to the security of Canada'.

[71] CSIS Act (1984) (Canada), s 21(1).

[72] ibid.

[73] ibid, s 21(1.1).

[74] ibid, s 21(2)(d.1).

Alongside this power of interception on the part of CSIS, the CSE may seek a Foreign Intelligence Authorization (FIA), permitting it to 'carry out, on or through the global information infrastructure, any activity specified in the authorization in the furtherance of the foreign intelligence aspect of its mandate'.[75] The aspect in question is 'to acquire, covertly or otherwise, information from or through the global information infrastructure, including by engaging or interacting with foreign entities located outside Canada or by using any other method of acquiring information, and to use, analyse and disseminate the information for the purpose of providing foreign intelligence, in accordance with the Government of Canada's intelligence priorities'.[76] 'Foreign intelligence' here means 'information or intelligence about the capabilities, intentions or activities of a foreign individual, state, organization or terrorist group, as they relate to international affairs, defence or security'.[77] Action under this aspect of the CSE's mandate does not per se require an FIA: instead, one will be required whenever CSE's activities in pursuit of that part of its mandate involve either the contravention of any Canadian statute or 'the acquisition by the Establishment of information from or through the global information infrastructure that interferes with the reasonable expectation of privacy of a Canadian or a person in Canada'.[78] This will not always be the case: indeed, the CSE's activities in pursuit of this aspect of its mandate must not be 'directed at a Canadian or at any person in Canada'.[79] Nevertheless, amongst the activities an FIA may authorise in pursuit of that aspect are to be found 'gaining access to a portion of the global information infrastructure' and 'acquiring information on or through the global information infrastructure, including unselected information'.[80] This is, then, what has been described above as 'bulk interception' and, as with all bulk interception, it is likely, if not in fact inevitable, that carrying it out will involve the incidental collection of information about Canadians or those living in Canada, with the Act in fact providing that the Establishment 'may acquire information relating to a Canadian or a person in Canada incidentally in the course of carrying out activities under', amongst other things, an FIA.[81] As a result of this apparent inevitability, it seems that the acquisition of an FIA 'may often be the default procedure for classes of foreign intelligence collection activities'.[82] Against this background, the Communications Security Establishment Act of 2019 requires – in general terms – that 'measures are in place to protect the privacy of Canadians and of persons in Canada in the use, analysis, retention and disclosure' of, amongst others things, information relating to such persons which acquired in the foreign intelligence aspect of its mandate.[83]

[75] Communications Security Establishment Act (2019) (Canada), s 26(1).
[76] ibid, s 16.
[77] ibid, s 2.
[78] ibid, s 22(3).
[79] ibid, s 22(1).
[80] ibid, s 26(2).
[81] ibid, s 23(4).
[82] Forcese and West (n 9) 451.
[83] Communications Security Establishment Act (2019) (Canada), s 24.

The granting of an FIA is by the Minister on the written application of the Chief of the CSE, with the Minister permitted to issue it only if he or she first concludes that 'there are reasonable grounds to believe that any activity that would be authorized by it is reasonable and proportionate, having regard to the nature of the objective to be achieved and the nature of the activities'.[84] In relation to FIAs – and not other types of authorisation under the Communications Security Establishment Act – the Minister must also conclude, if he or she is to issue one, that there are 'reasonable grounds to believe' three further things. One is that 'any information acquired under the authorization could not reasonably be acquired by other means and will be retained for no longer than is reasonably necessary'. The second is that, where the Authorization permits the acquisition of 'unselected information' – that is, information 'acquired, for technical or operational reasons, without the use of terms or criteria to identify information of foreign intelligence interest' – the 'unselected information' in question 'could not reasonably be acquired by other means'. The third is that measures the statute otherwise requires the CSE to put in place will ensure that 'information acquired under the authorization that is identified as relating to a Canadian or a person in Canada will be used, analysed or retained only if the information is essential to international affairs, defence or security'.[85] And so though the fact that is done in pursuit of the foreign intelligence aspect of CSE's mandate means that Canadians cannot be targeted by an FIA, there is ample scope for incidental collection, and then use, of information about them. Reflecting the level of their intrusiveness, and its implications for Canadians, FIAs must, once they have been made by the Minister, be passed for approval to the Intelligence Commissioner, who must review whether the Minister's conclusion as to the whether the relevant criteria are met is 'reasonable'.[86] FIAs are valid only once that approval has been given in writing.[87]

In Australia, where comprehensive legislation for the interception of communications was first put in place – and where much of the law is based on a somewhat baroque and unhelpful distinction between 'live' and 'stored' communications – the relevant legislation is now the (much-amended and notoriously complex) Telecommunications (Interception and Access) Act 1979,[88]

[84] ibid, s 34(1).

[85] ibid, s 34(2).

[86] Intelligence Commissioner Act (2019) (Canada), ss 12 and 13. For observations on when and why FIAs have not been approved, or approved only in part, see Intelligence Commissioner, *2023 Annual Report of the Intelligence Commissioner* (2024) 13–14. See in particular the claim that 'issuing an authorization is a ministerial responsibility that cannot be delegated. It is a heavy responsibility because authorized activities could contravene Canadian laws and intrude on the privacy interests of Canadians. Parliament is asking the Minister no less than to personally confirm that CSE is justified in carrying out unlawful activities.' (ibid).

[87] Communications Security Establishment Act (2019) (Canada), s 28(1).

[88] Speaking generally about the framework of which the Telecommunications (Interception and Access) Act 1979 is a prominent part, the *Comprehensive Review* noted that it is 'complex to the point of being opaque, creating challenges for agencies seeking to comply with the law, oversight bodies seeking to scrutinise agencies' conduct and the public seeking to understand agencies' powers': *Comprehensive Review* (n 27) [26.71]. A subsequent discussion paper noted that in order to 'keep pace

which (like its predecessors) prohibits interception and creates a number of exceptions, most importantly where the interception takes place under a warrant.[89] Two types of warrant are relevant. One is aimed at a 'telecommunications service' – such as a telephone number – and can be given where one of three conditions is met: either the service is being or is likely to be 'used by a person engaged in, or reasonably suspected by the Director-General of Security of being engaged in, or of being likely to engage in, activities prejudicial to security'; or the service is 'the means by which a person receives or sends a communication from or to another person who is engaged in, or reasonably suspected by the Director-General of Security of being engaged in, or of being likely to engage in, such activities';[90] or the service is 'used for purposes prejudicial to security'. Whichever circumstance is at issue, it must also be the case that intercepting communications made to or from that service 'will, or is likely to, assist the Organisation in carrying out its function of obtaining intelligence relating to security'.[91] Though this is not targeted interception in the sense of a specific person being named, a request for such a warrant must include 'a description of the service sufficient to identify it', including (amongst other things) 'the name, address and occupation of the subscriber (if any) to the service', and must specify 'the facts and other grounds on which the Director-General of Security considers it necessary that the warrant should be issued and, where relevant, the grounds on which the Director-General of Security suspects a person of being engaged in, or of being likely to engage in, activities prejudicial to security'.[92]

The primary criterion for the making of a warrant of the second type – a 'named person warrant', originally introduced in 2000 to address the problem that 'a person may subscribe to multiple services by acquiring several pre-paid mobile telephone services which may be used in one telephone handset, and swapped around and discarded at will'[93] – is that the granter of the warrant is satisfied that 'the person is engaged in, or reasonably suspected by the Director-General of Security of being engaged in, or of being likely to engage in, activities prejudicial to security'.[94] That named person warrants are logically secondary to telecommunication service warrants, however, is shown by the fact that for the Attorney-General to grant a named person warrant, he or she must also be satisfied that relying on a telecommunication service warrant would be 'ineffective'.[95]

with technology and the criminals who seek to exploit it, the Government has amended the [1979 Act] more than 100 times, with most amendments occurring in the past 15 years': Department of Home Affairs, *Reform of Australia's Electronic Surveillance Framework: Discussion Paper* (2021) 5.

[89] Telecommunications (Interception and Access) Act 1979 (Australia), s 7.

[90] For a discussion of the circumstances of the addition of this provision, and a critique, see D Hume and G Williams, 'Who's Listening? Intercepting the telephone calls, emails and SMS's of innocent people' (2006) 31 *Alternative Law Journal* 211.

[91] Telecommunications (Interception and Access) Act 1979 (Australia), s 9(1).

[92] ibid, s 9(2).

[93] Senate Legal and Constitutional Legislation Committee, *Inquiry into the Provisions of the Telecommunications (Interception) Legislation Amendment Bill 1999* (2000) [1.3] (note).

[94] Telecommunications (Interception and Access) Act 1979 (Australia), s 9A(1).

[95] ibid, s 9A(1)(c).

The general position is that a named person warrant authorises the interception of communications that are 'being made to or from any telecommunications service that the person is using, or is likely to use' or that are 'being made by means of a telecommunications device or telecommunications devices, identified in the warrant, that the person is using, or is likely to use'.[96] Interception warrants of whatever type also permit access to 'stored communications' such as voicemails.[97] In both cases, telecommunication service warrants and named person warrants, warrants are granted by the Attorney-General with – as discussed in section VI – no judicial involvement.

Analogues of both type of warrant are also available for the collection of foreign intelligence,[98] along with a third type, a 'foreign communications warrant',[99] with the relevant rules having been amended – quickly and with little scrutiny – by the Foreign Intelligence Legislation Amendment Act 2021.[100] In each case, the key criterion for the collection of foreign intelligence relating to the matter specified in the application for the warrant is that 'obtaining of foreign intelligence relating to that matter is in the interests of Australia's national security, Australia's foreign relations or Australia's national economic well-being'. In relation to foreign communications warrants, the Attorney-General must also be satisfied that 'relying on a telecommunications service warrant or a named person warrant to obtain the intelligence would be ineffective'.[101] A foreign communications warrant, as its name suggests, is one aimed ultimately at 'foreign communications', defined to mean communications 'sent or received outside Australia',[102] but it permits the interception of communications generally in order to acquire foreign intelligence from such communications.[103] There are no associated requirements of specification – not of telecommunications systems, nor of persons or anything else. This is therefore, at least potentially, and probably in practice, 'bulk' interception. Reflecting the fact that there is no limit on what is intercepted – and so communications that are not 'foreign' might lawfully be intercepted under a foreign communications warrant – a request for such a warrant must, amongst other things, 'specify how the interception of communications is proposed to be conducted under the warrant, including how the risk of intercepting domestic communications will be minimised'.[104] Domestic communications

[96] ibid, s 9A(1A).
[97] ibid, ss 9(1A) and 9A(1C).
[98] ibid, ss 11A and 11B.
[99] ibid, s 11C.
[100] See Parliamentary Joint Committee on Intelligence and Security, *Advisory Report on the Foreign Intelligence Legislation Amendment Bill 2021* (2021) [1.2], noting that the Committee had agreed the Government's request 'to expeditiously consider this legislation in a private inquiry' and (ibid [1.32]) that the Bill 'aligns Australia with the Five Eyes community but with a stronger set of safeguards'.
[101] Telecommunications (Interception and Access) Act 1979 (Australia), s 11C(1)(b)(iii).
[102] ibid, s 5.
[103] Under s 11(1), that is, such a warrant permits the interception of communications 'for the purpose of obtaining foreign intelligence relating to a matter specified in the notice from foreign communications intercepted under the warrant' – ie it is not limited to the interception of foreign communications.
[104] Telecommunications (Interception and Access) Act 1979 (Australia), s 11C(3)(a).

are, in this context, all communications that are not foreign communications.[105] Moreover, a procedure must be put in place for screening and destroying all domestic communications intercepted under a foreign communications warrant, other than one that 'relates, or appears to relate, to activities that present a significant risk to a person's life'.[106] Along with the other foreign intelligence warrants, foreign communications warrants cannot be sought for the purpose of collecting information about a citizen or permanent resident of Australia, unless the Director-General of ASIO 'reasonably suspects that the person is acting for, or on behalf of, a foreign power'.[107] Once again, there is general, heightened protection for those who 'belong' to the state, which is effectively denied to or withdrawn from those who are acting as foreign agents.

In the *Comprehensive Review* of the legislative framework applying to the Australian Intelligence Community, it was claimed that most of ASIO's powers were available only on an individual basis rather than on a class basis, but it was also noted that the UK and New Zealand, as described, have made provision allowing for the granting of class-based warrants for, amongst other things, the interception of communications. It is therefore striking that the *Review*, in the context of its recommendations that the statutory framework discussed above should be replaced by a new 'Electronic Surveillance Act', rejected the idea of making such class-based warrants available generally to ASIO:

> Currently, all of ASIO's warrant based powers are targeted, either in respect of a person, place or thing … this has a number of benefits. Importantly, it minimises the potential for innocent people to be intruded upon, and ensures the Attorney-General (rather than unelected officials) determines when, and against whom, use by ASIO of these powers will be justified. This helps to assure the public that these powers are only exercised in tightly limited and controlled situations. Class based warrants are, by definition, less targeted.[108]

In the context in which bulk interception has become normalised in some jurisdictions, it is striking to see this sort of resistance to the introduction of even 'class' warrants for the domestic security bodies, even if the changes made by 2021 Act indicate that this resistance was not shared by the Government, at least in so far as foreign intelligence was concerned. A subsequent discussion paper accepted the necessity for bringing the relevant legislation up to date, noting that parts of it 'reflect technological assumptions and definitions dating back to the 1960s':

> When the framework was designed, the Government owned telecommunications in Australia. Since then, the technological environment has evolved to the global telecommunications market we see today. The legislation was originally designed to protect the privacy of fixed line phone calls and telegrams. Over time, a patchwork

[105] ibid, s 11C(12).
[106] ibid, s 11C(6).
[107] iibd, s 11D(5).
[108] *Comprehensive Review* (n 27) [20.32].

of amendments has been necessary to uphold the same principles and address technological advances – including the use of computers, emails, texts, 'over-the-top' messaging applications and social media.[109]

Reflecting, however, the magnitude of the task, progress towards the goal of providing a new, comprehensive, legal framework for electronic surveillance in Australia appears to have been slow, the decision to enact the Foreign Intelligence Legislation Amendment Act 2021 indicating a desire to go ahead with changes perceived to be desirable without awaiting that larger project.

The other relevant legal framework for interception is that found in the Intelligence Services Act 2001, which governs both ASIS and the ASD. An interesting aspect of this regime has been identified. That is, we have noted above that in most cases the need for a warrant (or analogue) derives from the fact that what is being permitted thereunder is otherwise unlawful – the warrant cures the prima facie unlawfulness of what it authorises. The regime under the 2001 Act, however, has been claimed to operate on a different principle: 'Instead of authorising activities that would otherwise be unlawful, they allow additional ministerial control over intelligence collection activities because the legislature – and, through it, the public – has determined additional control to be desirable.'[110] This is given effect by a requirement, in the 2001 Act, that the relevant Minister make a direction requiring that the relevant SIA seek an authorisation in order to do certain things, including, for example, undertaking an activity for the purpose of 'producing intelligence on an Australian person', and a power to specify other activities or classes of activities for which authorisation is required.[111] Where that is the case, an authorisation can be given only where the Minister is satisfied, for example, that 'any activities which may be done in reliance on the authorisation will be necessary for the proper performance of a function of the agency concerned' and 'there are satisfactory arrangements in place to ensure that nothing will be done in reliance on the authorisation beyond what is necessary for the proper performance of a function of the agency'.[112] For many of the activities in question, the Minister must also be satisfied that the relevant Australian person (or, where relevant, class of such persons) is or is likely to be involved in one of a range of activities, including 'acting for, or on behalf of, a foreign power' or 'activities that are, or are likely to be, a threat to security'.[113] In keeping with the notion that this is primarily about ministerial control rather than legal permission, however, the presence of an authorisation is not required to immunise the relevant persons against any liability that might arise for these activities. Rather, the 2001 Act provides that members of staff are 'not subject to any civil or criminal liability for any act done outside Australia if the act is done in the

[109] Department of Home Affairs (n 88) 3.
[110] *Comprehensive Review*, Volume 2 (n 27) [19.110].
[111] Intelligence Services Act 2001 (Australia), s 8(1).
[112] ibid, s 9(1).
[113] ibid, s 9(1A).

proper performance of a function of the agency'.[114] This encompasses a range of activities that might be carried out without an authorisation, including – it seems inevitable – interception of communications, but only if carried out outside of Australia (which will of course then raise the question of the legality of those actions under the law of the jurisdiction in which those acts are carried out instead).[115]

The *Comprehensive Review* noted that authorisations under the 2001 Act can be granted on a class basis only in certain, limited circumstances, and endorsed a proposal to add to those circumstances already specified in the legislation. It rejected, however, a proposal to make class-based authorisations available to ASIS and the ASD on a general basis, noting that this would allow the Minister to designate a class of persons and then the relevant body to determine whether an individual fell within it, and rejected the proposal on the same sort of grounds that have been identified elsewhere:

> 20.66 … The minister would only be limited by his or her ability to identify a class of Australian persons who would all meet one of the grounds set out in the IS Act. This could be incredibly broad.
>
> 20.67 In addition, it would then be up to the IS Act agency to determine which individuals fall within that class. The minister would not have visibility of the individuals targeted by the IS Act agency until after the activities had already been undertaken, if at all.
>
> 20.68 Further, the public and legislature would have no oversight or visibility of the *class* the minister identifies, let alone the individuals an agency determines to have fallen within it …[116]

This, of course, does not affect the ability of the relevant SIAs to lawfully undertake activity – outside Australia – aimed at those who are not 'Australian persons', perhaps including what is elsewhere described as bulk interception. The only requirement for attracting general legal immunity is, we have seen, that the relevant act be 'done in the proper performance of a function of the agency'.

III. Bulk Data

The different legal regimes that govern interception of communications by the SIAs of the Commonwealth Five Eyes states demonstrate significant variation.

[114] ibid, s 14(1).

[115] Of possible relevance here – though the country in question is not named – is a report by the New Zealand's IGIS regarding the GCSB's 'hosting of a signals intelligence system deployed by a foreign agency and also taking part in a wider intelligence programme related to this capability', with the IGIS noting (at 10) that it 'seems clear the decision to sign the [Memorandum of Understanding] and host the capability was not put to the Minister responsible for the GCSB, or any other Minister' and that the hosting was therefore 'improper': Inspector-General of Intelligence and Security, *Inquiry into GCSB's hosting of a foreign capability* (2024).

[116] *Comprehensive Review*, Volume 2 (n 27) [20.66]–[20.68].

Whatever the common legal origin – and most considerations of the point, we have noted, are rightly sceptical of the claim that the practice possessed a foundation in the prerogative – the statutory bases have evolved in quite different directions, buffeted by historical contingencies and related to questions about when and where practices of interception were prohibited in the first place. Similar contingencies are reflected in the questions of what analogous powers exist and what specific form they take: whether distinct regimes are required, for example, in relation to access to metadata (the 'who', 'what' and 'when' of communications, separate from their content but no less revealing for it) or for the 'hacking' of electronic systems. Here, the various regimes would seem to differ too greatly, not only in their detail but also at the high level, in order to be usefully catalogued and contrasted. One question that is worth considering, however, is one that also relates to the vast technological environment that has driven evolution in both the law and practice of the interception of communications: the use of what we might call 'bulk data' by the SIAs. That is, in the modern world, vast amounts of data are created, stored and used by all manner of organisations – both those that are part of the state and those that are not. It is obvious that there are an infinite number of ways in which that data might be useful to the SIAs, and so the question arises of whether and under what conditions the SIAs might acquire that data in fulfilment of their functions, and what – if any regulation – exists of their own ability to retain and exploit bulk data of this sort. Again, we see the extent to which the SIAs' toolbox is framed in the first place by the question of what it is they require legal authority to do, and that in turn by the question of what it is prima facie unlawful to do. Where interception is barely and straightforwardly criminalised by each jurisdiction, however, there is in the context of (bulk) data much more variation, given the number of intersecting and overlapping regimes: the criminal law, the relevant law of fundamental rights, and the law of privacy or data protection or similar (from the ordinary operation of which the SIAs are in all cases at least partially exempt). The result of these differences in legal background – mapping the detail of which would take us far beyond the subject at hand – is that there are significant and interesting variations in the modern law and practice on what might nevertheless be understood as a single theme: the SIAs' use of bulk data and its treatment by law.

In New Zealand, as the IGIS has recently reaffirmed, in a report on the SIAs' use of bulk data, that SIAs can generally 'access, download, retain, and use publicly available information without doing anything unlawful and so with no need' for any sort of authorisation under the Intelligence and Security Act 2017.[117] That Act does, though – against the background of a statutory (re)recognition of the power of the SIAs to request information from public and private bodies, and

[117] Inspector-General of Intelligence and Security, *Review of the GCSB's acquisition and use of bulk personal datasets – Public Report* (2024) [8].

of those bodies (subject to limits) to provide it[118] – provide for direct access by the SIAs to certain databases storing public-sector information, as long as there exists a written agreement between the responsible Ministers.[119] These databases include, for example, those holding data about births, death and marriages, that which holds citizenship information and that which holds information about immigration.[120] This last example is particularly salient: an IGIS report published shortly after the enactment of the 2017 Act found that there had previously been 'systemic unlawful access on a large scale' by NZSIS to data regarding the movement of people and goods across the New Zealand border.[121] An agreement for access to these various databases can be made only if both the relevant Minister and that responsible for the agency in question, having consulted the Privacy Commissioner and the Inspector-General, are satisfied that: 'direct access to the information is necessary to enable the intelligence and security agency to perform any of its functions'; 'there are adequate safeguards to protect the privacy of individuals, including that the proposed compliance and audit requirements for the direct access, use, disclosure, and retention of the information are sufficient'; and 'the agreement will include appropriate procedures for direct access, use, disclosure, and retention of the information'.[122] Amongst the information that must be specified in such an agreement are the 'the circumstances (if any) in which the information may be disclosed to another agency (whether in New Zealand or overseas), and how that disclosure may be made'.[123] The default rule is that such agreements must be made public, but they can be withheld and a summary published instead.[124]

So, for example, the Direct Access Agreement between NZSIS and the Minister of Internal Affairs regarding access to birth (etc) information held by the Register General and citizenship information held by the Minister identifies a number of purposes for which NZSIS might access the relevant databases, including 'identifying persons of security or intelligence interest and their familial details by obtaining and corroborating their biographical or familial details and/or the details of family members (ie intelligence collection and analysis)'

[118] Intelligence and Security Act 2017 (NZ), ss 120–122. The language used here is that of 'agencies', but the statute provides (at s 118) that agency means 'any person, whether in the public sector or the private sector'.

[119] ibid, s 125. And see also the recommendations about reform of this regime in Arnold and Mahuika (n 51) recommendation 16, including that the relevant schedule to the 2017 Act should be amended 'to remove the list of databases accessible to the Agencies, but retain the names of the holder agencies … with which either the GCSB or the NZSIS may enter into direct access agreements' and that the Government 'should consider undertaking further policy work on the appropriateness of the Agencies having direct access to non-public sector agency databases containing information in respect of which there may be a reasonable expectation of privacy'.

[120] Intelligence and Security Act 2017 (NZ), sch 2.

[121] Inspector-General of Intelligence and Security, *Lawfulness of NZSIS access to data under the Customs and Excise Act 1996 and the Immigration Act 2009* (2017).

[122] Intelligence and Security Act 2017 (NZ), s 126.

[123] ibid, s 129.

[124] ibid, s 131.

and 'conducting searches in response to other information held by NZSIS', including 'target discovery, in which NZSIS would use indicators (or other relevant frameworks) to identify previously individual persons of concern'.[125] The Agreement refers to the existence of classified Ministerial Authorisation, which permits the sharing of intelligence, including information derived from these databases, with – most notably – 'a number of specified overseas public authorities (including agencies from Australia, Canada, the United Kingdom and the United States of America)'.[126] The fruits of the Direct Access Agreement might also, therefore, be made availableto SIAs in other Five Eyes states. The access of the New Zealand SIAs to publicly available information is also the subject of a Ministerial Policy Statement, which sets out – amongst other things – a range of principles (including privacy, necessity and proportionality) that must be taken into account when the two bodies are obtaining, collecting and using publicly available information.[127] A further Ministerial Policy Statement sets out principles for the management and use of information obtained by the SIAs in the course of performing their functions.[128] There is also, however, a statutory obligation to destroy 'irrelevant information' obtained under an authorisation, and the IGIS has observed that this is 'difficult to apply to bulk personal datasets':

> Most of the information in these datasets will likely be irrelevant, for intelligence purposes, at the time of acquisition or the initial retention decision, and will likely continue to be irrelevant. It will not always be clear to the agency what information in the dataset is relevant, and in some cases relevance will emerge in time, in light of other information.[129]

The IGIS therefore recommended that retention of data within a bulk dataset should be 'justified by a demonstrable value for the GCSB's functions, not the mere promise of potential value', with this approach enforced by 'a default presumption for deletion of irrelevant data after a certain time, unless a persuasive case is made for continued retention'.[130] The statute does not, however, appear to regulate directly the examination of data lawfully retained by NZSIS and the GCSB, and the agencies are exempted from many of the key provisions of New Zealand's Privacy Act.[131] The IGIS has observed that 'the more an intelligence agency makes use of "bulky" data (containing information on large numbers of

[125] NZSIS and Department for Internal Affairs, *Direct Access Agreement Under the Intelligence and Security Act 2017* (2022) [6].
[126] ibid [13.2.2].
[127] Minister Responsible for the Government Communications Security Bureau and Minister Responsible for the New Zealand Security Intelligence Service, *Ministerial Policy Statement: Publicly available information* (1 March 2022).
[128] Minister Responsible for the Government Communications Security Bureau and Minister Responsible for the New Zealand Security Intelligence Service, *Ministerial Policy Statement: Management and use of information* (1 March 2022).
[129] IGIS (n 117) [21].
[130] ibid [24].
[131] Privacy Act 2020 (NZ), s 28.

people who are not of security concern), the more important are post-collection controls on access to and use of that data', and that while NZSIS is 'developing systems and procedures to support its growing reliance on data holdings and analysis, … mature and fully satisfactory arrangements are still some way off'.[132]

The UK's SIAs are entitled, it appears, to acquire information – from whatever source – via what have been described as the 'information gateway provisions' in their governing statutes,[133] and are entitled to disclose it for the proper discharge of their functions and other functions relating to crime by a statute that also permits others to disclose information to those same SIAs, subject only to applicable data protection law.[134] Though they are in practice similarly exempted from complying with many of the key principles of data protection law,[135] the approach to regulating their use of data is very different from what we find in New Zealand, where the matter is regulated in a minimal way and to a considerable extent by non-statutory material. The context here is that, as has often been the case in relation to their activities, the UK's SIAs were making use of what are now known as 'bulk personal datasets' (BPDs) – that is, datasets that contain 'personal data about individuals, the majority of whom are unlikely to be of intelligence interest', and which are 'incorporated into an analytical system and used for intelligence purposes'[136] – for a long period on a very shaky legal foundation, which was held to have become compatible with the ECHR only following the avowal of the use of BPDs in 2015,[137] ahead of the enactment of the Investigatory Powers Act 2016, which provided that use with a new, significantly more robust, legal basis.[138] The 'Bulk Powers Review', published while the Bill that became the 2016 Act was before Parliament, was nevertheless clear as to the value of such datasets:

> I have no hesitation that BPDs are of great utility to the SIAs. The case studies that I examined provided unequivocal evidence of their value. Their principal utility lies in the identification and development of targets, although the use of BPDs may also enable swift action to be taken to counter a threat.[139]

The use of such datasets is now regulated by the 2016 Act, which does not contain any power to acquire BPDs but rather to retain and examine BPDs acquired via

[132] IGIS (n 57) 7.

[133] Security Service Act 1989 (UK), s 2(2)(a); and Intelligence Services Act 1994 (UK), ss 2(2)(a) and 4(2)(a).

[134] Counter-Terrorism Act 2008 (UK), ss 19 and 20, providing that – inter alia – a person 'may disclose information to any of the intelligence services for the purposes of the exercise by that service of any of its functions', that such a disclosure does not breach 'any obligation of confidence owed by the person making the disclosure' or 'any other restriction on the disclosure of information (however imposed)', but that this does not authorise a disclosure that 'contravenes the data protection legislation'.

[135] Data Protection Act 2018 (UK), pt 4.

[136] Quoted in *Privacy International v Secretary of State for Foreign and Commonwealth Affairs* [2016] UKIPTrib/15/110-CH, [5].

[137] ibid [101].

[138] For discussion, see Scott (n 32) 97–103.

[139] D Anderson, *Report of the Bulk Powers Review* (Cm 9326, 2016) [8.33]. Moreover (ibid [8.36]), 'In some areas, particularly pattern analysis and anomaly detection, no practicable alternative to the use of BPDs exists. These areas of work are vital, since they can provide information about a threat in the absence of any other intelligence seed.'

some other power,[140] including for example the use of bulk powers of some variety, or the purchase or even theft of data. The retention and use of these datasets must take place in accordance with a warrant, of which there are two types: class BPD warrants, which permit the retention and examination of BPDs falling within the class described in the warrant; and specific BPD warrants, which permit the retention and examination of (only) those specific BPDs described in the warrant.[141] Certain 'protected data' cannot be examined on the basis of a class BPD warrant but only where there is a specific BPD warrant in place. The double-lock process applies to both sorts of warrant, so that (except in cases of urgency) the conclusion of the relevant Minister that the conditions for the retention and examination of a BPD or class of BPDs are met must be approved by a Judicial Commissioner before the warrant may be issued.[142] The general scheme put in place by the 2016 Act in relation to BPDs has been held to be compatible with the same requirements of the ECHR that were, it seems clear, the original impetus for putting that scheme in place.[143]

Though the UK's is – relative to those applicable in the other Commonwealth Five Eyes states – an unusually restrictive and detailed regime, it contains some important limits. One already noted is that the 2016 Act regime does not directly regulate the acquisition of BPDs, only their retention and examination. Acquisition will in many cases take place in the exercise of other, separately authorised powers. Another is that it applies only to datasets that are or will be held electronically, and only where the 'the majority of the individuals are not, and are unlikely to become, of interest to the intelligence service in the exercise of its functions'.[144] Moreover, it did not in its original form regulate access by the SIAs to third-party databases,[145] either public or private, with a change to this position recommended early in the era of the 2016 Act by the Investigatory Powers Commissioner (IPC).[146] From the other direction, the regulation of BPDs by the 2016 Act has been identified as overly burdensome by the SIAs, not least in the context of an ever-growing use thereof: 'Both the size and the number of BPDs of interest to [the UK intelligence community] have increased massively since the advent of the internet, with the explosion of personal data stored on searchable electronic databases.'[147] That intelligence community therefore argued for the imposition of a lower level of safeguards relating to the retention and examination of BPDs in which individuals have low or no expectation of privacy, a case that was largely accepted by the review of the Investigatory Powers

[140] Investigatory Powers Act 2016 (UK), pt 7.
[141] ibid, s 200.
[142] ibid, s 204(3)(e) and s 205(6)(e).
[143] *R (National Council for Civil Liberties) v Secretary of State for the Home Department* [2023] EWCA Civ 926 [201]–[218].
[144] Investigatory Powers Act 2016 (UK), s 199(1).
[145] D Anderson, *Independent Review of the Investigatory Powers Act 2016* (2023) [3.20].
[146] Investigatory Powers Commissioner, *Annual Report for 2019* (HC 2019-21, 1039) [2.28]–[2.29].
[147] Anderson (n 145) [3.2].

Act 2016, five years after its coming into force.[148] This of course raises the question of how one determines whether or not a given BPD falls within that category. Notably, in the context of how the matter is handled elsewhere, the suggestions made by the SIAs to the reviewer as to the factors that might be taken into account in this regard excluded the question of where the persons whose data are contained in the BPD are located.[149]

Changes to this effect were made by the Investigatory Powers (Amendment) Act 2024. The result is that the SIAs will now be able to effectively self-authorise the retention (and retention or examination) of a BPD if its nature is such that 'individuals to whom the personal data relates could have no, or only a low, reasonable expectation of privacy in relation to the data'.[150] In determining whether that is the case, regard must be had to all the circumstances, but in particular to a set of specified considerations, including 'the nature of the data', the extent to which it was made public by the individuals to whom it relates (or the extent to which the making of it public was consented to by those individuals) and, 'if the data has been published or is otherwise in the public domain, the extent to which the data is widely known about'.[151] The SIAs can also self-authorise the retention and examination of classes of BPDs that meet this standard, with a class authorisation able to 'describe a category of bulk personal datasets by reference to (among other things) the use to which the datasets will be put'.[152] In either case the double-lock applies. The Act also puts access by the SIAs to third-party BPDs on largely the same footing as the retention and examination of BPDs they themselves hold,[153] which will no doubt include databases maintained by their Five Eyes partners.

In Canada, where a statute has been enacted specifically to permit governmental institutions to share information for security purposes,[154] it has been argued that CSIS has encountered difficulty in its approach to bulk data: criticised in the past for 'undershooting in its information retention policies', it later 'struggled to adjust to a new information-rich world' and 'overshot the mark, retaining too much'

[148] ibid [3.66].

[149] As the reviewer noted (ibid [3.51]), 'Two additional factors that seemed to me of possible relevance to the assessment are the anticipated use of the data and the location of the persons whose data is in issue. [The UK Intelligence Community] did not however seek to present a developed case to me on either of these factors, so I say no more about them.'

[150] Investigatory Powers Act 2016 (UK), ss 226A and 226B.

[151] ibid, s 226A(3).

[152] ibid, s 226BA.

[153] ibid, pt 7B.

[154] Security of Canada Information Disclosure Act, SC 2015, c 20, s 2 (Canada), s 3 of which states its purpose as being 'to encourage and facilitate the disclosure of information between Government of Canada institutions in order to protect Canada against activities that undermine the security of Canada'. A record must be kept of disclosures (and receipts) of information, which must be reported on an annual basis to the NSIRA. In 2022, four institutions made, in total, 173 disclosures to five recipient institutions, with 79% of those requested by the recipient and the other 21% made proactively: National Security and Intelligence Review Agency, *Review of Government of Canada Institutions' Disclosures of Information Under the Security of Canada Information Disclosure Act in 2022* (2023) [16].

and finding itself in legal difficulty as a result.[155] Both CSIS and the CSE are encompassed by Canada's Privacy Act, which nevertheless provides for predictable exceptions that will have the effect of preventing them from having to disclose sensitive information.[156] Following amendment in 2019 – aimed at 'finding a constitutionally compliant, civil-rights-respecting but security-useful solution'[157] – the CSIS Act contains rules relating to datasets containing personal information that 'does not directly and immediately relate to activities that represent a threat to the security of Canada',[158] and so does not meet the 'strictly necessary' threshold that applies to CSIS's primary power to retain and analyse information.[159] Datasets containing personal information that does so relate are not covered by these provisions, and CSIS may retain them without the relevant criterias' being met. The Service may collect a dataset relevant to its functions where it reasonably believes it to be publicly available, or to belong to a class of datasets collection of which has been approved, or that the dataset in question 'predominantly relates to non-Canadians who are outside Canada',[160] and – as we have seen – may seek permission to retain them following intercept. When it does so, it must evaluate within 90 days whether the dataset was in fact publicly available, and whether it is Canadian or a foreign dataset.[161]

Publicly available datasets may be retained, queried and exploited.[162] If a dataset is a Canadian dataset, it must be determined whether it falls within the class of datasets collection of which is authorised by the Minister (and approved by the Intelligence Commissioner) on an annual basis.[163] If it is not within one

[155] L West and C Forcese, 'Building Haystacks: Information Retention and Data Exploitation by the Canadian Security Intelligence Service' (2019) 57 *Alberta Law Review* 175, 200–01. Central to this legal difficulty was the 'ODAC decision', *X(Re)*, 2016 FC 1105, in which the Federal Court held that much of the metadata used by the 'Operational Data Analysis Center' had been unlawfully retained by CSIS. See also Security Intelligence Review Committee, *Building for Tomorrow: The Future of Security Intelligence Accountability in Canada – Annual Report 2017–2018* (2018), ch 3, including the observation that 'SIRC saw no evidence that CSIS had changed its policies and procedures with respect to the collection of bulk datasets in the wake of' that decision.

[156] Privacy Act, RSC, 1985, c P-21 (Canada), s 22(1), which provides that the head of a government institution (including CSIS and the CSE) may refuse to disclose any personal information under a broad range of circumstances, including where it was 'obtained or prepared by any government institution, or part of any government institution, that is an investigative body specified in the regulations in the course of lawful investigations pertaining to … activities suspected of constituting threats to the security of Canada', subject to a 20-year time limit. See also Communications Security Establishment Act (2019) (Canada), s 58, which provides that 'For the purposes of the Privacy Act, if any personal information, as defined in section 3 of that Act, of any other government institution, as defined in that section, or of any other organization is contained in or carried on the Establishment's information infrastructure on behalf of that institution or organization, the personal information is not held by the Establishment and is not under the Establishment's control'.

[157] West and Forcese (n 155) 201.

[158] CSIS Act (1984) (Canada), s 11.02.

[159] See the discussion in Security Intelligence Review Committee, *Review of CSIS's use of Data Management and Exploitation Activities*, SIRC Review 2015-02 (2015).

[160] CSIS Act (1984) (Canada), s 11.05.

[161] ibid, s 11.07.

[162] ibid, s 11.11(1).

[163] ibid, s 11.07(2). The Intelligence Commissioner has declined to approve classes that were 'defined so broadly that it was difficult, if not impossible, to determine which datasets would be excluded

of the approved classes, either it must be destroyed or further approval must be sought from the Minister and Intelligence Commissioner.[164] A judge may (following an application made with the Minister's approval) authorise the retention of a Canadian dataset if satisfied, in the first instance, that its retention is likely to assist the Service in performance of its key functions and duties.[165] The judge may, amongst other things, place conditions upon the querying and exploitation of the dataset; in any case, the authorisation can last a maximum of two years.[166] Whether no authorisation is given, the dataset must be destroyed.[167] Retention of a foreign dataset, on the other hand, can be authorised by the Minister or a person designated by him (including the Director or an employee of the Service), subject to authorisation by the Intelligence Commissioner, with the authorising person – whether the Minister or some other person – able to impose the same sorts of conditions as a judge considering an application to retain and exploit the data.[168] An authorisation of this sort, relating that is to a foreign rather than Canadian dataset, may last for up to five years.[169] Amongst the ongoing obligations of the Service are to remove from a foreign dataset information relating to Canadians or persons in Canada.[170]

Even once an authorisation is in place, the ability to query or exploit varies, depending upon whether a dataset is Canadian or foreign: the former may only be queried on grounds relating to threats to the security of Canada, while the latter may also be queried for the purposes of providing security assessments or advice relating to citizenship or immigration.[171] Either type may be queried for the purpose of assisting the Minister of National Defence or the Minister of Foreign Affair as regards 'information or intelligence relating to the capabilities, intentions or activities' of foreign states (or groups thereof) or non-Canadian persons.[172] There is, therefore, a clear set of distinctions between datasets that are publicly available and those that are not, and between datasets that relate predominantly to Canadians or persons within Canada on one hand and, on the other, those that relate predominantly to those who are not Canadian and who are outside Canada. This framework, it should be noted, does not apply to the CSE, which might, therefore, deal with datasets of whatever sort subject only to those aspects of the Privacy Act that apply to it. There have nevertheless arisen a number of issues relating to this new and complex regime, notwithstanding the involvement of CSIS in designing it: the NSIRA has suggested that 'CSIS's current application of the dataset

from the classes', stating that 'for the classes of datasets to be meaningful, they must be more precisely defined and include tangible examples of the types of information to be collected': Intelligence Commissioner (n 86) 23.

[164] CSIS Act (1984) (Canada), s 11.08(1).

[165] ibid, s 11.13.

[166] ibid, s 11.14.

[167] ibid, s 11.15(1).

[168] ibid, ss 11.17(1) and (2).

[169] ibid, s 11.17(3).

[170] ibid, s 11.10(1).

[171] ibid, ss 11.2(2) and (3).

[172] ibid, s 11.2(4).

regime is inconsistent with the statutory framework' and that CSIS has 'failed to fully apprise' the Federal Court, as it should have done, on its 'interpretation and application of the dataset regime'.[173]

The Australian position (where the SIAs with which we are concerned here are completely exempt from the Privacy Act 1988)[174] is interesting, because it provides an example of where the approaches elsewhere (which, as we have seen, vary significantly between them) have been considered and rejected, and so there, is as things stand, no direct regulation of the use of 'bulk data' or any equivalent by the Australian SIAs. Three reasons for which a regime on the lines of one or the other above might be put in place were identified by the *Comprehensive Review*: 'to overcome legal impediments that prevent [SIAs] from obtaining access to, and to retain and use reference information for intelligence purposes'; 'to introduce limits, controls or safeguards around [SIAs'] access to, and retention and use of reference information for intelligence purposes'; or 'to provide greater transparency around the limits, controls and safeguards that presently apply to [SIAs'] access to, and retention and use of, reference information for intelligence purposes'.[175] It was noted, however, that the bodies in question 'rarely face "hard" legal barriers that prevent them from collecting or receiving reference information, or dealing in reference information that they hold – in the sense that it would be unlawful for them to do so', and that the difficulties they encountered were usually 'the result of differing judgments between agencies as to the necessity, proportionality and propriety of sharing information, rather than being legal in nature'.[176] The *Review* therefore saw no need to recommend new rules permitting the sharing of information with the SIAs, suggesting that it was preferable that those bodies 'be required to return to the Parliament to seek amendments, should they require access to information that the Parliament has previously placed off limits'.[177] What of the use that might be made of data the SIAs come to possess in lawful exercise of their statutory powers? Here, emphasis was placed on the Guidelines for ASIO made in exercise of section 8A of the ASIO Act 1979, which provide that in performing its functions ASIO may:

a) collect, maintain, analyse and assess information relevant to security;
b) collect and maintain a comprehensive body of reference data to contextualise intelligence derived from inquiries and investigations, and;
c) maintain a broad database against which information obtained in relation to a specific inquiry or investigation can be checked and assessed.[178]

[173] National Security and Intelligence Review Agency, *NSIRA Review of CSIS Dataset Regime* (2024), ch 4.
[174] Privacy Act 1988 (Australia), s 7(1).
[175] *Comprehensive Review of the Legal Framework of the National Intelligence Community*, Volume 3: *Information, Technology, Powers and Oversight* (2019) [34.50].
[176] ibid [34.57].
[177] ibid [34.60].
[178] Minister for Home Affairs, *Minister's Guidelines in relation to the performance by the Australian Security Intelligence Organisation of its functions and the exercise of its powers* (2020) [3.2]. For a discussion, see G Carne, 'Guiding light or opaque filter?: The minister's guidelines for the Australian

These are subject to a variety of rules, amongst them that ASIO 'will only collect, use, handle, retain or disclose personal information for purposes related to the performance of its functions or exercise of its powers, or where otherwise authorised, or required, by law',[179] and that it will 'maintain policies about its access to, and retention of, personal information', with the content of these policies prescribed in various ways.[180] These rules do not apply to the other Australian SIAs with which we are concerned, though, which are also exempt from the Privacy Act 1988.

The *Comprehensive Review* declared itself satisfied that 'stronger and more consistent controls could be introduced for all Privacy Act-exempt agencies, to govern their collection, retention and use of reference information'.[181] It rejected, however, the idea that there was any need to put in place regimes for the prior approval of retention (as in Canada and the UK) or examination (as in the UK) of datasets retained by these bodies.[182] The agencies, it said,

> are subject to multi-layered controls, safeguards and accountability mechanisms – which include limited statutory functions for most agencies, and independent oversight of their activities by the IGIS and Ombudsman – that are designed to ensure that these agencies act lawfully and with propriety. In our view, additional controls, such as requirements for external authorisation, should be reserved for activities that would otherwise be unlawful, or that involve a significant interference with privacy or other human rights.[183]

Moreover, the extent of the reliance on data of this sort is such that a requirement of prior approval for using it 'would effectively operate as a tick-box requirement for [intelligence] agencies to obtain approval to perform their functions, providing the appearance of accountability and external control – but not substantive accountability or control'.[184] It nevertheless recommended that 'there should be opportunities for the Government, Parliament and public to revisit this issue, to ensure our approach remains valid over time'.[185] This approach is striking in its divergence from that taken elsewhere, and in particular in its contrast with an approach in the UK that the SIAs appear to have found overly restrictive in the period since its introduction. This, it seems, is one area in particular in which the influence of the ECHR has pushed the UK and its law in a direction in which the other Five Eyes states have no great desire to follow it.

Security Intelligence Organisation in performing its functions and exercising its powers as relevant to security' (2022) 43 *Adelaide Law Review* 814.

179 Minister for Home Affairs (n 178) [4.1].

180 ibid [4.3].

181 *Comprehensive Review*, Volume 3 (n 175) [34.103].

182 ibid [34.111]: '[W]e do not consider that controls of this kind are required, based on the kinds of reference information that these agencies collect, how they use it, and the privacy implications. We acknowledge that these facts may change over time, and have recommended that this issue be revisited periodically by future Independent Intelligence Reviews.'

183 ibid [34.123].

184 ibid [34.124].

185 ibid [34.128].

IV. Authorising Criminality

Many investigatory powers, we have noted, are carve-outs from general prohibitions on certain conduct – the SIAs require authorisation to do certain things only because those things are otherwise not permitted, not by them, nor by anyone else. So, for example, the interception of telecommunications or the interference with a computer system is generally prohibited conduct to which the powers of the SIAs to carry out such interception or interference stand as exceptions, either built into the prohibition (so that there is no prima facie violation of it) or simply cutting across it (so that the prima facie violation thereof is permitted in the circumstances). But the issue might be taken further: that is, one might wish to permit the SIAs at least the theoretical possibility of undertaking not specific activities that are otherwise prohibited by the criminal law, but rather undertaking unlawful activities – that is to say, committing crime – generally. And we might go further again, allowing for the authorisation of the commission of crimes not by the SIAs or their employees themselves, but instead by third parties working on their behalf – informants or the like. We see this in several of the Commonwealth Five Eyes states, though again with considerable divergence between the relevant frameworks.

In Australia, the National Security Legislation Amendment Act (No 1) 2014 inserted into the ASIO Act 1979 provisions relating to what are called in the legislation 'special intelligence operations' (SIOs).[186] The origins of the Act go back to 2012, when the Attorney-General requested that the Parliamentary Joint Committee on Intelligence and Security consider a set of possible reforms that included a regime like that which would later become law, which would – it was argued – 'significantly assist covert intelligence operations that require undercover ASIO officers or human sources to gain and maintain access to highly sensitive information concerning serious threats to Australia and its citizens', and would be modelled on an existing scheme applicable to ordinary police.[187] As noted above, an important part of the context was – or so it was claimed – the developing landscape of criminal law, which had worked to criminalise activity that ASIO previously undertook and for which, before then, no legal authority was therefore required. ASIO, for example, later told the *Comprehensive Review* that 'a successive series of criminal laws focused on national security and serious and organised crime, introduced over the last two decades, have had the unintended effect of criminalising activities commonly employed to collect

[186] Australian Security Intelligence Organisation Act 1979 (Australia), Division 4.

[187] Attorney-General's Department, *Equipping Australia Against Emerging and Evolving Threats: A Discussion Paper to accompany consideration by the Parliamentary Joint Committee on Intelligence and Security of a package of national security ideas comprising proposals for telecommunications interception reform, telecommunications sector security reform and Australian intelligence community legislation reform* (2012) 46. And see in response, endorsing the creation of such a scheme, Parliamentary Joint Committee on Intelligence and Security, *Report of the Inquiry into Potential Reforms of Australia's National Security Legislation* (2013) [4.104]–[4.120].

intelligence in the proper performance of its functions'.[188] And so at least some of the evolution of the power to commit crimes – here and perhaps elsewhere – is a function of changing the rules as to what is in fact a crime in the first place.

An SIO authority permits those identified therein 'to engage in the special intelligence conduct specified in the special intelligence operation authority in respect of that person',[189] and the effect of its existence is that a participant is not subject to any criminal or civil liability for acts, in effect, carried out in accordance with the authorisation.[190] An authority may be given by the Minister where satisfied that there are reasonable grounds to believe certain things. Two of these relate to the operation itself: that the circumstances are such as to justify the operation and that the operation will assist ASIO in one or more of what are described as its 'special intelligence functions',[191] a subset of its general functions that includes its functions of obtaining, correlating and evaluating intelligence relevant to security, communicating that intelligence for purposes relevant to security and in such manner as appropriate for those purposes, obtaining within Australia foreign intelligence and communicating that intelligence, and cooperating with and assisting various intelligence and law enforcement agencies.[192] Notwithstanding that they do not include the entirety of ASIO's functions, these are, then, very broad. Two of the other criteria for the making of an SIO authority are that 'any unlawful conduct involved in conducting the special intelligence operation will be limited to the maximum extent consistent with conducting an effective special intelligence operation' and that the operation so authorised 'will not be conducted in such a way that a person is likely to be induced to commit an offence against a law of the Commonwealth, a State or a Territory that the person would not otherwise have intended to commit'.[193] The final point on which the Minister must be satisfied that there are reasonable grounds to believe is that 'any conduct involved in the special intelligence operation' will not do one of the following things (a list that has evolved since the SIO regime was first put in place): cause the death of, or serious injury to, any person; constitute torture; involve the commission of a sexual offence against any person; or result in significant loss of, or serious damage to, property.[194]

These requirements are mirrored in those for enjoying the legal immunity an SIO authorisation is capable of providing, confirming that there can be no immunity for intentionally inducing a person to commit a crime that person would not otherwise have committed, or for committing a crime within one of the listed categories.[195] Where an SIO is authorised, that fact must be reported

[188] *Comprehensive Review*, Volume 2 (n 27) [24.97].
[189] ASIO Act 1979, s 35H.
[190] ibid, s 35K.
[191] ibid, s 35C(2)(a).
[192] ibid, ss 4 and 17.
[193] ibid, s 35C(2)(d).
[194] ibid, s 35C(2)(e).
[195] ibid, s 35K.

to the IGIS,[196] and reports on the effectiveness of the SIO, including whether it resulted in certain outcomes, must be provided by the Director-General to both the Attorney-General and the IGIS.[197] The giving of the authorisation is by the Attorney-General on the (usually written) application of the Director-General, a senior position holder or an ASIO employee.[198] Though it has been subject to significant criticism – as have the rules around secrecy associated with the regime[199] – the *Comprehensive Review* found that 'the special intelligence operations regime is an important part of the legal framework governing ASIO', rejecting in particular arguments against it founded on the concept of the rule of law:

> The special intelligence operations regime upholds the rule of law by ensuring that ASIO officers are not above the law, and are held to account for any unauthorised breaches. If anything, the alternative – which would require ASIO to rely on police or prosecutorial discretion – poses a greater threat to public confidence, by allowing the executive 'to dispense its own servants from obedience to laws made by Parliament'.[200]

This claim is particularly striking in light of the legal position that subsisted in the UK at that point in time, discussed below. Ultimately, the *Comprehensive Review* concluded 'the special intelligence operations regime is consistent with Justice Hope's concern that, in considering the role of ASIO, there be an appropriate balance between the rights of individual persons, on the one hand, and the preservation of the security of Australia as a nation, on the other'.[201] The Australian IGIS has, though, in the past identified 'several areas of concern relating to the management of legal risk, the completeness of information provided to the Attorney-General, and record keeping relating to management of a particular SIO',[202] which would seem to be particularly unacceptable given the extraordinary nature of the regime.

In Canada, the power to authorise the commission of crimes by CSIS is now found in the CSIS Act, having been inserted into it by the National Security Act of 2017. The rules in question provide first of all that there is no general right to act unlawfully: though the employees of CSIS have 'the same protection under the law as peace officers have in performing their duties and functions as peace officers', it is still of course possible for them to act unlawfully,[203] and if the Director

[196] ibid, s 35PA.
[197] ibid, s 35Q.
[198] ibid, ss 35B and 35C(1).
[199] See K Hardy and G Williams, 'Special Intelligence Operations and Freedom of the Press' (2016) 41 *Alternative Law Journal* 160; and Independent National Security Legislation Monitor, *Report on the impact on journalists of section 35P of the ASIO Act* (2015).
[200] *Comprehensive Review*, Volume 2 (n 27) [24.117].
[201] ibid [24.110].
[202] Inspector-General of Intelligence and Security, *Annual Report 2022–2023* (2023) 97.
[203] '[S]ince peace officers do not enjoy Crown immunity, this provision likely offers little protection to CSIS employees. Moreover, even if CSIS officers did possess Crown immunity, it seems very unlikely that it would extend to their human sources.' Forcese and West (n 9) 393.

is of the opinion that an employee has done so in 'the purported performance of the duties and functions of the Service under this Act' then he must report that fact to the Minister, with any report to be passed to the Attorney-General and then the NSIRA.[204] However, this is now subject to a provision that gives effect – we are told – to the principle that it is

> in the public interest to ensure that employees effectively carry out the Service's information and intelligence collection duties and functions, including by engaging in covert activities, in accordance with the rule of law and, to that end, to expressly recognize in law a limited justification for designated employees acting in good faith and persons acting under their direction to commit acts or omissions that would otherwise constitute offences.[205]

The provision in question was introduced following a period in which CSIS had been relying upon Crown immunity to authorise such activities, despite having been advised that it could not do so,[206] with the Federal Court concluding that CSIS had breached its duty of candour by applying for warrants and not disclosing that it was doing so on the basis of information that had been collected unlawfully.[207]

The recognition in law of the 'limited justification' referred to takes the form of a requirement that the Minister, at least once a year, make an order specifying 'the classes of acts or omissions that would otherwise constitute offences and that designated employees may be justified in committing or directing another person to commit if the Minister concludes that the commission of those acts or omissions is reasonable',[208] having regard both to the work of the Service and the relevant threats to the security of Canada. The Minister is required to notify the Intelligence Commissioner for his review and approval,[209] and so this is subject to the sort of 'double-lock' discussed in section VI. Employees may be 'designated' by the Minister on the recommendation of the Director, with a designated employee 'justified in committing an act or omission that would otherwise constitute an offence' if one of two sets of conditions is met, the most important such set being that the designated employee: (i) 'is engaged, in good faith, in an information and intelligence collection activity in relation to a threat to the

[204] CSIS Act (1984) (Canada), s 20(2).

[205] ibid, s 20.1(2). For background, see Security Intelligence Review Committee, *Annual Report 2015–2016: Maintaining Momentum* (2016) 19–20.

[206] 'SIRC reviewed the situation and concluded that CSIS had in fact been advised that Crown immunity could no longer be used as a legal defence. As a result, in its certificate, SIRC found that CSIS had knowingly broken the law. SIRC also made clear that although CSIS's operations could have been important from the standpoint of national security, this in no way excused it from adhering to the rule of law.' National Security and Intelligence Review Agency, *2019 Annual Report* (2020) [49].

[207] *Re Canadian Security Intelligence Services Act* 2020 FC 616.

[208] CSIS Act (1984), s 20.1(3).

[209] ibid, s 20.1(5). See Intelligence Commissioner, *Annual Report 2022* (2023) 34–35 for a discussion of some of the issues the Intelligence Commissioner has identified within the ministerial identification of classes of acts or omissions.

security of Canada'; and (ii) he or she 'believes on reasonable grounds that the commission of the act or omission, as compared to the threat, is reasonable and proportional in the circumstances, having regard to such matters as the nature of the threat, the nature of the act or omission and the reasonable availability of other means for performing the information and intelligence collection activity'.[210]

The Director (or a 'designated senior employee') might also give a written authorisation, subject to the same criteria and lasting for up to one year, that permits a designated employee to direct others to act in a way that would otherwise constitute a criminal offence.[211] A designated employee might also direct a person to commit an offence without an authorisation in place where certain urgent circumstances demand it.[212] In either case – where a designated employee is acting in a way that would normally be unlawful or directing some other person to do so – the employee is only justified if the offence in question is one of those identified by the Minister and approved by the Intelligence Commissioner.[213]

The effect of all this is that there is a broad capacity for employees of CSIS to commit criminal offences or direct others to do so. Where the relevant process has been adhered to – approval of the classes of acts and omissions, designation of the employee and so on – an act that would otherwise attract criminal liability is stated by law instead to be justified. There are two sets of limits upon this power, though. One is that it is provided by the CSIS Act, that nothing within the procedure justifies any of the following:

(a) causing, intentionally or by criminal negligence, death or bodily harm to an individual;
(b) wilfully attempting in any manner to obstruct, pervert or defeat the course of justice;
(c) violating the sexual integrity of an individual;
(d) subjecting an individual to torture or cruel, inhuman or degrading treatment or punishment, within the meaning of the Convention Against Torture;
(e) detaining an individual; or
(f) causing the loss of, or any serious damage to, any property if doing so would endanger the safety of an individual.[214]

The other is that nothing within the relevant provision 'justifies the commission of an act or omission that would infringe a right or freedom guaranteed by the Canadian Charter of Rights and Freedoms',[215] which therefore acts – where it applies – as an overarching limit on how this regime might be used. Reporting by the NSIRA shows that these powers are widely used, with 172 authorisations

[210] CSIS Act (1984), ss 20.1(6) and (11).
[211] ibid, ss 20.1(12) and (15).
[212] ibid, s 20.1(15)(b).
[213] ibid, s 20.1(17).
[214] ibid, s 20.1(18).
[215] ibid, s 20.1(20).

given in 2022, with 61 relevant acts or omissions committed by CSIS employees that year and 132 directions given to others to commit such an act or omission.[216] It is important to underscore, however, that even if this 'justification framework', as it is referred to, now works to provide a clear legal basis for the activity in question, it does so in the context of prior, seemingly pervasive, illegality.

Much the same story – of a weak or absent legal basis relied upon for far longer than it should have been – can also be told of the UK, in which the matter is now governed by the Covert Human Intelligence Sources (Criminal Conduct) Act 2021, enacted in response to the so-called 'third direction' litigation, before the Court of Appeal (to which the matter had at that point been appealed) decided that it would uphold the split decision of the Investigatory Powers Tribunal.[217] The regime approved by the courts in that litigation was subject to a paradox: a set of guidelines by which MI5 authorised participation in criminality was held to possess an adequate legal basis, but only because it did not in fact provide any genuine immunity to those so 'authorised'.[218] The effect of an authorisation under that regime, that is, was that MI5 would, where a crime had been committed in accordance with an authorisation, make representations to the prosecuting authorities that the prosecution of the authorised individual for the relevant act(s) or omission(s) was not in the public interest. This was the sort of reliance on prosecutorial discretion the Australian Comprehensive Review likened to the effective dispensing of the law by the executive, in the manner of the Stuart Monarchs (though the Investigatory Powers Tribunal rejected a claim that this was the effect of that regime).[219] The regime put in place by the 2021 Act moves beyond this sort of pseudo-authorisation, neither one thing nor the other and so highly unsatisfactory even if – as the Court of Appeal eventually said – it was lawful. It involved the insertion of a new provision into the Regulation of Investigatory Powers Act 2000, once the centrepiece of the landscape of investigatory powers in the UK but now a shell of its former self. This addition provides for the making of a 'criminal conduct authorisation' (CCA) where there already exists a 'CHIS authorisation', which authorises a person to act as a 'Covert Human Intelligence Source' and where it is necessary on one of the standard trifecta of grounds and proportionate to what is sought to be achieved by the conduct being authorised.[220] Conduct authorised by a CCA – which might be granted to a range of policing and non-policing bodies over and

[216] National Security and Intelligence Review Agency (n 67) [49]–[50] and table 5.

[217] *Privacy International v Secretary of State for Foreign and Commonwealth Affairs* [2021] EWCA Civ 330.

[218] See the discussion in PF Scott, 'Authorising Crime: The Covert Human Intelligence Sources (Criminal Conduct) Act 2021' (2022) 85 *Modern Law Review* 1218, 1229–37.

[219] *Privacy International v Secretary of State for Foreign and Commonwealth Affairs* [2019] UKIPTribIPT/17/186/CH, [72]–[85].

[220] Regulation of Investigatory Powers Act 2000 (UK), s 29B, as inserted by the Covert Human Intelligence Sources (Criminal Conduct) Act 2021 (UK).

above the SIAs[221] – will be 'lawful for all purposes' – both civil and criminal.[222] These authorisations, notwithstanding their potentially drastic effect, are not granted by an independent figure or even, as is standard for more intrusive powers, a Minister of the Crown. Instead, they are granted by an actor internal to the relevant organisation. Nor are they subject to the so-called 'double-lock', by which the original decision-maker's decision that the conditions for the grant of many types of warrant are met must be approved by a senior judicial figure before those warrants can take effect. Rather, it is sufficient to notify the IPC of the grant of an authorisation, including the grounds for believing that the requirements for its grant are met and details of the conduct that it authorises.[223] 'What is elsewhere a substantive and crucial oversight role,' I have previously suggested, 'is substituted here with a data-gathering exercise which is likely to be of benefit – if at all – only in assessing the operation of the CCA regime as a whole, rather than in excluding abuse in particular cases.'[224]

The relative weakness of the oversight regime is particularly notable in light of the fact that there are no substantive limits, on the face of the statute, on the conduct that might be authorised under this regime; though some limits might be imposed by ministerial order, this has not so far been done.[225] The Government came under significant pressure to include some such limits during the legislative process, but it resisted this on the basis that it might be used to test the bona fides of those tasked by the UK authorities with infiltrating prohibited organisations or criminal gangs: if a CHIS could be authorised to commit any crime other than, say, murder, then – the logic goes – a person could prove that he was not a CHIS by carrying out a murder.[226] Though it was frequently noted in this discussion that Canada (as described above) manages with such limits – as does, we might note, ASIO in Australia – the argument did not win out, perhaps due to what were described as 'the unique challenges faced in Northern Ireland'.[227] On the human rights point, the Government originally argued that 'there would not be State responsibility under the Convention for conduct where the intention is to disrupt and prevent that conduct, or more serious conduct, rather than acquiesce in or otherwise give official approval for such conduct, and/or where the conduct would take place in any event'.[228] This seemed a hopeless argument, and the Government later appeared to accept that the ECHR, through the HRA

[221] Regulation of Investigatory Powers Act 2000 (UK), sch 1, pt A1.
[222] ibid, s 27(1).
[223] ibid, s 32C.
[224] Scott (n 218) 1239.
[225] Regulation of Investigatory Powers Act 2000 (UK), s 29B(10).
[226] Scott (n 218) 1240.
[227] Joint Committee on Human Rights, *Legislative Scrutiny: Covert Human Intelligence Sources (Criminal Conduct) Bill: Government Response to the Committee's Tenth Report of Session 2019–21* (HC 2019–21, 1127), 2.
[228] Home Office, 'Covert Human Intelligence Sources (Criminal Conduct) Bill – European Convention on Human Rights Memorandum' (nd) [16].

1998, would in general apply to authorisations under the new regime.[229] But the UK is only obliged to secure the rights under the ECHR (and so the HRA 1998) of those within its jurisdiction. Jurisdiction's being primarily territorial, this means that those abroad who are the targets of the efforts of the UK SIAs do not enjoy the protection of the Convention, and acts aimed at them need not as a rule comply with its requirements. This will have particular implications for MI6, much of whose work will be targeted at persons outside the UK, and indeed we know that MI6 'runs' CHISs, including – no doubt – authorising them to commit crimes, under the much broader authority of section 7 of the Intelligence Services Act 1994.[230] In both cases, however, the ability to authorise the commission of crimes will also benefit those who do the authorising in question, meaning that they do need not be concerned about whatever secondary or parasitic liability might otherwise arise from their involvement. Already in 2022, we know that 326 criminal conduct authorisations were given under the new powers introduced by the 2021 Act.[231]

In keeping with the points made above, New Zealand's Intelligence and Security Act 2017 confirms what is elsewhere sometimes only implicit: no authorisation is required to carry out lawful activity; unlawful activity can be carried out only where it is authorised activity; and, where it is authorised, activity can be carried out regardless of what any other statute might say.[232] The statute provides criminal immunity for acts done in good faith in order to obtain an intelligence warrant or to carry out an authorised activity – as long as the relevant party reasonably believed that the act was necessary and the activity in question was done in a reasonable manner – but there is no general immunity available outside of the regime of the sort that now exists in all of the other Commonwealth Five Eyes states, and the review that prefigured the reform of the law in 2017 did not argue for one:

> We do not consider it necessary or appropriate to extend the Agencies' criminal immunity to acts outside the scope of an authorisation (for example, to any act necessary for the proper performance of the Agencies' functions), as has been done in some

[229] See Scott (n 218) 1242–43.

[230] 'SIS have eight class-based Authorisations under Section 7 of the Intelligence Services Act. These remove liability under UK law for day-to-day activity undertaken in pursuit of SIS's statutory functions, such as the identification and use of Covert Human Intelligence Sources, Directed Surveillance and interference with, and receipt of, property and documents': Intelligence and Security Committee, *Privacy and Security: A modern and transparent legal framework* (HC 2014–15, 1075) [233]; 'SIS is primarily a humint (human intelligence) organisation. They operate overseas under a section 7 class authorisation for agent running (CHIS) … I am satisfied that although [the Regulation of Investigatory Powers Act 2000] does not apply, SIS seek to apply the same principles and that the relevant points are being considered in relation to authorising a CHIS': Intelligence Services Commissioner, *Report of the Intelligence Services Commissioner for 2014* (HC 2014–15, 225) 21.

[231] Investigatory Powers Commissioner, *Annual Report of the Investigatory Powers Commissioner 2022* (HC 2023–24, 364), table 19.2. See also ibid [19.10]: 'It is worth noting that a single authorisation for criminal conduct may involve multiple operatives and a single operative might be authorised on a number of operations throughout the year.'

[232] Intelligence and Security Act 2017 (NZ), ss 48 and 49.

> other jurisdictions. Under the new authorisation regime we are proposing, some level of authorisation will be available and required for all of the Agencies' intrusive activities. Unlike under the current legislation, there will no longer be gaps in the activities that are covered by the authorisation regime. As such, there should be no reason for employees to commit unlawful acts in the pursuance of unauthorised activities.[233]

One thing that an authorisation might permit is 'any human intelligence activity to be carried out for the purpose of collecting intelligence',[234] with the key formulation defined to mean 'activities that involve the use of any person to gather intelligence'.[235] This is framed very broadly, and only two specific exceptions to it are identified: the ability to authorise human intelligence activities excludes such activity as (i) 'involves the use or threat of violence against a person' or (ii) 'perverts, or attempts to pervert, the course of justice',[236] clearly suggesting that, even if it falls short of the sorts of general scheme for the authorisation of criminal activity now found in various forms in the other Commonwealth Five Eyes schemes, it might permit other sorts of activity that would otherwise constitute a criminal offence. It is, however, subject to the general duties that apply to the New Zealand SIAs when performing their functions.

V. Geography and Citizenship

We have noted at various points so far in this chapter a matter about the regulation of the investigatory powers on which there is interesting, and seemingly significant, divergence between the four Commonwealth Five Eyes states. That is, all of them draw a distinction between – we might say, putting the point deliberately loosely – what is 'inside' and what is 'outside'. The difference matters, because what is recognised as being 'inside' attracts a higher level of protection than that which is 'outside': the most intrusive powers are often reserved for the latter context, and even where the powers available are superficially identical, the level of safeguards associated with the use of intrusive powers is usually lower when they are exercised 'outside' as opposed to 'inside'. But though the line between inside and outside is often, as that metaphor suggests, a geographic one, it is not always so. Sometimes it is drawn on some other basis, and especially on the basis of the division between citizens (and perhaps permanent residents) and non-citizens (and those who are not permanent residents), or (perhaps most frequently) on a mixture of these two criteria – geography and status.

To illustrate the point by reference to a particularly striking example, in the UK there is a distinction, noted in section II.B, between powers that are 'targeted'

[233] Cullen and Reddy (n 8) [6.126].
[234] Intelligence and Security Act 2017 (NZ), s 67(1)(g).
[235] ibid, s 4.
[236] ibid, s 67(1)(g).

in nature and those that are 'bulk'. Bulk powers, broadly, are distinguished by the fact that they result in intrusion into the privacy of persons who are not, and never will be, targets of the security and intelligence agencies. Bulk interception of communications might, for example, sweep up the communications of many thousands of people, few or none of whom would ever have been capable of meeting the criteria for the interception of their communications via a targeted interception warrant. Though bulk interception warrants must be aimed primarily at the interception of 'overseas-related' communications (which are either sent from or to a person who is outside the British Islands),[237] it is accepted, in practice and in law,[238] that they will result in the collection of a range communications that are not so related, being both sent and received within the British Islands. But there are limits on what might be done with the material acquired via the bulk interception of communications, which work to ensure that bulk interception cannot be employed in order to bypass the requirements of targeted interception: specifically, the need to show that the criteria for the granting of a warrant for the interception of communications are met in relation to a specific (group of) person(s). The most important of these limitations, however, is itself subject to a geographic distinction. That is, material acquired via bulk interception may not be selected for examination using criteria 'referable' to a person known to be within the British Islands at the time, if the purpose of the search is to identify the content of communications sent to or from that person.[239] The SIAs, therefore, may not search through their vast quantities of intercepted communications using your name, or email address or telephone number, in order to access your communications, if it knows you to be within the relevant geographic area. Instead, if they wish to do so they must acquire a targeted interception warrant applicable to you and your communications. This is the case whether you are a UK citizen, a Commonwealth citizen or neither. Conversely, however, if you are known to be outside of the British Islands, they may search through that bulk intercept material for the content of your communications using, say, your email address, regardless of your citizenship, residency or other features, without any further authorisation. Location is what matters; citizenship status is irrelevant.

Why exactly this approach was taken in the UK is not wholly clear, but it seems very likely that the key influence was the position under the ECHR, whereby the UK – as a signatory to the Convention – is obliged by Article 1 to secure to the relevant rights to 'everyone' within its jurisdiction. It will be remembered, of course, that it was the UK's membership of the Convention system that first prompted the introduction of a statutory basis for interception in the mid-1980s (albeit that the initial statutory scheme made an exception to the basic scheme

[237] Investigatory Powers Act 2016 (UK), ss 136(2) and (3).
[238] ibid, s 136(5).
[239] ibid, ss 152(3)(a) and (4).

where terrorism was at issue).[240] It would not be possible, therefore, to exclude such persons from the protection of the Convention, with the effect that interferences with the (primarily) Article 8 rights of such persons must take place only where necessary and proportionate. A distinction based at least in part on geography is therefore in effect a direct consequence of the ECHR and the understanding of jurisdiction thereunder. Two points might though be made about this situation. One is that the question of jurisdiction under the ECHR would not seem to prevent the UK from treating its own citizens outside the jurisdiction 'better' (that is, applying to them greater safeguards) than it does non-citizens outside its territory, and yet this has never been done in law.[241] A second is that the background understanding of jurisdiction reflected in this position may over time be undermined by the 2023 decision of the Fourth Section of the European Court of Human Rights in *Wieder and Guarnieri v United Kingdom*, that where the UK intercepted the communications of non-resident non-citizens, the interference with Article 8 ECHR nevertheless took place within the UK's territory and therefore within its jurisdiction.[242]

Elsewhere, the situation is different, with the key distinction resting at least in part on legal status instead of, or in addition to, physical location. In New Zealand, for example, we observed in section II.B that the Intelligence and Security Act 2017 provides for two varieties of intelligence warrant, known as Type 1 and Type 2 warrants.[243] The former are subject to more demanding safeguards: in particular, they are granted on the joint authority of a Minister and the Commissioner of Intelligence Warrants, whereas Type 2 warrants are granted by the Minister acting alone.[244] And the key difference between the two – the motive for which Type 1 warrants are subject to these greater safeguards – is that though both permit the carrying out of unlawful activity 'for the purpose of collecting information about, or to do any other thing', Type 1 warrants permit the doing of those things in relation to a New Zealand citizen or permanent resident, or to a class of persons including a person who is one of those two things.[245] A Type 2 warrant, conversely, is one that is aimed at any other persons: individuals who are neither New Zealand citizens nor permanent residents of the country, or

[240] Interception of Communications Act 1985 (UK), s 3(3).

[241] Though the Intelligence and Security Committee (n 230) [116], discussing the previous legal regime, noted that 'GCHQ recognise the particular sensitivities around the targeting of UK nationals, and this policy position is reflected in their operational approach: GCHQ have implemented an additional system of internal authorisations for the communications of UK nationals overseas to provide that further assurance.'

[242] *Wieder and Guarnieri v United Kingdom* App Nos 64371/16 and 64407/16 (ECtHR, 12 September 2023).

[243] The report from which this distinction emerged noted that 'The government, as part of its role in protecting national security, has an obligation to protect the rights of its citizens and permanent residents. We consider this is appropriately achieved by applying a higher threshold for authorising activities directed at New Zealanders than in respect of foreign citizens, whose own states are responsible for protecting their rights.' Cullen and Reddy (n 8) [5.61].

[244] Intelligence and Security Act 2017 (NZ), ss 57 and 60.

[245] ibid, s 53.

a class of persons that does not include any such citizens or permanent residents.[246] Here, then, what is crucial is legal status rather than physical location – a New Zealand citizen enjoys the greater safeguards, regardless of whether he or she is inside the country or not; a person who is neither a citizen nor a permanent resident enjoys less protection, even while located within the territory of New Zealand itself.

The previous law governing the GCSB prevented it from intercepting the private communications of New Zealanders and permanent residents of New Zealand, subject to limitations that were widely, it seems, misunderstood,[247] including where a New Zealander or permanent resident counted as a foreign person because acting on behalf of a foreign organisation.[248] The report by Cullen and Reddy that led to the 2017 Act argued that 'this restriction, while intended to protect New Zealanders, is a blunt tool and does not provide the best means of protecting individual rights in situations where there is a threat to national security'.[249] They recommended it be removed, to be replaced by an authorisation regime that would, they said, provide clearer protections to New Zealanders: in effect, that requiring dual approval of Type 1 warrants. The distinction, therefore, was to be retained, but the consequences of it were to change. As we have seen, however, it has since been argued that the distinction between Type 1 and Type 2 warrants – a distinction rooted in the recommendation of Cullen and Reddy, if not perfectly aligned with it – should be abandoned, with the procedure that the 2017 Act applies to Type 1 warrants used for all warrants:

> The result would be that New Zealanders and non-New Zealanders would be treated alike in relation to warrants for the protection of national security, and non-New Zealanders would benefit from the higher standard presently applicable only to New Zealanders.[250]

Even this, however, would not abolish the further distinctions, including in the granting of warrants for international relations or economic well-being purposes, which rest upon whether a person is a New Zealand citizen or permanent resident or not, with warrants only available against such a person on these bases where there are reasonable grounds for thinking that he or she is a foreign agent.[251]

[246] ibid, s 54.

[247] See the discussion in Cullen and Reddy (n 8) [5.13]–[5.14].

[248] Two exceptions seem to have been relied upon by GCSB: one where it was assisting NZSIS under a NZSIS warrant (in which case the relevant provision did not apply 'because GCSB was acting as the agent of the requesting agency and was therefore operating under the legal authority of the warrants') and another where it was acquiring not the content of the communications but related metadata and 'metadata was not a "communication" for the purposes of the prohibition expressed in section 14 of the GCSB Act': R Kitteridge, *Review of Compliance at the Government Communications Security Bureau* (2013) [23]. Kitteridge concluded (ibid [34]) that 'the GCSB Act is not (and probably has never been) completely fit for purpose'. Following this report, changes to the rules in question were made by the Government Communications Security Bureau Amendment Act 2013 (NZ).

[249] Cullen and Reddy (n 8) [5.67].

[250] Arnold and Mahuika (n 51) [E.26].

[251] ibid [E.27].

We have seen that in Canada, bulk interception powers belong to the CSE in pursuit of the foreign intelligence aspect of its mandate. The Communications Security Establishment Act of 2019 provides that activities carried out by the CSE in furtherance of that and most other parts of its mandate 'must not be directed at a Canadian or at any person in Canada and must not infringe the Canadian Charter of Rights and Freedoms',[252] with 'Canadian' defined so as to include both citizens and permanent residents.[253] This is a mixture of the citizenship and geographic distinctions of a sort we have already encountered: foreigners acquire the same degree of protection simply by virtue of their presence in Canda, while Canadians retain it even if they leave the state. 'Directed at' is of course crucial language and leaves open the possibility that such persons might be caught by surveillance under those headings indirectly by virtue of their communications with people outside Canada or foreigners, as the case may be. This is therefore augmented by provisions relating to different aspects of the CSE's mandate, including that the Establishment's foreign intelligence activities must not involve 'the acquisition by the Establishment of information from or through the global information infrastructure that interferes with the reasonable expectation of privacy of a Canadian or a person in Canada', unless they are carried out in pursuit of an FIA or an emergency authorisation.[254] They cannot, that is, be targeted directly, but they may nevertheless be caught by the work of the CSE where it is acting for this end.[255] Even here there are limits as to what might be done with information relating to such a person: an authorisation might be made only where the Minister is satisfied that measures are in place to ensure that 'information acquired under the authorization that is identified as relating to a Canadian or a person in Canada will be used, analysed or retained only if the information is essential to international affairs, defence or security'.[256] Moreover, specific powers exist to permit the Minister to designate persons to whom the CSE might disclose 'information that could be used to identify a Canadian or a person in Canada' if it concludes that to do so 'is essential to international affairs, defence, security or cybersecurity'.[257] It might also use and disclose information relating to a Canadian or person in Canada in cases where to do so might help prevent death or serious bodily harm.[258] The work of CSIS, however, which is focused upon security rather than foreign intelligence, did not for the most part originally reflect these sorts of distinctions as to legal status or geography,[259] though – as we have seen in section III – they are now reflected in the rules about the retention and examination of datasets by CSIS.

[252] Communications Security Establishment Act (2019) (Canada), s 22(1).
[253] ibid, s 2.
[254] ibid, s 22(3).
[255] 'The Establishment may acquire information relating to a Canadian or a person in Canada incidentally in the course of carrying out activities' under, amongst other things, an FIA: ibid, s 23(4).
[256] ibid, s 34(2)(c).
[257] ibid, ss 43 and 45.
[258] ibid, s 46.
[259] One exception was the provision that permits CSIS to assist the Minister for National Defence or the Minister for External Affairs (but only within Canada) 'in relation to the defence of Canada or

In Australia too, the question of citizenship or permanent residence is made relevant to the question of intrusive investigatory powers, though in a more minor way. The distinction was first introduced by the Australian Security Intelligence Organisation Act 1979, reflecting the recommendations of Justice Hope, and in particular his belief that it would not be desirable to prohibit the collection of foreign intelligence (as opposed to security intelligence) within Australia itself.[260] Though Hope gave no reason for his associated belief that this capacity should not extend to Australians, it reflects, it was later claimed, a set of considerations about the distinctive political implications of targeting Australians:

> The treatment of Australians by intelligence collection agencies generally engages higher political risk considerations. Accordingly, the exercise of intrusive, covert or other powers against Australians can require additional procedural steps – including ministerial authorisation – before intelligence activities occur.[261]

The *Comprehensive Review*, however, was at pains to emphasise that the rules reflecting these considerations were largely procedural in nature. Moreover, the language of 'Australians' in this passage should not be allowed to mislead: the statutory language used in most cases is that of 'Australian person', which includes not only citizens but also permanent residents.[262] And, finally, the distinction is used only partially: ASIO's security intelligence collection activities within Australia take no account of citizenship; its foreign intelligence activities, however, do.[263] As with New Zealand, certain warrants can be used to collect information about a person who is an Australian citizen or a permanent resident of

the conduct of the international affairs of Canada', which excluded citizens and permanent residents: CSIS Act (1984) (Canada), s 16. When the CSIS Act was being enacted, suggestions were made that such a distinction be included in the rules on intrusive powers, on the basis that 'foreign nationals are more likely to be involved in security-threatening activity, and that Canadians who are so involved are much more amenable to less intrusive techniques or to the ordinary processes of the criminal law'. This was rejected by the Committee considering the Bill: 'The Committee entertains some doubt as to the legal propriety of such a distinction between citizens and non-citizens. It is generally undesirable. Further, it would prove to be a difficult distinction to make in practice.' Special Committee of the Senate on the Canadian Security Intelligence Service, *Delicate Balance: A Security intelligence Service in a Democratic Society* (1983) [63].

[260] 'I am satisfied that Australia has a need to collect foreign intelligence which relates to its national security and its other national interests. Considerations of the national interest, national independence, costs, and practical difficulties have led me to conclude that it would be highly advantageous for Australia to be able to collect foreign intelligence within its own territory where this is possible.' Royal Commission on Australia's Security Intelligence Agencies, *Report on the Australian Security Intelligence Organization* (1984) [6.80].

[261] *Comprehensive Review of the Legal Framework of the National Intelligence Community*, Volume 1: *Recommendations and Executive Summary; Foundations and Principles; Control, Coordination and Cooperation* (2019) [10.2]. In 2017, it has been observed that 'the traditional distinction between foreign and security intelligence underpinned an emphasis on the special rights to privacy and civil liberties of Australian persons in the Hope Royal Commissions. That underpinning continues to be important and the privileging of Australian persons in the mandates of particular Australian intelligence agencies and in Australian law remains strong.' M L'Estrange and S Merchant, *2017 Independent Intelligence Review* (2017) [2.22].

[262] See, eg, Intelligence Services Act 2001 (Australia) ss 9 and 3.

[263] ASIO Act (Australia), s 27A(9).

the country only if it is reasonably suspected that the person is acting on behalf of a foreign power.[264] The agencies – ASIS and the ASD – set up under the Intelligence Services Act can be authorised to produce intelligence on an Australian person only under certain conditions, and subject to a more onerous authorisation procedure.[265] Nevertheless, as is the case in the UK, Australians outside of Australia generally attract no special protection: 'in most circumstances the Government is able to authorise the same intelligence activities offshore against Australians that those agencies undertake against non-Australians – including, in very rare circumstances, the production of intelligence that would enable targeting for lethal action in accordance with the laws of armed conflict'.[266] The effect would seem to be that the Australian use of the geographic and citizenship distinctions is more varied, and more subtle, than is the case elsewhere.

The *Comprehensive Review* of the legal framework of the intelligence community in Australia recommended that the legislative framework should continue to distinguish between Australians and non-Australians. It found, however, and perhaps unsurprisingly in light of what has just been said, that the procedural requirements contained within the legislative framework 'do not apply in a consistent or principled fashion'.[267] It therefore suggested certain changes to the picture sketched briefly above. One would require the introduction of a ministerial approval process for Australians abroad, giving them the same – procedural – protection they would enjoy while in the country.[268] Another change, not purely procedural, that was recommended involved the removal of the special protection that Australians enjoyed against foreign intelligence collection while within the country, which it suggested 'has cost Australia valuable intelligence where an Australian [is] acting for, or on behalf of, a foreign power, and that it will continue to do so unless it is changed'.[269] The *Review* therefore recommended that the collection of foreign intelligence on Australians be permitted where the person in question was acting on behalf of a foreign power, bringing the rule in line with the one that will exist in New Zealand even if the distinction between Type 1 and Type 2 warrants is abolished there.

The upshot of this overview would seem to be that there is a consistency between the different jurisdictions only in that they all appear to draw lines of this sort. Everything else varies: where they are drawn, in relation to what and whether there is one line or many. Sometimes the line is purely geographic. Elsewhere the line is drawn based on legal status – citizenship or citizenship and permanent

[264] Telecommunications (Interception and Access) Act 1979 (Australia), ss 11A(3), 11B(4) and 11C(3A).

[265] Intelligence Services Act 2001 (Australia), s 9(1A).

[266] *Comprehensive Review*, Volume 1 (n 261) [10.3].

[267] ibid [3.37].

[268] 'It is not sufficient for ASIO to have robust internal accountability frameworks for authorising offshore activities. A ministerial authorisation framework for ASIO's offshore activities is required to ensure appropriate ministerial control of, and accountability for, those activities concerning Australians where those activities would require a warrant if undertaken in Australia.' ibid [16.13].

[269] ibid [10.74].

residence. Sometimes it is drawn in relation to all of the activities of the SIAs; at others times, only in relation to certain aspects of their mandate. Sometimes it is used to render certain powers unavailable; elsewhere its implications are procedural, requiring more approvals or approvals from different actors. We can therefore make only hesitant general claims about the phenomenon of differentiation as it exists in the Commonwealth Five Eyes states. It reflects, it seems clear, the sense that certain powers of the SIAs are highly intrusive, such that it would not be appropriate to make them available without differentiation. Whether that is a legal claim, however, as it seems to be in the UK, where the line appears to reflect the requirements of the ECHR, or a political one, where activities directed at those with a sufficiently close connection to the state are more politically sensitive, and so either not undertaken at all or taken only with executive approval, varies. One striking element of this picture is that where a distinction is drawn (explicitly or implicitly) between security and foreign intelligence, the former is seen as the more important, with additional limits likely to appear (if at all) on activities undertaken for foreign intelligence purposes. If, as I suggest in chapter 7, we are in the process of a shift back to viewing hostile states rather than terrorism as the primary threat to national security, the assumptions underlying that position may be called into question.

VI. The 'Double-Lock'

One of the ways in which distinctions based on citizenship and geography are used – we have noted – is to determine the level of safeguards that apply to particular (uses of) powers. One of these safeguards is particularly significant to the argument of the present work. Though they are not the only safeguards that apply to the various investigatory powers that now exist, there were two key safeguards included in the UK's Investigatory Powers Act 2016. The first was the IPC, an individual responsible for the review of the use to which the various powers are put, who replaced the fragmented landscape that existed before the 2016 Act and who is assisted by other Judicial Commissioners. That role and its analogues are discussed in chapter 5. The other was the so-called 'double-lock', which requires a two-stage process to take place when the SIAs wish to use many of their powers. At the first stage, the Secretary of State grants the warrant or other authorisation. At the second stage, one of the Judicial Commissioners must approve that grant, assessing the conclusions as to necessity and proportionality. In doing so, the Commissioner must 'apply the same principles as would be applied by a court on an application for judicial review',[270] a requirement that has been interpreted by the Commissioner as requiring – at least in most cases – that he be independently satisfied of the necessity for and proportionality

[270] See, eg, Investigatory Powers Act 2016 (UK), s 23(2).

of the warrant, even as the Minister is given far greater latitude on questions of policy.[271] In normal circumstances, a warrant – or other authorisation – may not be issued until approval is given by a Judicial Commissioner.[272] This represents a significant departure from the historic norm, noted repeatedly in this chapter, whereby the authorisation of interception of communications in the UK was given by the Minister, with no judicial involvement. The particular significance of the double-lock, for present purposes, is that it appears to have become highly influential within Commonwealth national security constitutionalism, with the other Commonwealth Five Eyes states – which, as we saw in section II.A, generally adopted the model of solely executive approval in their initial regimes for the interception of communications – either adopting it or feeling obliged to justify the decision not to do so. It thus operates to illustrate the existence of a model of Commonwealth national security constitutionalism even in a context where there is considerable divergence between the Commonwealth Five Eyes states, and where many of those resemblances that we have nevertheless identified might otherwise be attributed to some combination of a functional logic and the fact that the states in question shared and share a number of constitutional fundamentals.

Different views on the matter had been expressed in the various reports leading up to the enactment of the Investigatory Powers Act 2016, which first broke with the model of executive approval in the UK, though with most seeking to draw some sort of distinction between purely legal questions and those considered to have a substantial policy element. The ISC's report, *Privacy and Security*, recommended that responsibility for granting warrants remain with Ministers, these being 'able to take into account the wider context of each warrant application and the risks involved, whereas judges can only decide whether a warrant application is legally compliant'.[273] *A Question of Trust*, the report of the Independent Reviewer of Terrorism Legislation, David Anderson, recommended purely judicial authorisation for interception warrants, though with the Secretary of State responsible for certifying (where necessary) that a warrant was required in the interests of the defence or foreign policy of the UK.[274] The report of the Royal United Services Institute's Independent Surveillance Review came closest to arguing for the double-lock as ultimately implemented, saying that while crime-fighting warrants should be given by Judicial Commissioners acting alone, where a warrant was given 'for purposes relating to national security (including counter-terrorism, support to military operations, diplomacy and foreign policy) and economic

[271] For discussion of what that means in practice, see PF Scott, 'Hybrid Institutions in the National Security Constitution: The Case of the Commissioners' (2019) 39 *Legal Studies* 432, 450–53 and the document considered there: Investigatory Powers Commissioners Office, *Advisory Notice 1/2018: Approval of Warrants, Authorisations and Notices by Judicial Commissioners* (8 March 2018).

[272] See, eg, Investigatory Powers Act 2016 (UK), s 19(2)(d).

[273] Intelligence and Security Committee (n 230) 73–76.

[274] D Anderson, *A Question of Trust: Report of the Investigatory Powers Review* (2015), recommendations 30 and 31.

well-being, the warrant should be authorised by the secretary of state subject to judicial review by a judicial commissioner'.[275] Possibly influential in the decision to adopt the double-lock in the face of these disagreements was the spectre of the ECHR, and the possibility that one day it would be held to be incompatible with Article 8 of the Convention for the executive to have sole responsibility for authorising interferences with the right to private and family life.[276]

That the UK model – and its terminology – has achieved the prominence that it has is telling, for the double-lock was not wholly novel when included in the 2016 Act. In New Zealand, the approach was at first that of ministerial approval, as recommended (for the approval of all forms of otherwise unlawful action) in the Powles report in 1976 and justified in part on comparative grounds:

> The argument that an independent judicial officer should have the power is a strong one; our constitutional history has examples of strong reaction against executive warrants. Nevertheless, I recommend that, as in the United Kingdom, Australia, and Canada, the Minister should have the power, first and principally, because as I have stressed throughout this section he is responsible for the Service; secondly because (unlike the situations where a judicial officer grants a warrant) the grant is likely to be part of an ongoing intelligence exercise not resulting in court proceedings; thirdly because of the problems of properly briefing a person issuing a warrant and, fourthly, because judicial officers should not be involved in what is essentially executive business.[277]

Nevertheless, a form of double-lock later existed under both the New Zealand Security Intelligence Service Act 1969 and the Government Communications Security Bureau Act 2003, with warrants issued by the relevant Minister and an independent Commissioner of Security Warrants. In the case of the 1969 Act, for example, by an amendment of 1999,[278] which introduced the Commissioner – who was required to have previously held the role of Judge of the High Court[279] – the original Act was amended to provide that the Minister and the Commissioner could 'jointly issue a domestic interception warrant, authorising a person to intercept or seize any communication, document, or thing not otherwise lawfully obtainable by the person' if both were satisfied, 'on evidence on oath given by the applicant for the warrant', that the conditions for its granting were satisfied.[280] The New Zealand Privacy Commissioner welcomed the introduction of this process, suggesting that it would 'enhance controls over the SIS, emphasise the Service's

[275] Royal United Services Institute, *A Democratic Licence to Operate: Report of the Independent Surveillance Review* (2015), recommendation 10.

[276] As the point was put in *Zhakarov v Russia* (2016) 63 EHRR 17 [275], decided in 2015, 'although it is in principle desirable to entrust supervisory control to a judge, supervision by non-judicial bodies may be considered compatible with the Convention, provided that the supervisory body is independent of the authorities carrying out the surveillance, and is vested with sufficient powers and competence to exercise an effective and continuous control'.

[277] Powles (n 15) [15].

[278] New Zealand Security Intelligence Service Amendment Act (No 2) 1999 (NZ).

[279] New Zealand Security intelligence Service Act 1969 (NZ), s 5A(3).

[280] ibid, s 4A(1), as amended by the New Zealand Security Intelligence Service Amendment Act (No 2) 1999 (NZ).

political neutrality and go some way to provide reassurance as to the protection of civil liberties'.[281] Similarly, when the 2003 Act was amended in 2013, a new provision was introduced whereby the ability of the Minister to grant certain warrants upon application was made subject to the rule that applications had to be made jointly to, and warrants be issued jointly by, the Minister and the Commissioner if 'anything that may be done under the warrant or authorisation is for the purpose of intercepting the private communications of a New Zealand citizen or permanent resident of New Zealand'.[282] In both cases, in fact, the system put in place was perhaps more demanding than that in the UK's Investigatory Powers Act 2016: the two actors were formally equal within it, rather than the judicial actor's being – as in the case of the modern double-lock in the UK – secondary, if to a somewhat ambiguous extent, to the Minister, who remains the primary decision-maker.

Against this background, the authors of the review that prefigured the major reform of the law in New Zealand in 2017 distinguished between three tiers of warrant, reflecting the different levels of intrusiveness of the activities they permitted, with different procedures applying to different tiers. Tier 1 and 2 warrants should, they said, be approved by the Attorney-General rather than the Minister responsible for the Agencies, with those in Tier 1 also requiring the approval of a Judicial Commissioner.[283] There would be a slight distinction between the roles, though. Where both would have to be satisfied that the statutory criteria were met, only the Attorney-General would have to be satisfied that it was appropriate to issue the warrant.[284] This amounted to a slight rewriting of the prior practice, ensuring – in remarks that recall some of the views expressed in the UK in the run-up to the enactment of the 2016 Act – that 'judicial approval is appropriately focused on legal factors'[285] rather than on questions about, say, foreign policy, which were considered to be ultimately political rather than legal. In endorsing this dual approach rather than a purely judicial approval process of the sort for which some had argued, the reviewers drew on the example of the Investigatory Powers Act, then in preparation, which – they noted – introduced 'a process of approval by a secretary of state and review by a judicial commissioner on judicial review grounds for most of the intelligence agencies' activities'.[286] The review did

[281] Privacy Commissioner, *Report to the Minister of Justice: New Zealand Security Intelligence Service Amendment Bill (No 2)* (1999) 7, quoted in A Sandberg, 'Keeping a Watch on Big Brother: The SIS and the Court of Appeal' (2000-2003) 9 *Auckland University Law Review* 257, 265. A few years later, the New Zealand Government itself claimed that the creation of the Commissioner role involved recognising that 'the Prime Minister alone should no longer exercise the great power of issuing an interception warrant directed against New Zealand citizens or permanent residents' and that it had been 'a substantial check on the power of the Executive'. Department of the Prime Minister and Cabinet, *Securing our nation's safety: How New Zealand manages its security and intelligence agencies* (2000).

[282] Government Communications Security Bureau Act 2003 (NZ), s 15B, as amended by the Government Communications Security Bureau Act 2013 (NZ).

[283] Cullen and Reddy (n 8) [6.28].

[284] ibid [6.78].

[285] ibid [6.79].

[286] ibid [6.83].

not, however, recommend the extension of this double-lock to the foreign intelligence activities of the reformed SIAs, with the reviewers' remarks on this point endorsing the sort of hierarchy of intrusiveness founded on distinctions of legal status that we have noted previously:

> There is a balance to be struck between placing sufficient safeguards on the Agencies' activities, which are by their nature intrusive, while providing the Agencies with enough flexibility to perform their functions … The benefits of increased oversight must be weighed against the corresponding decrease in efficiency and increase in compliance costs. In our view, this balance is best struck by requiring judicial approval of activities targeting New Zealanders, but not the Agencies' other activities.[287]

These recommendations were accepted by the New Zealand Government and implemented, with modifications, in the Intelligence and Security Act 2017. The basic scheme of the 2017 Act, as we have seen, is to distinguish between two types of warrants: Type 1 warrants, which target New Zealand citizens or permanent residents, or a class of persons including at least one such person; and Type 2 warrants, which do not. Applications for the former must be made to both the authorising Minister and the Chief Commissioner of Intelligence Warrants, and both must be satisfied that the criteria for the issuance of the warrant are met. Applications for Type 2 warrants need be made only to the Minister, who alone need be satisfied that the criteria are met. As we have also seen in section V, the trend since the enactment of the 2017 Act seems to be away from the Type 1/Type 2 distinction, with the specific shift being argued for involving the extension to non-New Zealanders of the higher level of procedural protections currently only enjoyed by New Zealanders. The domain of the double-lock – in its particular New Zealand instantiation – would in this event expand significantly.

In Canada, the National Security Act of 2017 enacted – inter alia – the Intelligence Commissioner Act. The Commissioner, who must be a retired judge of a superior court,[288] is responsible thereunder for 'reviewing the conclusions on the basis of which certain authorizations are issued or amended, and certain determinations are made, under the Communications Security Establishment Act and the Canadian Security Intelligence Service Act' and, 'if those conclusions are reasonable, approving those authorizations, amendments and determinations'.[289] The authorisations in question include (as discussed in section II.B) FIAs under the Communications Security Establishment Act of 2019, as well as determinations about the retention of datasets under the CSIS Act of 1984[290] and determinations under that same statute as to classes of acts or omissions that might be carried out even though they would normally constitute offences.[291] This is, in effect, the double-lock, in a form that mirrors the

[287] ibid [6.86].
[288] Intelligence Commissioner Act (2019) (Canada), s 4(1).
[289] ibid, s 12.
[290] CSIS Act (1984) (Canada), s 11.03(2) and 11.17(1).
[291] ibid, s 20.1(3).

approach taken in the text of the UK's Investigatory Powers Act 2016, if not necessarily in practice thereunder: the role of the Commissioner is secondary, and is restricted to assessing not whether the criteria are met but whether the initial judgement that they are is a reasonable one. The process was not, however, introduced for the first time in 2019. Rather, there had long been a two-stage process, involving both Ministers and judges, for the issue of some warrants in Canada, with the judicial element – the review by David Anderson noted in its overview of comparative practice – 'introduced following a series of reports into abuses carried out by the Canadian Police Security Services in the 1970s'.[292] The reference is to the McDonald Commission, which recommended (against the background of a legal regime in which, as noted previously, approval was solely by a Minister) both a ministerial role[293] and a judicial one. This latter might, it suggested, be considered 'an unacceptable extension of judicial authority into decisions which should be reserved for responsible Ministers', but the Commission denied that this was the case, partly because of the sort of concern for the appropriate distribution of labour between policy and legality that is attested to in more recent considerations,[294] but also for the sorts of reasons that underpin so much of modern national security oversight in the Commonwealth Five Eyes states, whereby the felt imperative of secrecy means that the normal methods of testing, and so ensuring, the legality of governmental action are largely unavailable in practice:

> Under our proposal, the judiciary's role would be to determine whether or not a statutory standard established by Parliament as a condition for exercising certain extraordinary powers has been satisfied by the facts of a particular case. In normal situations of public law, the judiciary is involved when the exercise of a power is challenged after the fact. However, because of the secrecy inherent in the exercise of investigative powers by the security intelligence agency this practice becomes unrealistic, because the person affected does not normally learn of the use of this power and therefore cannot challenge its validity.[295]

These recommendations were implemented in the CSIS Act as enacted in the mid-1980s, and provided that where CSIS was seeking certain a warrant under

[292] Anderson (n 274) Annex 15, [47].

[293] The decision to subject an individual to intrusive techniques for national security purposes, it said, 'is a decision with important policy implications which in our view ought to have the approval of a responsible Minister. Indeed, it is through his participation in these decisions that the Minister responsible for a security intelligence agency is most likely to have the "window" he needs into the agency's activities.' Commission of Inquiry Concerning Certain Activities of the Royal Canadian Mounted Police, *Second Report – Volume 1: Freedom and Security Under the Law* (1981), 525.

[294] 'As we see it, the ministerial role with respect to these powers is to make policy decisions … He might refuse to authorize an application even though convinced that it met the statutory standard. The Solicitor General should by no means be indifferent as to whether the legal requirements were satisfied by a proposed application: on the contrary, he should not approve the application for a judicial warrant unless satisfied that the legal requirements have been met. However, our proposals give the judiciary, not the Minister (or his legal advisers), the final decision whether the law is being properly applied.' ibid 525–26.

[295] Commission of Inquiry (n 293) 525.

section 21 of that Act – including for the interception of communications – it would have to seek approval from the Minister and then make an application to a judge, who was able to issue a warrant if satisfied that the statutory criteria were satisfied.[296] This involved judges' acting specifically in a directly judicial role and not, as is now more common, performing a role which, though restricted to serving or retired judges, is discrete and special to the intelligence sphere – as an Intelligence Commissioner (as in modern Canada), say, or a Judicial Commissioner (as in the UK). In that context, it is notable that the CSIS Act also permitted the Governor in Council to make regulations governing – amongst other things – 'the practice and procedure of, and security requirements applicable to, hearings of applications for such warrants'.[297] Judges continue to play this role to this day, with one result being the existence of a substantive body of (often highly redacted) case law on questions relating to warrantry under the CSIS Act, and have an equivalent role in relation to warrants enabling the Service to take measures 'to reduce a threat to the security of Canada', where the measures involve certain actions or would limit a right or freedom guaranteed by the Charter of Rights and Freedoms.[298] The double-lock, then, or something very like it, has a much longer history in the Commonwealth Five Eyes states than modern discourse, in which that label and the UK example from which it derives have become predominant, might suggest.

In Australia, where the usual model remains sole authorisation of ASIO's investigatory powers by the Attorney-General,[299] much ink has been spilt on the question of whether the double-lock or some equivalent should be introduced. The Independent National Security Legislation Monitor, James Renwick, was tasked with reviewing the Telecommunications and Other Legislation Amendment (Assistance and Access) Act 2018.[300] In a speech discussing his work on the issue, he expressed his belief that certain authorisations under that Act should 'be issued, or at least subject to a "double lock" approval system, by a judge, serving or retired rather than an agency head or the Attorney'.[301] He noted too that 'the technical complexity of what is being authorised requires senior lawyers with access to top level technical advice' and that an 'excellent operating model' was to be found in the UK.[302] Having previously met with the Investigatory Powers Commissioner's Office (IPCO), he felt able to recommend the double-lock system:

> It works in this way: there is a double-lock system, so that if you can imagine a warrant or authorisation application is given first to the Minister, the same paperwork is then

[296] CSIS Act, s 21 (as enacted).

[297] ibid, s 28 (as enacted).

[298] ibid, s 21.1.

[299] See, eg, Telecommunications (Interception and Access) Act 1979 (Australia), ss 9 and 9A (providing for the Attorney-General to issue telecommunications service warrants and named persons warrants).

[300] Telecommunications and Other Legislation Amendment (Assistance and Access) Act 2018 (Australia).

[301] J Renwick, 'What are the Right Encryption Laws for Australia?', Speech at the Lowy Institute, Sydney (5 March 2020).

[302] ibid.

given to IPCO. IPCO doesn't look at all the matters the Minister looks at, for example, effects on international relations, but does ask, looking at the same material the Minister did, is the application lawful, proportionate, and reasonable? And if it's not, then the request is ineffective hence the 'double lock'.[303]

Drawing on his interactions not only with IPCO but also with the SIAs and police in the UK, Renwick suggested that the double-lock has been 'very well-received, not least because it has raised the level of trust'.[304] Rather than replicating IPCO in Australia, however, Renwick suggested that task of opening the second lock might be handed to the Security Division of the Administrative Appeals Tribunal.[305] Note that a model that had existed in Canada for all of the modern history of its SIAs, and which had been introduced in New Zealand long before the Investigatory Powers Act 2016, had already by this point in time become identified almost entirely with the UK.

When, later that year, Renwick's review of the Act was published, he noted therein that he had had extensive contacts with oversight figures in the UK,[306] and outlined in detail the work of IPCO and the operation of the double-lock in the UK. He described attempts to recast the Australian system, whereby both 'the Attorney-General and the Minister for Communications must both agree' on the use of certain powers, as a 'double-lock'.[307] This – in effect the claim that Australia already had the double-lock – Renwick rightly rejected, on the basis that 'one Cabinet minister's approval of another's decision to [issue the relevant notice] does not, in substance or perception, amount to an independent or external review of the decision to issue the notice'.[308] He argued, however, not for a double-lock of the

[303] ibid.
[304] ibid.
[305] ibid. The Australian Department of Home Affairs cast doubt on the suitability of the Administrative Appeals Tribunal (AAT) to perform this role: 'As a primary decision-making exercise, the approval of technical assistance notices and technical capability notices would be a significant departure from the merits review function performed by the AAT. A similar function is not conferred on AAT members in their official capacity by any other piece legislation. Therefore, the proposed Investigatory Powers Division would operate differently to any other AAT division and may require significant legislative amendments to the Australian Administrative Appeals Tribunal Act 1975, including modifying the basic objectives of the AAT and creating an entirely new function for the AAT.' Quoted in Parliamentary Joint Committee on Intelligence and Security, *Review of the amendments made by the Telecommunications and Other Legislation Amendment (Assistance and Access) Act 2018* (2021) [7.31].
[306] 'I have been able to consult with Lord Anderson throughout my tenure, including in relation to this review. Having met the inaugural Investigatory Powers Commissioner, Lord Justice Fulford, in a previous visit, in November 2020 I spent nearly 2 days with the IPCO – notably, with the new Commissioner, the Rt Hon Sir Brian Leveson, formerly President of the Queens's Bench Division and Head of Criminal Justice in the High Court of England and Wales, various judicial commissioners and members of IPCO's Technology Advisory Panel, including its Chair, Sir Bernard Silverman FRS.' Independent National Security Legislation Monitor, *Trust but Verify: A report concerning the Telecommunications and Other Legislation Amendment (Assistance and Access) Act 2018 and related matters*, 9th Report (2020) [2.31].
[307] Independent National Security Legislation Monitor (n 306) [10.5].
[308] ibid [10.29].

sort that exists under the Investigatory Powers Act 2016, but rather for a genuinely independent system, with the relevant decision as regards certain types of authorisations made by (and only by) a new IPC.[309] But even here the UK influence was crucial: Renwick rejected arguments for a continued ministerial role, using the exact arguments considered and accepted by David Anderson in *A Question of Trust*,[310] which preceded the 2016 Act. And so the influence of UK oversight mechanisms is palpable in arguments from both directions.

In the meantime, the *Comprehensive Review of the Legal Framework of the National Intelligence Community*, completed in 2019 but made public only at the end of 2020, had been published, and pushed in exactly the opposite direction. A key recommendation of that report was that much of the existing framework for investigatory powers be replaced by 'a single new Act governing the use of electronic surveillance powers – telecommunications interception, covert access to stored communications, computers and telecommunications data, and the use of optical, listening and tracking devices – under Commonwealth law'.[311] That of course raises the question of what safeguards should apply to warrants authorising use of these intrusive powers. The author – Dennis Richardson – noted that he had 'carefully weighed the arguments for and against an additional approval for warrants and authorisations, independent of the Executive (commonly known as a "double lock")' and did not recommend its introduction:

> It is a solution in search of a problem. There was no evidence before us – including from the Inspector-General of Intelligence and Security – of partiality or lack of rigour in the process for ministerial issue of warrants or authorisations such that an independent officer need also consider the legality and propriety of proposed activities. We are satisfied that Ministers engage with the applications put to them and the issues at play.[312]

Noting that the double-lock (or a close analogue) was used in 'comparable democracies', the report concluded that 'the mere existence of comparable arrangements elsewhere has been insufficient to convince us that such arrangements are needed in Australia': 'Each country has its own unique arrangements, including very different constitutional requirements and oversight structures.'[313] In late 2021, the Parliamentary Joint Committee on Intelligence and Security produced its own report on the Act that Renwick had been discussing, in which it offered the opinion that 'there would be benefits to a "double-lock" model,

[309] ibid [10.36].

[310] ibid [10.35].

[311] *Comprehensive Review*, Volume 1 (n 261) [3.22]. See also the recommendations in Parliamentary Joint Committee on Intelligence and Security, *Report of the Inquiry into Potential Reforms of Australia's National Security Legislation* (2013), ch 2.

[312] *Comprehensive Review*, Volume 1 (n 261) [3.105].

[313] ibid [3.106]. For discussion and some criticism of the *Review*'s recommendations on this point, see B Walker-Munro, 'The Richardson Review: Reviving the "Purpose" of Law Enforcement and Intelligence Legislation' (2023) 46 *University of New South Wales Law Journal* 268, 274–75.

given the success of the Investigatory Powers Commissioner's Office model in the United Kingdom'.[314] That is, and notwithstanding that the mechanism appears to originate not in the UK but in Canada, and has long existed in New Zealand, the terms of the debate are being set by the specific reforms introduced by the Investigatory Powers Act 2016, which has emerged as the dominant model within this aspect of Commonwealth national security constitutionalism. This, we can reaffirm, is an example of borrowing and sharing between the Commonwealth Five Eyes states that goes beyond what the shared functional logic operative in this domain, and the shared constitutional context within which it unfolds, might demand.

VII. Conclusion

It is no surprise that the SIAs of each state enjoy a range of highly intrusive powers, nor that certain issues or dilemmas turn out to be common to many or all of the four states under consideration. They are expected to acquire intelligence about threats emanating from (potentially) every part of the globe, and so are entrusted with highly intrusive capacities and the ability to act outside the confines of the home jurisdiction. Because threats might emerge even from those of whom the SIAs have no knowledge – persons and groups not known to them – some of these powers must, they say, be 'bulk' in nature, exercisable against vast groups of people and their communications, the overwhelming majority of which are not and never will be a threat to the security of the state on even the broadest conception thereof. How exactly those powers are framed differs greatly between the various jurisdictions. Though all reflect the basic idea that legal authority is required only for things that are prima facie unlawful, how that idea unfolds varies in practice. All of them now criminalise the interception of communications, and so must provide positive authority for such interception by the SIAs. The rules governing the use of data are much more variable, however, and sometimes amorphous, with the result that there is more variation as how the use of data by the SIAs is regulated in law. Though all of the jurisdictions now possess a – by definition more limited – power to authorise criminality generally, the power in question has been implemented in a variety of ways, and with varying substantive limits on what might be authorised thereunder. The threats posed by such powers and such capacities as are possessed by the modern SIAs are obvious, and not usually denied even by those who are certain that all of those powers and capacities are genuinely required. The result is the need to draw lines: to distinguish between those people and those places who can be exposed to their full weight; and those who, for political or legal reasons, cannot be so exposed and who must enjoy a higher level of protection. How those lines are drawn

[314] Parliamentary Joint Committee on Intelligence and Security (n 305) [7.90].

varies, but a key aspect is the interaction of factors relating to geography and those relating to status. Alongside these lines, new safeguards against abuse are argued for and sometimes granted, with one example – the 'double-lock', or some variant thereof, often described using exactly that term – now present in multiple systems, indicating very clearly the persistence of a Commonwealth approach to national security constitutionalism that transcends what the combination of functional logic and shared constitutional heritage might lead us to expect, and the transmission of which between jurisdictions can – as a result of the sorts of growing formalisation and transparency described in earlier chapters – be traced more easily and more precisely than was the case in the past.

5

Oversight Institutions

I. Introduction

The standard institutional apparatus of modern constitutions is usually a function of the traditional division of powers – there is a legislature, an executive and a judicial branch – though of course the Westminster model, discussed in the Introduction to this book, involves a significant degree of overlap between the legislature and executive – with the latter being formed out of and accountable to the former – of a sort which the classical doctrine in its stronger forms would not countenance.[1] Alongside this traditional division, and attracting increasing attention in recent years, are fourth-branch or integrity institutions, which seek to ensure the proper functioning of the democratic process or the upholding of standards of conduct within the other branches of government.[2] Like the judiciary, these fourth-branch institutions are usually to some degree separated from, and even insulated against, the democratic elements of the constitutional order. Unlike the judiciary, they do not apply, or do not solely apply, legal standards but also those rooted in other forms of constitutional norm; more significantly, and again unlike the judiciary in common law states, they do not wait for disputes to be brought before them but have an ongoing, 'watchdog' role, which means that they are not reliant for their functioning on the existence of suitably-qualified litigants.

An important feature of the constitutionalisation of national security in the four states that are our subject, however – formalising and giving to the national security apparatus of each state a solidity it lacked through much of the twentieth century – is that the institutional forms of the traditional Westminster model have had to be adapted in a number of ways in order to provide the sort of oversight or accountability that was, for much of the Cold War period, ostentatiously absent. We discuss in chapter 6, for example, the various parliamentary

[1] The literature on the separation of powers ideal is vast: see, for a historical overview of its development, MJC Vile, *Constitutionalism & the Separation of Powers*, 2nd edn (Liberty Fund, 1998).

[2] See M Tushnet, *The New Fourth Branch: Institutions for Protecting Constitutional Democracy* (Cambridge University Press, 2021). Tushnet calls those that are his focus 'institutions for protecting democracy' and identifies (ibid 3) as their conceptual underpinning the fact that 'the Montesquieian tradition cannot provide sufficient guarantees for constitutional democracy in a political world where political parties play central roles', and their functional underpinning is the fact that 'that difficulty is created by conflicts or convergences of interests in such a world'.

or quasi-parliamentary bodies that exist in the Commonwealth Five Eyes states in order to provide oversight of the work of the security services, and the often crucial fashions in which they differ from orthodox parliamentary committees, held in the past and even still at times in the present to be unsuited on a range of grounds for oversight of these matters. We might also observe the special judicial procedures that have been introduced into some of those states in order to accommodate the requirements of justice without jeopardising those of security.[3] In each of these cases, however, the bodies at issue remain recognisable variants of existing institutions, which can be, without excessive difficulty, attributed to one or another of the three branches of state for the purpose of analysis. Another, more striking feature of modern Commonwealth national security constitutionalism is the existence of bodies that do not so belong, or which cut across the traditional distinction: what I have previously described as 'hybrid' institutions.[4]

II. The Separation of Powers and 'Hybrid Institutions'

To explain the label 'hybrid institutions', we might categorise the different institutions of the constitution within the tripartite separation of powers by taking a functional approach – crudely, legislative institutions are those that make the law (and, in a parliamentary democracy, as the Westminster states are, hold the executive to account), executive institutions those that give effect to or execute it, and judicial institutions those that interpret the law and resolve disputes as to its application in particular cases. Not only, traditional separation of powers theory holds, does the division of responsibility in this way protect individual freedom against excessive (or, perhaps more precisely, arbitrary) governmental interference, but each (type of) institution has structural features that render it particularly suited (or, as the case may be, unsuited) to the performance of certain tasks, such that all three are a necessary part of a coherent and effective system of government. Legislatures, which might rewrite the law on a given topic in its entirety, are capable of taking whatever evidence they may desire before deciding whether or not to do so, and if so how. Decisions will be made, or at least might be made, after consultation and debate, and with inevitable consideration of the political desirability of whatever is being proposed as compared not only to the status quo but also to other options for action. Given that lack of structural constraints on their power to make law, they are accountable to the people of the state, via periodic general elections and the ongoing mechanisms by which public sentiment is formed and communicated, and indeed they might choose to exercise their legislative power

[3] Though now somewhat out-of-date, see D Jenkins, 'The handling and disclosure of sensitive intelligence: Closed material procedures and constitutional change in the "Five Eyes" nations' in G Lennon and C Walker (eds), *Routledge Handbook of Law and Terrorism* (Routledge, 2015) 266.

[4] PF Scott, 'Hybrid institutions in the National Security Constitution' (2019) 39 *Legal Studies* 432.

for no reason other than how their doing so will be received by these actors. Courts, on the other hand, might resolve only those live questions of law and fact necessary to resolve a dispute that comes before them, and are limited in the evidence they might accept, and from whom they might accept it, while simultaneously being subject to significant (if sometimes imprecise) limitations upon their ability to act on motives of policy. They are structurally insulated against democratic sentiment, whether acting directly or via the political organs of the state, openness to the relevance of which might undermine their performance of their role and the legitimacy they require to be allowed to continue to perform it. The executive, which controls directly or indirectly many of the actors and institutions that make up the coercive apparatus of the state, as well as its vast bureaucracy, is capable of acting quickly and decisively, with a high degree of discretion, implementing a unity of will the other branches of the state cannot easily find and often without being subject to the sorts of procedural requirements that are necessitated by the nature of the task those other bodies are tasked with performing.

Within this picture, what I call hybrid institutions are those that cut across these distinctions, performing a mix of those tasks normally performed by multiple separate (types of) constitutional institutions. Though I make no claim that they are exclusive to that context, within the national security constitution, such hybrid institutions are a vital part of the modern oversight landscape, generally carrying out a range of tasks, some of which would more usually have been performed by political institutions (executive and legislature); some of which would seem, within the traditional separation of powers model, to be best suited to the judicial branch. In particular, though they were introduced into the national security constitution with, effectively, a complaint-handling jurisdiction – which served to counteract the practical and sometimes legal difficulties of bringing a case against the SIAs to court, and in some cases persist, even if now often eclipsed in practice by other elements of their remits – they in most cases now provide a broad oversight of the work of the SIAs and the use of some or all of the investigatory powers enjoyed by some or all of those SIAs, as well as (in some cases) a broader review jurisdiction. Unlike courts, that is, they do not consider merely those situations in which there exists some live dispute that is brought before them for resolution. Such review is of course common: modern constitutional orders are replete with examples of the review of the work of public actors of various stripes, being carried out by a range of bodies. What is distinctive about the hybrid institutions that are the subject of this chapter, however, is that they carry out the oversight in question not (or not solely) by reference to policy or prudence, but with specific reference to legal questions, and for that reason they are often staffed at a high level by members or former members of the judiciary or others with relevant legal expertise, who are trusted to have access to secret material about the work of the SIAs and their use of their intrusive capacities. For these reasons, they differ both from courts or other judicial bodies – which might assess the legality of specific uses of those powers – and from bodies providing generalised oversight (such as the parliamentary bodies considered in chapter 6) – which consider broader questions, not limited to, or even necessarily concerned with, the specific issue of legality. One early consideration of the phenomenon therefore identified amongst the factors prompting their institution not only the obvious, primary factor – that is, scandal, and the need to respond to it and avoid its recurrence – but also what it described as the rise of 'rights-based' societies,[5] with these sorts of bodies working not only to address the threat of rights violations by the SIAs of the relevant jurisdiction but also, in the UK example, to bring the jurisdiction as a whole into compliance with the ECHR. Hybrid institutions, that is, are in part a function of the changing constitutional context noted in chapter 4, which made it politically and perhaps also legally intolerable to leave the SIAs in the constitutional black hole in which they had previously existed, with no direct or open accountability for their work.

Such hybrid bodies now exist in each of the four Commonwealths Five Eyes states, though the institutions in question vary in terms of their composition, the role they play and, in particular, in terms of whether certain functions – discussed in section IV.B – are performed by the hybrid body itself or a separate body. In Australia, there is an Inspector-General of Intelligence and Security (IGIS).[6] In New Zealand, there is an IGIS and a Commissioner of Intelligence Warrants.[7] In the UK, the relevant figure is the IPC.[8] In Canada, there is a National Security and Intelligence Review Agency (NSIRA),[9] but also an Intelligence Commissioner.[10]

Several of these bodies are the successors of previous bodies with analogous, but usually more limited, remits. The New Zealand IGIS, for example, replaced a Commissioner for Security Appeals established under the New Zealand Security Intelligence Service Act 1969,[11] which seems to have been the first body of this type in the Commonwealth Five Eyes states, but which was limited to investigating certain complaints about the NZSIS and so was more obviously a court substitute than is its modern successor. In Canada, the NSIRA replaced the SIRC, set up in 1984 by the statute that created CSIS and possessed of (amongst other things) a complaints jurisdiction,[12] while also taking on – alongside the Intelligence Commissioner – some of the functions of the Communications Security Establishment Commissioner, created in 1996. An earlier office that was a more direct predecessor of the modern bodies – that of Inspector General – had

[5] GR Weller, 'Comparing Western inspectors general of intelligence and security' (1996) 9 *International Journal of Intelligence and Counter Intelligence* 383, 385–86.
[6] Inspector-General of Intelligence and Security Act 1986 (Australia).
[7] Both under the Intelligence and Security Act 2017 (NZ).
[8] Investigatory Powers Act 2016 (UK), pt 8, ch 1.
[9] National Security and Intelligence Review Agency Act, SC 2019, c 13, s 2 (Canada).
[10] Intelligence Commissioner Act (2019) (Canada).
[11] New Zealand Security Intelligence Service Act 1969, ss 14–24.
[12] CSIS Act (1984) (Canada), ss 34–55.

also been set up by the original CSIS Act,[13] but disbanded prior to the creation of NSIRA. In the UK, the IPC replaced a range of Commissioners with narrower remits.[14] This chapter considers not only these various institutions in their own right and in relation to one another, but also uses them to demonstrate the emergence within the Commonwealth Five Eyes states of a discrete model of national security constitutionalism.

III. The Institutions of the Modern National Security Constitution

The institutions with which we are concerned in this section are described briefly before we go on to compare them along certain specific dimensions. Then, in section IV, we consider the work these institutions carry out and their contribution to the contemporary picture of national security oversight.

Though not the first to be introduced, the oldest of these institutions to still exist (albeit in modified form) is the IGIS in Australia, which was created by the Inspector-General of Intelligence and Security Act 1986,[15] subsequent to the second Hope Royal Commission.[16] Hope's work, as noted in chapter 2, was commissioned in response to a series of scandals, many of which either arose from or prompted the concern that ASIO was hostile to the Australian Labor Party. Hope produced a series of reports, making recommendations not only about the organisation of ASIO but also about the oversight of its work, including (and as had been argued for in particular by the Labor Party) for the introduction of what would eventually become the IGIS, that is,

> an independent person with power to maintain a close scrutiny of ASIO's performance of its functions, and to look into complaints, in order to give greater assurance to the Attorney-General, and through him Parliament and the public, that ASIO is acting with propriety and within its charter.[17]

The three subjects the IGIS would be empowered to look into in relation to ASIO were 'its compliance with the law', 'the propriety of its actions in more general

[13] ibid, ss 30–33. Key functions of the Inspector General included monitoring CSIS's compliance with its operational policies and reviewing its operational activities. For an early consideration of its work, see JF Ryan, 'The Inspector General of the Canadian Security Intelligence Service' (1989) IX *Conflict Quarterly* 33.

[14] See Scott (n 4) for an overview.

[15] For an early assessment, see HP Lee, PJ Hanks and V Morabito, *In the Name of National Security: The Legal Dimensions* (LBC Information Services, 1995) 232–40.

[16] Royal Commission on Australia's Security Intelligence Agencies, *General Report* (1984) Parliamentary Paper No 231/1985, [3.19]–[3.26]; and Royal Commission on Australia's Security Intelligence Agencies, *Report on the Australian Security Intelligence Organization* (1984) Parliamentary Paper No 232/1985 ('*ASIO*') [16.76] et seq.

[17] Royal Commission, *ASIO* (n 16) [16.84].

terms', and 'the appropriateness and effectiveness of its internal procedures', with the typical mixture of concern for legal and non-legal factors therefore built into this model from very early on; the IGIS would consider those matters both on his or her own initiative and in response to complaints.[18] He or she would report both on particular matters and on an annual basis, with reports laid (in redacted form if necessary) before Parliament.[19] If this recommendation were to be accepted, said Hope,

> the public interest in knowing whether ASIO (or indeed any intelligence service) is conforming with the requirements of the law and of propriety will be met by that officer's investigations and reports. The public's curiosity about the facts may not be satisfied, but the public will know whether it can have confidence in the integrity of the security and intelligence services; and the interests of any individual who might be adversely affected will be protected.[20]

This recommendation, that is, is a direct response to the need to ensure public confidence about the use of power in a context characterised by pervasive secrecy. Some points about the specifics of this original recommendation are worth noting. The position should, Hope said, be established by legislation, with any appointment to it supported by Parliament (and so 'there should be consultation before it is made between the Prime Minister and the Leader of the Opposition, as is required now for the position of Director-General of Security');[21] the IGIS should have security of tenure ('but not for so long a term as might give rise to any feeling that he had, through familiarity, become too close to those whom he is charged to inspect')[22] and 'full access to files and other materials held by ASIO and the power to require answers to questions from its officers'.[23] Though amongst the 'obvious prerequisites' for appointment to the role Hope identified '[i]ntegrity, independence of mind and a capacity for rigorous inquiry', he felt, for reasons that are not spelled out, that – notwithstanding that the primary plank of the role would be monitoring ASIO's compliance with the law – it would 'generally not be appropriate that the Inspector-General be a judge'.[24]

The origins of this vision appear, from the Hope report, to be twofold: one is the Inspectors-General 'who are a well-established feature of many departments and agencies, including security and intelligence agencies, in the United States'; these, however, appeared to Hope 'to be designed primarily to work internally to provide the executive head of each agency with "eyes and ears", removed from regular line management, to what is happening in the agency',[25] whereas he foresaw the IGIS as providing a broader political accountability for the work of the SIAs.

[18] ibid [16.91].
[19] ibid [16.94]–[16.97].
[20] Royal Commission, *General Report* (n 16) [2.10].
[21] Royal Commission, *ASIO* (n 16) [16.87].
[22] ibid [16.89].
[23] ibid [16.90].
[24] ibid [16.86].
[25] ibid [16.99].

In this way too, his proposal differed in a small but crucial manner from the other example he relied upon,[26] that of the Inspector-General provided for in Canada by the, at that point recently enacted, CSIS Act (and who was also not required to be a former or serving judge). That figure was designed – it was once said – to provide, 'for the political masters of the agency, ongoing information as to its functioning';[27] and it was abolished without fanfare as a 'cost-cutting measure' in 2012.[28] One of the Canadian Inspector-General's functions was to certify, each time the Director of CSIS submitted a report on its operational activities to the Minister, the extent to which he was satisfied with the report and whether any act done by the Service in that context was either not authorised by the CSIS Act or contravened a direction issued by the Minister, or involved 'an unreasonable or unnecessary exercise by the Service of any of its powers'.[29] This point is crucial: as we shall see in chapter 6, when (quasi-)parliamentary bodies were first introduced in the national security domain, allowing for oversight of the SIAs by political actors, they were (and in many cases have remained) unable to consider the operations of those SIAs. Hybrid institutions, on the other hand, were, from the beginning, not merely permitted but required to consider those operations. A few years later, when the CSIS Act was reviewed by a special committee of the House of Commons, it noted that the first Inspector-General's certificates 'tended to be fairly lengthy documents, running on occasion to nearly 300 pages … partly because they sometimes contained extensive legal analyses'.[30] But though it had a role focused primarily on compliance, the impact of the Inspector-General was argued to be broader:

> The CSIS Act does not specifically require the Inspector General to examine the effectiveness and efficiency of the Service. The examination of compliance with the standards imposed by the CSIS Act, ministerial directions, Federal Court warrants and operational policies may, however, cause the Inspector General to raise issues of effectiveness and efficiency as well as those of legality and propriety.[31]

[26] ibid [16.101].

[27] Special Committee of the Senate on the Canadian Security Intelligence Service, *Delicate Balance: A Security intelligence Service in a Democratic Society* (1983) [90]. See also Ministry of the Solicitor General, *On Course: National Security for the 1990s* (1991) 21, explaining that the post was created 'to provide the Minister with an independent window on the operational activities of the Service. In effect, the Inspector General serves as the Minister's internal auditor for CSIS, supplementing the advice the Minister receives from the Deputy with an independent means of assurance that the Service is complying with the law, Ministerial direction, and its own policies.'

[28] L West, 'Review and Oversight of National Security in Canada' in S Carvin, T Juneau and C Forcese (eds), *Top Secret Canada: Understanding the Canadian Intelligence and National Security Community* (University of Toronto Press, 2020) 257, 259. The role was 'quietly eliminated by means of a clause slipped into an omnibus budget bill, which was not the subject of debate in Parliament': R Alford, 'Bill C-59 and the Former Bill C-22: Compromised Oversight and Continuing Threats to Non-Derogable Rights' (2018) 69 *University of New Brunswick Law Journal* 57, 74.

[29] CSIS Act (1984) (Canada) (as enacted), s 33(2).

[30] Special Committee on the Review of the CSIS Act and the Security Offences Act, *In Flux But Not in Crisis* (1990) 140. The post was said, in the Government's response to this report, to be 'functioning to the full satisfaction of the Minister': Ministry of the Solicitor General (n 27) 21.

[31] Special Committee (n 30) 138.

Though it in turn influenced the Australian position, the origins of the Canadian model itself are less clear: neither the Inspector-General nor the SIRC – also introduced by the CSIS Act – was recommended by the McDonald Commission, whose report prompted the creation of CSIS. McDonald had recommended instead the creation of an Advisory Council on Security and Intelligence and a Joint Parliamentary Committee, and it has been suggested that the system put in place instead – comprising the SIRC and the IGIS, together identified by the Solicitor General as 'perhaps the most innovative features of our legislation' and 'an effective and credible guarantee that intelligence operations remain within the rule of law'[32] – 'was felt by many at the time to be a weaker system'.[33] This was a particular theme of debates on the resulting Bill, with one speaker noting – before the introduction of parliamentary oversight in any Commonwealth Five Eyes states – that 'In other countries, including countries with security problems that are far worse than ours, these parliamentary committees do exist' and that 'In the United States and West Germany, parliamentary committees oversee security services, and have access to all information in the possession of these services.'[34] Nevertheless, the Canadian preference at this point in time was for the dual institutions of the Inspector-General and the SIRC, and it was on the former that Hope then drew in recommending a new oversight model for Australia. One historian of ASIO suggests that Hope, in doing so, 'seemed to appreciate that an Inspector-General' of this sort 'was the lesser of two evils', in that its creation meant that 'ASIO escaped the attentions of oversight agencies that other government departments were exposed to'.[35] Viewing it as a means by which Labor MPs would acquire 'inside knowledge' of ASIO's working, the opposition of the day sought – unsuccessfully – to have the role limited to a duration of three years.[36]

Having been created by the 1986 Act, the role of the Australian IGIS was initially held by the journalist and public servant Neil McInnes,[37] with several of his successors being career civil servants.[38] McInnes, who described his role as 'protecting the public from the invasion or oppression of rights by intelligence agencies', noted what was described as 'a lack of enthusiasm within the Australian intelligence community for his new office'.[39] In time, however, it became a prominent feature of the accountability landscape surrounding the Australian SIAs,[40]

[32] House of Commons Hansard (Canada) vol 2, 1274 (10 February 1984).

[33] Ryan (n 13) 33.

[34] House of Commons Hansard (Canada) vol 4, 4595 (12 June 1984) (Lynn McDonald).

[35] F Cain, *The Australian Security Intelligence Organization: An Unofficial History* (Frank Cass, 1994) 272. Cain suggests (ibid 275) that the IGIS has already had a 'considerable impact' on ASIO.

[36] ibid 274.

[37] Inspector-General of Intelligence and Security, 'Past Inspectors-General' at www.igis.gov.au/about/past-inspectors-general.

[38] ibid.

[39] Commission of Inquiry into the Australian Secret Intelligence Service, *Report on the Australian Secret Intelligence Service – Public Edition* (1995) [9.13]–[9.14].

[40] See the discussion of some of its work in I Carnell and N Bryan, 'Watching the Watchers: How the Inspector-General of Intelligence and Security Helps Safeguard the Rule of Law' (2006) 57

with one of the periodic reviews of those agencies that have taken place in the twenty-first century suggesting that it was valuable in particular for its 'power to investigate deeply into the conduct of the agencies'.[41] More recently, and without any change to the rules as to eligibility, the post appears to have become more juridical in nature, with recent holders including Margaret Stone, who, like the current holder Christopher Jessup,[42] had previously been a judge of the Federal Court.[43] This tracks with what the IGIS told the *Comprehensive Review* of the legal framework governing the Australian intelligence community: that fulfilling aspects of the role 'requires a rigorous, independent assessment [of] the legal positions adopted by agencies in support of their actions' and 'often involves consideration of legal advices prepared or obtained by the agencies'.[44] Indeed, it was noted by that *Review* that the Australian SIAs occasionally sought views about questions of law from the IGIS, treating those views as legal advice – potentially suggesting an excessively close relationship between the 'regulator' and the bodies it oversaw. This the *Review* deprecated: 'a perception that the IGIS is closely involved in pre-operational decision-making must be avoided', for failing to do so 'could undermine IGIS' actual or perceived independence and thus undermine the entire system'.[45]

In New Zealand, there exist both an IGIS and Commissioners of Intelligence Warrants. The IGIS was created by the Inspector-General of Intelligence and Security Act 1996, replacing the Commissioner for Security Appeals that had been included in the New Zealand Security Intelligence Services Act 1969. That latter role, which had to be held by a lawyer but not necessarily a judge, but which was in fact held for much of its existence by the judge Sir Thaddeus Pearcey McCarthy, had in the original scheme the limited role of inquiring into complaints 'by any person ordinarily resident in New Zealand that his career or livelihood is or has been adversely affected by an act or omission of the New Zealand Security Intelligence Service'.[46] The 1996 Act, passed together with the New Zealand Security Intelligence Service Amendment Act 1996 (which amended the mission

Admin Review 34. The authors, the IGIS and an investigator in his office, identified amongst the key features of the role that it was 'independent and apolitical' and that it carried out 'a thorough and rigorous inspection program that identifies matters of potential concern and has a substantial normative effect'. See also V Thom, 'Reflections of a Former Inspector-General of Intelligence and Security' (2016) 83 *AIAL Forum* 11.

[41] P Flood, *Report of the Inquiry into the Australian Intelligence Agencies* (2004) 59.

[42] Inspector-General of Intelligence and Security, 'The Inspector-General of Intelligence and Security' at www.igis.gov.au/about/inspector-general-intelligence-and-security.

[43] Inspector-General of Intelligence and Security (n 37).

[44] *Comprehensive Review of the Legal Framework of the National Intelligence Community*, Volume 3: *Information, Technology, Powers and Oversight* (2019) [41.69].

[45] ibid [41.85].

[46] New Zealand Security Intelligence Services Act 1969 (NZ), s 17(1). Sir Guy Powles noted, however, his understanding that 'the Commissioner has read this provision widely and has considered issues, especially relating to citizenship, which have only an indirect link with the career or livelihood of the complainant'. G Powles, *Security Intelligence Service: Report by Chief Ombudsman*, Appendix to the Journals of the New Zealand House of Representatives (1976) 85.

of NZSIS and introduced new protections for political impartiality and freedom of expression) and the Intelligence and Security Committee Act 1996 (which introduced the Committee of the same name), provided that it was creating the role in question, which would ensure that 'complaints relating to that intelligence and security agency are independently investigated' but would also assist the Minister responsible for the SIAs in ensuring that their activities complied with the law.[47] To that end, a new function of the IGIS compared to its predecessor was to inquire (autonomously or at the Minister's request) 'into any matter that relates to the compliance by an intelligence and security agency with the law of New Zealand'.[48] This, then, was much more like the modern approach of using hybrid institutions to promote compliance with the law in circumstances where the ordinary means of doing so could not be relied upon to operate effectively in relation to the SIAs – and this was the SIAs plural, with the new IGIS (unlike the Commissioner for Security Appeals) possessing a jurisdiction in relation to not only the NZSIS but also the Government Communications Bureau.[49] Also notable was that as the role had expanded, the criteria for appointment had been tightened compared to those for the Commissioner of Security Appeals: a person could only be appointed to the post of IGIS if he or she had previously held office as a Judge of the High Court of New Zealand.[50] A few years into the existence of the role, the IGIS wrote that the 'fact that there are very few complaints and little need for any inquiry into the activities of the New Zealand Security Intelligence Service or the Government Communications Security Bureau indicates … that the performance of their activities does not impinge adversely on New Zealand citizens'.[51] We might, though, see an implicit criticism in the later claim that this view indicates that not only were Inspectors-General for a long time reactive – 'they did not tend to initiate their own inquiries or audits, but waited for complaints to which to respond' – but that in fact they 'equated a lack of complaints with compliance'.[52] Around this same time, however, 'the credibility of the Inspector-General was thrown into question' by an incident in which the NZSIS broke into and searched the home of a political activist.[53] Where the IGIS considered the Service to have acted lawfully in doing so, the New Zealand Court of Appeal disagreed.[54]

[47] Inspector-General of Intelligence and Security Act 1996 (NZ), s 4.

[48] ibid, s 11(a).

[49] ibid, s 2.

[50] ibid, s 5(3). 'Some submissions questioned the requirement for a nominee to be a retired High Court Judge. We recommend that there be no change to this requirement. The sensitive nature of the position requires the appointee to be demonstrably a person of the utmost integrity and independence with the advantage of a judicial background. We are of the view that a retired High Court Judge will have these qualities and will be perceived by the public as having them.' Committee on the Intelligence and Security Agencies Bill, *Intelligence and Security Agencies Bill* (1996) vi.

[51] Inspector-General of Intelligence and Security, *Annual Report 1998–99* (1999) [1].

[52] R Kitteridge, *Review of Compliance at the Government Communications Security Bureau* (2013) [85].

[53] GR Weller, 'Change and Development in the New Zealand Security and Intelligence Services' (2001) 21 *Journal of Conflict Studies* 1.

[54] See *Choudry v Attorney-General* [1999] 3 NZLR 399; and A Sandberg, 'Keeping a Watch on Big Brother: The SIS and the Court of Appeal' (2000–2003) 9 *Auckland University Law Review* 257.

The IGIS involved was Laurence Greig, the first holder of the role.[55] Greig resigned as IGIS following a decision of the New Zealand High Court, in circumstances that indicate some of the dangers of mixing up generalised oversight, designed to provide reassurance to the public at large, with the duty to make decisions having legal effect in relation to specific individuals. Another part of Greig's role as Inspector-General involved reviewing the decisions of the Minister of Immigration to rely on the certification of the Director of the NZSIS that individuals were a security risk. In this context, Greig had upheld on an interim basis such a decision made in relation to one Ahmed Zaoui, an Algerian national who had arrived in New Zealand travelling on a false passport and who sought refugee status there. Zaoui sought judicial review of this interim decision, and while that (and the Inspector-General's final decision) was pending, Greig gave an interview and carried out other acts that – the High Court held – raised the 'real possibility of apparent bias against Mr Zaoui', with the effect that Greig should not have any further involvement in the review of the decision under challenge.[56] Greig resigned from the role and was replaced by Justice Paul Neazor, a former Solicitor General, immediately following his retirement from the High Court.[57] The current New Zealand IGIS is Brendan Horsley, a lawyer with considerable governmental experience.

The New Zealand IGIS was compared unfavourably to that of Australia in an important report in 2013,[58] and changes were made that were aimed, the Government said, at making the role 'a more proactive overseer of the intelligence community':[59] these included removing the requirement that the IGIS be a retired High Court judge and creating a Deputy Inspector-General.[60] The functions – much expanded – of the modern New Zealand IGIS are discussed in section IV. The Intelligence and Security Act 2017 also provides for the existence, in addition to the IGIS and his Deputy, of up to three Commissioners of Intelligence Warrants, one of whom must be appointed the Chief Commissioner.[61]

[55] Inspector-General of Intelligence and Security, 'Who is the IGIS' at https://igis.govt.nz/about-us/who-is-the-igis/.

[56] *Zaoui v Greig*, High Court of New Zealand (31 March 2004).

[57] Prime Minister of New Zealand, 'Justice Neazor appointed Inspector-General of Intelligence and Security' (27 April 2004).

[58] Kitteridge (n 52) [83]–[94]: 'The overwhelming impression one gets about the Office of the IGIS in Australia is that it is very muscular. All parties to whom I spoke described it consistently as robust and assertive … In my view, incorporating elements of the Australian IGIS model would provide strengthened oversight of GCSB, which would be positive for the Bureau and welcomed by the New Zealand public.'

[59] Quoted in T Arnold and M Mahuika, *Taumaru: Protecting Aotearoa New Zealand as a free, open and democratic society* (New Zealand Ministry of Justice, 2023) [4.32]. Rogers quotes a holder of the role as noting that the 2013 changes significantly strengthened the role: 'Previously the Inspector-General had been a retired Judge, working part-time, with no investigatory capacity. Under the amendments it became a fulltime role and the powers and resources of the office now more closely match the mandate.' D Rogers, 'Intelligence and Security Act 2017: A Preliminary Critique' [2018] *New Zealand Law Review* 657, 684.

[60] See Inspector General of Intelligence and Security Amendment Act 2013 (NZ), which also expanded the range of circumstances in which an inquiry could take place.

[61] Intelligence and Security Act 2017 (NZ), s 112.

As discussed further in section IV.B, the Commissioners perform an approval role in (parts of) the warrantry process, which in the UK is performed within the IPCO itself rather than by a separate body. Given this role, it is unsurprising that a person must previously have held office as a Judge of the High Court to be eligible for appointment,[62] and the current Chief Commissioner is Bruce Robertson, formerly of the New Zealand Court of Appeal.

In the UK, the office of the IPC was created by the Investigatory Powers Act 2016, but the precursors of that role go back to 1985 (and so pre-date the Australian but not the Canadian institutions) in the form of the Interception of Communications Commissioner,[63] which was part of the original settlement introduced in response to the decision of the European Court of Human Rights in *Malone v UK*.[64] Even before that decision, though, there had been a few years of annual (but informal, and partly unpublished) reporting on the use of interception powers, first by Lord Diplock and later by Lord Bridge of Harwich.[65] When the Government first proposed to legislate to fill the gap the Strasbourg Court had identified, it said that it believed that 'the safeguards offered by the statutory scheme would be significantly reinforced if this office was incorporated within it':

> The functions of the person appointed to this office, who will be called the Commissioner, will be enlarged to cover all kinds of authorised interception. His tasks will be to review, on a continuing basis, the exercise of the functions conferred on the Secretary of State and the associated procedures in respect of the authorised interception of all communications falling within the ambit of the Act. As now, he will report annually to the Prime Minister and will be able to report at any time if he believes that powers conferred under the Act have been improperly exercised.[66]

The Commissioner was put in place by the Interception of Communications Act 1985, with its being suggested in the following decade that 'in practice it is probably the knowledge in Whitehall that the office exists, rather than the weak standard of review applied, which exerts most influence to ensure that the Act is followed carefully'.[67] The European Commission of Human Rights later held that the role of the Commissioner, and the work performed by him, played an important part in ensuring compatibility of the Interception of Communications Act 1985 with the ECHR.[68] The first Interception of Communications Commissioner was Lord Justice Lloyd, whose first report was published at the start of 1987. It was 13 pages long, which the Commissioner attributed to the need

[62] ibid, s 113.

[63] Interception of Communications Act 1985 (UK), s 8. The Commissioner was required to be someone who 'holds or has held a high judicial office'.

[64] *Malone v United Kingdom* (1984) 7 EHRR 14.

[65] See, eg, Lord Diplock, *The Interception of Communications in Great Britain* (Cmnd 8191, 1981). Later reports were not published.

[66] Home Office, *The Interception of Communications in the United Kingdom*, (Cmnd 9438, 1985) [16].

[67] L Lustgarten and I Leigh, *In from the Cold: National Security and Parliamentary Democracy* (Oxford University Press, 1994) 62–63.

[68] *Campbell Christie v United Kingdom* App no 21482/93 (ECtHR, 27 June 1994).

to set out the relevant procedures in his own words for those not already familiar with them from the 1985 White Paper. The following year's report, he hoped, would be 'much shorter'.[69]

The office of the Interception of Communications Commissioner was augmented within the broader landscape by, first, a Security Service Commissioner and, later, an Intelligence Services Commissioner, as the various SIAs were given a statutory footing.[70] When what became the Regulation of Investigatory Powers Act 2000 was proposed, the Government stated that it believed 'that the role of the Interception Commissioner is an essential one and proposes no change to this effective means of oversight'.[71] These actors had only a secondary role in the investigation or resolution of complaints against the SIAs, most of which were handled in the first place by specialist tribunals created by those same statutes. Another function of the Commissioners was to 'keep under review' the exercise by the relevant Minister of the powers to grant warrants or authorisations under the relevant statutes.[72] The ISC therefore described them as providing 'retrospective review of the Agencies: their role is to provide an independent "audit" of the Agencies' compliance with the law'.[73] Though annual reports were published by each of these figures, and some of them contain – by accident or design – interesting details about the legal framework within which the relevant SIAs were operating, they were generally short and, within that, highly repetitive.[74] These various separate roles were folded into an expanded role of the IPC, who would enjoy 'new powers and resources' and be part of a 'world-leading oversight regime'[75] when the law in this area was reformed by the Investigatory Powers Act 2016.[76] The first IPC was Lord Justice Fulford, who was succeeded by Sir Brian Leveson.[77] The statute originally provided for the appointment of a series of Judicial Commissioners to whom the IPC might delegate the exercise

[69] Interception of Communications Commissioner, *Report of the Commissioner for 1986* (Cm 108, 1987).

[70] Security Service Act 1989 (UK), s 4; and Intelligence Services Act 1994 (UK), s 8.

[71] Home Secretary, *Interception of Communications in the United Kingdom: A Consultation Paper* (Cm 4368, 1999) [9.1].

[72] Security Service Act 1989 (UK), s 4(3); and Intelligence Services Act 1994 (UK), s 8(3). Promoting the inclusion of a Commissioner in the Bill that became the Security Service Act 1989, the Home Secretary described his experience of giving warrants under the 1985 Act thus: 'In making my decision, I know that the interception commissioner is looking over my shoulder. He has access to all the warrants and has the right to call for any document or file relating to those warrants.' HC Deb 15 December 1988, vol 143, col 1108.

[73] Intelligence and Security Committee, *Privacy and Security: A modern and transparent legal framework* (HC 2014–15, 1075) [207].

[74] The only Security Service Commissioner in the period of that role's existence was Lord Justice Stuart-Smith, who was appointed to the role of Intelligence Services Commissioner when it was created several years later. For discussion of these roles see Scott (n 4).

[75] Home Office, *Investigatory Powers Bill: Government Response to Pre-Legislative Scrutiny* (Cm 9219, 2016).

[76] Investigatory Powers Act 2016 (UK), pt 8, ch 1.

[77] Investigatory Powers Commissioner's Office, 'PM appoints new Investigatory Powers Commissioner' (3 October 2019).

of most of his functions,[78] though later changes introduced a differentiation of those functions that might be delegated: some could be delegated only to those performing the newly created role of Deputy IPC, of whom up to two might be appointed.[79] When the compatibility of the 2016 Act regime with the ECHR was challenged, the High Court – in rejecting that challenge – pointed to a range of 'inter-locking safeguards' against the abuse of the powers introduced or reformed by it, including the general oversight provided by the IPC,[80] a view that was largely echoed when that judgment was appealed.[81] Where they exist, therefore, these oversight bodies will at times make a crucial contribution to ensuring that the overall regime of investigatory powers is compatible with relevant human rights norms.

In Canada there now exists both an NSIRA and an Intelligence Commissioner. The NSIRA, created by the National Security and Intelligence Review Agency Act (2019) as part of the omnibus National Security Act, 2017, replaced a number of institutions – including the SIRC,[82] a Committee of Privy Councillors that reviewed only the activities of the CSIS, and the Office of the CSE Commissioner, which reviewed the activities of the CSE,[83] the other institution to which it might be considered a successor – the Inspector General – having, as previously noted, been abolished a number of years beforehand.[84] The SIRC, set up by the same enactment that first gave CSIS a legislative basis and comprising between three and five members of the Privy Council for Canada who did not sit in either chamber of the Canadian Parliament, had as it primary function that of reviewing 'generally the performance by [CSIS] of its duties and functions',[85] as well as a range of related

[78] Investigatory Powers Act 2016 (UK), s 227(8).

[79] Investigatory Powers (Amendment) Act 2024 (UK), ss 7 and 8.

[80] *R (Liberty) v Secretary of State for the Home Department* [2019] EWHC 2057 (Admin) [174].

[81] See, eg, in its discussion of the position of bulk interception, *R (Liberty) v Secretary of State for the Home Department* [2023] EWCA Civ 926 [118]–[128].

[82] On which see Special Committee on the Review of the CSIS Act and the Security Offences Act, *In Flux but Not in Crisis* (September 1990) ch 11. For an early, but largely positive, appraisal of the body and its work, see P Gill, 'Symbolic or real? The impact of the Canadian security intelligence review committee, 1984–88' (1989) 4 *Intelligence and National Security* 550. For a brief post-mortem, see West (n 28) 258–60.

[83] See M Rudner, 'Canada's Communications Security Establishment, Signals Intelligence and counter-terrorism' (2007) 22 *Intelligence and National Security* 473, discussing the Commissioner's work and noting (ibid 487), in relation to the Commissioner and other oversight actors, that 'reassurances about probity and proficiency from review bodies apparently have not sufficed to overcome those latent public ambiguities and scepticism about intelligence and national security'.

[84] The loss of which was bemoaned during debates on what became the Anti-terrorism Act (Canada) of 2015 – see, eg, relying on a distinction between oversight (real-time consideration of operations) and review (consideration of it after the fact) that is more prominent in Canada than elsewhere, E May, House of Commons Hansard (Canada) vol 147, 1720 (5 May 2015): 'We can say that SIRC provides review … but there is no oversight. We used to have an inspector general for CSIS. The inspector general for CSIS was done away with …'.

[85] CSIS Act (1984) (Canada) (as enacted), s 38(a). The SIRC was discussed by Lustgarten and Leigh (n 67) 463–66, and was described there as 'a constitutional innovation which stands in unusual relation to both executive and legislative branches of government'.

matters, and would – it was said when the Bill was being enacted – 'perform the crucial review function, seeking to ensure that the whole superstructure set up by the legislation operates within the bounds of the law'.[86] It also heard complaints against CSIS, both in general – though after a complaint had first been made to the Service itself – and specifically in relation to decisions about security clearance.[87] Writing in the 1990s, from a mostly British perspective, Leigh and Lustgarten painted a very positive picture of the SIRC, which – they said – meant 'having significant impact on an organization whose operations are perforce hidden from public view, and altering the climate of public opinion and interest within which the organization functions'.[88] Their account, however, confirms the impression that notwithstanding its extra-parliamentary status (and the non-parliamentary status of its members), the SIRC is best thought of as a precursor to the sorts of parliamentary or quasi-parliamentary bodies considered in chapter 6: Leigh and Lustgarten identify one of the institutional characteristics that contributed to SIRC's success as its independence from the executive, and note that it had been described (in a phrase apparently coined by SIRC itself) as 'Parliament's surrogate'.[89] It could, however, direct CSIS or the Inspector General – before that latter post was abolished – to 'conduct a review of specific activities of the Service and provide the Committee with a report of the review'; where it considered that a review by one or the other would be 'inappropriate', it could carry out the review itself.[90]

The CSE Commissioner, an office formalised by the same Anti-terrorism Act that first gave the CSE a statutory basis via amendment of the National Defence Act, had the following functions: 'to review the activities of the Establishment to ensure that they are in compliance with the law'; to investigate where a complaint had been made against the CSE; and 'to inform the Minister and the Attorney-General of Canada of any activity of the Establishment that the Commissioner believes may not be in compliance with the law'.[91] In light of the highly legalistic nature of this mandate, it is unsurprising that the Commissioner was required to be either a supernumerary judge or a retired judge of a superior court.[92] In the Commissioner's final report after the office had been abolished,

[86] Special Committee of the Senate on the Canadian Security Intelligence Service, *Delicate Balance: A Security intelligence Service in a Democratic Society* (1983) [93].

[87] CSIS Act (1984) (Canada) (as enacted), s 41.

[88] Leigh and Lustgarten (n 67) 462.

[89] ibid 463.

[90] CSIS Act (1984) (Canada) (as enacted), s 40. The SIRC's first annual report contains a thoughtful consideration of the review landscape put in place by the CSIS Act, which observes that there is 'little doubt that Parliament would not have given the CSIS its extraordinary powers if Parliamentarians had not been satisfied that the use of those powers was to be subject to continuous and thoroughgoing review'. Security Intelligence Review Committee, *Annual Report 1984–85* (1985) 3–5.

[91] National Defence Act, RSC, 1985, c N-5 (Canada), s 273.63(2), as inserted by the Anti-terrorism Act, SC 2001, c 41 (Canada), s 102.

[92] National Defence Act (Canada), s 273.63(1).

the Commissioner noted that in the period of its existence, Commissioners had submitted to the Minister 122 review reports:

> Of the 175 recommendations contained in these reports, CSE has accepted and implemented, or is working to address, 166 or 95% of these recommendations. The office can be pleased with its contribution to the overall accountability of CSE to Parliament and the public, and to improvements in CSE policies and practices.[93]

It has been pointed out, however, that only on one occasion over two decades of its existence did the Commissioner conclude that the CSE had failed to comply with the law, 'and even in that case the non-compliance was ascribed to a failure of due diligence rather than determined to be an intentional violation of the law'.[94]

When the Canadian Government undertook a series of consultations on issues around national security and the protection of freedoms starting in 2016,[95] a central theme that emerged from them was that of accountability, 'with the vast majority of participants stressing the importance of ensuring that Canada's national security agencies are subjected to sufficient oversight to prevent unnecessary or excessive surveillance and protect Canadians' Charter rights and freedoms'.[96] There was strong support for some form of independent review in addition to the Committee of Parliamentarians being proposed at that point, including for 'the creation of a "super" review body to consolidate all oversight functions now conducted' not only by the SIRC and Commissioner of the CSE, but also by the body charged with oversight of the RCMP.[97] The result was the NSIRA, the creation of which has been claimed to have brought to an end a persistently 'siloed' approach to review in Canada.[98] The NSIRA's first Chair was Murray Rankin, a lawyer who had been legal counsel to the SIRC and was at that time a Member of the Canadian Parliament, and who had been made a member of the National Security and Intelligence Committee of Parliamentarians (NSICOP) on its creation.[99] Rankin stepped down a year later and the Chair is now Marie Deschamps, a retired judge of the Canadian Supreme Court.[100] The statute that created the Agency requires that it have between three and six additional members, and four of the original six members of the NSIRA had previously been members of the SIRC, the body from which it took over.[101]

[93] Communications Security Establishment Commissioner, *2018–19 Departmental Results Report* (2019) 1.

[94] B Robinson, 'The Communications Security Establishment' in Carvin, Juneau and Forcese (eds) (n 28) 72, 82.

[95] See Government of Canada, *Our Security, Our Rights: National Security Green Paper, 2016* (2016).

[96] Government of Canada, *National Security Consultations What We Learned Report* (2017) [2.2.1].

[97] Government of Canada (n 95) [2.2.1].

[98] West (n 28) 262.

[99] National Security and Intelligence Committee of Parliamentarians, 'NSICOP Congratulates Murray Rankin on Appointment as Chair of NSIRA' (1 August 2019).

[100] National Security and Intelligence Review Agency, 'Who We Are' at https://nsira-ossnr.gc.ca/who-we-are.

[101] Prime Minister of Canada, 'Prime Minister announces members of the new National Security and Intelligence Review Agency' (24 July 2019).

The last of these original members was the academic Craig Forcese,[102] a leading authority on Canadian national security law.[103] Also introduced by the National Security Act was the Intelligence Commissioner – required to be a retired judge of a superior court[104] – who performs a review (described, usually, as a 'quasi-judicial review') of certain decisions relating to the use of intrusive powers,[105] as described in chapter 4. As in New Zealand, that is, a separate body (here, the Intelligence Commissioner) carries out, in effect, one of two parts of the double-lock review process that in the UK is carried out by the hybrid institution – the IPC – itself, rather than by a distinct institution. We discuss this issue further in section IV.B. The first holder of the Intelligence Commissioner post was Jean-Pierre Plouffe, a long-time Judge of the Superior Court of Québec, who had previously been Communications Security Establishment Commissioner.[106] Before his new role had even been legislated for, Plouffe had visited the UK's IPC to discuss the work he would be required to do as Intelligence Commissioner,[107] indicating the sort of interaction between oversight actors in the Commonwealth Five Eyes states that has been normalised and, as discussed further in section V, formalised in the modern era. Plouffe's successor, Simon Noël, was similarly experienced in the domain of national security law.[108]

A. The Status of Oversight Institutions

The hybridity of these institutions – their positioning in a space between legislatures and courts – is a function of the fact that they are often addressing not only the propriety of what the SIAs (or those authorising their activities) do, and its prudence, but also its lawfulness: at times in terms of whether those agencies are at the macro level acting within the legal boundaries laid down for them (mostly) by statute, but also – and increasingly – the question of whether they have been acting lawfully in relation to specific acts, and specific exercises of intrusive powers. Again, the use of these powers is usually not known to, or perhaps even suspected by, those at whom they are targeted, and so the likelihood that they will be adjudicated upon by a court (or court-surrogate) is, in ordinary circumstances, low. A key implication of using hybrid institutions to fill this accountability gap is

[102] ibid.

[103] See, eg, C Forcese and L West, *National Security Law*, 2nd edn (Irwin Law Inc, 2020).

[104] Intelligence Commissioner Act (2019) (Canada), s 4(1).

[105] ibid, ss 13–19.

[106] Office of the Intelligence Commissioner, 'The Honourable Jean-Pierre Plouffe' (nd) at www.canada.ca/en/intelligence-commissioner/thehonourablejeanpierreplouffe.html.

[107] IPCO, 'Office of the Communications Security Establishment Commissioner Visit' (30 July 2018).

[108] Having been counsel to the Royal Commission of Inquiry into certain activities of the RCMP (1979–81) and 'represented the interests of the Security Intelligence Review Committee for over 15 years'. Office of the Intelligence Commissioner, 'The Honourable Simon Noël' (nd) at www.canada.ca/en/intelligence-commissioner/honourablesimonnoel1.html.

that they either have a strong juridical element or, if they do not have such a thing by design, they in practice tend towards it. We have already noted, for example, that the role of IGIS in Australia has over time come to be performed by senior judges rather than the public servants of its early years. In this section, I consider what the relevant statutory frameworks say about who may (or must) perform the various roles described so far, and the related question of security clearances, which has particular significance in light of the role of these bodies in overseeing operational matters, as well as the ways – if any – in which the independence of these bodies is protected against the executive of the day.

The Australian IGIS is appointed by the Governor-General on the nomination of the Prime Minister, who is obliged to first consult the Leader of the Opposition.[109] Appointment, which may be on a full- or part-time basis, is for a period of up to five years, which is renewable only once,[110] a rule that calls to mind the fear expressed by Justice Hope in the report that proposed the role: that a long period of appointment might give rise to the apprehension that the IGIS 'had, through familiarity, become too close to those whom he is charged to inspect',[111] and also carries with it the danger that the prospect of the mandate's being – or not being – renewed might influence how it is fulfilled. Within the period of appointment, there is a degree of protection for the independence of the IGIS, in the form of protection of security of tenure: the IGIS's appointment may be terminated only on limited grounds, most importantly 'by reason of misbehaviour or physical or mental incapacity'.[112] The governing statute foresees but does not require that the IGIS might be a judge, providing (for example) that appointment as IGIS does not affect a judge's 'tenure as the holder of a judicial office' nor 'rank, title, status, precedence, salary, annual or other allowances or other rights or privileges as the holder of the judicial office', and that if the person appointed as IGIS is a judge and ceases to be so then the Governor-General may terminate his or her appointment as IGIS.[113] As already noted, practice has varied over time, with a clear trend apparent: though a number of those who have held the post since its inception were not judges, nor even (it seems) legally qualified, the current IGIS is a (former) judge, and his predecessor was during her tenure a serving judge. As a result, perhaps, the statute appears to make no provision for security clearance of the IGIS, but only of his or her staff.[114]

The absence of any reference to security vetting also applies in the UK, where – as has been the case with all of the various Commissioners that have existed within the modern national security framework – to be eligible for

[109] Inspector-General of Intelligence and Security Act 1986 (Australia), s 6.
[110] ibid, s 26.
[111] Royal Commission, *ASIO* (n 16) [16.89].
[112] Inspector-General of Intelligence and Security Act 1986 (Australia), s 30.
[113] ibid, s 7.
[114] ibid, s 32(6): 'Unless the responsible Minister otherwise agrees in relation to a particular inquiry, the person proposed to be employed in relation to the inquiry must be cleared for security purposes to at least the same level, and at the same frequency, as staff members of ASIS.'

appointment as the IPC or a Judicial Commissioner, a person must hold (or have held) 'high judicial office', meaning a post as a High Court judge (or its equivalents in Scotland or Northern Ireland) or above.[115] The IPC is appointed by the Prime Minister, and must be recommended jointly for appointment by the Lord Chancellor and the senior territorial judges,[116] and so must be acceptable to the government of the day;[117] the other Commissioners must be recommended not only by those same figures but also by the IPC, giving the IPC at least a theoretical veto over new Judicial Commissioners.[118] The Scottish Ministers must be consulted, but there is no requirement, of a sort that exists in other jurisdictions, that the Leader of the Opposition be consulted.[119] The term of appointment for each post is three years, though this is renewable on an indefinite basis.[120] Though the IPC and Judicial Commissioners therefore do not enjoy the protection of tenure that they do or previously did in their judicial roles, where appointment is until the fixed retirement age, within that three-year period they enjoy a degree of protection that resembles it. They may, that is, be removed from post by the Prime Minister only on limited grounds or – like a senior judge in his or her judicial role – if both Houses of Parliament pass a resolution approving removal.[121] The distinction from the Australian position regarding the possibility of renewal is notable, if counter-balanced by the shorter term of office enjoyed by the IPC, and various advantages and disadvantages to each approach might be identified.

In Canada, the Intelligence Commissioner is appointed by the Governor in Council on the recommendation of the Prime Minister, and must, as already noted, be a 'retired judge of a superior court'.[122] Appointment is for a term of five years, which is renewable once, and the Commissioner holds office on good behaviour.[123] Appointment to NSIRA is on the same basis – by the Governor in Council on the advice of the Prime Minister, on good behaviour for a term of up to five years, again renewable only once[124] – and may take place only after a range of mandatory consultations with the leaders or facilitators of political parties.[125] A Chair of the Agency must be designated by the Governor in Council; a Vice-Chair may also be designated.[126] As well as the Chair, there must be between three

[115] Investigatory Powers Act 2016 (UK), s 227(1).
[116] That is, the Lord Chief Justice of England and Wales, the Lord President of the Court of Session and the Lord Chief Justice of Northern Ireland.
[117] Investigatory Powers Act 2016 (UK), s 227(3).
[118] ibid, s 227(4). And when the Investigatory Powers (Amendment) Act 2024 introduced the category of Deputy IPC, it left their appointment in the hands of the IPC: Investigatory Powers (Amendment) Act 2024 (UK), s 7.
[119] Investigatory Powers Act 2016 (UK), s 227(5).
[120] ibid, ss 228(2) and (3).
[121] ibid, s 228(5).
[122] Intelligence Commissioner Act (2019) (Canada), s 4(1).
[123] ibid, ss 4(1) and (2).
[124] National Security and Intelligence Review Agency Act (2019) (Canada), s 4.
[125] ibid, s 4(2).
[126] ibid, ss 4(5) and (6).

and six other members.[127] The Chair and Vice-Chair might be appointed on a full-time basis; other members are appointed on a part-time basis.[128] There are no criteria with which a person must comply to be eligible for membership of the NSIRA – in particular there is no obligation to have held judicial office or even to be legally qualified. Perhaps, again, as a logical correlate of this, each member of NSIRA (as well as employees of the associated secretariat) must 'maintain the security clearance required by the Government of Canada'.[129] Nevertheless, of the seven current members of the NSIRA, four appear to have a legal background,[130] suggesting – like the example of the Australian IGIS – that lawyers will come to dominate oversight bodies, whether or not the statute specifically requires their involvement. This in turn suggests that one possible advantage of drawing a distinction between the body charged with approving warrants (here, the Intelligence Commissioner) and that which provides more general oversight (here, the NSIRA) – that is, that one can seek to avoid domination of the more general oversight institution by questions of law, to the exclusion of those other standards by which the appropriateness of the work of the SIAs might be judged – may not in fact manifest in practice.

That division also exists, as noted, in New Zealand, where up to three people must be appointed, by the Governor-General on the recommendation of the Prime Minister, as Commissioners of Intelligence Warrants, with one appointed the Chief Commissioner,[131] in order to carry out a range of warrantry work. A person, the 2017 Act provides – again reflecting the highly legalistic nature of this particular work – may be appointed as a Commissioner 'only if that person has previously held office as a Judge of the High Court'.[132] Commissioners are appointed for renewable three-year terms, and can be removed only on limited grounds (including neglect of duty and misconduct) on address from the House of Representatives.[133] The appointment of the New Zealand IGIS is by the Governor-General on the recommendation of the House of Representatives; before a recommendation is made, the Prime Minister must consult the ISC about the appointment that is proposed and inform that House of the outcome of that consultation.[134] Appointment is for up to five years and may be renewed for a (single) further term of up to three years.[135] Removal or suspension is possible only via the same process as might be used to remove a Commissioner of Intelligence Warrants, and the grounds for doing so are the same, except that they also include the ground of 'failure to hold the appropriate

[127] ibid, s 3.
[128] ibid, s 4(7).
[129] ibid, s 50.
[130] National Security and Intelligence Review Agency (n 100). These include Marie Deschamps, Craig Forcese, Foluke Laosebikan and Colleen Swords.
[131] Intelligence and Security Act 2017 (NZ), s 112.
[132] ibid, s 113.
[133] ibid, sch 3, pt 1.
[134] ibid, s 157.
[135] ibid, sch 3, para 6.

security clearance'.[136] This is because the IGIS need not now be a judge or legally qualified but – note again the connection between these two points – must 'hold a government-sponsored security clearance of a level determined by the Prime Minister'.[137] The distinction between the IGIS and the Commissioners is reaffirmed by the fact that the IGIS, his or her Deputy, and any of his or her employees do not – unlike the Commissioners – enjoy the immunities of a Judge of a High Court but, rather, 'are not personally liable for any act done or omitted to be done in good faith in the performance or intended performance of the Inspector-General's functions or duties'.[138] On paper, it would again appear that the separation of the general oversight and the warrantry functions allows the IGIS, which performs the former, to take account of a range of considerations beyond the purely legal – after all, the IGIS is tasked not only with reviewing compliance with law by the New Zealand SIAs but also, in certain circumstances, with conducting an inquiry into 'the propriety of particular activities of an intelligence and security agency',[139] understood by at least one IGIS to mean 'whether the agencies have acted in a way that a fully-informed and objective observer would consider appropriate and justifiable in a free and democratic society'.[140] In practice, however, the post of IGIS appears to have been held, again, exclusively by lawyers, with the change made in 2013 to end the requirement that the holder be a judge resulting in a preference for the appointment of public sector lawyers. Bodies that possess a role in assessing lawfulness, even if it is one role amongst many, seem frequently, perhaps inevitably, to come to be dominated by that function, with – one might think – possibly deleterious effects on the wider range of interests they were intended by their creators to promote and protect.

IV. The Work of the Hybrid Institutions

The various bodies that now exist in each state perform a variety of tasks, both regular and ad hoc. In this section I outline the range of work they carry out, which – we shall see – has evolved significantly since the original introduction of the New Zealand Commissioner for Security Appeals in 1969. Where that role was focused on investigating complaints against NZSIS, and some of the bodies discussed here retain a complaints-handling jurisdiction of greater or lesser scope, the bulk of these bodies' efforts – and certainly, I submit, that which is most impactful – now involves reviewing in more general terms the work of the SIAs, and doing so with specific reference to the lawfulness of that work; where

[136] ibid, sch 3, para 8.
[137] ibid, s 157(4).
[138] ibid, sch 3, para 12.
[139] ibid, s 158(1)(c).
[140] Inspector-General of Intelligence and Security, *Annual Report for the year 1 July 2018 to 30 June 2019* (2019) 4.

complaints handling remains, it appears in most cases to be a less prominent aspect of their work than are those with a broader focus. I consider here some aspects of that review work before going on to consider the specific question of warrantry.

A. Review Work

The UK's IPC has no complaint-handling jurisdiction, though the Commissioner may be called upon to assist the Investigatory Powers Tribunal, which does have such jurisdiction.[141] The IPC must, the 2016 Act provides, keep under review ('including by way of audit, inspection and investigation') the exercise by public authorities generally of statutory functions relating to certain activities, including the interception of communications and the acquisition or retention of communications data, but also a series of more specific issues – including, for example, the 'giving and operation' of 'national security notices'.[142] A particular point that is to be kept under review in this process is the operation of safeguards intended to protect privacy.[143] Some general rules are included to shape this reviewing work: it does not, for example, encompass the exercise of the functions of judicial authorities,[144] and in exercising these functions the Commissioner must not act in way he or she considers to be contrary to the public interest generally or prejudicial to one of the core interests: national security, the prevention or detection of serious crime, or the economic well-being of the UK.[145] In particular, the IPC and other Judicial Commissioners must ensure (subject to logical exclusions) that they do not 'jeopardise the success of an intelligence or security operation or a law enforcement operation', 'compromise the safety or security of those involved', or 'unduly impede the operational effectiveness of an intelligence service, a police force, a government department or Her Majesty's forces'.[146] This effectively confirms what is implied by all of this: the IPC and those who work under him or her may – indeed must – take a close interest in the operations of the SIAs, a right that was originally denied to the ISC, the other major element of the modern oversight landscape. For the purpose of these functions, a Judicial Commissioner (including the IPC) may carry out 'such investigations, inspections and audits' as he or she considers appropriate,[147] with a broad range of persons obliged to furnish information and assistance to the Commissioner.[148]

[141] Investigatory Powers Act 2016 (UK), s 232(1). The Tribunal was created by the Regulation of Investigatory Powers Act 2000 (UK), replacing multiple tribunals of more limited jurisdiction.
[142] Investigatory Powers Act 2016 (UK), s 229.
[143] ibid, s 229(5).
[144] ibid, s 229(4)(b).
[145] ibid, s 229(6).
[146] ibid, s 229(7).
[147] ibid, s 235(1).
[148] Including 'any person who holds, or has held, an office, rank or position with a public authority' and 'any telecommunications operator or postal operator who is, has been or may become subject to a requirement imposed by virtue of' the 2016 Act: ibid, s 235(7).

The Investigatory Powers Act 2016 also provides for the Prime Minister to direct the IPC to keep under review, in addition to those issues specified in the statute itself, 'any aspect of the functions of' either one of the UK's SIAs, 'a head of an intelligence service' or 'any part of Her Majesty's forces, or of the Ministry of Defence, so far as engaging in intelligence activities'.[149] Such a direction may be given at the request of the IPC, at the request of the ISC, or without such a request from either party.[150] Though the general rule is that a direction of this sort must be published, there are broad exceptions to that requirement where the Prime Minister considers that publication would be contrary to the public interest or prejudicial to not only one of the standard three interests but also 'the continued discharge of the functions of any public authority whose activities include activities that are subject to review by the Investigatory Powers Commissioner'.[151] The effect is that it is not possible to know for sure what additional functions might have been given to the IPC over and above those provided for in the 2016 Act itself. It is notable, though, that a number of additional functions have been added via amendment of the 2016 Act, rather than via such a direction: these include, for example, reviewing the compliance of public authorities with the UK–US 'CLOUD Act' Agreement,[152] compliance by certain persons with *The Principles relating to the detention and interviewing of detainees overseas and the passing and receipt of intelligence relating to detainees* (2019)[153] and 'the process operated by GCHQ for determining whether information about vulnerabilities in technology should be disclosed'.[154] The effect is that a vast, and growing, range of issues are brought within the remit of the IPC and other Judicial Commissioners, and that the IPC's annual reports – required by law to contain certain data[155] – are a valuable source of information about the work of the SIAs and the legal and other problems that have been identified in connection with it. Two other sorts of reports might be carried out: 'any report' that is requested by the Prime Minister; and a report ('on any matter relating to the functions of the Judicial Commissioners') the IPC considers it appropriate to make.[156] While reports in these categories (or parts thereof) are published only at the discretion of the Prime Minister, the annual reports of the IPC must be published and laid before Parliament, though they might be redacted on the same grounds upon which directions requiring the Commissioner to take on new functions might be withheld from publication.[157] In practice, they appear to be

[149] ibid, s 230(1).
[150] ibid, s 230(3).
[151] ibid, s 230(4).
[152] ibid, s 229(3A). And see T Cochrane, 'Digital Privacy Rights and CLOUD Act Agreements' (2021) 47 *Brooklyn International Law Journal* 1.
[153] Investigatory Powers Act 2016 (UK), s 229(3C). And see PF Scott, 'Law, Non-law, and Torture: From the Consolidated Guidance to the Principles' [2020] *Public Law* 488.
[154] Investigatory Powers Act 2016 (UK), s 229(3B).
[155] ibid, s 234.
[156] ibid, s 234(3).
[157] ibid, ss 234(6) and (7).

sent to the Prime Minister with a confidential annex, which can then be neatly excluded from publication without the need for redaction of the main part of the report. No reports by the IPC other than the annual reports have been published in the period since the role was created.[158] These reports are important sources of information on the extent of the use to which the SIAs and others have put their powers, which historically was disclosed only occasionally and reluctantly.

The Australian IGIS has both inquiry and complaints functions. The former varies, depending upon which of the Australian SIAs is at issue. In relation to ASIO, the primary function of the IGIS is to inquire – at the request of the Attorney-General or the responsible Minister, on the IGIS's own motion, or in response to a complaint – into 'any matter' that relates to one of a number of issues: ASIO's compliance with the laws of the Commonwealth and of the States and Territories; its compliance with 'directions or guidelines' given to it by the responsible Minister; the propriety of particular of its activities; the 'effectiveness and appropriateness' of ASIO's procedures 'relating to the legality or propriety' of its activities; its compliance with human rights and anti-discrimination laws.[159] Propriety is not defined ('I found this to be a good thing. While administrative law experts might angst over the difference between judicial and merits review the IGIS has scope to look at almost anything under "propriety".'[160]), but one Australian IGIS has endorsed an understanding offered by one of her New Zealand counterparts: 'The standard of propriety encompasses whether the agency acted in a way that a fully informed and objective observer would consider appropriate and justifiable in the circumstances.'[161] Again, many of these are functions that cannot be performed without close consideration of the actual operations of ASIO. The scope of the equivalent function as regards ASIS and the ASD differs in two ways: the complaints in response to which an inquiry might be carried out may be made only by an Australian citizen or a permanent resident, while the IGIS has no jurisdiction over these bodies' procedures in the context of an inquiry responding to a complaint.[162] Where the responsible Minister has given a direction to ASIO on one of two points – whether 'the collection of intelligence concerning a particular individual is, or is not, justified by reason of its relevance to security' or 'the communication of intelligence concerning a particular individual would be for a purpose relevant to security' – then the IGIS is to

[158] At least one such report was published by one of the IPC's predecessors, the Interception of Communications Commissioner. See Interception of Communications Commissioner, *IOCCO inquiry into the use of Chapter 2 of Part 1 of the Regulation of Investigatory Powers Act (RIPA) to identify journalistic sources* (2015). The Commissioner explains (ibid [1.2]) that 'Due to the serious nature of the concerns reported in the media about the protection of journalistic sources, and the allegations that the police had misused their powers under the Act to acquire communications data, the Commissioner considered it necessary to undertake this inquiry and make an additional report to the Prime Minister.'

[159] Inspector-General of Intelligence and Security Act 1986 (Australia), s 8(1).

[160] Thom (n 40) 12.

[161] ibid.

[162] Inspector-General of Intelligence and Security Act 1986 (Australia), s 8(2).

inquire (automatically, it appears) into whether what the Minister has directed is in fact the case,[163] this process presumably working to disincentivise or outright exclude the abuse of this example of ministerial control of the SIAs. Other inquiries may be requested by the Prime Minister: if the Prime Minister requests that the IGIS carry out an inquiry into 'an intelligence or security matter relating to a Commonwealth agency' then the IGIS must do so.[164] In keeping with the notion, that has sometimes been expressed, that the IGIS exists to assist the Minister, the Minister's own actions are largely excluded from the scope of this inquiry's remit.[165]

Where the IGIS has carried out an inquiry then he or she must produce a report setting out his or her conclusions and recommendations and give a copy to the Agency to which it relates and to the responsible Minister, as well as to the Prime Minister or the Attorney-General if they request it[166] or if the IGIS otherwise considers it appropriate to do so.[167] If, in response, the head of the SIA proposes to take action as a result of the conclusions and recommendations then details must be given to the IGIS; if the SIA does not take, within a reasonable period following the report, action that is 'adequate and appropriate' then the IGIS may discuss the matter with the responsible Minister and report on it.[168] The IGIS's functions, in relation to the SIAs, also include conducting 'at such times as the Inspector-General determines in consultation with the head of the agency, such other inspections of the agency as the Inspector-General considers appropriate' for the purpose of giving effect to the objects of the statute that creates the post.[169] A report on an inspection may be prepared for the responsible Minister or the head of the agency in question.[170] In its annual reports, the IGIS publishes details of the inspections conducted in relation to each agency, 'compliance incidents' that have been reported to it and any inquiries it has conducted. The scope of these inquiries ranges widely: in recent years, for example, they have included an inquiry into 'the conduct and details of a multi-faceted, multi-agency foreign intelligence collection operation led by ASIO, including whether certain intelligence collection activities conducted by ASIO as part of that operation were lawful',[171] one into 'the adequacy of mental health support provided by an intelligence agency to one of its former employees'[172] and one into the application of national security classifications within the six agencies under the IGIS's jurisdiction.[173]

[163] ibid, s 8(1)(d). If the IGIS concludes that it is not then, as well as reporting to the relevant Minister, he or she must give a copy of the report to the Attorney-General and may, if he or she considers it appropriate, give a copy also to the Prime Minister: ibid, s 25.
[164] ibid, s 9(3).
[165] ibid, s 9AA.
[166] ibid, s 22.
[167] ibid, s 24.
[168] ibid, s 24.
[169] ibid, s 9A(1).
[170] ibid, s 25A.
[171] Inspector-General of Intelligence and Security, *2018–2019 Annual Report* (2019) 25.
[172] ibid.
[173] Inspector General of Intelligence and Security, *2020–2021 Annual Report* (2021) 24.

The New Zealand IGIS also possesses both inquiry and complaint functions, alongside a reviewing function. There are three types of inquiry that the IGIS might carry out: an inquiry into 'any matter relating to an intelligence and security agency's compliance with New Zealand law, including human rights law'; an inquiry into 'any matter where it appears that a New Zealand person has been or may be adversely affected by an act, omission, practice, policy, or procedure of an intelligence and security agency'; and an inquiry into 'the propriety of particular activities of an intelligence and security agency',[174] making clear that it is understood that the SIAs 'may act in a way that is lawful but, when viewed from the perspective of morality or social acceptability, is improper'.[175] All three types of inquiry might take place at the request of either the responsible Minister or the ISC, or on the initiative of the IGIS. The third type of inquiry might also be requested by the Prime Minister, who is no longer the Minister responsible for the New Zealand SIAs but is now – as well as being Prime Minister – Minister for National Security and Intelligence. The IGIS must also review, at least every 12 months, 'the procedures of each intelligence and security agency to ensure compliance with this Act in relation to the issue and execution' of authorisations, as well as 'the compliance systems of each intelligence and security agency for operational activities',[176] a much broader mandate than is possessed by some of the role's equivalents elsewhere. A previous prohibition on inquiring into operationally sensitive matters is not retained in the 2017 Act,[177] bringing the New Zealand IGIS into line with its counterparts elsewhere. Another function involves reviewing (after the fact, rather than within the process) the issue of authorisations and the carrying out of the activity authorised thereunder.[178] In carrying out these and other functions, again the IGIS is not looking solely at legal questions but must also take into account any relevant ministerial direction and the SIAs' compliance with it.[179]

Where an inquiry has been completed, a written report containing the IGIS's conclusions and recommendations must be prepared and sent to the relevant Minister and the head of the relevant SIA, as well as to the Prime Minister or the ISC if the inquiry was conducted at their request.[180] If the inquiry was not requested by the ISC, the report can be sent to it only if the relevant Minister (or the Prime Minister if he or she requested the inquiry) permits it.[181] The IGIS may advise the Minister who receives the report on 'the compliance by an

[174] Intelligence and Security Act 2017 (NZ), s 158.

[175] Arnold and Mahuika (n 59) [4.38].

[176] Intelligence and Security Act 2017 (NZ), s 158(1)(f).

[177] A point noted by Rogers (n 59) 683. The original formulation in what had become the 1996 Act used instead the phrase 'day-to-day operations' and was changed at the behest of the Committee that reviewed the Bill: Committee on the Intelligence and Security Agencies Bill (n 50) vii.

[178] Intelligence and Security Act 2017 (NZ), 158(1)(i).

[179] ibid, s 158(2).

[180] ibid, s 185.

[181] ibid, s 185(4).

intelligence and security agency with the recommendations in that report' and 'the adequacy of any remedial or preventative measures taken by an intelligence and security agency following an inquiry'.[182] The Minister must respond as soon as possible.[183] Reports are to be published subject to a requirement not to disclose information that fulfils certain criteria, including where its disclosure would prejudice 'the continued performance of the functions of an intelligence and security agency' or 'the security or defence of New Zealand or the international relations of the Government of New Zealand'.[184] In the period of its existence, a number of IGIS reports have considered high-profile or important issues. In the late 1990s, for example, the IGIS inquired – at the request of the Prime Minister – into the question of whether GCSB was suitably subject to control by the New Zealand Government or whether (as had been alleged) it was instead operating for the benefit – or even at the direction – of foreign partners.[185] Another inquiry related to misleading claims that NZSIS had made about its contacts with the Leader of the Opposition, following allegations about Israeli intelligence activity in New Zealand at the time of the Christchurch earthquake in 2011.[186] A number of these reports have been published in the years since the major reform of the New Zealand intelligence community, alongside the annual report of the New Zealand IGIS. These include (for example) a report of the review of a warning issued to a New Zealand citizen by the NZSIS against carrying out foreign interference in New Zealand (the IGIS accepted that the warning was lawful, but recommended that a new policy be adopted)[187] and a report of a review of the use and sharing of vetting information by NZSIS (the IGIS found that NZSIS had at times sought to make use of vetting material in ways the law did not permit).[188] Perhaps the most important report of recent years, however, related to possible New Zealand involvement with the CIA's infamous detention and interrogation programme in the years after the 9/11 attacks,[189] an issue that has been addressed by oversight bodies in several jurisdictions. As with the Australian IGIS, then, the New Zealand IGIS in practice roams much more widely than does the UK's

[182] ibid, s 186.
[183] ibid, s 187.
[184] ibid, s 188. The IGIS has noted that the relevant provision 'encompasses but goes beyond "classified" material' and so published details of the procedure for determining whether it applies and, in particular, whether 'public disclosures in the report might affect New Zealand's international relations': Inspector-General of Intelligence and Security, *International relations: the Inspector-General's process under s 188 ISA for finalising a public inquiry report* (2020).
[185] Inspector-General of Intelligence and Security, *Report on Inquiry into National Control of SIGINT Collection and Reporting by the Government Communications and Security Bureau* (1999).
[186] Inspector-General of Intelligence and Security, *Report into the release of information by the New Zealand Security Intelligence Service in July and August 2011* (2014).
[187] Inspector-General of Intelligence and Security, *Review of an NZSIS Warning – Public Report* (2022).
[188] Inspector-General of Intelligence and Security, *Review of NZSIS Use and Sharing of Vetting Information – Public Report* (2023).
[189] Inspector-General of Intelligence and Security, *Inquiry into possible New Zealand intelligence and security agencies' engagement with the CIA detention and interrogation programme 2001–2009* (2019).

IPC, carrying out reviews of a sort that in the UK would be carried out instead by the ISC or some third actor. The functions of the other New Zealand body, the Commissioners of Intelligence Warrants are discussed in section IV.B.

Also discussed in that section are the functions of the Canadian Intelligence Commissioners, which exist alongside the NSIRA. The mandate of the NSIRA is defined in four (very broad) parts: it is to review 'any activity carried out by the Canadian Security Intelligence Service or the Communications Security Establishment', 'any activity carried out by a department that relates to national security or intelligence' and 'any matter that relates to national security or intelligence that a minister of the Crown refers to the Agency'.[190] In the course of its review work on the activities of CSIS, it must review, each year, 'at least one aspect of the Service's performance in taking measures to reduce threats to the security of Canada'.[191] It must also review the implementation of what are described as 'significant aspects of every new or modified ministerial direction' that is issued to CSIS, the CSE or 'any other department if the ministerial direction relates to national security or intelligence'.[192] In its reviews, NSIRA may make 'any finding or recommendation that it considers appropriate', including – but not limited to – findings or recommendations regarding 'a department's compliance with the law and any applicable ministerial directions' and 'the reasonableness and necessity of a department's exercise of its powers'.[193] It must make annual reports to the relevant Minister on the activities of CSIS and the CSE, which must contain information relating to their compliance with the law and relevant ministerial directions, as well as the reasonableness and necessity of each body's exercise of its powers.[194] It may also submit a report to the relevant Minister regarding 'any matter that relates to a department and that is the subject of a review by the Agency'.[195] A report must be made to the relevant Minister of any national security and intelligence and activity that NSIRA considers may not be in compliance with the law, with any report – and the Minister's response – to be passed to the Attorney-General.[196] These reports are not made public, but NSIRA must report to the Prime Minister each year on its activities and the findings and recommendations it has made.[197] This annual report is to be laid before each house of the Canadian Parliament.[198] The Agency may also, if it considers it to be in the public interest to do so, make a special report on 'any matter

[190] The fourth part of the mandate involves investigating certain complaints, as well as reports made to it and matters referred to it under specific provisions of the Citizenship Act and the Canadian Human Rights Act. National Security and Intelligence Review Agency Act (2019) (Canada), s 8(1).

[191] National Security and Intelligence Review Agency Act (2019) (Canada), s 8(2).

[192] ibid, s 8(2.1).

[193] ibid, s 8(3).

[194] ibid, ss 32 and 33.

[195] ibid, s 34.

[196] ibid, s 35.

[197] ibid, s 38(1).

[198] ibid, s 38(2).

related to its mandate' to the relevant Minister.[199] These reports must also be laid before Parliament.[200] In the relatively short period of its existence, NSIRA has carried out a number of reviews, albeit with some of them having been initiated by its predecessor institutions, including – for example – a review of 'Ministerial Authorizations' given to the CSE under the Communications Security Establishment Act, which permit the CSE to engage in activity that risks contravening an Act of Parliament or 'interfering with a reasonable expectation of privacy of a Canadian or person in Canada', the published version of which was very heavily redacted.[201] Again, it is clear that this work involves a close consideration of the SIAs' work: as part of that review, the NSIRA received 'comprehensive briefings on activities authorized' by each Ministerial Authorization.[202]

B. Approving Warrants

We have noted at various points in this chapter the difference that exists between the Commonwealth Five Eyes jurisdictions as regards the 'double-lock' – the involvement of hybrid institutions or their analogues in deciding whether the decision of some executive actor that the criteria for the granting of a warrant authorising the use of intrusive powers of some sort or other were met – whose origins and diffusion were discussed in chapter 4. That is, in three of the four jurisdictions a double-lock (of sorts) now exists. In one of those jurisdictions, the UK, the double-lock is exercised by the same institution that carries out the general oversight of the SIAs and their actions that exists in all four jurisdictions. In two of them, the double-lock exists but is carried out by separate bodies, the existence of which we have noted at various points: in Canada the Intelligence Commissioner and in New Zealand the Commissioners of Intelligence Warrants. In Australia, despite considerable discussion of the point, no double-lock has (yet) been introduced.

When David Anderson – later Lord Anderson of Ipswich – carried out a review of the investigatory powers landscape in the UK ahead of the reforms made by the Investigatory Powers Act 2016, he recommended the creation of an Independent Surveillance and Intelligence Commission to replace the existing Commissioners, made up of a Chief Commissioner and other Judicial Commissioners. This new body would take on the functions of the existing Commissioners, audit and inspection functions, and, most significantly,

> the warrant-issuing powers currently vested in the Secretary of State, to be exercised only by Judicial Commissioners who must hold or have held high judicial office, or

[199] ibid, s 40(1).

[200] ibid, s 40(2).

[201] National Security and Intelligence Review Agency, *Review of the CSE ministerial authorizations and ministerial orders under the CSE Act* (NSIRA Review 08-501-5) (2023).

[202] ibid [3].

> Assistant Judicial Commissioners who have themselves held judicial office … and after hearing submissions from independent standing counsel where necessary.[203]

Anderson considered whether it would be 'difficult' to combine these different functions and concluded that it would not – in fact, there might be some advantage to placing these two distinct functions in the same institution:

> Whilst the judicial function is obviously a distinct one, there is considerable benefit in dialogue: the Judicial Commissioners could advise the inspectorate on matters to look out for on their inspections, and the inspectors could in turn suggest that a warrant be referred back to the Judicial Commissioners if they formed the impression that it was not being implemented as it should be, and that the Judicial Commissioners might wish to consider modifying or cancelling it.[204]

This nevertheless still involves the internal separation of those functions within the relevant institution. In the Bill that followed from Anderson's work not only was the role of the Judicial Commissioners in addition to that of the Secretary of State rather than in place of it, but no such separation between the inspectorate and warrantry functions of the IPC's Office (as it was now to be called) was evident. One of the Commissioners the Bill sought to replace argued that without such an operational distinction, the regime being put in place 'could be construed as the Judicial Commissioners "marking their own homework" which would dilute the credibility and independence of the new body'.[205] Nevertheless, no change was made and the double-lock, as discussed chapter 4, is carried out by the same IPC and Judicial Commissioners as carry out the various audits and reviews discussed in section IV.A. If there is an internal separation of these functions, it has no statutory basis and is not visible to external observers.

We also noted in chapter 4 that something very like the double-lock had existed in New Zealand long before the UK introduced it. There, however, the secondary role introduced in 1999 was not to be played by the IGIS, introduced a few years earlier, but rather by a new Commissioner of Security Warrants. This distinction was carried over into the reforms of 2017, which provide for the appointment of up to three Commissioners of Intelligence Warrants, one of whom must be made Chief Commissioner of Intelligence Warrants and all of whom must have previously held office as judges of the New Zealand High Court.[206] A similar separation exists also in Canada, which – as noted – has for many decades had a system of even greater judicial involvement than even now exists elsewhere, with judges the primary decision-makers on applications made to them (with ministerial approval) by CSIS for a range of warrants. When national security law was being reformed, however, and the decision taken

[203] D Anderson, *A Question of Trust: Report of the Investigatory Powers Review* (2015) [14.95].
[204] ibid [14.98].
[205] Office of the Interception of Communications Commissioner, *Written Evidence on the Draft Investigatory Powers Bill*, IPB0101 (2015) [16].
[206] Intelligence and Security Act 2017 (NZ), ss 112 and 113.

to move to something more akin to the UK double-lock for certain authorisations, the approach adopted was not to grant decision-making authority to those same judges, or to any of the oversight bodies then in existence, nor even to the NSIRA that was being created, but to grant it instead to a new entity called the Intelligence Commissioner. The Commissioner, as we have seen, is responsible for 'reviewing the conclusions on the basis of which certain authorizations are issued or amended, and certain determinations are made, under the Communications Security Establishment Act and the Canadian Security Intelligence Service Act' and, 'if those conclusions are reasonable, approving those authorizations, amendments and determinations'.[207] Both New Zealand and Canada have therefore chosen in recent years not to adopt the UK model to the extent that it involves the fusion of general oversight and the approval of warrants in the same body. Though the double-lock has not been implemented in Australia, it is notable that the primary recommendation that it be implemented involved the Security Division of the Administrative Appeals Tribunal[208] as the additional decision-maker – the holder of the second key – rather than the existing IGIS or a new specialist body akin to those in New Zealand and Canada.

What is at stake in this issue? Not, that is, whether the double-lock should exist at all, or what the specific division of labour should be within it, but whether, where it exists, it should be carried out by the same body that undertakes the sort of generalised oversight that is now a prominent feature of Commonwealth national security constitutionalism. We have already noted the concern that the absence of any such separation gives rise to a situation in which the body in question 'marks its own homework'. Though there seems little positive basis for criticising on this ground the work of the UK's IPC (and other Judicial Commissioners) since the office's introduction, it is true that perception is significant, particularly where the underlying substantive work of these bodies – the content of their warrantry decisions – is, for good reason, kept from public view. Perhaps, then, the issue is not so much what the fusion of roles means for the oversight of the warrantry process, but what the warrantry role means for the rest of the body's work. That is, we have seen that the UK's IPC and the other Judicial Commissioners – in whose hands warrantry and oversight are fused – must be or have been senior judges. This in turn goes hand in hand with an oversight role that appears to prioritise legal questions over other standards and norms. Elsewhere, and without taking a view on causation, the design of oversight bodies has been able to be more flexible. Members of Canada's NSIRA, for example, which does not play a role within the warrantry process, need not be or have been judges, and the Agency's review work ranges far beyond questions about compliance with existing law. Given the bias towards issues of legality that is evidenced by so much oversight of national security constitutionalism, the separation of warrantry functions from

[207] Intelligence Commissioner Act (2019) (Canada), s 12.

[208] J Renwick, 'What are the Right Encryption Laws for Australia?', Speech at the Lowy Institute, Sydney (5 March 2020).

other sorts of review may, this suggests, be necessary in order to make room for considerations of prudence or propriety that are informed by familiarity with the activities of the SIAs; to make room, that is, for the idea that there is more to oversight of the SIAs and their work than the mere question of their compliance with the law.

V. Networks of Oversight Actors

We see, then, that though there have been and remain important differences between the status and work of these actors, there has been a clear convergence upon a particular model, whereby one or more individuals, usually with legal qualifications or expertise, carry out oversight and review of the work of the SIAs, considering in particular – but by no means solely – the question of their compliance with the relevant legal regime(s). On one hand, it is perhaps more difficult here than in other contexts to demonstrate the ways in which, and specific moments at which, one jurisdiction has influenced another as regards the institution and evolution of these bodies. On the other hand, however, stepping back, the mutual influence is clear, not least in the occurrence of similar terminology across jurisdictions. Of course, some degree of convergence is perhaps unsurprising, if not in fact inevitable, for the same reasons one might identify in the context of the parliamentary or quasi-parliamentary institutions discussed in chapter 6. That is, there is a dual commonality to the contexts in which these institutions arise. One is the background context not only of the constitutional fundamentals shared by the Commonwealth Five Eyes states, but also of the similar national security institutions created and empowered, eventually, by the legislatures of the four states at issue. The other is the policy context, the exigencies (secrecy) and particularities (legal complexity) of which shape to a considerable (though, as we have seen, by no means absolute) degree the design of any institution by which oversight might be carried out, especially against the background of the underlying constitutional fundamentals. What is striking, however, and what I consider in this section, is the ways in which the existence of these actors in the contemporary age – overseeing the work of the security and intelligence agencies but by design independent of them – works to promote further evolution, and potentially further convergence, in the domain of national security constitutionalism: not only at the level of oversight and review mechanisms, but also at that of what we have called elsewhere the positive dimension of the national security endeavour – the capabilities and powers the SIAs possess, and the conditions under which they are permitted to make use of them. The mechanism by which this occurs is the various networks of oversight actors that have emerged now that each jurisdiction possesses a hybrid oversight or review body that might participate in such networks. These networks include the Intelligence Oversight Working Group, a network of European oversight bodies including (as a founding member) the UK's IPC,[209] the aims of which include exchanging 'knowledge, experiences and best practices of oversight' and providing 'a platform for developing new and/or more effective oversight methods'.[210] Another is the International Intelligence Oversight Forum, an initiative of the UN Special Rapporteur on the Right to Privacy, the first edition of which was held in Bucharest in 2016, discussing such themes as 'respect for fundamental human rights, a need for standardization and professionalization of oversight activities, safeguards without borders and remedies across borders, accountability and transparency, good and bad practices and the need for more fora in which a high-level discussion can be held'.[211] For obvious reasons, though, we are most interested in the network that brings together oversight actors from the Five Eyes states – noting, however, that there appear to have been connections between these actors for much of their existence, such that it is the formalisation of these exchanges rather than their simple fact that gives this modern phenomenon its distinctiveness.[212]

A. Five Eyes Intelligence Oversight and Review Council

The Five Eyes Intelligence Oversight and Review Council (FIORC), was set up in 2017 by agreement of the relevant bodies in each of the Five Eyes states.[213] Its members include all of the bodies discussed so far in this section – the UK's IPCO, the Australian Office of the Inspector-General of Intelligence and Security, the New Zealand Commissioner of Intelligence Warrants and the Office of the Inspector-General of Intelligence and Security, and Canada's NSIRA and the Office of the Intelligence Commissioner – along with body that seems to have helped inspire this set of institutions: the US Office of the Inspector General of the Intelligence Community. The founding agreement of FIORC (made within 'the framework and in the spirit of the existing Five Eyes partnership') provides that the Council 'is established with the purpose of creating a forum where Council

[209] Intelligence Oversight Working Group, *Charter of the Intelligence Oversight Working Group*, signed by its members in The Hague (12 December 2019). The others were the Belgian Standing Intelligence Agencies Review Committee, the Danish Intelligence Oversight Board, the Review Committee on the Intelligence and Security Services (from the Netherlands), the Norwegian Parliamentary Intelligence Oversight Committee and the Independent Oversight Authority for Intelligence Activities of Switzerland.

[210] ibid [2].

[211] Special Rapporteur on the Right to Privacy, 'Statement by Mr. Joseph Cannataci, Special Rapporteur on the right to privacy, at the 71st session of the General Assembly' (24 October 2016).

[212] So, to take one example amongst many, the New Zealand IGIS described, in his second annual report, having attended the 'first international meeting of Inspector-Generals of Intelligence and Security' hosted by the IGIS of Australia in November 1997, alongside representatives (including 'Inspector-Generals and members of Parliamentary and other review committees') from Canada, the UK, the USA and South Africa: Inspector-General of Intelligence and Security, *Annual Report 1997/98* (1998) [25].

[213] Five Eyes Intelligence Oversight and Review Council, *Charter of the Five Eyes Intelligence Oversight and Review Council* (2 October 2017).

Members may', amongst other things, 'exchange views on subjects of mutual interest and concern', 'explore areas where cooperation on reviews and the sharing of results is permitted where appropriate', 'encourage transparency to the largest extent possible to enhance public trust', and 'maintain contact with political offices, oversight and review committees, and non-Five Eyes countries as appropriate'.[214] Most interesting for present purposes is the explicit reference to the comparing of 'best practices in review and oversight methodology',[215] which makes clear the possibility that FIORC will work to enhance oversight processes.

Physically, FIORC meets at least once a year, and there are, in addition, quarterly meetings 'by means of secure communication'.[216] The Council's operational guidelines note that 'each country has a variation of law on security of information or official secrets binding officials to secrecy' but that the Council's various members 'commit to facilitating information sharing and collaboration between themselves to advance the stated purposes where appropriate and within the respective limits imposed by law, executive or ministerial direction, or other binding authority'.[217] Though there is no formal hierarchy within the Council, there exists an 'Executive Secretariat' that resides in the Office of the Inspector General of the Intelligence Community of the United States,[218] giving that body what may in practice be an influence greater than that of the other member bodies, in keeping – it must be noted – with the general dominance of the US in the intelligence field. The Secretariat produces summaries of FIORC's annual meetings. From those, certain information about the Council's work – largely anodyne, of course – can be extracted. The 2018 meeting took place in Canberra, Australia,[219] with the report of the meeting containing a list of topics discussed and indicating – amongst other things – the desire of the various oversight bodies to share information and the 'challenges and successes' associated with doing so.[220] Also noted was a desire to 'cooperate on reviews and share results', including by sharing employees, and the security challenges posed by doing so. Even without detail of the substance of the discussions, therefore, the multiplicity of mechanisms by which innovations in one state might come to be replicated, with or without variation, in another becomes clear.

In 2019, the Council met in London, with a number of points of interest emerging from the Secretariat's report on the meeting.[221] After the different

[214] ibid [2].
[215] ibid.
[216] ibid [3].
[217] ibid [4].
[218] ibid [5].
[219] Office of the Inspector General of the Intelligence Community of the United States, 'Executive Summary: 2018 Annual Meeting of the Five Eyes Intelligence Oversight and Review Council, National Library of Australia, Canberra, Australia October 8–9, 2018' (nd).
[220] ibid 2.
[221] Office of the Inspector General of the Intelligence Community of the United States, 'Executive Summary: 2019 Annual Meeting of the Five Eyes Intelligence Oversight and Review Council Middle Temple, London October 15–17, 2019' (nd).

oversight bodies had provided updates on developments within their respective jurisdictions, we are told that Lord Anderson – the former Independent Reviewer of Terrorism Legislation – 'presented his reflections on three recent reviews', including those which influenced the Investigatory Powers Act 2016 and helped to justify the inclusion within it of 'bulk' powers.[222] The 2020 meeting, 'due to take place in New Zealand in October 2020, was replaced by virtual meetings throughout 2020 with a focus on progressing the joint work that was agreed at the 2019 conference.'[223] At that conference, the members of FIORC agreed to set up working groups on three specific topics: 'automated data processing and Artificial Intelligence; methods to mitigate risks of mistreatment from sharing information with foreign entities; and jurisdictional or territorial constraints on the review/oversight activities of FIORC partners that create a gap in coverage over the cumulative activities of the Five Eyes agencies'.[224] The 2021 meeting was also held virtually[225] and included discussion of – amongst other things – lessons learned 'from adapting to widened and altered review and oversight mandates' and, strikingly, the issue of accountability gaps: 'potential gaps where there is limited or no independent accountability in terms of oversight of Intelligence Community agencies, or other areas where accountability could be strengthened'. In that latter context, five themes were – we are told – identified: jurisdiction; technology; access to information; resourcing; and physical presence.[226] The year 2022 saw a return to in-person meetings for FIORC, with the working groups on 'Accountability Gaps' and 'Assurances' retired, and new ones established on 'Transparency and Public Engagement' and 'Work Planning and Methodology'.[227]

We have already seen the manner in which the key feature of the UK's Investigatory Powers Act 2016 – the double-lock – has influenced reform elsewhere (whether or not it has eventually been adopted) and might yet influence further reform. Though in a number of cases the specific mechanism of this influence seems to have been bilateral,[228] it is nevertheless easy to see how the work of FIORC might in the past have contributed, and may in the future

[222] ibid 3.

[223] Investigatory Powers Commissioner, *Annual Report of the Investigatory Powers Commissioner 2020* (HC 2020–21, 897) [5.20].

[224] Inspector-General of Intelligence and Security, *2019–2020 Annual Report* (2020) 66.

[225] Office of the Inspector General of the Intelligence Community of the United States, 'Executive Summary: 2021 Annual Meeting of the Five Eyes Intelligence Oversight and Review Council' (nd).

[226] ibid 3.

[227] Office of the Inspector General of the Intelligence Community of the United States, 'Executive Summary 2022 Annual Meeting of the Five Eyes Intelligence Oversight and Review Council' (nd).

[228] See, eg, the Australian IGIS: 'In early May 2019 the Inspector-General and a senior officer travelled to the United Kingdom to meet with the Investigatory Powers Commissioner and members of his office. Discussions covered the formation and functioning of the Investigatory Powers Commissioner's Office and the "double-lock" mechanism, the Technology Advisory Panel, oversight of covert effects and bulk data, oversight of policing bodies, and dealings with civil society groups. This engagement also saw the Inspector-General meet with agencies within the oversight jurisdiction of the Investigatory Powers Commissioner's Office.' Inspector-General of Intelligence and Security, *2018–2019 Annual Report* (2019) 64.

contribute, to the transmission of the law of investigatory powers from one jurisdiction to another. The various oversight bodies come together annually and are exposed to developments from other jurisdictions. They bring that knowledge home with them, and it would hardly be surprising if they drew on it when called upon to feed into, as they often do, the process of reviewing and reforming the law of investigatory powers or national security law more generally. After all, the direction of travel is in one sense clear: the reforms in question seem almost invariably to promote the status and powers of the bodies that make up the network, as part of a wider process of constitutionalisation of national security that has been ongoing, as this book shows, for many decades. A key point, however, is that these developments are not necessarily positive: though the double-lock may in practice be an unambiguous good, the transfer of these norms is equally capable of having a net negative effect, either by allowing for the honing of powers, or by providing the mechanisms necessary in order to render powers, new or existing, politically palatable or, perhaps, compatible with the relevant rules of human rights protection.

VI. Conclusion

Achieving accountability for the work of the state in the domain of national security has long been a difficult task, to which neither the traditional political nor legal organs of the modern state are usually considered to be suited. Though, as we shall see again in chapter 6, attempts have been made to adapt both political and legal institutions to, amongst other things, the need for sensitive methods and capabilities to remain secret, one of the key themes of modern national constitutionalism in the Commonwealth Five Eyes states is the attempt to make up for the shortcomings of these institutions in the national security context via the introduction of oversight institutions that marry legal and political accountability in a distinctive fashion. Usually legally qualified figures who enjoy privileged access to sensitive material, and who are permitted or even required to consider the specific operations of the SIAs, they do not (as they do when acting judicially) resolve individual legal disputes but rather consider the SIAs' pursuit of their mandates, and the operation of their various intrusive powers, in the round, identifying – and perhaps contributing to the resolution of – issues that are likely never to be identified within the ordinary processes of accountability given the secrecy that prevails, and perhaps also inquiring into specific themes that emerge only over time. They have, that is, moved very far from the original, and very limited, complaint-handling form in which they were first introduced into the national security constitution, to become a centrepiece of the modern accountability landscape.

When the Inspector-General of the CSIS was being introduced – the first time one of these bodies took on the sort of generalised review jurisdiction that is now standard – it was suggested that the role was primarily about enhancing ministerial responsibility:

> If the Solicitor General is to be politically responsible he must know what is going on in the agency, through his deputy. The Inspector General will be the ministry's 'eyes and ears' on the Service. He will very much be the 'minister's man', in order to maintain an appropriate degree of ministerial responsibility, and is not to be regarded as a functionary of the CSIS.[229]

When Justice Hope argued for the creation of a similar model in Australia, he suggested, however, that the 'eyes and ears' approach (associated by him with the US) should be deprecated in favour of a broader contribution to political accountability. Developments since would seem to have vindicated Hope: nowadays, it seems unlikely that the relevant Minister would ever be identified as the sole or even primary audience for the work of hybrid institutions, which instead are aimed at informing and reassuring a much wider group – politicians and the public, as well as perhaps external observers – that the SIAs of each jurisdiction are acting appropriately and, crucially, lawfully. What the courts cannot do, or cannot do easily or consistently, these hybrid institutions now try to do, armed with a range of powers to access information that is not available to the usual organs of political accountability.

Though there are important differences between the hybrid institutions in question, all of them appear to reflect the same dual intuitions: (i) that the absence of oversight that historically prevailed is no longer acceptable; and (ii) that the traditional forms of accountability are not capable of providing such oversight. Stepping back, a number of points might be made, relating both to national security constitutionalism and to the comparative exercise. One is that though their work varies – both in terms of their mandates and powers, but also, it would seem, in terms of the alacrity and more general attitude with which they perform it – the existence of these bodies represents in all cases at least a formal improvement upon the status quo ante. They are capable of shedding light on the actual work of the various SIAs and, often, their exercise of their most intrusive powers, even where there is no legal dispute. Their activities are informed both by access to sensitive material and by legal expertise, even if one danger we have identified is that questions of legality will tend in practice to crowd out the more general considerations of propriety or appropriateness to which these bodies are at least in some cases more or less clearly directed. While there are no doubt (possibly significant) improvements that might be made, this position is of course better than the sort of bare gaps that previously existed, when legislatures and courts were less interested and no other institutions existed to take up the constitutional slack: only ad hoc bodies, which were convened (and not convened) at the discretion of the executive and worked to terms of reference that were set by that executive, which often placed

[229] Special Committee (n 86) [90].

an unsubtle thumb on the scales employed by them. But these hybrid institutions were not for the most part introduced out of some abstract commitment to values of constitutionalism – openness and accountability, or whatever else – but in response to political demands that themselves reflected a changing conception of when and to what extent the sort of national security exceptionalism that previously prevailed remained appropriate; demands that were informed by an intuition and sometimes a knowledge that previous arrangements had not sufficed to exclude the misuse or outright abuse of power. In some cases, at least, they were introduced specifically to temper fears about what the consequences might be of introducing new bodies, new mandates or new powers, and so contributed, overall, not to the reining in of the national security state but rather to its ongoing expansion.

Once in place, these bodies act as models for other jurisdictions: testing grounds on which new approaches might be tried out, with each jurisdiction learning from and influenced (positively or negatively) by the experience of others. Here as elsewhere, the Commonwealth Five Eyes states appear once more to act as a distinct ecosystem; one that is not, or has not been, hermetically sealed (the model, we noted, seems to have originally entered this ecosystem from the US, which would nowadays be a less likely source of inspiration in the domain of national security constitutionalism) but within which the special linkages that exist means that learning spreads more quickly and with greater fluency from one to another, a process which seems to be accelerating over time and which the networks of oversight actors discussed in section V might further promote. On the broader point, one of the recurring criticisms of comparative constitutional law is its excessive focus on courts and their judgments (a criticism, to be fair, that one might make also of the study of constitutional law within individual jurisdictions). The institutions described in this chapter offer an example of the sort of innovation that a focus on courts (or even on legislative or executive bodies in their paradigmatic form) will miss. They challenge the traditional separation of powers model, demonstrating that the impulse underlying the constitutionalist project may require an openness to novel institutional forms – in the national security context but also, perhaps, elsewhere. If, at the same time, this provokes a greater level of attention within the mainstream of constitutional scholarship rather than merely at the margins thereof to the areas of policy where such institutional innovation is encountered, then all the better.

6

Parliamentary Accountability

I. Introduction

The four Commonwealth Five Eyes states are, in accordance with the Westminster model they exemplify, parliamentary democracies. The executive is formed out of the legislature, with the Prime Minister the person capable of commanding (or most likely to be able to command) the confidence of the relevant chamber of that legislature. Though the legislature has the role of legislating, it also has the role of scrutinising and holding that executive to account, a task that is framed, ultimately, by the ability of the relevant chamber to withdraw confidence from the executive and force the formation of a new or renewed government or, as the case may be, a General Election. This involves an ongoing process not necessarily of open and direct contestation, but of requiring the executive to explain, asking it to justify and criticising it where those explanations and justifications are considered to fall short. This has an ex post aspect – allowing for decisions taken and acts carried out to be scrutinised after they have happened, especially when there is no legal requirement of prior notification to or approval by the legislature – but also one based on anticipation: the knowledge that one might have to explain or to justify a given act at some future point must logically influence, perhaps very strongly, the decision to act in a particular way. That, at least, is the theory. Many of the factors we have canvassed elsewhere in this book have historically worked to prevent this process from applying, in part and sometimes at all, in the domain of national security.

We have already noted that many of the security and intelligence agencies in the Commonwealth Five Eyes states operated in the past – and sometimes in the recent past – without statutory authority, meaning that the legislature was not called upon to approve their existence and whatever (often shaky) legal basis they enjoyed did not require notification of their creation to the legislature or even the avowal of their existence. Even where statutory authority was put in place, the guiderails within it were, initially at least, loose, providing a legal mandate to the SIAs from which it would often be impossible to infer anything significant about how they might make use of that new authority. There was, therefore, little or no prior scrutiny of these bodies or their work: only, at best, and at certain discrete moments in time, the possibility of endorsing their legislative basis, including whatever arrangements that legislation did or did not include for oversight or review of them outside of the legislature itself. Nor, however, in the context of pervasive factual secrecy – if not absolute, then certainly significant – was there the same anticipatory dimension to the decision-making about national security, its exigencies and the action that would be taken to protect it. If neither parliamentarians nor the press and wider public would ever know that some action or other was taken in pursuit of national security, there was no need to worry about what sort of explanations and justifications might be offered to them, or what they might say or do in response. Combined with the very limited role recognised for (including by the courts themselves) and played by the courts in this area, the result was that the work of the SIAs was often shielded against any accountability emanating from outside the executive itself. Though the executive was formally accountable to the legislature in this as in other areas of policy, the practical lines of executive responsibility were often unclear, and executives usually denied to legislatures information about the SIAs and their work.

Though consideration was occasionally given to instituting some form of more direct parliamentary oversight of the legislative endeavour, the prospect was not usually welcomed by authorities. Writing in the late 1960s, the Mackenzie Commission in Canada accepted, for example, that 'an effort should be made to provide some public reassurance that the activities and operations of the Security Service are not immune from responsible scrutiny apart from that exercised by the government of the day', and considered as one way of providing that reassurance the creation of a parliamentary committee. This it rejected, in part because – a point with some resonance –

> if the committee were to carry out its tasks in a meaningful way, its members would need formal security clearance. On general grounds we think it inappropriate to subject private Members of Parliament to these procedures, and in addition we foresee great complications if a Member nominated by a political party were ever deemed unacceptable on security grounds.[1]

Its other reason, however, was much more general, and expressed in a remarkably conclusory fashion: 'we think', said the Commissioners, in a statement of what would seem to have been the (only sometimes tacit) consensus of the era, 'that the legislature should not be directly involved in these executive matters'.[2] Indeed, the first Hope Royal Commission in Australia the following decade took a similar line. Though the 'problem of the accountability of the Director-General and of the organization generally to the Parliament' had – Justice Hope said – given him 'very great trouble', he had come to the same conclusion as the Mackenzie Commission: that he 'should not recommend that there should be a parliamentary committee to scrutinize or supervise ASIO's activities'.[3]

[1] Royal Commission on Security, *Report (Abridged)* (1969) [65].
[2] ibid.
[3] Royal Commission on Intelligence and Security, *Fourth Report – Volume 1*, Parliamentary Paper No 248/1977 (1977) [457]. He noted, however (ibid [461]), that 'The absence of express Parliamentary supervision is correlative to a bipartisan approach to security matters. If security is to be the subject of a partisan approach, the basis of what I have recommended about supervision goes.'

The pattern we have observed earlier in this book, of scandal followed by ad hoc review followed (in many cases) by legislative reforms aimed at addressing the causes of the underlying issue, appears in many ways a function of the limits of ordinary processes and mechanisms of political accountability in the context of the national security endeavour. Had there been ongoing accountability, that is, and ongoing consideration of the legal framework within which the SIAs were operating, it seems plausible that some of these scandals would not have arisen in the first place. Only some of those limits on the subjection of the SIAs to ordinary political accountability, however, are inherent in the enterprise of protecting national security. Others are the result of deliberate choices of the relevant bodies, which reflect more or less directly a series of contingent background assumptions as to, for example, the position of national security within the separation of powers ideal and the level of secrecy the success of that enterprise necessitates (and so, conversely, the level of transparency it can tolerate). What we have seen, therefore, is that as these assumptions – on the part of the state, but also on the part of the public – have shifted, a greater level of ongoing political accountability has become a standard part of the landscape of Commonwealth national security constitutionalism: not only in the form of the sort of hybrid oversight bodies discussed in chapter 5, but also in terms of parliamentary accountability – provided not, or not always, by the ordinary parliamentary processes but by new bodies designed and instituted especially for that task. It is those bodies that this chapter discusses.

II. Parliamentary Oversight

One reason, we can reaffirm, that scandal and intrigue often resulted in some sort of ad hoc inquiry into the SIAs, their work and the governing law, was that there were no standing bodies that provided the sort of accountability to which other parts of the state are – at least in principle – subject. This situation no longer holds. In each of the Commonwealth Five Eyes states, there now exists a body that seeks to balance the need for parliamentary scrutiny in the field of national security with the special sensitivities applicable to this field of policy, chief amongst them the dangers of revealing information the dissemination of which might harm the national security of the state directly or indirectly and so increase (or appear to increase) democratic accountability in the domain of national security only at the cost of undermining that security. In chronological order of the founding of their current iterations, these bodies are the Parliamentary Joint Committee on Intelligence and Security (Australia) (PJCIS),[4] founded in 2001 as successor

[4] Founded by the Intelligence Services Act 2001 (Australia) and originally named the Parliamentary Joint Committee on ASIO, ASIS and DSD. See, for discussion of various aspects of its work, R Bolto,

to the Parliamentary Joint Committee on the Australian Security Intelligence Organisation, which had been instituted in 1988;[5] the ISC of Parliament (United Kingdom), founded in 1994 and reformed in 2013;[6] the ISC (New Zealand), founded in 1996 and reformed in 2017;[7] and, finally, the National Security and Intelligence Committee of Parliamentarians (Canada), founded in 2017.[8] Alongside the various independent reviewers that now exist – the hybrid institutions discussed in chapter 5 – these parliamentary security committees now bear much of the burden of ensuring accountability in the domain of national security by carrying out a range of reviews on questions relating thereto. Indeed, one important question raised by their existence is that of when and where, in the domain of national security, the new standing bodies, hybrid or parliamentary, are taken to be insufficient:, what matters will be so high-profile, complex or politically salient that it is felt necessary for consideration of them to be carried out by, say, a judge in a public inquiry or a Committee of Privy Councillors or similar?

A. Status and Composition

When first created (its establishment being 'a highly contentious issue'),[9] the Parliamentary Joint Committee on the Australian Security Intelligence Organisation was limited – as its name suggests – to inquiring into issues relating to ASIO and not to any of the other Australian SIAs, and it was able to inquire into matters only if they were referred to it by either the Minister or a House of Parliament.[10] The introduction of a committee of this sort had been considered but not recommended – for a second time – by the second Hope Royal Commission in the 1980s. Some of the Commission's reasons for doing so are of ongoing interest. One was that 'the lack of publicity for most of ASIO's activities may restrict the

'Accountability and secrecy in the Australian Intelligence Community: the Parliamentary Joint Committee on Intelligence and Security' (2019) 85 *International Review of Administrative Sciences* 137; and S Moulds, 'Forum of choice?: The legislative impact of the Parliamentary Joint Committee of Intelligence and Security' (2018) 29 *Public Law Review* 87.

[5] Founded in 1988, via amendment to the ASIO Act 1979 (Australia).

[6] Intelligence Services Act 1994 (UK); and Justice and Security Act 2013 (UK). See, most fully, H Bochel, A Defty and J Kirkpatrick, *Watching the Watchers: Parliament and the Intelligence Services* (Palgrave McMillan, 2014).

[7] Intelligence and Security Committee Act 1996 (NZ); Intelligence and Security Act 2017 (NZ).

[8] Founded by the National Security and Intelligence Committee of Parliamentarians Act, SC 2017, c 15 (Canada) (NSICOP Act). For background, see Interim Committee of Parliamentarians on National Security, *Report* (May 2004–October 2004), recommending (at 5) 'the creation of a Parliamentary Intelligence Committee in the form of an innovative joint committee of Parliament' over other options that had been canvassed. Notably, the Committee 'met with legislators, oversight bodies, security and intelligence agencies, and academics in Canada and abroad' and 'visited Australia, the United Kingdom and the United States'.

[9] HP Lee, 'The Australian Security Intelligence Organisation – New Mechanisms for Accountability' (1989) 38 *ICLQ* 890, 903.

[10] The Committee was created by the Australian Security Intelligence Organization Amendment Act 1986 (Australia), amending the ASIO Act 1979 (Australia).

issues that attract parliamentary attention'.[11] This remains a problem: even where parliamentary oversight bodies have an ability to launch investigations on their own initiative, as most now do, they will not be able to inquiry into a phenomenon the existence of which they have no knowledge nor any reason to suspect. Another difficulty was the question of access to information, as 'the requirements of security often limit the information which can be provided by the Government to Parliament in respect of issues which do attract its attention'.[12] Though at that point in time the Australian Government had shown itself more willing than in the past to provide information about ASIO to Parliament – which Hope said was commendable – this had logical limits:

> [V]ery careful judgment is required to avoid obvious dangers in such disclosure. The ready answering of questions to which a response can be made without damage, or with little damage, may compound the difficulty of dealing with another question which raises more sensitive implications for national security.[13]

As we shall see in sections II.B and II.C, various mechanisms of differing ambition have been found to address this persistent difficulty, at least in part. Hope's preference, therefore, was to 'suggest ways in which the capacity of Ministers to account to parliament for the activities of intelligence agencies could be strengthened' rather than create new and separate lines of accountability such as via a parliamentary committee.[14] The Australian (Labor) Government, however, believed that improvements to the oversight of ASIO could be achieved

> by directly involving the Parliament … in imposing the discipline of an external scrutiny of the intelligence and security agencies quite independent of the Executive. While the Government has been conscious also of the need to carefully protect intelligence and security information, it believes that appropriate arrangements can be made to ensure that a small but informed parliamentary committee would operate effectively in the public interest.[15]

The (limited) functions of the original Committee were laid out in a provision inserted into the ASIO Act 1979, which introduced the rule whereby the Committee could review only those matters referred to it. Though the Committee could request that the Minister refer a matter to it for review, there was no obligation to do so.[16] And even in relation to ASIO's work, the Committee's remit was notably limited: its functions did not include 'reviewing a matter that relates to the obtaining or communicating by the Organization of foreign intelligence',

[11] Royal Commission on Australia's Security Intelligence Agencies, *Report on the Australian Security Intelligence Organization*, Parliamentary Paper No 232/1985 (1985) [17.5].

[12] ibid.

[13] ibid [17.9].

[14] Royal Commission on Australia's Security Intelligence Agencies, *General Report* (December 1984) [3.28].

[15] House of Representatives Hansard (Australia) no 142, 2886 (22 May 1985) (Robert Hawke).

[16] ASIO Act 1979 (Australia), s 92C(3), inserted by the Australian Security Intelligence Organization Amendment Act 1986 (Australia).

'reviewing an aspect of the activities of the Organization that does not affect any person who is an Australian citizen or a permanent resident', 'reviewing a matter, including a matter that relates to intelligence collection methods or sources of information, that is operationally sensitive' or 'originating inquiries into individual complaints concerning the activities of the Organization'.[17] A fair degree of scepticism seems to have greeted the Committee's creation. One commentator suggested that it should be recognised as 'very much a token gesture from the government to the critics of ASIO from within the Labour Party, for in reality the Committee has little in the way of effective review powers; and is placed firmly under government control in its membership, its agenda and its investigative powers'.[18] Another noted, presciently, that whether or not they succeeded on their own terms, these mechanisms – the Committee and the role of IGIS created simultaneously – would certainly be of interest to other countries that were seeking to resolve the dilemma of how to balance national security and civil liberties.[19] The Australian opposition, believing (it has been claimed) that the Committee 'would become a device for the [Labor Party's] probing into ASIO secrets', promised to dissolve it on coming to power.[20]

The remit of the original Committee's replacement, the Parliamentary Joint Committee on ASIO, ASIS and DSD ('PJCAAD'), which was created by the Intelligence Services Act 2001, was far broader, also taking in the other SIAs included in the title of the new body, which were given – as we have seen in chapter 3 – a statutory basis in that same Act.[21] The PJCAAD no longer required a reference for the carrying out of a review – of the 'administration and expenditure' of the three SIAs – but could still be tasked with reviewing 'any matter' in relation to those bodies if referred to it by the Minister or either House of Parliament.[22] It remained the case, however, that the Committee was precluded from reviewing a range of the most sensitive issues, including 'particular operations that have been, are being or are proposed to be undertaken' by the SIAs.[23]

[17] ASIO Act 1979 (Australia), s 92C(4), inserted by the Australian Security Intelligence Organization Amendment Act 1986 (Australia).

[18] P Hanks, 'Accountability for Security Intelligence Agencies: Australia' (paper delivered at a conference on 'Domestic Security: Issues for Democracy' at Osgoode Hall Law School, York University on 8 May 1987), cited in Lee (n 9) 904.

[19] Lee (n 9) 905.

[20] F Cain, *The Australian Security Intelligence Organization: An Unofficial History* (Frank Cass, 1994) 276.

[21] See the report that had been the ultimate progenitor of the 2001 Act: 'Parliamentary oversight through a special committee is the appropriate vehicle for ASIS because of the sensitivity of the issues involved and the associated need to ensure the security of information provided ... It would be anomalous if ASIS were to be subject to more extensive parliamentary review than ASIO. Since both are small organisations with similar needs for secrecy, it would seem sensible for a single committee to oversee them both.' Commission of Inquiry into the Australian Secret Intelligence Service, *Report on the Australian Secret Intelligence Service – Public Edition* (1995) [40]–[45].

[22] Intelligence Services Act 2001 (Australia), s 29(1).

[23] ibid, s 29(3).

It was now obliged to produce an annual report on its activities.[24] Following the recommendations of Philip Flood's Inquiry into Australian Intelligence Agencies,[25] this remit was expanded once more by the Intelligence Services Legislation Amendment Act 2005 to include what were then called the Defence Imagery and Geospatial Organisation, the Defence Intelligence Organisation and the Office of National Assessments, with the Committee's new incarnation renamed the 'Parliamentary Joint Committee on Intelligence and Security'.[26] Further recommendations as to the reform of the Committee – and continued expansion of its remit – were made by the Independent Intelligence Review of 2017.[27] The later *Comprehensive Review* of the legislative framework governing the Australian Intelligence Community agreed with these recommendations but noted that the Australian Government had not yet responded to them.[28]

Currently, then, the relevant parliamentary body remains the Australian PJCIS, which (statute provides) is 'to be established after the commencement of the first session of each Parliament', has seven members – three of them senators and four members of the House of Representatives – with its being required by statute that a majority of its members are government members.[29] These members are appointed by resolution of the relevant chamber of the Commonwealth Parliament on nomination of the Prime Minster (for those four of its members who are members of the House of Representatives) or the Leader of the Government in the Senate (for the three who are members of the Senate).[30] There is a requirement of prior consultation with the leaders of each non-government party represented in the relevant chamber.[31] Government Ministers cannot be members of the PJCIS, but apart from that, the 2001 Act provides only that the nominating individual must, in making nominations, have regard to the 'desirability of ensuring that the composition of the Committee reflects the representation of recognised political parties in the Parliament', which is a notably weak obligation.[32] The Chair of the

[24] ibid, s 31.

[25] 'Effective oversight and accountability of intelligence agencies is critically important for a healthy democracy. The more relevant intelligence becomes to government, the greater the need and public demand for strong and transparent oversight and accountability. To the greatest extent possible, these mechanisms should be similar to those of other government agencies. In particular, greater parliamentary scrutiny is necessary to enhance public confidence in Australia's intelligence agencies. Because security issues will preclude full parliamentary scrutiny of the operations and output of the intelligence agencies, the role of the Parliamentary Joint Committee on ASIO, ASIS and DSD, extended to cover all agencies, should be supplemented by periodic review.' P Flood, *Report of the Inquiry into Australian Intelligence Agencies* (2004) 164–65.

[26] Intelligence Services Legislation Amendment Act 2005 (Australia), sch 1.

[27] M L'Estrange and S Merchant, *Independent Intelligence Review* (2017), recommendations 21 and 23.

[28] *Comprehensive Review of the Legal Framework of the National Intelligence Community*, Volume 3: *Information, Technology, Powers and Oversight* (2019) [42.12]–[42.13].

[29] Intelligence Services Act 2001 (Australia) s 28.

[30] ibid, sch 1, cl 14.

[31] ibid.

[32] ibid.

Committee is selected by its Members, but must be a government member of the Committee.[33] Though the Act provides that members of the Committee's staff 'must be cleared for security purposes to the same level and at the same frequency as staff members of ASIS',[34] it does not make any reference to the question of security clearance for members of the Committee itself, the practical import of which is of course likely diminished to some extent by the level of government control over appointments thereto: if there is a doubt about some person's suitability for the Committee, he or she will simply not be nominated to it. The *Comprehensive Review* of Australian intelligence legislation considered arguments in favour of changing the rules relating to the composition of the Committee but concluded that the governing legislation provided 'sufficient flexibility for the membership of the Committee' and that 'the Committee's composition is, and rightly remains, a matter for the Parliament'.[35]

The UK's ISC was originally set up (as what was described as a 'committee of parliamentarians' rather than a parliamentary committee) in 1994 in order to 'examine the expenditure, administration and policy' of the three SIAs,[36] attempts at forcing the creation of such a Committee or an equivalent having taken place already during the process of enacting the Security Service Act 1989.[37] Inevitably, discussion of the proposed oversight during the Bill's enactment involved a range of comparisons to other jurisdictions, including not only the Commonwealth Five Eyes states but also the United States.[38] The Committee originally consisted (as it still does now) of nine members of the House of Commons or House of Lords who were not Ministers of the Crown,[39] with the proportion from each chamber not specified in statute and so liable to vary over time. Originally appointment to the Committee was directly by the Prime Minister (after consulting the Leader

[33] ibid, sch 1, cl 16.

[34] ibid, sch 1, cl 21.

[35] *Comprehensive Review* (n 28) [42.88].

[36] Intelligence Services Act 1994 (UK), s 10(1). Andrew traces its origins back to the Franks Report of 1983 on the events leading up to the Argentinian invasion of the Falkland Islands, noting that when he himself had suggested the idea a few years earlier, Peter Hennessy had noted that it had 'been received in Whitehall … with all the enthusiasm normally reserved for insulting references to the Royal Family': C Andrew, *The Defence of the Realm: The Authorized History of MI5* (Allen Lane, 2009) 755. Leigh and Lustgarten quote 'officials' as noting at the time that they 'would have been delighted' to introduce instead a Committee of Privy Councillors along the lines of Canada's SIRC, 'if we though we could have got away with it': L Lustgarten and I Leigh, *In from the Cold: National Security and Parliamentary Democracy* (Oxford University Press, 1994) 514–15.

[37] See the discussion in Bochel, Defty and Kirkpatrick (n 6) 58–59, quoting one peer as claiming that 'we are the only English-speaking democracy without some independent oversight', and noting a separate attempt to set up a body modelled on the Canadian SIRC.

[38] Compare Chris Mullin MP ('What is proposed falls a long way short of what is taken for granted in the United States, Canada, Australia and other democracies which we profess to admire. One of the ironies is that the Russians always seem to know more about our security services than do Parliament or the British people.') with the Chancellor of the Duchy of Lancaster ('If the Bill is passed, we shall be in a position not unlike that in Australia and Canada. There will be differences, but the positions will be comparable.'): HC Deb 22 February 1994, vol 238, cols 153–240.

[39] Intelligence Services Act 1994 (UK), s 10(2); and Justice and Security Act 2013 (UK), s 1(2) and (4).

of the Opposition), as was appointment of the Chair of the Committee.[40] The Prime Minister was also in effect entitled to force a person to leave the Committee by appointing another person in its place.[41] The Committee was 'something of a constitutional anomaly',[42] though, and calls for its reform were made on a frequent basis, with a number of (non-legislative) changes made as part of a broader set of constitutional reforms subsequent to the *The Governance of Britain* Green Paper of 2007.[43] A more ambitious proposal to consult on how the Committee's statutory basis might be changed, so as to 'bring the way in which it is appointed, operates and reports as far as possible into line with that of other select committees, while maintaining the necessary arrangements for access to, and safeguarding of, highly-classified information on which effective security depends',[44] came to nothing in the short term.

The reformed Committee's current, parliamentary status was given to it instead by the Justice and Security Act 2013,[45] largely in line with proposals made by the ISC itself for its own reform.[46] The prospect of transforming the ISC into a departmental select committee – deriving its authority from the standing orders of the two Houses of Parliament rather than an Act of Parliament – was rejected by the Government. Its reasoning was that, on the basis that, if it did not possess a statutory veto on the publication of material by the Committee, there would be 'a real risk that … Agency Heads would find it hard to reconcile their statutory duty to protect information with their statutory duty to facilitate parliamentary oversight', possibly resulting in a 'reduction in both the credibility and effectiveness of the oversight the committee provided'.[47] Instead, then, the Committee is described as a 'statutory Committee of Parliament', with the 2013 Act providing that members of the Committee are appointed by the House in which they sit, though only those nominated by the Prime Minister (again, after consultation with the Leader of the Opposition) are eligible,[48] perpetuating an effective Prime Ministerial veto over membership. The Chair of the Committee is now appointed by members of the Committee themselves,[49] though the Government is liable to try – and has indeed tried in the recent past – to use its majority on the Committee in order to influence

[40] Intelligence Services Act 1994 (UK), s 10(3).
[41] ibid, sch 3, para 1(2).
[42] 'Although it was a committee of parliamentarians, it was not a parliamentary committee. It was appointed by and reported to the Prime Minister, met in secure premises away from the parliamentary estate and was staffed by officials from the Cabinet Office, rather than parliamentary staff. The committee's mode of operation was also markedly different to parliamentary committees, meeting entirely in secret and submitting reports for approval by the Prime Minister before publication.' A Defty, 'Coming in from the cold: bringing the Intelligence and Security Committee into Parliament' (2019) 34 *Intelligence and National Security* 22, 22.
[43] Secretary of State for Justice and Lord Chancellor, *The Governance of Britain* (Cm 7170, 2007).
[44] ibid [92].
[45] Justice and Security Act 2013 (UK), pt 1 and sch 1. For an account of the background to the changes, see Defty (n 42) 24–27.
[46] Intelligence and Security Committee, *Annual Report 2010–2011* (Cm 8114, 2011) 81–82.
[47] Secretary of State for Justice, *Justice and Security Green Paper* (Cm 8194, 2011) [3.19].
[48] Justice and Security Act 2013 (UK), s 1.
[49] ibid, s 1(6).

the selection of the Chair.[50] A member of the ISC vacates office if appointed as a Minister, or if a resolution for his or her removal is passed by the House of Parliament in which the person sits,[51] and so the Prime Minister can no longer remove a member unilaterally. The question of security vetting of Committee members – a central concern, as noted, of the Mackenzie Commission in Canada – is unclear: the website of the ISC previously stated that its members were not vetted,[52] but it no longer does so, and reports frequently attribute the slowness with which the Committee is constituted following General Elections in part to the need to vet those who will be its members.[53] Nor is any statutory provision made regarding its staff, presumably because – as Andrew Defty has noted – the reformed ISC 'continues to meet at secure premises in Victoria rather than on the parliamentary estate and is staffed by officials seconded from the Cabinet Office, rather than parliamentary clerks'.[54] Its members need not be members of the Privy Council but are 'notified' for the purposes of the Official Secrets Act 1989.

In New Zealand, the equivalent body is also the ISC, having been created in 1996,[55] and so shortly after the UK's own Committee, which was a clear if imperfect influence on it. On introducing the Bill that became the 1996 Act, the Prime Minister Jim Bolger said that:

> In developing the proposal for the establishment of the committee, close attention has been paid to the practice adopted by like Governments overseas. It is significant that in both Australia and Britain parliamentary oversight committees for intelligence and security agencies have been established by legislation. The British Intelligence Service Act provided, for the first time in the United Kingdom, a means by which the British intelligence and security services could be made accountable to Parliament.[56]

The New Zealand Committee is subject to far greater and more direct influence by the executive than are its equivalents elsewhere. It previously had five members, including the Prime Minister, the Leader of the Opposition, two members of the House of Representatives nominated by the Prime Minister after consultation with other party leaders, and one member of that House nominated by

[50] See J Devanny, 'The government has mishandled the appointment of the ISC' *King's College London* (17 July 2020), discussing the apparent (and so apparently failed) attempt by the Government to have Chris Grayling MP elected as Chair of the ISC: 'That the government tried and failed to appoint a preferred candidate to chair it, and felt sufficiently confident to publicly punish the disloyalty of a more independent-minded Conservative MP for pursuing the chairship for himself, further brings into disrepute the government's treatment of the ISC and apparent respect for the integrity of its independence.'

[51] Justice and Security Act 2013 (UK), sch 1, para 1(2).

[52] See the discussion in PF Scott, 'The Contemporary Security Vetting Landscape' (2020) 35 *Intelligence and National Security* 54, 60.

[53] See, eg, N Eardley, 'Government criticised for delay in setting up security committee' *BBC News* (19 June 2020): 'Sources said there had been enough time for relevant vetting to be carried out for new members.'

[54] Defty (n 42) 29.

[55] See Committee on the Intelligence and Security Agencies Bill, *Intelligence and Security Agencies Bill* (1996) ii–v, for discussion of the proposals and comments on them from a range of actors.

[56] House of Representatives Hansard (New Zealand), vol 552 (19 December 1995).

the Leader of the Opposition after consultation with the leaders of other parties that were not in government.[57] Each of the Prime Minister and the Leader of the Opposition was capable of revoking the nomination of the members he or she had nominated.[58] Those members of the Committee other than the Prime Minister and the Leader of the Opposition required the endorsement of the House of Representatives before they could take their seats.[59] The Prime Minister (or his or her appointee) would chair the Committee,[60] though an amendment made in 2013 provided that the Prime Minister was not to chair meetings where the Committee was discussing certain matters relating to the Agency for which he or she was responsible.[61] The 2016 Report of the Independent Review of Intelligence and Security in New Zealand recommended that the ISC remain a statutory committee – rather than being reconstituted as a parliamentary select committee, as some had argued for – but that its membership be expanded and it be permitted to 'request (but not require) the Inspector-General to inquire into any matter relating to the Agencies' compliance with the law, including human rights law, and into the propriety of particular activities of the Agencies' – including, as discussed further in section II.B, operationally sensitive matters.[62]

Thus, though the Committee was reformed in 2017 as part of the major reform of the New Zealand intelligence and security framework, the degree of executive control remains high. The ISC now has a membership of between five and seven. The Prime Minister and Leader of the Opposition still sit on the Committee and are joined there by other members of the House of Representatives. If there are five members in total, (as before) two of the other three are the Prime Minister's nominees; if there are six or seven in total then two of the others (either four or five) are to be the Leader of the Opposition's nominees, with the remainder (two or three, as the case may be) the Prime Minister's.[63] The members of the Committee other than the Prime Minister and the Leader of the Opposition still require the endorsement of the House of Representatives.[64] It remains the case that the Prime Minister and the Leader of the Opposition may revoke, at any time, the membership of the Committee of a member for which he or she was responsible.[65] The fact that the Prime Minister, who is also the Minister for National Security and Intelligence, chairs the Committee means – it has been argued – that the oversight it performs 'is compromised because the committee is holding itself to account'.[66]

[57] Intelligence and Security Committee Act 1996 (NZ), s 7(1).
[58] ibid, s 9.
[59] ibid, s 8.
[60] ibid, s 7(3).
[61] ibid, s 7A, inserted by the Intelligence and Security Committee Amendment Act 2013 (NZ).
[62] M Cullen and P Reddy, *Intelligence and Security in a Free Society* (2016) [4.76]–[4.82].
[63] Intelligence and Security Act 2017 (NZ), s 194.
[64] ibid, s 196.
[65] ibid, sch 3, cl 17.
[66] D Rogers, 'The anatomy of political impunity in New Zealand' in D Bigo, E McCluskey and F Tréguer (eds), *Intelligence Oversight in Times of Transnational Impunity: Who Will Watch the Watchers?* (Routledge, 2024) 211.

The matter of the Committee's future is by no means closed, however. A major review of the 2017 Act, published in 2023, was highly critical of its effectiveness, noting three ways in which it is lacking. On of these was exactly that lack of independence from the executive that is, in comparative perspective, the Committee's most striking feature. This was criticised from multiple angles:

> First, while the Committee's present structure may have been appropriate when the Committee was first established, it is no longer fit for purpose as a matter of principle. The dominance of the Executive on the Committee cannot, in our view, be defended. Second, even if there was not that problem of principle, it would be impractical for the Committee as presently constituted to do what the Canadian and UK committees do and what we think the New Zealand Committee should do, given the other commitments of its members. The Prime Minister, other senior Ministers and the Leader of the Opposition do not have the time that would be needed to be a member of an intelligence and security committee that provides the type of oversight we envisage.[67]

The report of that review therefore made a series of detailed recommendations regarding reform of the ISC, summed up in the ambition of reconstituting it 'along the lines of the Canadian and UK committees', while accepting that it would 'not fully replicate those Committees'.[68] Again, comparison with other Commonwealth Five Eyes states clearly drove a set of recommendations aimed at making (and indeed, if implemented, likely to make) oversight of the SIAs more effective.

Canada's National Security and Intelligence Committee of Parliamentarians (NSICOP) is the newest addition to this lineup. The introduction of a body along these lines had been recommended, though, as long ago as the early 1980s by the McDonald Commission,[69] which suggested rather pointedly that it 'should be constituted of parliamentarians whose commitment to Canada's democratic system of government is unquestionable'[70] and believed the problems identified by the earlier Mackenzie Commission, which had seen it reject such a body – especially the issue of vetting, noted above – could be overcome.[71] With its

[67] T Arnold and M Mahuika, *Taumaru: Protecting Aotearoa New Zealand as a free, open and democratic society* (Ministry of Justice, 2023) [12.33] (references omitted).

[68] ibid [12.43]–[12.63].

[69] Commission of Inquiry Concerning Certain Activities of the Royal Canadian Mounted Police, *Second Report: Volume 2 – Freedom and Security under the Law* (1981) 896–905. The role of Parliament in relation to security matters was considered in a study prepared for the Commission, which observed that Committees had played a surprisingly small role in security matters, but this was explained in part by the fact that security matters had been intensely partisan in Canada: 'Committees are ill-adapted to dealing with highly charged matters. The opposition attacks; the government uses its powers to protect witnesses and prevent inquiry; the opposition is frustrated and makes wild accusations; and both sides become upset and bitter. These problems are especially acute when members can grandstand in front of the media, but whether the House would be prepared to allay these problems by handling highly partisan issues through in camera meetings is doubtful.' CES Franks, *Parliament and Security Matters* (Canadian Government Publishing Centre, 1980) 36.

[70] Commission of Inquiry (n 69) 897.

[71] 'Our position is that, while parliamentarians should not be subjected to the formal security screening process, the security intelligence agency should be asked to report in advance to a party leader as to whether it has information about a Member the leader is proposing to name to the Committee

introduction, it is now the case that each body has a parliamentary or quasi-parliamentary committee responsible for oversight of certain matters relating to the intelligence endeavour.[72] The NSICOP is very much in the latter category – a committee of parliamentarians rather than a parliamentary committee. The point is made bluntly in the statute that established it, which provides that the Committee 'is not a committee of either House of Parliament or of both Houses'.[73] Its members must sit in one or the other of those Houses of Parliament, but Ministers are ineligible.[74] Along with the Chair of the Committee, there might be up to 10 other members – not more than three of whom may be appointed from the Senate and not more than eight of whom may sit in the Commons.[75] No minimum number of members is provided for. Of the (up to) eight NSICOP members who are appointed from the Commons, no more than five may be members of the government party[76] – a rule that appears compatible with a situation in which only five are appointed, all of them from the governing party. And there is no limit on the number from the Senate who might be members of the government party. Appointment to the Committee is by Governor in Council, on the recommendation of the Prime Minister, with requirements for consultation – with party leaders generally as regards members of the Senate, and with the leader of the relevant party as regards members of the Commons.[77] Members hold office 'during pleasure' and so might, it seems, be removed from their position on the Committee at any time.[78] The Chair of the Committee is chosen not by its members, as is usually the case elsewhere, but by the Prime Minister.[79]

It was noted above that one difficulty that has arisen in the UK context is recurring and considerable delays in the formation of the ISC after a General Election, with predictable implications for its work: here, in contrast, the statute (now) provides that the NSICOP must be appointed within 60 days of a General Election.[80] Notwithstanding the effective government control on membership, in

which indicates a significant association of that member with an activity threatening the security of Canada … In addition to this security check, Members might be asked to take an oath similar to that taken by Privy Councillors, and they should receive a security briefing from the Director General of the security intelligence agency.' ibid 901–02.

[72] A point made by the Liberal Party in its 2015 manifesto, where it noted that Canada was 'the sole nation among our Five Eyes allies whose elected officials cannot scrutinize security operations', leaving the public 'uninformed and unrepresented on critical issues'. Liberal Party of Canada, 'A New Plan for a Strong Middle Class' (2015) 31. And see L West, 'Review and Oversight of National Security in Canada' in S Carvin, T Juneau and C Forcese (eds), *Top Secret Canada: Understanding the Canadian Intelligence and National Security Community* (University of Toronto Press, 2020) 266–69.

[73] NSICOP Act (2019) (Canada), s 4(3).

[74] ibid, s 4(1).

[75] ibid, s 4(2).

[76] ibid, s 4(2).

[77] ibid, s 5.

[78] ibid, s 5(1).

[79] ibid, s 6(1).

[80] ibid, s 5(1.1). See A Defty, 'From committees of parliamentarians to parliamentary committees: comparing intelligence oversight reform in Australia, Canada, New Zealand and the UK' (2020) 35 *Intelligence and National Security* 367, 374, noting contacts between the Canadian Government and

the form of a requirement for nomination by the Prime Minister, the statute also provides that members of the Committee must 'obtain and maintain the necessary security clearance' from the Canadian Government,[81] a requirement that – as noted earlier – the Mackenzie Commission thought would be a bar to the creation of a body of this sort, and which other jurisdictions either do not require or do not require openly. Another issue relates to how one enforces obligations of secrecy against members of the Committee, preventing the leaking of information acquired by virtue of one's membership of the body or its use for political gain. Outside of Parliament there is no difficulty: the criminal law will cover unauthorised disclosure. But for communications made in Parliament, privilege generally applies, and so the criminal law cannot be relied upon to address the threat of such disclosures. For that reason, the NSICOP Act purports to disapply parliamentary privilege in relation to disclosures made by Committee members contrary to their obligations under that statute or the Security of Information Act.[82] Though this was originally held unconstitutional,[83] potentially undermining in large part the original justification for constituting the NSICOP as an executive rather than parliamentary body, that judgment was overturned on appeal.[84] Endorsing the Bill that eventually created the Committee, a member of the Standing Committee on Public Safety and National Security engaged in a detailed process of comparing and contrasting the proposed body with its equivalents elsewhere, and told Canada's House of Commons that '[w]e have taken some of the best practices from our allies and gone further to establish a strong, accountable, and transparent review of Canada's security and intelligence community's activities',[85] demonstrating once more the extent to which the other (Commonwealth) Five Eyes states invariably loom large when reforms are suggested or carried out.

B. Mandates

It is clear that there has been a considerable degree of convergence, not least in the fact that these bodies now exist at all. This is evident also in considering the work

members of the UK ISC and observing that it was 'unlikely that the UK parliamentarians' undoubted frustration at the delays in nominating members to the UK committee was not passed on to their Canadian counterparts'.

[81] NSICOP Act (2019) (Canada), s 10.

[82] ibid, s 12.

[83] *Alford v Canada (Attorney-General)* 2022 ONSC 2911. The Ontario Superior Court of Justice held that 'Parliament's legislative authority to "define" parliamentary privilege pursuant to s 18 of the Constitution Act, 1867 does not provide Parliament with the constitutional competence to abrogate or restrict parliamentary privilege in the circumstances set out in s 12 of the [NSICOP Act], absent a constitutional amendment pursuant to s 38 of the Constitution Act, 1982.'

[84] *Alford v Canada (Attorney General)* 2024 ONCA 306, noting (at [48]) that 'this is a situation in which Parliament has chosen, through legislation, to limit its own privileges, powers, and immunities to enhance Parliament's ability to oversee certain government activities'.

[85] House of Commons Hansard (Canada) vol 148, col 1324 (10 March 2017).

that the Committees do: they are (largely) similar bodies, doing (largely) similar work. Nevertheless, there are important differences in their mandates – both in terms of how they are set by the relevant statutory (and other) frameworksm and in terms of how they those mandates are executed. Some of that difference in execution is a function of the structure of the bodies, discussed in section II.A; other elements are a function of their powers, discussed in section II.C, to acquire and disseminate information about the SIAs and their work. Of particular significance, and on which there remains an important degree of divergence, is the question of whether, and if so to what extent, they have been and are now entitled to inquire into the operations of the SIAs of which they provide oversight. We shall return to that question at a number of points in what follows.

The functions of the Australian PJCIS were originally the narrow one of reviewing 'the administration and expenditure of ASIO, ASIS and DSD, including the annual financial statements' of those SIAs, as well as any matter in relation to those Agencies referred by the Minister or Parliament, and then to report its comments and recommendations to the relevant Minister and Parliament.[86] Over the years, however, a range of other reviews have been added to the statute, some which the Committee is obliged to carry out and some which it is given discretion to undertake. Many of these new powers and obligations involve the reviewing of the 'operation, effectiveness and implications' of particular pieces of legislation or parts thereof.[87] In this way, the Committee has become something of a standing law reform body in the domain of national security, avoiding a situation – as happens in other jurisdictions – where that task is instead entrusted to a range of ad hoc bodies that may lack the institutional memory and policy expertise (but also the political status) of the relevant parliamentary or quasi-parliamentary committee. It has also, 'as a matter of practice', taken to reviewing proposed legislation in the domain of national security and counter-terrorism.[88] It may request that the relevant Minister or the Attorney-General refer a particular matter relating to the activities of the SIAs to it, though there is no obligation that the person to whom such a request is made make the referral.[89] The effect would seem to be that the Government is able to deploy the PJCIS as it sees fit while being under no obligation to accede to the Committee's own understanding of what might be a valuable use of its time. And though it has been recommended on multiple occasions, there is no power for the PJCIS to initiate its own inquiries.[90]

There is a list of exclusions from the oversight of the PJCIS, including, for example, reviewing the 'intelligence gathering and assessment priorities' of the

[86] Intelligence Services Act 2001 (Australia), s 29(1).
[87] ibid, s 29(1) (as amended).
[88] *Comprehensive Review*, Volume 3 (n 28) [42.4].
[89] Intelligence Services Act 2001 (Australia), s 29(2).
[90] See, echoing the recommendation of the 2017 Independent Intelligence Review, *Comprehensive Review*, Volume 3 (n 28) [42.12].

various SIAs, reviewing particular operations 'that have been, are being or are proposed to be undertaken' by the SIAs, reviewing 'information provided by, or by an agency of, a foreign government where that government does not consent to the disclosure of the information' and reviewing an aspect of their work that 'does not affect an Australian person'.[91] Some of these exclusions relate to issues within the remit of other oversight bodies; others appear to be considered unsuited to oversight from any institution outside of the SIAs themselves. When the 2001 Act was first being debated, the Joint Select Committee on the Intelligence Services recommended that the words 'have been' be removed from the provision relating to operations, so that the Committee would be able to examine 'the generality of past operations',[92] but this was not done, and the matter was later considered in more detail by the *Comprehensive Review* of the intelligence community framework. The *Review*, which explicitly considered the position in the other Five Eyes states, noted that public submissions had highlighted

> that the exercise of agency powers is not subject to the same level of scrutiny as other government departments due to the inherent secrecy of agencies' work. The underlying concern raised by public submissions is that responsible ministers and possibly the IGIS (as an executive body) have a close relationship with the agencies they oversee, risking bias or inability to bring a sufficiently critical approach to oversight.[93]

Despite this, the *Review* also observed the limitations of the parliamentary oversight of SIA operations – noting in particular some of the specific difficulties encountered by the UK's ISC in practice – and concluded that 'operational oversight is currently effectively provided by the IGIS' and that there was a benefit to having a single body responsible for such oversight,[94] The limit in question therefore remains in place. Though the Committee may conduct a review in public, it may only do so with the consent of the Ministers responsible for the SIAs.[95]

The original task of the UK's ISC, when it was put in place by the statute giving MI6 and GCHQ a formal basis, was to examine the 'expenditure, administration and policy' of the three SIAs,[96] no such committee's having been put in place when MI5 was first given statutory basis five years earlier. This remit was broadened by the 2013 Act to include also those Agencies' operations.[97] The 2013 Act's reference to 'operations' represents, on paper, a significant increase to the work of the Committee of a sort that, we have just seen, has not so far been permitted in Australia. There are two caveats, however. One is that, according to the Committee

[91] Intelligence Services Act 2001 (Australia), s 29(3).

[92] Joint Select Committee on the Intelligence Services, *An advisory report on the Intelligence Services Bill 2001, the Intelligence Services (Consequential Provisions) Bill 2001 and certain parts of Cybercrime Bill 2001* (2001) [3.18]–[3.21].

[93] *Comprehensive Review*, Volume 3 (n 28) [42.46].

[94] ibid [42.60].

[95] Intelligence Services Act 2001 (Australia), sch 1, cl 20(2).

[96] Intelligence Services Act 1994 (UK), s 10(1).

[97] Justice and Security Act 2013 (UK), s 2(1).

itself, it had already 'for many years reported on operations, both publicly and in confidence to the Prime Minister', carrying out inquiries into 'specific operations that gave rise to public concern and significant national interest' and for which the ISC had access to 'specific, detailed, operational material'.[98] For this reason, the ISC considered the 2013 change to merely represent a formalisation of existing practice. The second point is that the ISC's right to consider SIA operations is still limited: the ISC may consider any particular operational matter if the Prime Minister asks it to, or if both it and the Prime Minister agree that the matter 'is not part of any ongoing intelligence or security operation' and 'is of significant national interest' (effectively giving the Prime Minister a veto), or the consideration of the matter by the ISC is limited to material provided to it voluntarily by the SIAs or a government department.[99] The Committee may also, the statute provides, 'examine or otherwise oversee such other activities of Her Majesty's Government in relation to intelligence or security matters' as are set out in a Memorandum of Understanding between it and the Government.[100] The original version of that Memorandum of Understanding, agreed at the time of the 2013 Act on this basis, provides for the Committee to oversee certain activities of the Ministry of Defence, the Cabinet Office (including the Joint Intelligence Organisation), and the Home Office (specifically, the activities of the Office for Security and Counter-Terrorism).[101] This has been a source of tension between the Committee and the Government. Though it was said at the time of that statute's passage that the Government's intention was that 'the ISC should have oversight of substantively all of central Government's intelligence and security activities to be realised now and in the future',[102] the Memorandum of Understanding has not been updated to reflect the creation, over the last decade, of new bodies with national security responsibility.

The effect is that the ISC – which, it has been noted, is 'the only Committee of Parliament with regular access to classified information, and to which the UK Intelligence Community has a statutory duty to provide information' – is unable to oversee those new bodies and their work.[103] Though a Memorandum of Understanding, being 'flexible', and so capable of being 'changed much more easily than primary legislation', was, it has been claimed, originally preferred for that reason over an exhaustive statutory list of bodies the ISC might oversee,[104] the ISC has had to resort to seeking to have a statutory obligation to update the Memorandum of Understanding placed upon the Government, ultimately succeeding only in achieving a much weaker obligation on the Prime Minister

[98] Intelligence and Security Committee, *Annual Report 2011–2012* (Cm 8403, 2012) [169]–[171].
[99] Justice and Security Act 2013 (UK), s 2(3).
[100] ibid, s 2(2).
[101] See Intelligence and Security Committee, *Annual Report 2021–2022* (HC 2022–23, 922), Annex C.
[102] Justice and Security Bill [HL] (19 July 2012).
[103] ISC (n 101) [33].
[104] Justice and Security Bill [HL] (19 July 2012).

and the Committee itself to 'consider whether' the existing Memorandum 'should be altered (or replaced) to reflect any changes arising out' of the National Security Act 2023 (but no other changes in the intervening decade).[105] The result is both an increasingly large gap in national security oversight and potential damage to the reputation of the ISC, which cannot promote public confidence if the Government is willing to undermine it and its work so openly over such a long period. Though a case might be made that the ISC is unsuited to overseeing some or all of these bodies – such as, for example, the Investment Security Unit created by the National Security and Investment Act 2021, and the Department of Health's Joint Biosecurity Unit[106] – it seems clear that the current position, whereby those bodies are either not subject to external political scrutiny, or are (as in the case of the Investment Security Unit) subject to such scrutiny only by a departmental select committee with no access to sensitive material (and so, as the ISC has put it, 'when the Government informs the Committee that a classified topic falls within the remit of those Committees, it is clear that this topic will not be subject to effective oversight'),[107] is unacceptable. A remit that is broad in one sense might, we must recall, be limited in others, with obvious implications for the overall scrutiny of the national security endeavour.

The UK's ISC, as previously noted, was a direct influence on that of New Zealand when it was introduced just a couple of years later. The original functions of the New Zealand Committee included examining 'the policy, administration, and expenditure of each intelligence and security agency' – the same terms as used in the UK legislation, though in a different order – considering their annual reports and matters ('not being a matter relating directly to the activities of an intelligence and security') referred to the Committee by the Prime Minister 'by reason of that matter's security or intelligence implications'.[108] However, the New Zealand ISC was prevented from intruding on the jurisdiction of the Inspector-General or inquiring into 'any matter that is operationally sensitive, including any matter that relates to intelligence collection and production methods or sources of information'.[109] This limit also encompassed another of its functions: that of considering 'any bill, petition, or other matter in relation to an intelligence and security agency referred to the Committee by the House of Representatives'.[110] Rather than arguing for an expansion of the ISC's jurisdiction, the Cullen and Reddy review recommended that the ISC should be granted the power to request (not require) the Inspector-General – discussed in chapter 5 – to inquire into 'any matter relating to the Agencies' compliance with

[105] National Security Act 2023 (UK), s 93.
[106] For a full list of the bodies that the ISC would wish to oversee in addition to those it currently oversees, see ISC (n 101) Appendix D.
[107] ibid [36].
[108] Intelligence and Security Act 1996 (NZ), s 6(1).
[109] ibid, s 6(2).
[110] ibid, s 6(1)(b).

the law, including human rights law, and into the propriety of particular activities of the Agencies', including operational matters.[111] It also cast doubt on the role of the ISC in legislative scrutiny and its ability to perform the work normally carried out by a select committee:

> We do not think the ISC should replace the role of a subject select committee when considering proposed legislation in relation to the Agencies. We think the government should in general refer proposed legislation relating to intelligence and security matters to an appropriate subject select committee. However, if there is classified material that needs to be considered in the context of the proposed legislation, the government should consider placing this before the ISC. The ISC would then report its conclusions on that material to the select committee. This process would allow all relevant information to be taken into account, while also helping the ISC to build its knowledge of intelligence and security matters.[112]

The 2017 reform ultimately expanded the remit of the ISC only slightly, and in line with these other recommendations: it is, amongst a few other things, to 'examine the policy, administration, and expenditure of each intelligence and security agency', receive from them their annual reports and carry out an annual review of them, and to carry out reviews (including of Bills) of matters referred to it either by the House of Representatives or the Prime Minister.[113] Unlike before, it is permitted to request that the IGIS conduct an inquiry into either 'any matter relating to an intelligence and security agency's compliance with New Zealand law, including human rights law' or 'the propriety of particular activities of an intelligence and security agency',[114] and the Committee is to consider and discuss with the IGIS his or her annual report.[115] It remains the case, however, that the New Zealand Committee is – like its Australian counterpart, but unlike its namesake in the UK – precluded generally from inquiring into matters that are 'operationally sensitive' (including 'any matter that relates to intelligence collection and production methods, or sources of information'), while its jurisdiction is again subject to that of the IGIS: if a matter is within the Inspector-General's jurisdiction then the ISC may not inquire into it.[116] In the review of the 2017 Act published in 2023, the reviewers therefore considered the two bodies and their interaction, noting that even taken together, they left an important gap in the oversight of the New Zealand SIAs, in the form of a failure to consider the effectiveness of those SIAs in fulfilling their statutory mandates. Despite what they identified as 'clear statutory indications that the effectiveness of the Agencies in fulfilling their essential functions should be subject to oversight under the [Intelligence and Security Act 2017], no such assessment

[111] Cullen and Reddy (n 62) [55].
[112] ibid [4.82].
[113] Intelligence and Security Act 2017 (NZ), s 193.
[114] ibid, s 193(1)(e).
[115] ibid, s 193(1)(g).
[116] ibid, s 193(2).

is presently occurring through the ISA's oversight mechanisms'.[117] Their specific recommendations encompassed not only filling this particular gap – which they clearly specify might involve examination of operational activities[118] – but also the expansion of the ISC's remit beyond the core SIAs to include, for example, Defence Intelligence, Customs Intelligence, Immigration Intelligence and Police Intelligence,[119] reflecting the same sorts of concerns that are evident in the UK, where the expansion of intelligence functions to bodies other than the traditional SIAs potentially leaves gaps in oversight.

The NSICOP in Canada, the newest of these bodies, reviews the following: first, the 'the legislative, regulatory, policy, administrative and financial framework for national security and intelligence', as well as 'any activity carried out by a department that relates to national security or intelligence, unless the activity is an ongoing operation and the appropriate Minister determines that the review would be injurious to national security'.[120] The statute also requires the Committee to review 'any matter relating to national security or intelligence' that is referred to it by a Minister of the Crown.[121] Where a Minister determines that the Committee cannot review an activity carried out by his or her department because a review would be injurious to national security (something that is only possible where it relates to an ongoing operation) then the Minister must give NSICOP reasons,[122] but the determination is final and the Committee's only recourse is to note its dissatisfaction in its report.[123] If the situation changes – either because the operation is no longer ongoing or review of it would no longer be injurious to national security – then the Minister must inform the Committee of that,[124] clearing the way for its review of the activity at issue. The NSICOP mandate is therefore defined more broadly than are those of some of its equivalents elsewhere, with operational sensitivity acting only as a contingent and time-limited bar to the Committee's consideration.

C. Powers

The PJCIS in Australia is bound by a broad, overarching requirement that it must not require disclosure of 'operationally sensitive information or information that would or might prejudice Australia's national security or the conduct of Australia's foreign relations'.[125] Subject to that rule, it has two separate powers to require a person to give evidence to it or to produce documents. One relates to persons

[117] Arnold and Mahuika (n 67) [4.73].
[118] ibid [12.51].
[119] ibid recommendation 30.
[120] NSICOP Act (2019), s 8(1).
[121] ibid, s 8(1)(c).
[122] ibid, s 8(2).
[123] ibid, s 31.
[124] ibid, s 8(3).
[125] Intelligence Services Act 2001 (Australia), sch 1, cl 1.

generally but cannot be used in relation to the heads and staff of the Agencies, the IGIS and its staff; the other relates to the heads of the Agencies it oversees.[126] The former might be used where the Committee has reasonable grounds for believing that the person in question is capable of giving evidence or producing documents relevant to a matter the Committee is reviewing or which has been referred to it; the latter only where the Committee has reasonable grounds to believe that the Agency Head is capable of doing one or the other thing relevant to a matter which has been referred to it.[127] It is therefore unavailable in relation to own-initiative reporting by the PJCIS. Where the latter power – that relating to the head of the Agency – is used, the Agency Head in question may nominate a member of staff to give evidence alongside or instead of him or her.[128] The Minister has broad powers, exercised by certification, to intervene in the giving of evidence or disclosure of documents (whether or not required by the Committee in exercise of its powers) where he or she believes it necessary to prevent the disclosure of 'operationally sensitive information'.[129] In relation to a person other than an Agency Head, the effect of the certificate can be to stop the person from giving evidence altogether; otherwise, it prevents the production of documents, or of documents of a particular kind.[130] A copy of a certificate must be provided to the President of the Senate and the Speaker of the House of Representatives, and is protected against judicial review.[131] The powers to require the giving of evidence or the production of documents are backed by criminal sanctions, including for knowingly giving false or misleading evidence, though the offence of refusing or failing to produce a document does not apply if 'the producing of the document would tend to incriminate the person'.[132]

The UK's ISC has a prima facie right of access to information from the SIAs and from government departments. This applies, however, to information relating to a 'particular operational matter' only where certain of the conditions for the consideration of such a matter by the ISC are met – that is, that the Prime Minister has asked the ISC to consider the matter or the ISC and the Prime Minister are both satisfied that the matter 'is not part of any ongoing intelligence or security operation' and is 'of significant national interest'.[133] Effectively, therefore, the Prime Minister has a veto over the ISC's access to information about particular operational matters. Otherwise, if the head of the relevant SIA or a government department is asked for information by the ISC, it must be disclosed to the Committee in accordance with the Memorandum of Understanding, unless the Secretary of State has decided that it should not be disclosed.[134] This can

[126] ibid, sch 1, cls 2 and 3.
[127] ibid, sch 1, cls 2 and 3.
[128] ibid sch 1, cl 3(5).
[129] ibid, sch 1, cl 4.
[130] ibid, sch 1, cl 4(1).
[131] ibid, sch 1, cls 4(3) and (4).
[132] ibid, sch 1, cl 10.
[133] Justice and Security Act 2013 (UK), sch 1, para 4(1) and s 2(3).
[134] ibid, sch 1, paras 4(2) and (3).

happen only where the Secretary of State considers that one of two sets of criteria are met. One is that the information requested is both 'sensitive information' and information that, 'in the interests of national security, should not be disclosed to the ISC'.[135] 'Sensitive information' has three prongs: (i) information that 'might lead to the identification of, or provide details of, sources of information, other assistance or operational methods available to' the SIAs or other parts of the state involved in intelligence work; (ii) information about the particular operations – previously undertaken or merely proposed – by those bodies; (iii) information provided by a foreign government or its agencies, where that government does not consent to its disclosure.[136] The effect is that the ISC may seek such information, with the Government able withhold it only where the interests of national security – albeit as adjudged by the government of the day – justify doing so. The relative narrowness of this right to withhold (and corresponding breadth of the power on the part of the ISC to compel disclosure) is, however, undercut by the second circumstance in which disclosure may be refused: where, that is, the Secretary of State considers that 'it is information of such a nature that, if the Secretary of State were requested to produce it before a Departmental Select Committee of the House of Commons, the Secretary of State would consider (on grounds which were not limited to national security) it proper not to do so',[137] which would seem to be a very broad rule.[138]

The Memorandum of Understanding that exists between the ISC and the UK Government states that 'no decision will be taken to withhold information from the ISC without the ISC being informed of that decision'.[139] In practice, the ISC has had evident difficulty in getting access to information it considered necessary to complete some of its inquiries. Perhaps most notably, in the context of its inquiry into UK drone strikes in Syria – one of them significant because it involved the targeting of a suspected terrorist who was a UK national outside of an ongoing military operation – the ISC was unable to assess with any certainty whether an armed attack against the UK was imminent, as the Government had claimed in asserting the strike's legality. In a footnote to its report, the ISC observed:

> The National Security Secretariat has made clear that the Committee has not been provided with all the intelligence, but only the 'main primary intelligence reports

[135] ibid, sch 1, para 4(4)(a).

[136] ibid, sch 1, para 5.

[137] ibid, sch 1, para 4(4)(b).

[138] 'Select committees have occasionally argued that there should be a procedure to enable them to challenge in the House a department's decision to withhold papers. Governments have opposed recommendations for a formal procedure to give them that opportunity, but have instead relied on the terms of the House's Resolution on Ministerial Accountability of March 1997, and in particular its provision that "Ministers should be as open as possible with Parliament, refusing to provide information only when disclosure would not be in the public interest".' M Hutton et al, *Erskine May: Parliamentary Practice*, 25th edn (LexisNexis Butterworths, 2019) [38.32] (references omitted).

[139] Intelligence and Security Committee, *Annual Report 2013–2014* (HC 2014–15, 794), Annex A, [31].

> specifically drawn upon in compiling the contemporaneous assessments and a selection of supplementary reports'. We requested sight of any further intelligence reports which would disprove our statement, but the National Security Secretariat declined to provide any such material.[140]

In the following Parliament, the Committee was forced to bring its inquiry into detainee mistreatment and rendition between 2001 and 2010 to an early conclusion, because the Government refused to provide access to relevant witnesses and said that those witnesses who would be made available would not be permitted 'to talk about the specifics of the operations in which they were involved, nor fill in any gaps in the timeline of events', and the Committee would not be permitted to quote from their evidence in its report.[141] As well as these specific issues, the Committee has frequently commented on the unwillingness of successive Prime Ministers to appear before it,[142] and about delays in the Government's response to its reports,[143] which the Memorandum of Understanding says the Government should aim to do within 60 days.[144] So far, however, this sort of attempt to enforce compliance via shaming of the relevant persons and bodies appears to have had little success, indicating the dangers of reliance on anything other than statute to create a meaningful norm in this context.

New Zealand's ISC may require the Director-General of an SIA to appear before it, and may 'request' any other person to attend and give evidence to it, or to produce documents or information relevant to its work.[145] The Director-General must disclose documents or information relevant to the Committee's work unless he or she considers that it is (or contains) 'sensitive information'. This is turn is subject to an exception where the Director-General considers it safe to disclose the information or documents.[146] 'Sensitive information' is information falling in one of four categories, the disclosure of which would have one of four effects. The four categories are: (i) information that might lead to the identification of an Agency's sources of information or operational methods; (ii) information about 'particular operations that have been undertaken, or are being or are proposed to be undertaken, in performing any of the functions of an intelligence and security agency'; (iii) information provided to an Agency by another government

[140] Intelligence and Security Committee, *UK Lethal Drone Strikes in Syria* (HC 2016–17, 1152) [37] and fn 22.

[141] Intelligence and Security Committee, *Detainee Mistreatment and Rendition: 2001-2010* (HC 2017–18, 1113) [10]–[14].

[142] See, eg, Intelligence and Security Committee, *Annual Report 2022–2023* (HC 2023–24, 287) [58]: 'Since its establishment in 1994, and for 20 years thereafter, the Committee met annually with the Prime Minister to discuss its work, report on key issues, and raise any concerns. However, the Committee has not had a meeting with a Prime Minister since December 2014.'

[143] ibid [8]: 'The Committee is concerned that the Government did not provide a substantive response [to its report on Extreme Right-Wing Terrorism] until 30 March 2023, 261 days after the Report was published, and that no explanation has been provided as to the reasons for the delay.'

[144] ISC (n 101) Annex C, [38].

[145] Intelligence and Security Act 2017 (NZ), s 201.

[146] ibid, s 203(1) and (2).

department whose consent is needed for its disclosure; and (iv) information provided by a foreign government or its Agency whose consent is required for the information to be disclosed.[147] The effects in question are where the information's disclosure would be likely: 'to prejudice the security or defence of New Zealand or the international relations of the Government of New Zealand'; 'to prejudice the entrusting of information to the Government of New Zealand on a basis of confidence by' a foreign government (or its Agency) or an international organisation; 'to prejudice the maintenance of the law, including the prevention, investigation, and detection of offences and the right to a fair trial'; or 'to endanger the safety of any person'.[148] Of the four types of information, however, a distinction is drawn between the first three and the fourth. The Prime Minister (who, we must remember, is a member of the ISC in New Zealand) can require disclosure of information if he or she considers it to be in the public interest.[149] Information in category (iv) – that disclosure of which would require the consent of the foreign government (or its Agency) that provided it – is excluded from this override, and so if its disclosure would have one of the relevant effects, the Director-General may not supply it to the ISC regardless of where the Prime Minister thinks the public interest lies. The powers of the ISC in New Zealand were not subject to any detailed consideration either in the review that preceded the enactment of the Intelligence and Security Act 2017, or in the review of that Act in 2023. It seems likely that the Committee's shortcomings, and in particular its lack of independence from the executive, are, as discussed in section II.A, so fundamental that the specific question of what powers it does or does not possess are currently of only secondary import.

Canada's NSICOP is by statute 'entitled to have access to any information that is under the control of a department and that is related to the fulfilment of the Committee's mandate', including that which is subject to various forms of legal privilege,[150] and may therefore request that information from the relevant department.[151] Leah West has noted, however, that the language of 'control' is a term of art, and that a security body may have information in its possession that is not in its control because it is subject to the control of a foreign body which was its originator.[152] There are two (sets of) exceptions to the general rule. One is that the Committee is not entitled to have access to 'a confidence of the Queen's Privy Council for Canada';[153] information about the identity of a person in witness protection; the identity of an intelligence source; or information 'relating directly to an ongoing investigation carried out by a law enforcement agency that

[147] ibid, s 202(2).
[148] ibid, s 202(1).
[149] ibid, s 203(2).
[150] NSICOP Act (2019) (Canada), s 13.
[151] ibid, s 15(1).
[152] West (n 72) 267–68.
[153] On which see Canada Evidence Act, RSC 1985, c C-5 (Canada), s 39, which protects (an expansive understanding of) Cabinet confidentiality for a period of 20 years.

may lead to a prosecution'.[154] And even outside of those categories, a Minister may refuse to disclose information requested by the NSICOP where it constitutes what is known as 'special operational information' (generally, information about the sources and methods of the Canadian Government and its intelligence services)[155] and 'provision of the information would be injurious to national security'.[156] The NSICOP has observed that when it was first set up, departments that were new to being the subject of oversight responded in varying ways: some engaged well with it, while others 'required more time to achieve an ability to provide the Committee with information that was comprehensive and timely'.[157] It has also identified a number of specific issues it has encountered in seeking access to information, including departments citing reasons for not supplying information other than those identified in the statute as exceptions to their obligations,[158] and at times simply refusing to supply information requested by the Committee.[159] Finally, it observed that the exception for Cabinet confidences was being broadly interpreted by some departments, with potentially significant implications:

> If departments continue to broadly interpret the definition of Cabinet confidence to withhold information and are not required to inform the Committee of what relevant information has been withheld and why, then the Committee's ability to transparently and comprehensively review the governance frameworks which support Ministerial accountability risks being compromised.[160]

Again, it seems clear that the effectiveness of the various Committees' powers to acquire information (and exceptions thereto) might be undermined by the practices of those they are overseeing, with the Committees' ability to fight back against such recalcitrance itself potentially undermined by the degree of control the executive enjoys over their membership.

D. Reporting

Just as the different Committees vary in terms of their composition, mandates and powers, they differ in terms of their reporting powers and requirements, and in the extent to which they are able to and do produce reports other than those the governing statute demands. The Australian PJCIS has as one of its functions that of reporting 'the Committee's comments and recommendations to each House of the Parliament, to the responsible Minister and to the Attorney-General',[161] and must

[154] NSICOP Act (2019), s 14.
[155] The definition is contained in the Security of Information Act, RSC 1985, c O-5 (Canada), s 8(1).
[156] NSICOP Act (2019), s 16(1).
[157] National Security and Intelligence Committee of Parliamentarians, *2022 Annual Report* (2023) [9].
[158] ibid [11].
[159] ibid [12].
[160] ibid [13].
[161] Intelligence Services Act 2001 (Australia), s 29(1)(c).

give an annual report to Parliament on its activities.[162] There are limits on what may be disclosed in a report it makes to Parliament: it must not disclose information about the identity of those working either as staff or agents of the SIAs, or 'from which the identity of such a person could reasonably be inferred', though the head of an agency can waive these restrictions. Also prohibited is disclosure of 'operationally sensitive information or information that would or might prejudice' either 'Australia's national security or the conduct of Australia's foreign relations' or 'the performance by an agency of its functions'.[163] On this point as on the others, the Committee must seek the advice of the responsible Minister or Ministers and is effectively bound by it.[164] For this and other reasons, it has been suggested that 'the public must often trust that the PJCIS is using its limited powers to hold the intelligence agencies to account, rather than knowing this to be the case'.[165] There are no other specific requirements to produce reports, though the PJCIS does produce a large number of additional reports on a range of topics, some of which are discussed further in section II.E.

The UK's ISC is required to make an annual report to Parliament on the discharge of its functions, and 'may make such other reports to Parliament as it considers appropriate concerning any aspect of its functions'.[166] In either case, it must send the draft report to the Prime Minister before making a report to Parliament, and must exclude from the report any matter that the Prime Minister – after consultation with the Committee itself – considers would be 'prejudicial to the continued discharge of the functions' of the SIAs or others carrying out intelligence or security functions.[167] A report made to Parliament must state whether any information has been excluded on that basis, though in practice this is not usually necessary – ISC reports are often visibly, and highly, redacted. The Committee may also make a report not to Parliament but to the Prime Minister in relation to matters that would have to be excluded if the report were made to Parliament.[168] Though the Memorandum of Understanding between the Government and the ISC does not make reference to the point, it is often said – not least by the Committee itself – that there is a 'convention' that the Prime Minister will respond to its draft reports with a decision as to what needs to be redacted within 10 days of receiving the drafts.[169] In practice,

[162] ibid, 31.
[163] ibid, sch 1, cl 7.
[164] ibid, sch 1, cl 7(3).
[165] K Hardy and G Williams, 'Executive Oversight of Intelligence Agencies in Australia' in ZK Goldman and SJ Rascoff (eds), *Global Intelligence Oversight: Governing Security in the Twenty-First Century* (Oxford University Press, 2016) 315, 317–18.
[166] Justice and Security Act 2013 (UK), s 3(1) and (2).
[167] ibid, s 3(4).
[168] ibid, s 3(7).
[169] ISC (n 142) [36]: 'By convention, the deadline requested for the Prime Minister to provide such a confirmation is ten working days.' The Memorandum of Understanding (ibid, Annex C, [37]) merely says that the Government and the ISC 'will work together to apply a reasonable process for identifying, in consultation with the ISC, sensitive material that must be removed from ISC reports prior to publication.'

however, this seems to be breached more often than it is adhered to, so that the notion that it might constitute a convention is difficult to accept. In particular, there is a strong suspicion that the approval process has been used for political purposes – the delay of the publication of the ISC's high-profile Russia report until following the 2019 General Election is the key example.[170]

The New Zealand ISC too must present an annual report to the House of Representatives on its activities,[171] and may make other reports. In each case, it must in doing so 'have regard generally to security requirements'.[172] There are limits on what might be disclosed in its reports. Most notably, the Committee must not disclose in any of its reports 'any information that, if publicly disclosed, would be likely to prejudice the entrusting of information to the Government of New Zealand on a basis of confidence' by foreign governments (or agents thereof) or international organisation, nor any information that, 'if publicly disclosed, would be likely to endanger the safety of any person'.[173] Any 'sensitive information' disclosed to the Committee as an exception to the general rule against disclosure of such information, on the say-so either of the Director-General of the relevant SIA or of the Prime Minister, may not be disclosed by it in its reports.[174] Other information can be disclosed only if the ISC considers that there are 'compelling reasons in the public interest' for it to be disclosed. This includes the identity of officers, employees or agents of the SIAs (other than the Director-General), as well as any information the disclosure of which is likely to prejudice either 'the continued performance of the functions of an intelligence and security agency' or 'the security or defence of New Zealand or the international relations of the Government of New Zealand'.[175] Any reader of the Committee's annual reports of its own activities will immediately be struck by how short and devoid of detail they are. The substantive part of its report on its activities in 2022, for example, runs to three pages, one of which is used in order to recapitulate its legal framework.[176] The reports of the annual reviews of the New Zealand SIAs are even less informative, amounting (in apparently all cases) to no more than a statement that the ISC has carried out a review and a recommendation that the House of Representatives take note of the report.[177] Whatever the value of the work the New Zealand ISC does, the communication of that work to the public would

[170] D Sabbagh, 'Russia report to be released on Tuesday after nine-month delay' *The Guardian* (20 July 2020). And see Intelligence and Security Committee, 'Russia' press release (21 July 2020): 'This Report is the result of an extensive Inquiry by the previous Committee … it is a matter of great regret that it was not published last November, ahead of the General Election.'

[171] Intelligence and Security Act 2017 (NZ), s 223(1).

[172] ibid, s 224(1).

[173] ibid, s 224(2).

[174] ibid, s 224(2)(c).

[175] ibid, s 224(3).

[176] Intelligence and Security Committee, *Activities of the Intelligence and Security Committee in 2022*, G.21 (2023).

[177] See, eg, Intelligence and Security Committee, *2021/22 Annual review of the New Zealand Security Intelligence Service* (2023).

appear to be incapable of contributing to public confidence in the SIAs, and indeed to belief in the propriety and value of the national security endeavour in New Zealand more generally.

Canada's NSICOP must report to the Prime Minister annually on the reviews it has conducted in that year, including details of its findings and recommendations, as well as information relating to the number of occasions on which certain ministerial veto powers have been used in the relevant period.[178] It may also, if it considers it necessary, submit a special report on 'any matter related to its mandate' to the Prime Minister and the relevant Minister.[179] It may prepare a summary of its special reports for inclusion within its annual report, notifying the Prime Minister of its intention to do so.[180] In either case, the Prime Minister may require the submission of a revised version if he or she considers the report to include 'information the disclosure of which would be injurious to national security, national defence or international relations or is information that is protected by litigation privilege or by solicitor–client privilege or the professional secrecy of advocates and notaries'.[181] A revised version must note that it is such a thing, and indicate 'the extent of, and the reasons for, the revisions'.[182] This is not necessarily helpful information: in a special report on the federal policing mandate of the RCMP, for example, the note in question simply repeats the statutory language, indicating that revisions had been made to remove information 'the disclosure of which the Prime Minister believes would be injurious to national security, national defence or international relations or which constitutes solicitor–client privilege' – the revisions taking the form of a mix of redactions and summaries of sensitive material.[183] Reports must be laid before each House of Parliament within the first 30 sitting days after their submission,[184] a statutory rule again being used to avoid the difficulties that have been encountered in the UK. Even in the short period since the institution of the NSICOP, reporting practice has evolved: the Committee in 2021 decided to provide its future reviews as special reports, thus separating them from the annual reporting cycle and 'permitting the Committee to conduct complex reviews over varying timeframes and to provide its reports to the Prime Minister as soon as they are ready'.[185] Annual reports would as a result, it said, focus 'more narrowly' on the Committee's activities and its statutory reporting requirements.[186]

[178] NSICOP Act (2019) (Canada), s 20(1).
[179] ibid, s 20(2).
[180] ibid, s 21(3).
[181] ibid, s 21(5).
[182] ibid, s 21(5.1).
[183] National Security and Intelligence Committee of Parliamentarians, *Special Report on the Federal Policing Mandate of the Royal Canadian Mounted Police* (2023).
[184] NSICOP Act (2019) (Canada), s 21(6).
[185] National Security and Intelligence Committee of Parliamentarians, *Annual Report 2021* (2022) [2].
[186] ibid.

E. The Work of Parliamentary Security Committees

The various parliamentary security committees also vary, in a manner that cannot be explained entirely by variation in their formal characteristics, in the work they do and the attitude to their role that the work in question manifests. Australia's PJCIS, as already noted, does much more legislative scrutiny work than do any of its equivalents elsewhere,[187] those equivalents seeming to engage in legislative scrutiny only infrequently if at all. The PJCIS also, relatedly but distinctly, is charged with carrying out the sort of (post-enactment) periodic scrutiny often done in other jurisdictions by other or even ad hoc bodies,[188] including – for example – a review of the Foreign Influence Transparency Scheme Act 2018 discussed in chapter 7.[189] In accordance with its statutory mandate, it produces periodic reports on the 'administration and expenditure' of the SIAs. These different activities make up the bulk of its published output: given its dependence upon other actors to refer matters to it for it to inquire into, it has produced relatively few thematic reports.[190]

As well as its annual reports, over the 30 or so years of its existence, the UK ISC has published a considerable number of special reports. Some relate to terrorism, amongst which are numbered several relating to specific acts of terrorism in the UK or abroad – what the SIAs knew or should have known of the threat[191] – as well as others relating to more general phenomena within the domain of terrorism.[192] A number of them deal with the fall-out from the War on Terror, sometimes in areas also covered by public inquiries but sometimes in other areas in which the ISC was in the end the only institution able and permitted to consider the issues – the key example being that of rendition and the mistreatment of detainees, where a first attempt at a judge-led inquiry was abandoned

[187] In the 46th Parliament of Australia, for example, between 2019 and 2022, the Committee produced 10 of what it calls 'advisory reports' on a Bill or multiple Bills before the Parliament. See, for discussion of this aspect of its work, see D Dalla-Pozza, 'The Parliamentary Joint Committee on Intelligence and Security: A Point of Increasing Influence in Australian Counter-Terrorism Law Reform?' in R Levy et al (eds), *New Directions for Law in Australia: Essays in Contemporary Law Reform* (ANU Press, 2017) 397.

[188] See, for one recent example, Parliamentary Joint Committee on Intelligence and Security, *Review of the Counter-Terrorism (Temporary Exclusion Orders) Act 2019* (2023), a review of the 'operation, effectiveness and implications' of that Act, which the Committee was obliged to undertake three years after its enactment.

[189] Parliamentary Joint Committee on Intelligence and Security, *Review of the Foreign Influence Transparency Scheme Act 2018* (2024), as required by s 70 of that Act.

[190] In the 46th Parliament of Australia, for example, between 2019 and 2022, two inquiries were referred to it: see Parliamentary Joint Committee on Intelligence and Security, *Inquiry into the impact of the exercise of law enforcement and intelligence powers on the freedom of the press* (2020); and Parliamentary Joint Committee on Intelligence and Security, *Inquiry into national security risks affecting the Australian higher education and research sector* (2022).

[191] See, eg, Intelligence and Security Committee, *Review of the Intelligence on the London Terrorist Attacks on 7 July 2005* (Cm 7617, 2009).

[192] See, eg, Intelligence and Security Committee, *Extreme Right-Wing Terrorism* (HC 2021–22, 459).

and a promise to hold another later reneged upon.[193] Though the reports in question are in their own way impressive, it is necessary to note that they took place against a background in which the ISC's own previous attempt to get to the heart of these issues was widely discredited.[194] Other special reports have addressed general issues relating to or within the intelligence community.[195] Reflecting the origins of the ISC in the aftermath of the Cold War, the focus on terrorism was in the first two decades of its existence largely to the exclusion of the question of 'state threats', though this pattern has, it would seem, begun to go into reverse in recent years, in keeping with the legislative pivot back to state threats, which we will discuss in chapter 7. One example of this, the ISC's Russia report,[196] was particularly (and perhaps unusually) high-profile: it was followed by a report on China,[197] with an inquiry into Iran also in progress. The Committee has reported on the powers of the SIAs and produced one of the reports that was influential on the design of what became the Investigatory Powers Act 2016.[198] It therefore might be considered to have ranged widely, if not always successfully, across the majority of the landscape of national security issues – considering both the legal frameworks of and (despite the original absence of a remit to inquire into operational matters) specific activities undertaken by the SIAs.

Alongside its annual reports, which are relatively short but nevertheless informative, the NSICOP has in the few years since its formation produced six special reports.[199] Some of these have a quite particular focus, such as its first special report in which it addressed issues arising out of a trip by the Canadian Prime Minister to India in 2018.[200] Others involve much broader and more diffuse (sets of) issues, suggesting that the Committee will in the future pursue the same approach as the UK's ISC in terms of the variety of its reports and the depth and breadth of their focus. Though these reports – the fact of their being produced as well as their content – are of course of interest, it is notable that as published,

[193] See PF Scott, *The National Security Constitution* (Hart Publishing, 2018) 296–97. For discussion, see P Gill, 'Twenty years on: Intelligence and Security Committee and investigating torture in the "war on terror"' (2023) 38 *Intelligence and National Security* 799.

[194] Intelligence and Security Committee, *Rendition* (Cm 7171, 2007).

[195] Intelligence and Security Committee, *Women in the UK Intelligence Community* (HC 2014–15, 970); and *Diversity and Inclusion in the UK Intelligence Community* (HC 2017–19, 1297).

[196] Intelligence and Security Committee, *Russia* (HC 2019–21, 632).

[197] Intelligence and Security Committee, *China* (HC 2022–23, 1605).

[198] Intelligence and Security Committee, *Privacy and Security: A modern and transparent legal framework* (HC 2014–15, 1075).

[199] The six are as follows: *Special Report on the Prime Minister's Trip to India in February 2018* (2018); *Special Report on the Collection, Use, Retention and Dissemination of Information on Canadians in the context of the Department of National Defence and the Canadian Armed Forces Defence Intelligence Activities* (2020); *Special Report on the Government of Canada's Framework and Activities to Defend its Systems and Networks from Cyber Attack* (2022); *Special Report on the National Security and Intelligence Activities of Global Affairs Canada* (2022); *Special Report on the Federal Policing Mandate of the Royal Canadian Mounted Police* (2023); *Review of the dissemination of intelligence on People's Republic of China political foreign interference, 2018–2023* (2024).

[200] National Security and Intelligence Committee of Parliamentarians, *Special Report on the Prime Minister's Trip to India in February 2018* (2018).

several of them have been subject to very considerable redaction. As with the UK's ISC, therefore, the question arises of who is the intended audience of the NSICOP's work; and whether, if it is the public at large rather than the legislature, the confidence of that public can be secured by the work the NSICOP in fact produces.

In terms of the quality of material published, and its helpfulness, then, the clear outlier amongst the four bodies under consideration here is New Zealand's Intelligence and Security Committee. That Committee produces annual reports on each of the intelligence services; but even after the reform of the oversight landscape in 2017, these reports provide no information whatsoever about the NZ SIAs and their work.[201] Perhaps the only thing that might be said in favour of these reports is that they are based on evidence sessions that take place partly in public. The Committee also produces a short and uninformative report on its own activities each year, the majority of which is devoted to identifying its statutory obligations and noting that they were complied with.[202] It has also in the past carried out some legislative scrutiny, but none of the sorts of thematic reporting that is common in the UK, becoming so in Canada and which has taken place occasionally in Australia. Though there is no necessary connection between the composition of these bodies and their output, it seems highly likely that to achieve a more effective ISC in New Zealand would require reforming the Committee to address the question of executive dominance outlined in section II.A. As it stands, it operates largely to demonstrate the distinction between parliamentary accountability's formal existence and its meaningful operation – in this domain as, no doubt, in others.

III. Patterns of Mutual Influence

In concluding, in the early 1980s, that it was 'neither necessary nor appropriate' to establish a special parliamentary committee for oversight of ASIO that would shortly be given a statutory basis, Justice Robert Hope had no model from any other Commonwealth (or Westminster) constitutional order to which to refer. Though the creation of such a committee had been recommended in Canada by the McDonald Commission – following Hope's own rejection of the idea in his first Royal Commission – it had been rejected by the Special Committee of the Canadian Senate that scrutinised the resulting CSIS Bill. Hope noted that proponents of such a committee 'generally refer to Congressional oversight of the intelligence community in the United States of America' and that the 'relevant experience in that country over the last decade is certainly of great interest', that

[201] See, eg, Intelligence and Security Committee, *2021/22 Annual review of the New Zealand Security Intelligence Service* (2023).

[202] See, eg, Intelligence and Security Committee, *Activities of the Intelligence and Security Committee in 2022* (2023).

period having seen 'a marked increase in Congressional interest in, and oversight of, the relevant agencies'.[203] Though he identified a number of limitations of the Congressional oversight in question, Hope suggested that the 'essential relevant difference' between the constitutional position in the US and in Australia (and indeed in Canada) was that

> in our system the responsible Minister is a member of Parliament and is directly answerable to it … This is no small difference when considering the case for a special committee. Perhaps this difference helps to explain why in the United States tension between Congress and the Executive appears to be greater, but partisan differences seem less marked, than under the Australian system.[204]

The correctness of that supposition is neither here nor there: what matters instead is the manner in which the parliamentary status of the Australian constitutional order was used in order to distinguish it (and by implication all the other Commonwealth Five Eyes states) from the United States, a presidential system. This allowed Hope to resist the institution of parliamentary oversight now that the argument once made by the Mackenzie Commission and which we noted at the start of this chapter – that these matters belonged to the executive, and the legislature should simply not be involved – was, as a result of the institution of Congressional intelligence oversight in the United States the 1970s, no longer as compelling as it might once have been. The resistance, we might suggest, was perhaps deeper-rooted than the specific justification offered for it at any particular point in time might have indicated.

Going back to the Canadian context, the McDonald Commission – reporting a few years before Hope's second Royal Commission – seems, in recommending such a committee, to have treated the point as one of pure practicality, not drawing directly on any other model (from the US or elsewhere):

> Parliament requires an enhanced capacity to scrutinize security and intelligence activities. The necessarily secret nature of these activities makes it impossible for Parliamentary scrutiny to be exercised effectively through any mechanism other than a small committee whose members either include the party leaders or are specially selected by them. This committee's effectiveness will depend on its capacity to develop and maintain the confidence of all parliamentary parties, as well as that of the government and the security agency.[205]

The Commission considered, it said, 'the possibility of a Committee of parliamentarians (rather than a Committee of Parliament) which, rather like the British Committees of Privy Councillors, would not die with each dissolution of Parliament', but it rejected that model because 'such an arrangement would,

[203] Royal Commission on Australia's Security Intelligence Agencies, *Report on ASIO* (n 11) [17.23].
[204] ibid [17.30].
[205] Commission of Inquiry Concerning Certain Activities of the Royal Canadian Mounted Police, *Second Report: Volume 1 – Freedom and Security under the Law* (1981) 426.

in our view, go too far towards detaching this Committee from Parliament'.[206] The 'prime function' of the model being recommended 'should be to scrutinize the activities of the security intelligence organization with a view to ensuring that it fulfills the intentions of Parliament as set out in the organization's legislative charter', and it should be 'as much concerned with the effectiveness of the security intelligence organization as with the legality or propriety of its operations'.[207] The Commission openly noted that no such equivalents existed at that point in time in most other comparable states. In Australia, one reason it had not been done was the practice of electing members of parliamentary committees, but consultation with the Leader of the Opposition had been used to foster a bipartisan approach.[208] In the UK too, there was no such committee but instead reliance on Committees of Privy Councillors to inquire into issues relating to security.[209] This model was not transplantable to Canada at that point in history:

> This is scarcely a feasible option in Canada until such time as the balance of power in federal politics shifts much more frequently from one party to another. Indeed, one important function which the existence of a parliamentary committee on security and intelligence would perform is to provide much more opportunity for at least a few leading opposition Members of Parliament to become reasonably well-informed about security and intelligence matters than has been possible in recent years.[210]

The McDonald Commission nevertheless noted that in

> embarking on the experiment in parliamentary oversight which we have proposed, Canada would not be breaking entirely new ground. Nearly all of the western democracies in one way or another have been moving away from the position taken by the Canadian Royal Commission on Security … 13 years ago that the legislature should not be directly involved in security matters. The trend has been towards a greater role for Members including those who do not belong to the governing party or coalition, to review secret security and intelligence activities.[211]

The two states identified as having made most use of committees of the legislature in this context were the US and the Federal Republic of Germany,[212] a pairing indicative of the manner in which the Commonwealth Five Eyes states once drew with some regularity on arrangements of states outside that group of states – something that is much less likely with the passage of time and the emergence of arrangements within it that might instead be drawn upon. As we have noted, however, this experiment did not in fact take place at that point with the Special

[206] Commission of Inquiry Concerning Certain Activities of the Royal Canadian Mounted Police, *Second Report: Volume 2 – Freedom and Security under the Law* (1981) 897–98.

[207] ibid 898–99.

[208] ibid 903.

[209] An important example of the genre, the Birkett Committee, which examined the interception of communications, is discussed in ch 4.

[210] Commission of Inquiry (n 206) 904.

[211] ibid 902.

[212] ibid 902–03.

Committee of the Senate rejecting it on a range of grounds, some of them effectively the same practical grounds that had usually been identified as making the national security endeavour unsuitable for parliamentary oversight.[213] Instead, what was implemented was the SIRC, a committee of Privy Councillors outside of Parliament, of exactly the sort that McDonald had suggested was unsuited to the Canadian context. Though it was claimed to be the 'most obvious example of a unique approach to intelligence oversight' in these jurisdictions, it was one no other jurisdiction felt compelled to emulate.[214] Conversely, as we have seen, though the second Hope report in Australia counselled against a parliamentary body, the Australian Committee was introduced shortly thereafter.

When the UK's Home Affairs Committee carried out its inquiry into the accountability of the Security Service, MI5, at a point in time when it but neither MI6 nor GCHQ had a statutory basis, it noted that 'despite the formal responsibility for MI5 which we believe that we have … we are unable to exercise any effective scrutiny' of the Service, with the Home Secretary forbidding its Director-General from appearing before it and declining to answer any of what he described as the 'tantalising questions' it wished to put to him.[215] The Committee noted that the systems of accountability in other countries were 'instructive', starting with Canada's SIRC and also taking in, perhaps most importantly, Australia's Parliamentary Joint Committee on ASIO (as it was then). These it drew on to consider how parliamentary oversight of the Security Service might be improved, notwithstanding the resistance of the Home Secretary:

> Though he was unwilling to be specific, the Home Secretary told us that there had been operational difficulties for the Security Services in Canada, Australia, Germany and the USA as a result of their systems of parliamentary scrutiny. However, he was not prepared to say that the Security Services in those countries had been weakened in consequence … [I]t seems to us that the examples from abroad demonstrate that there are a number of ways in which parliamentary scrutiny of the Security Service in the United Kingdom might be improved.[216]

[213] 'A parliamentary committee would likely duplicate much of the efforts of the SIRC. Further, parliamentary committees are notoriously subject to vagaries of time, changes in membership and overwork. There is also the problem of maintaining the security of information. This has reference in part to the possibility of partisan motivations in some members; but it also refers to the general question of whether that type of committee can maintain the requisite confidentiality by reason of the nature of its proceedings. In view of these considerations, the Committee believes that it would not be advisable to establish a parliamentary committee with special access to CSIS operations and information.' Special Committee of the Senate on the Canadian Security Intelligence Service, *Delicate Balance: A Security intelligence Service in a Democratic Society* (1983) [100].

[214] Defty (n 80) 372.

[215] House of Commons Home Affairs Committee, *Accountability of the Security Service* (HC 1992–93, 265) [17]. For the Government's response, see *Accountability of the Security Service* (Cm 2197, 1993), noting at [5], that the Government 'does however believe that it is a mistake to follow overseas models too readily'. Amongst the factors making foreign models inapplicable it identified 'the nature and extent of the threats to national security which it is the duty of the Security Service to work against' and 'the nature of the general arrangements for Ministerial accountability to Parliament'.

[216] Home Affairs Committee (n 215) [24].

Again, therefore, even when foreign models were not explicitly being drawn on by those charged with reforming the oversight mechanisms, they were being drawn on by critics of the status quo. And indeed, the point was conceded in the context of the Intelligence Services Act 1994 shortly thereafter, which first created the ISC.[217] That Committee, as we have seen, then directly influenced the creation of its namesake in New Zealand just a few years later.[218] Much more recently, the Canadian equivalent's belated creation was justified on the basis that Canada was, prior to its introduction, 'the sole nation among our Five Eyes allies whose elected officials cannot scrutinize security operations', leaving the public 'uninformed and unrepresented on critical issues'.[219] Finally, recent arguments for the reform of New Zealand's ISC rest heavily on the (undoubtedly correct) belief that the arrangements in place there have fallen behind those of comparable states – primarily its Commonwealth Five Eyes counterparts – as those have developed in recent times.[220]

And so, it seems undisputable, the evolution of parliamentary mechanisms of national security oversight, though it may have entered the Commonwealth Five Eye states from outside, has since Australia first introduced such a mechanism been driven largely by the influence of each of these four states upon the others. Whether to introduce such a body, how to design it, and whether and how to reform it, all are determined in large part by a perception as to what the position is elsewhere in the Commonwealth Five Eyes and, perhaps to a lesser extent, how it is unfolding in practice. Certainly, for all the limits, both on paper and perhaps more so in practice, of the bodies that now exist, it seems impossible to argue – as was once the commonsense position – that national security is inherently unsuited to legislative oversight. All of the various reasons for so thinking – most strikingly, the need to maintain secrecy – have been addressed, and solutions in one jurisdiction are liable to be taken up quickly in another. Sometimes there is vetting of members of the committees in question; more usually there are limits – often broad – on what they can require to be divulged to them, and what they in turn can divulge to the public, as well as considerable government control over their membership. Moreover, the model of oversight provided by these bodies has developed, so that what was once particularly unthinkable – oversight of operational matters – now takes place in a number of jurisdictions and may in time become standard. The four Commonwealth Five Eyes states have, we see again, acted as something of

[217] 'It seemed to me [in 1989] either one put such a parliamentary group inside the ring of secrecy, in which case what its members could say to the world outside, including the House, would be strictly limited, or one kept them outside the ring of secrecy, in which case they would have nothing especially important to communicate … I believe that the House will judge that, with the hindsight derived from four years' experience of the Security Service Act, and since the avowal of SIS, we have now found a way of overcoming the difficulty and reconciling those considerations. I believe that the committee proposed in the Bill will provide welcome additional and effective monitoring of the agencies, without putting national security at risk.' HC Deb 22 February 1994, vol 238, col 161 (Douglas Hurd).

[218] Bolger (n 56).

[219] Liberal Party (n 72) 31.

[220] Arnold and Mahuika (n 67) [12.29].

a constitutional microclimate in which the shared constitutional and cultural background has seen a model of national security constitutionalism emerge and spread over what is, in constitutional terms, a relatively short period.

IV. Conclusion

There now exist in each of the Commonwealth Five Eyes states parliamentary or quasi-parliamentary bodies charged with reviewing aspects of the national security endeavour as carried out by the SIAs of that jurisdiction. Though there remain a range of important and less important differences between the four – with Canada's NSICOP housed within the executive and New Zealand's ISC notable for its lack of day-to-day independence from the country's government – it seems obvious that there has been convergence on what we can now identify as a shared model of parliamentary scrutiny, which we might go so far as to consider an aspect of the Westminster model of constitutional ordering in its contemporary form. On the one hand, the functional element of this picture – that these bodies are trying to solve a similar problem, which arises in the context of broadly similar constitutional orders – means that it would have been possible that these bodies might have emerged independently, without reference to the other jurisdictions. On the other hand, simply to describe these bodies – their status, their powers, their work – is to immediately suggest a very strong degree of mutual influence between them. The similarities are too great, and the divergences now mostly too minor, for us to believe that the institution and evolution of these bodies took place in isolation one from the other. In practice, however, and as repeatedly noted throughout this chapter, we do not need to speculate on this point. The public record is clear as to the ways in which and reasons for which the bodies discussed in this chapter have developed. We can therefore go beyond noting the similarities between them and speculating as to how they arose, which might be the limit of our ambition in some other contexts, and instead seek to identify more specific ways in which the pattern of mutual influence that a comparison strongly suggests exists might be evidenced.

Throughout, but especially at certain key moments, there is unambiguous evidence of the use of the various bodies' existence and specific status in order to argue for, respectively, the creation or reform of counterparts in other jurisdictions. Though their entry into this ecosystem took place under the influence of states outside of it – and in particular the US – as elsewhere in this book, what we find is a process in which as time has passed the field of reference has become more limited, so that now each of the Commonwealth Five Eyes states frequently refers (and refers only) to arrangements in each of the others. What we have seen, indeed, much more so than in the other contexts we have considered, is something like a race to the top, where any consideration of the position in one of the Commonwealth Five Eyes states now quickly resolves into a process of identifying the position in other states and, very often, arguing for a move towards the most ambitious model currently in existence. There is, we might suggest, an upwards spiral of parliamentary scrutiny for national security, and though New Zealand's ISC has not yet succumbed to the momentum thus created, history suggests that it will do so sooner rather than later. Two points might be made. One is that it is not clear how much further this model might plausibly develop, given that the exigencies of security and secrecy, which were originally used in order to argue against parliamentary oversight of the national security endeavour altogether, persist. We may, that is, have reached its logical endpoint already, without yet knowing it. The other is that the process of development is not so one-sided as this description might make it appear. That is, we have spent considerable time exploring the various institutional characteristics and formal powers of these (quasi-)parliamentary bodies, and in that context the history has always been one of expanded mandates and greater powers over time.

But a consideration focused on these formal characteristics and ignorant of the actual operation of these bodies will mislead: we have also noted at a number of points the manner in which executive bodies appear to have in recent years resisted more or less openly some of the oversight to which they are subject by the bodies discussed in this chapter. Though the level of compliance and cooperation will no doubt ebb and flow with changes of politics and personnel, one question that arises, therefore, is whether it is preferable to insist on more rigorous oversight institutions if to do so comes at the cost of increasing the degree of constitutional friction, and so works to undermine the aim that one is seeking to achieve. The likelihood of such push back is exacerbated, I will argue in chapter 7, by the apparent return, after a period in which national security was largely synonymous with counterterrorism, to a situation (like that which prevailed during the Cold War) when the most prominent threat is instead that posed by hostile states. That is, we quoted in section II.A the claim – striking to modern eyes – from the McDonald Commission in Canada that the Committee for which it was arguing – but which was not in fact created at that point in time – 'should be constituted of parliamentarians whose commitment to Canada's democratic system of government is unquestionable'. Whether the danger that some parliamentarians did not possess such a commitment was a genuine one, or whether it was merely an example of Cold War paranoia, is largely irrelevant. What matters instead is that this sort of thinking was a prominent aspect of the case against parliamentary oversight in the Cold War era but has been largely absent in the post-Cold War era, dominated by the threat of terrorism, in which such oversight has become a standard part of Commonwealth national security constitutionalism.

7

National Security Constitutionalism in the Commonwealth Five Eyes States

I. Introduction

This book, I said in its opening pages, is a work of comparative constitutionalism. It has sought to examine the manner in which the modern constitutional orders of the four Commonwealth Five Eyes states – the UK, Canada, Australia and New Zealand – have in the past addressed and now address the topic of national security: how those constitutional orders create, structure and empower those bodies – the SIAs – that bear primary responsibility for protecting the national security of their respective states, and what forms of oversight and accountability they include in order to guard against the threat posed to their citizens and, perhaps, the broader democratic order by the existence of bodies that possess a range of highly intrusive capabilities and operate largely in secret. Having first oriented the project within the broader literature on constitutional law and comparative constitutional law in particular, we have considered these topics under a number of headings, including: the reasons for, and manner in which, the SIAs of the Commonwealth Five Eyes states were first given statutory bases; the form they take in the contemporary constitutional orders, including the concepts that frame their mandate and the limits to which they are subject, as well as their relationship to the political element of the executive branch; the powers they possess and the manner in which the danger that those powers will be misused or abused is or is not addressed; the oversight to which the SIAs are now usually subject, both by specialist bodies I have described as hybrid in nature because they consider (amongst other things) compliance with the law and do so in the round rather than in relation to specific disputes, and bodies with a parliamentary or quasi-parliamentary status, which seek to provide – and at their best may succeed in providing – in the domain of national security, and despite the special features of that domain, the sort of accountability the pursuit of which is taken for granted in other policy areas.

The focus of this work on only four of the five states that are party to what seems widely agreed to be the most important intelligence-sharing agreement in existence, and perhaps that has ever existed, was justified by the shared constitutional structures of those four, which separate them from the fifth – the US. Three of them (New Zealand, Australia and Canada) emerged out of an Empire belonging to the fourth (the UK) and so, though there are important differences between these states and their constitutional orders, the four constitutions share several fundamental features that have influenced the creation and subsequent evolution of their national security constitutions. This is compounded by the considerable borrowing and sharing that has taken place over the last 70 or so years, which takes us beyond what the dual factors of that shared constitutional heritage and the functional logic of the national security endeavour might demand. What emerges from the account offered in the book, I suggest, is that we can understand the object of our study not only as four distinct but related national security constitutions, but also as a single model of Commonwealth national security constitutionalism with four different instantiations in the Commonwealth Five Eyes states. Though considerable differences remain, they are diminishing over time as a result of ongoing processes of borrowing and sharing, and a state that now declines to adhere to those patterns evident in the national security constitutions of its counterparts appears, increasingly, to feel compelled to justify that decision.

In this final chapter, which acts as a conclusion to the book, I discuss a number of themes or (sets of) issues that arise out of what has gone before. The first is the model of national security constitutionalism that now predominates in the Commonwealth Five Eyes states: how it differs from the model that historically prevailed, how it relates to and reflects the underlying commonalities between the constitutional orders of these states, what the significant variations or discrepancies are, and what (if anything) is at stake in those variations. A second theme is the way in which the model I describe in section II has emerged, and in particular the mechanisms – to the extent that they are publicly visible – by which legal and constitutional innovation in the domain of national security has come to migrate or be transplanted from one of these jurisdictions to the others. A third theme seeks, against the background of this account of Commonwealth national security constitutionalism, to go beyond the framing used so far in the book, of four states and their influence on one another, to consider what we know about how they interact and how the law facilitates, limits or otherwise frames that interaction. That is, the very existence of the Five Eyes alliance implies there will be considerable sharing of intelligence (at least) between the SIAs of the four states under discussion and the US. What does the law say about such intelligence sharing and other forms of international cooperation between SIAs, both within Five Eyes and beyond them, and how does it prevent such cooperation, in whatever form, from either undermining the safeguards associated with intrusive powers in domestic law or resulting in complicity in wrongdoing outside of the jurisdiction? What we see, I suggest, is that notwithstanding that the modern national security enterprise in the Commonwealth Five Eyes states appears to have an inescapably transnational dimension, the relevant cooperation appears to be regulated inconsistently and often in a minimalist fashion, and in a manner that potentially undermines many of the safeguards that exist within the individual jurisdictions. Finally, I consider the question of democracy as it relates to national security law in light of what appears to be a trend towards – a return to – considering the primary threat to national security to be other states rather than, as has been the case in recent decades, (international) terrorism.

II. A Commonwealth Model of National Security Constitutionalism

At various points in this work, I have noted claims about the existence of a 'new Commonwealth' model of human rights protection, according to which a number of Commonwealth states have instituted a recognisable model of rights protection that seeks a third way between the competing logics of legislative supremacy on one hand and constitutional or judicial supremacy on the other. This is a model in the sense that it involves a recognisable set of institutions and processes that are now common to multiple states, and which can be – perhaps, must be – assessed not only in relation to those other models they (seek to) transcend but also in relation to one another, being in effect variations on a single constitutional theme. We are now in a position to consider what we might, on the same logic, call the Commonwealth model of national security constitutionalism. This is again a set of institutions and practices that are common to the four Commonwealth Five Eyes states and that reflect certain exigencies of constitutionalism as applied to the specific context of national security: the need both to act to protect the state against threat from within and without, and to provide sufficient oversight of those endeavours to be confident that the work done by the bodies charged with that responsibility, much of which by definition must be kept secret, at least at the level of specifics, does not lapse into the arbitrary or otherwise abusive use of power. This model does so, more specifically, against the background of the set of shared constitutional forms and practices that make up the so-called Westminster model of constitutional structure.

The key features of the Commonwealth model of national security constitutionalism, we now see, comprise a range of security and intelligence agencies that are under the ultimate authority of a member of the executive formed out of the relevant legislative body, but subject to the day-to-day control of some sort of chief. Where once not only the powers but also the very existence of these SIAs were traced, loosely but persistently, to the prerogative transferred by the UK to these states as part of the British Empire, they have now all been given statutory form, and the opportunity has been taken to limit the threat posed by these bodies to the democratic order, through either their intervention in the (domestic) political process or the pursuit of their mandates in a fashion at odds with rights of freedom of assembly or other forms of democratic participation, or both. The statutory recognition of these bodies brought with it the opportunity to clarify and immediately expand upon their powers, which have been frequently rewritten to reflect both the changing threat matrix and the changing technological environment. The felt need for secrecy in this domain has meant that it has never been considered possible for the SIAs of each state to be subject to the ordinary processes by which the legislature holds the executive, in its myriad forms, to account. Instead, there have been developed – carried out sometimes but not necessarily in parallel – two related and interlocking models of accountability specially designed for the national security context and its particular sensitivities. One is what I have described as 'hybrid' institutions: independent bodies that review the work of the SIAs in a fashion that bridges the standard division between legal and political mechanisms of accountability. That is, they consider in the round, as political mechanisms of accountability generally do, the work of the SIAs, while being mandated to consider, in a fashion more usually associated with legal mechanisms of accountability, the lawfulness of that work, and so are usually staffed with judges or other legally qualified figures. Though the origins of these institutions reflect the idea that they might assist the executive in ensuring that the SIAs were acting lawfully and properly, in circumstances where the courts could not be relied upon to do so, they tend nowadays to have – de facto if not de jure – a wider reassurance function, including in many cases the right to inquire on their own initiative into the work of the SIAs. The other model of accountability is the parliamentary or quasi-parliamentary bodies that fill the gap historically left by the insistence of executives, often accepted by legislatures, that the national security endeavour was not suited to normal, open processes of political scrutiny and contestation. In its stead, these bodies see Parliamentarians given access to information that is not publicly disclosed or disclosable, allowing them to report on the issues that information raises without undermining the work of the SIAs. Given the dangers associated with disclosure even to this small subset of political actors, these bodies usually involve a degree of executive control of their membership greater than that which applies to normal parliamentary committees. In recent years, a further aspect to this picture seems to be crystallising: the role of independent bodies (sometimes the hybrid oversight body itself; sometimes an additional, more strictly judicial, companion institution) in authorising the use of some or all intrusive powers as part of what has become known as a 'double-lock'. Though in some jurisdictions a process of this sort has a longer history, and in others it represents not an advance on but rather a retreat from the historic position as regards the role of the judiciary, it appears clear that the double-lock has in the last decade or so entered the shared understanding of policy-makers in the Commonwealth Five Eyes states, such that where a reform does not include the mechanism, it cannot be because its inclusion was not considered but must instead result from its conscious and deliberate rejection – a rejection that will require considerable justification, given that it goes against the general pattern of convergence we can identify in this arena.

We might make two points about this model of Commonwealth national security constitutionalism. One is that, as emerges clearly out of the chapters discussing individual elements of the model as it now exists, it did not develop in a single bound but rather via a series of incremental moves that took place at different times, and for different reasons, in each of the four states. At what point it might be considered to have become a model in the sense I am using it here is therefore debatable. There are of course signs of it from the earliest years of the Cold War, as the UK's MI5 sought to encourage other states to create domestic security bodies modelled on itself, but when and why those bodies were given a statutory basis varies considerably, with MI5 itself in fact the last of the domestic security bodies to be granted such a basis. I would venture to suggest, therefore, that it is only in the early 2000s, when the final steps were taken to give a legislative basis to those SIAs that did not already have one, that the model unambiguously crystallises. At that point in time, there is sufficient legal and policy material publicly available that almost every decision – to codify a body, and if so how, or to grant it certain powers, or to create (or not) oversight institutions, and of what type, with what powers – appears to take place in the context of a clear knowledge and understanding, often publicly communicated and discussed, of how the other Commonwealth Five Eyes states have or have not dealt with the same matter.

Developments since then would seem largely to have confirmed that status, not least – and this is a second point – because they demonstrate ever more clearly the way in which developments in each of the four individual states are being openly and directly influenced, negatively and positively, by arrangements in the other three. That is, there is an obvious rejoinder to the portrayal of the constitutional arrangements relating to national security in the Commonwealth Five Eyes states as a model in the sense that it is used by Stephen Gardbaum in his work on new Commonwealth constitutionalism, which was discussed in the book's Introduction: that it does not constitute a model at all, for it lacks the fundamental neatness of the new Commonwealth model of constitutionalism, reducible as that phenomenon is to two specific elements – pre-enactment political rights review and post-enactment weak-form judicial review – that are clearly distinguishable from the alternatives (or from their absence). In the context of what I am calling Commonwealth national security constitutionalism, the picture is significantly messier: there are more aspects to it, more variation between the states as regards these specific aspects, and more areas in which there remain, despite considerable convergence, real and important differences between the four states. Moreover, what similarities do exist might in many cases be reasonably attributed to the confluence of two factors I have repeatedly stressed: the shared constitutional fundamentals of the states in question and the demands of the functional logic of national security – that is, that the arrangements I have sought to describe in this book are seeking to discharge a common task. My reason for claiming, nevertheless, that they amount to a distinct model is that there is, as we have repeatedly seen and can now summarise, evidence of very considerable borrowing amongst these Commonwealth Five Eyes states. I am not, that is, identifying it as a model by mere description of constitutional commonalities, but rather because of the causal influence we can clearly see these states play on each other in the domain of national security constitutionalism – over the entirety of the period since the Second World War, certainly, but ever more so as we approach the present day – with other states, including but not limited to the US, contributing initially to the stock of norms and institutional forms but now almost entirely squeezed out. Where once, that is, official reports produced in one of the Commonwealth Five Eyes states might make reference to arrangements in Sweden or West Germany, they now almost invariably make reference to – and only to – arrangements in the other three of those states. This is not to say there is a perfect symmetry between them, but rather that the stock of appropriate comparators is now, it appears, clearly defined and tightly circumscribed.

III. Transmitting the Commonwealth Model of National Security Constitutionalism

There is no reason to believe that the modern degree of convergence visible within the Commonwealth Five Eyes states is somehow the result of a deliberate attempt on the part of any person or group of people. The national security context, including the manner in which that context has evolved over time, with geopolitical shifts and the emergence and decline of certain threats, in addition to the shared constitutional fundamentals of the Commonwealth Five Eyes states, is sufficient to explain much of the convergence upon shared institutions and shared approaches we have identified. Nevertheless, as observed at a number of points, it is possible to identify examples where one or more jurisdictions exert direct and unambiguous influence on one another, and the explicit borrowing, often with no significant modification, by one of the four states of institutional forms and constitutional innovations that originally emerged elsewhere. That is, as with the new Commonwealth model of rights protection, which Gardbaum has noted has taken 'a self-consciously comparative approach' that involves 'looking at, and learning from, jurisdictions deemed most similar and relevant', giving the sense of the new Commonwealth model as what he calls 'a shared work in progress',[1] the Commonwealth model of national security constitutionalism is openly and explicitly comparative, and – crucially – appears to be becoming ever more so.

There has been, that is, significant transmission of norms – used broadly, so as to encompass specific legal rules, but also the design of processes and institutions – in the domain of national security: in the early Cold War, from the UK to the other Commonwealth Five Eyes states; from those jurisdictions to one another; and, more recently and perhaps still to a lesser extent, from them back to the UK. The question for this section is how that norm transfer has come about. In other contexts, the spread of legal rules and legal tools in this way is not direct but rather would represent the shared influence of some common but external factor. So, for example, we have noted in chapter 3 the harmonising influence of the United

[1] S Gardbaum, *The New Commonwealth Model of Constitutionalism* (Cambridge University Press, 2012) 8.

Nations in the field of counter-terrorism.[2] In the more general field of national security law, an important influence on the UK has been the European Court of Human Rights, which has imposed a series of requirements upon surveillance, including the oversight thereof, that the UK previously struggled to meet, and has shown signs of developing those further. As noted in chapter 4, the approach is in effect one that requires a certain level of what we might call 'signposts and safeguards'. The specific safeguards most prominent in the Investigatory Powers Act 2016 – the IPC and the 'double-lock' – are not explicitly required by the Convention jurisprudence, but this general approach prizes both of them. If, as has been the case so far, the European Court of Human Rights accepts these as integral parts of a package of measures that render the UK's surveillance powers compatible with the ECHR, then other states against which litigation has not (yet) been brought will have a clear incentive to adopt the same or equivalent measures (just as the fact that the Strasbourg Court has not held bulk surveillance to be per se incompatible with the Convention might tempt some of those states that do not yet carry out such surveillance to begin to do so). And given that contemporary human rights regimes cross-pollinate via judicial citation of foreign jurisprudence,[3] it may be that even states that are not themselves subject to the ECHR nevertheless find themselves adopting safeguard mechanisms that originated in an attempt to meet its requirements, as those requirements are read into or otherwise influence the interpretation of other instruments of rights protection. Human rights treaties might act, that is, as mechanisms of norm transmission, including in the field of national security, even without the sort of explicit harmonising intent evidenced by the work of the United Nations in the field of counter-terrorism. Neither of these things, however, is the case in the context we are dealing with in the present work. The rationalisation, expansion and progressive empowerment of the SIAs in the Commonwealth Four Eyes states, and the development of oversight regimes special to those bodies and their work, have in no way taken place at the direct or indirect prompting of the United Nations. No binding human rights regime applies to all four of the states whose national security law has been considered here, and though there is cross-pollination between those jurisdictions evident in the case law of their courts on questions of human rights, that jurisprudence appears to have had little impact upon the legal frameworks discussed in the present work. And yet the influence that these jurisdictions have exercised upon one another – originally largely in one direction, but later in a more complex and multi-directional fashion – is nevertheless clear to see.

[2] See in particular F de Londras, *The Practice and Problems of Transnational Counter-Terrorism* (Cambridge University Press, 2022).

[3] See, from the UK perspective, H Tyrrel, *Human Rights in the UK and the Influence of Foreign Jurisprudence* (Hart Publishing, 2018). For an older study of the phenomenon taking in examples from a range of jurisdictions, see C McCrudden, 'Common Law of Human Rights?: Transnational Judicial Conversations on Constitutional Rights' (2000) 20 *Oxford Journal of Legal Studies* 499.

Turning to the operative mechanisms, and in light of the scope of the present work, an initial point that needs to be made is that it is striking how little of this mutual influence between the Commonwealth Five Eyes states is – as far as one can tell – a direct function of their membership of the alliance. Five Eyes is centred on intelligence sharing, and the alliance has – again, in so far as can be known – never involved any direct attempt to harmonise the legal regulation of intelligence gathering within its member states. Nevertheless, there are reasons to think that the existence of the alliance and the relationships that are crystallised by it must in the past have influenced the development of the law in the individual states in a way over and above the causal relationships that one would expect to exist between (largely) common law, anglophone states, the majority of which were the Dominions of the UK within the last 100 years and whose constitutional fundamentals remain similar. That is, a key point is that – as I emphasised in chapter 2 – though the formal links between them are now largely gone, three of these states were, well into the twentieth century, part of an Empire possessed by the fourth. The UK, no doubt in large part for that reason, therefore played a dominant role even into the period following the Second World War, by which time the Empire had – as far as Australia, Canada and New Zealand were concerned – given way to the modern Commonwealth. It did not merely influence these countries but actively sought to do so, effectively exporting, or so it would seem, its own incipient model of national security constitutionalism.

But this pattern of influence continues later than the fact of an imperial past would seem capable of explaining, becoming more complex and more egalitarian than in the early years of the Cold War, when Britain's relative economic and geopolitical superiority was still palpable, and becomes in fits and starts something like a reciprocal process. A useful contrast might be drawn between other former Dominions that are not within the Five Eyes alliance. South Africa, Ireland and Sri Lanka (under the name 'Ceylon') were all British Dominions – as, for much shorter periods, were India and Pakistan – but none of these appears to demonstrate the sort of cross-pollination of national security constitutionalism we have identified in a range of areas in the context of the second half of the twentieth century. Some of this no doubt reflects the time at which and circumstances in which the states in question became independent. Some of it may, however, reflect other considerations: when, as often happened, reports and reviews on questions of what I have called national security constitutionalism in the Five Eyes states were engaging in comparison, they seemed to (as they usually still do) turn almost by default to what were sometimes identified as comparable jurisdictions. As we have noted, in practice, these were almost invariably references to the other Five Eyes states, with some consideration, early in this period, of West Germany or Sweden. What rendered them comparable, then, seemed to reflect a range of (often unspoken) factors, including their capitalist status (of particular import during the Cold War), geopolitical significance and, perhaps, whiteness, but surely also the same closeness in intelligence cooperation that was reflected in the Five Eyes Agreement. What was good enough (or even desirable) for one was likely good enough – with the usual exception of the inherently exceptional US – for all.

What of the specific mechanisms by which norm transfer occurred? We noted in chapter 3 that in the immediate aftermath of the Second World War – at the beginning, that is, of the Cold War – MI5 was central to the project of having the Dominions set up a domestic security body, and of ensuring that the bodies in question were modelled directly on MI5 itself. Where the early inquiries into and reports on national security (and in particular espionage) issues in Canada and Australia paid relatively little attention to other jurisdictions, the latter resulted in a statute that drew indirectly on (non-statutory) UK material and brought these issues out into the open, offering concepts and language that could be adapted or amended as necessary, or even simply copied directly over into new regimes. Later bouts of public concern resulted in further evolutions, including the introduction of the modern oversight regimes. That borrowing was sometimes done without formal acknowledgement, though it was often no less apparent to any informed observer as a result. As time passes, however, the process of comparing and then borrowing, with or without adaptations, becomes ever more clear and ever more exhaustive, so that – for example – while the Mackenzie Commission in Canada in the late 1960s makes minimal reference to the position in the other Commonwealth Five Eyes states, the McDonald Commission reports published a little over a decade later make extensive such reference, to the position in Australia in particular.[4]

That process has continued ever since, to the extent that it is now entirely standard for independent reviews in the domain of national security in the Commonwealth Five Eyes states (of whatever sort, and on whatever question) to contain a detailed, at times perhaps even excessive, consideration of how the matter under discussion is dealt with by the other such states, quoting legislative provisions and citing the work of the standing review bodies in those states. That is, innovations in the domain of oversight or review not only could be – and were – taken up elsewhere, but also themselves put into the public domain a range of material, growing over time, that acted as the backdrop to, or which assessed or critiqued the substance or operation of, the relevant legislation, with the effect that an interested observer could learn about the legal position of the SIAs and even, at times, their work, without having to wait for some scandal to take place and an inquiry to be instituted. The result has been, I suggest, to create the conditions for ever more borrowing and sharing. Those who wish to see the security enterprise in a given state subject to further 'constitutionalisation' – made, that is, more rational, more procedurally limited or subject to greater oversight – will usually be able to find, amongst the other Commonwealth Five Eyes states, an example of where such constitutionalisation has already happened, it is hoped without adverse effect, or has merely been suggested by some suitably authoritative

[4] Royal Commission on Security, *Report of the Royal Commission on Security (Abridged)* (1969); and Commission of Inquiry Concerning Certain Activities of the Royal Canadian Mounted Police, *First Report: Security and Information* (October 1979), *Second Report: Volume 1 – Freedom and Security under the Law* (1981), *Second Report: Volume 2 – Freedom and Security under the Law* (1981), *Third Report: Certain RCMP Activities and the Question of Governmental Knowledge* (1981).

body created as part of some previous round of constitutionalisation. Where in the past there might have been secret Orders in Council or unpublished Directives, now there will be statutes they can assess, and reports they can study in order to make their case. States in which wrongdoing or incompetence has been exposed will come under pressure to do what certain of their Commonwealth Five Eyes counterparts have already done, and might well accede to that pressure. The process of constitutionalisation therefore appears to have an inescapably inflationary dimension. The networks of oversight actors that have grown up, and which are discussed in chapter 5, are not, that is, distinctive in being possible mechanisms of further norm transfer; rather, in likely contributing to the increase of the pace of such transfer, they are merely the latest example of a much longer-standing pattern in this domain.

What is crucial, then, is that the borrowing and sharing in question did not end with MI5's post-war attempts to export its own model elsewhere in the Commonwealth but carries on to the present day, now taking place not only in one direction – from centre to periphery, as it were – but in multiple directions, and driven not by direct interaction between the apparatus of one state and that of another but rather often operating in plain sight via the work of actors inside and outside of the national security apparatus in its broadest sense. And so, to sum up the point, the constitutionalisation of national security in the states that are the subject of this work – firming up the legal bases of the SIAs and providing for review of their frameworks and operations that is ongoing rather than sporadic – is not, and never has been, a self-regarding endeavour. Rather, that constitutionalisation has always contributed to an expanding and accelerating process of norm transfer – of frequent borrowing and occasional refusal to do so – which has increased the pace of legal evolution in the domain of national security and contributed, as noted, to the emergence (or, perhaps, consolidation) of a model of Commonwealth national security constitutionalism. Examples of the migration of constitutional and legal ideas – institutions, norms and so on – in the field of national security constitutionalism include all three of the aspects of the picture to which consideration has been given in this work: the SIAs themselves; the intrusive and investigatory powers enjoyed by them; and the institutions by which oversight of their work and the use of their powers is carried out. One final point, therefore, is that though it is tempting to treat this as unambiguously positive – a race, as it were, to the constitutional top – there is no reason that this should be the case. As we have seen, just as safeguards and procedural innovations can be taken up by admirers elsewhere, so too can (and have been) new powers and new taskings for the SIAs. The process of constitutionalisation has often been a positive one from the point of view of, say, individual liberty or the minimisation of arbitrary power, but there is no reason to believe that it must necessarily be so.

Given this account, one question is how it might develop in future: whether, that is, the model as I have described it will remain that of Commonwealth national security constitutionalism, or whether it will expand to encompass some bigger grouping of states. The correct way to think about this, I would suggest, is to accept the inevitability of other, perhaps often smaller, states' borrowing aspects of national security constitutionalism from the Commonwealth Five Eyes states, with or without modifications. It seems likely, in fact, that such a thing is already happening, perhaps at scale, in states that do not feature prominently, for whatever reason, in the literature on comparative constitutionalism. That alone, however, will not suffice to make them part of the ecosystem I am describing here. Only if and when the (authorities of) Commonwealth Five Eyes states are routinely considering the arrangements employed in states outside of that grouping, and perhaps even borrowing those approaches, will it make sense to think of those other states as part of the phenomenon at issue. At this point in time, such an eventuality seems – given how self-contained the Commonwealth Five Eyes grouping seems to be, and the closeness of the links between them – remote.

IV. Domestic Regulation of National Security Cooperation

The framing of the present work rests in large part upon the common membership of the four Commonwealth states in question of the Five Eyes alliance: this membership pre-dates largely but not quite entirely the process I have described as the constitutionalisation of national security in the Commonwealth Five Eyes states, and has therefore acted as part of the shared background against which that constitutionalisation has taken place. In section III, I considered how the process of constitutionalisation has resulted in convergence into what I described as a shared model, and how the borrowing and sharing that gave rise to that convergence privileged – from the beginning, but increasingly over time, to the point that they are nowadays almost exclusively considered – arrangements in other Commonwealth Five Eyes states over those in all other states. But the Five Eyes alliance is not, of course, designed as a mechanism for importing and exporting developments in the field of national security law or constitutionalism. Rather, as we saw from consideration of the original UKUSA Agreement in this book's Introduction, it involves direct cooperation between its members in the form of the sharing of intelligence (and perhaps also, still, of methods and techniques). In this section, I consider briefly the ways in which, and the extent to which, the law in the Commonwealth Five Eyes states seeks to regulate transnational cooperation. Before considering some examples of that phenomenon, however, it is important to note that in no case I can find is the formal legal position sensitive to the identity of the state with whose SIAs the 'home' SIAs are cooperating. That is, where the law in the Commonwealth Five Eyes states makes open provision (of whatever sort) for such cooperation (again, of whatever sort), it always and everywhere applies in a facially neutral fashion rather than applying solely or even distinctively to cooperation within the Five Eyes alliance. Though there is no longer any attempt to hide membership of that grouping – indeed, contemporary official publications are filled to the brim with references to Five Eyes and its centrality to the contemporary national security enterprise[5] – it remains the case that it has no formal status within the various domestic legal frameworks at issue. It must nevertheless be assumed that in many cases where provision is made for transnational cooperation, it is intended that the provision will be – and the provision in fact is – made use of in the first place, and most importantly, to facilitate cooperation with other Five Eyes states.

Some contemporary examples of the phenomenon are worth considering. First, however, we should note that the statutes governing the SIAs in the UK do not themselves seek to regulate – either positively or negatively – transnational cooperation by them, and so there is no formal provision made either for ministerial approval of such cooperation or for any sort of parliamentary oversight of the cooperation that does take place, though information sharing is governed in a variety of ways, and Ministers will be involved both in 'setting high-level strategy' and, where necessary, 'providing formal ministerial direction and legal authorisation for international activity, usually through the approval of warrants, authorisations and submissions'.[6] This contrasts strongly with the position in the other Commonwealth Five Eyes states. For example, the Canadian Communications Security Establishment Act (2019) provides that the CSE

> may enter into arrangements with entities that have powers and duties similar to the Establishment's – including entities that are institutions of foreign states or that are international organizations of states or institutions of those organizations – for the purposes of the furtherance of its mandate, including for the purposes of sharing information with them or otherwise cooperating with them …

though ministerial approval (granted after consultation with the Minister of Foreign Affairs) is required where the institutions with which arrangements are entered into are those of foreign states or (institutions of) international organisations.[7] Unsurprisingly, the CSE asserts that its 'closest intelligence-sharing relationships are with the other Five Eyes countries'.[8] Subject to the same approval process, CSIS too may 'enter into an arrangement or otherwise cooperate with the government of a foreign state or an institution thereof or an international organization of states or an institution thereof'.[9] In accordance with this latter rule, the

[5] See, eg, Intelligence and Security Committee, *International Partnerships* (HC 2023–24, 288) 53–77, starting with the claim that 'The Five Eyes alliance is the UK Intelligence Community's most important partnership. Consisting of Australia, Canada, New Zealand, the UK and the United States (US) – countries with a shared language and history, and with common values and similar legal systems – it is of a "fundamentally different nature" to the other relationships maintained by the Intelligence Community.'

[6] ibid [36].

[7] Communications Security Establishment Act (2019) (Canada), s 54.

[8] Communications Security Establishment, *Annual Report 2022–23* (2023) 9.

[9] CSIS Act (1984), s 17(1)(b). Under s 17(2), a copy of any written arrangement entered into under this provision must be supplied to the NSIRA. In *Mahjoub (Re)* 2013 FC 1096, it was argued – unsuccessfully – that this provision was unconstitutional because it authorised intelligence sharing with foreign agencies with poor human rights records. And see also *Mahjoub (Re)* 2013 FC 1097 and *Mahjoub v Canada (Citizenship and Immigration)* 2017 FCA 157.

Minister for Public Safety has authorised 'more than 300 foreign relationships in over 150 countries',[10] offering a clear sense of the extent to which the modern national security enterprise is an inherently transnational one that, though it no doubt gives the other Five Eyes states a central position, reaches far beyond them.

In New Zealand, one of the functions of (all of) the SIAs is to 'collect and analyse intelligence in accordance with the New Zealand Government's priorities' and to 'provide any intelligence collected and any analysis of that intelligence' to the Minister, the Chief Executive of the Department of the Prime Minister and Cabinet, and to 'any person or class of persons (whether in New Zealand or overseas) authorised by the Minister to receive the intelligence and any analysis of that intelligence'.[11] The Intelligence and Security Act 2017, which governs those bodies, provides that in performing its collection and analysis function an SIA 'may co-operate with, and provide advice and assistance to' either 'any public authority' (whether in New Zealand or overseas) or any other person or class of persons authorised by the Minister to receive that intelligence.[12] 'Public authority' includes a 'foreign public agency'.[13] In order for an overseas person (or class of persons) to be authorised to receive intelligence or analysis, the Minister must be satisfied that 'in providing the intelligence and analysis, the intelligence and security agency will be acting in accordance with New Zealand law and all human rights obligations recognised by New Zealand law'.[14] Here again, the primary procedural hurdle is ministerial authorisation, and it is known that, shortly before the 2017 Act came into force, 'the agencies sought, and the Minister granted, two very broad standing authorisations for information sharing and cooperation with foreign States and agencies'.[15]

Several points might be made about the regime. One is that it refers only to the compliance by the New Zealand bodies with New Zealand law: whether the persons in question are complying or will comply with their home law is not required to be considered in authorising the provision. Another is that the condition of which the Minister must be satisfied does not appear to apply to cooperation with the person or class of persons in question: once sharing with them has been authorised then cooperation with them may take place without the Minister's being satisfied of anything in particular about that cooperation. Finally, the requirement does not apply to the provision of intelligence or analysis to public authorities – even those that are foreign public agencies. There is

[10] Canadian Security Intelligence Service, *Avoiding Complicity in Mistreatment by Foreign Entities Act – Annual Report to the Minister of Public Safety* (2023) [4].

[11] Intelligence and Security Act 2017 (NZ), s 10(1).

[12] ibid, s 10(2). For the underlying recommendations, see M Cullen and P Reddy, *Intelligence and Security in a Free Society: Report of the First Independent Review of Intelligence and Security in New Zealand* (2016) [58]–[59].

[13] Intelligence and Security Act 2017 (NZ), s 4.

[14] ibid, s 10(3).

[15] Inspector-General of Intelligence and Security, *Inquiry into possible New Zealand intelligence and security agencies' engagement with the CIA detention and interrogation programme 2001–2009* (2019) [268].

no requirement for ministerial authorisation, and so no criteria of which the Minister must be satisfied, though of course New Zealand law continues to apply to the actions of the SIAs, and the obligation upon them to act 'in accordance with New Zealand law and all human rights obligations recognised by New Zealand law' is reaffirmed within the 2017 Act itself.[16] Further provision is made for cooperation in the context of imminent threats to the life of safety of persons with a suitable connection to New Zealand, or to 'any person outside the territorial jurisdiction of any country'.[17] As discussed further in section IV.C, the responsible Minister must issue to the relevant SIA one or more policy statements relating to cooperation with overseas public authorities, providing 'advice and assistance' to such a body and sharing intelligence with them, and indeed has done so.[18] This followed from the recommendation, in the review leading up to the 2017 Act, that the legislation be amended so as to 'clearly enable the Agencies to co-operate and share intelligence with foreign jurisdictions and international organisations where that is consistent with the purposes' of that Act.[19] Not implemented, however, was the recommendation that there be added a process allowing for parliamentary scrutiny of these arrangements:

> Any future bilateral or multilateral arrangements entered into with foreign jurisdictions or international organisations should be referred to the Intelligence and Security Committee to be noted. This would help ensure that such arrangements are consistent with the Agencies' obligations to act in accordance with New Zealand law, including human rights standards. It would also enable a level of Parliamentary oversight of the Agencies' international engagement.[20]

In Australia, ASIS and the ASD may (subject to any 'arrangements made or directions given by the responsible Minister') cooperate with (inter alia) 'authorities of other countries approved by the Minister as being capable of assisting the agency in the performance of its functions', to the extent that doing so 'is necessary for the agency to perform its functions, or so far as facilitates the performance by the agency of its functions'.[21] (A similar provision applies to ASIO.[22]) An approval of this type must be in writing[23] and is subject to certain limits, which can be transcended only if the Minister has, before giving the approval, consulted with the Attorney-General and Prime Minister. These limits (not present in the Act as enacted) include cooperating with the authorities of another country in planning or undertaking activities that involve paramilitary activities, violence against

[16] Intelligence and Security Act 2017 (NZ), s 17(a).
[17] ibid, s 14(1).
[18] ibid, s 207.
[19] Cullen and Reddy (n 12) [4.30].
[20] ibid [4.30]–[4.31].
[21] Intelligence Services Act 2001 (Australia), s 13(1)(c).
[22] ASIO Act 1979 (Australia), s 19(1)(c). Unlike that which applies to ASIS and (to a limited extent) the ASD, that applicable to ASIO also provides (in s 19(1)(d)) for cooperation with 'any other person or body whether within or outside Australia'.
[23] Intelligence Services Act 2001 (Australia), s 13(2).

the person or the use of weapons.[24] The requirement for ministerial approval was endorsed by the *Comprehensive Review* of the intelligence community's legislative framework:

> Foreign intelligence cooperation generally engages a degree of foreign relations risk, as well as the risk of compromise to covert intelligence operations. As ministers have ultimate responsibility for agencies within their portfolio, they should have the opportunity to consider and appropriately engage with this risk.[25]

The logic seems sound, and would apply equally to the SIAs of those states in which there is not currently statutory provision for ministerial approval (and by implication, veto) of cooperation between the home SIAs and foreign partners, to say nothing of parliamentary involvement. A later insertion, however, partially disapplies the requirement for ministerial approval in relation to the ASD, which may now – subject to 'arrangements made or directions given by the responsible Minister' – 'cooperate with authorities of other countries if they are capable of assisting ASD in the performance of' its information security function, with its Director-General obliged to report 'any significant cooperation' to the Minister on an annual basis.[26] No direct provision is made for parliamentary oversight or approval of these arrangements.

A. Transnational Cooperation and the Circumvention of Safeguards

Given that perhaps the primary form of transnational cooperation involves the simple sharing of data, a particular concern that arises is that it will be carried out in such a way as to undermine the sorts of limitations on the SIAs and their powers discussed in previous chapters. That is, we have noted that a number of limits exist on the SIAs' pursuit of certain aspects of their mandates within the boundaries of their home states, or against those who are its citizens or permanent residents. Some of these limits are procedural; others substantive. Some are written into their general mandates or the schemes that grant them intrusive powers; others derive from the application to them of human rights norms. Though, as was made clear in chapter 4, the picture that emerges is complex and inconsistent, such line-drawing is a standard and highly significant part of the modern national security landscape. And yet much of that picture will be meaningless if the transnational cooperation involves receiving from one's partners material

[24] ibid, s 13(1A).

[25] *Comprehensive Review of the Legal Framework of the National Intelligence Community*, Volume 1: *Recommendations and Executive Summary; Foundations and Principles; Control, Coordination and* Cooperation (2019) [15.86].

[26] Intelligence Services Act 2001 (Australia), s 13(4) and (5), inserted by the Intelligence Services Amendment (Establishment of the Australian Signals Directorate) Act 2018 (Australia).

that one could not lawfully acquire oneself, especially once one recalls that those partners include not only the four states that are the subject of this work but also the US, whose intelligence capabilities are widely assumed to outstrip the rest of them by a considerable margin. Such a practice has been alleged across time and space, and concerns about it were revived in the aftermath of the Snowden leaks, when the extent of US surveillance was brought into focus. It is important to note, therefore, that the Five Eyes states have previously – and strongly – denied that this is the effect of their cooperation. As it was put by the UK's ISC, 'long-standing agreements between the Five Eyes countries mean they cannot ask each other to target each other's citizens or individuals that they cannot themselves target, or in any other way seek to circumvent their own or each other's legal and policy obligations'.[27]

One key question, though, relates to the extent to which these 'agreements' – note the plural, but also the lack of specificity – are reflected in the domestic law of the states in question. In relation to Canada, Forcese and West have noted the CSE's claim that it is 'prohibited from requesting that an international partner undertake activities that CSE itself is legally prevented from conducting', and said that this is 'the only reasonable construction of CSE's statutory framework'.[28] If it is correct – as often claimed – that the Five Eyes states do not target those who 'belong' to their Five Eyes partners, or people in the territory of those partners (described as 'second parties'), then this framework would seem to suffice to avoid the potential mischief identified: the other Five Eyes states do not target Canadians autonomously, and the CSE cannot ask them to do so if it could not lawfully do so itself. In New Zealand, the Ministerial Policy Statement on overseas cooperation – not legally binding, but which the Directors-General and employees of the SIAs are obliged to take into account – provides:

> When cooperating with overseas public authorities, GCSB and NZSIS must continue to apply the same protections that would normally apply in New Zealand in relation to the specific activity. GCSB and NZSIS must not cooperate with an overseas public authority for the purposes of avoiding or circumventing those protections.[29]

In the UK, the ISC's consideration of the Snowden leaks examined the allegation that GCHQ had 'circumvented UK law by using the NSA's PRISM programme to access the content of private communications'. This the Committee rejected: 'From the evidence we have seen,' the ISC said, 'we have concluded that this is unfounded.'[30] And in litigation relating to the previous legal framework for bulk interception of communications, and in relation to the broader question of whether

[27] ISC (n 5) [214].
[28] C Forcese and L West, *National Security Law*, 2nd edn (Irwin Law Inc, 2020) 480.
[29] Minister Responsible for the Government Communications Security Bureau and Minister Responsible for the New Zealand Security Intelligence Service, *Ministerial Policy Statement Cooperating with overseas public authorities* (1 March 2022) [35].
[30] Intelligence and Security Committee, 'Statement on GCHQ's Alleged Interception of Communications under the US PRISM Programme' (17 July 2013).

data sharing might be used in order to circumvent the safeguards applicable to that regime, it was disclosed to the Investigatory Powers Tribunal that a request might be made to a foreign government 'for unanalysed intercepted communications (and associated communications data), otherwise than in accordance with an international mutual legal assistance agreement', only in one of two circumstances. Either a warrant under that previous regime was in place, or one was not in place but

> making the request for the communications at issue in the absence of a … warrant does not amount to a deliberate circumvention of [the Regulation of Investigatory Powers Act 2000] or otherwise contravene the principle established in Padfield v Minister of Agriculture, Fisheries and Food [1968] AC 997 (for example, because it is not technically feasible to obtain the communications via RIPA interception), and it is necessary and proportionate for the Intelligence Services to obtain those communications.[31]

It was also disclosed that '[a]ny such request would only be made in exceptional circumstances, and has not occurred as at the date of this statement'.[32] This position – again, applying to a request for 'unanalysed intercepted communications content (and secondary data)' other than under an international mutual assistance agreement – is also reflectedby the relevant Code of Practice under the 2016 Act,[33] with that Act further making clear that the authorities of another state or territory can be requested 'to carry out the interception of communications sent by, or intended for, an individual who the person making the request believes will be in the British Islands at the time of the interception' only if one of the relevant warrants – a targeted interception or a targeted examination warrant – is in place.[34] The result is that the danger in question has been identified and addressed, in a manner of ways, and with greater or lesser precision, across the Commonwealth Five Eyes states. There remains, however, considerable room for the matter to be dealt with more directly, and more fully, than is currently the case.

B. Transnational Cooperation and the Limits of Accountability

Transnational cooperation, whether or not provided for directly by law, and whether or not requiring executive approval, is also significant in acting as a limitation on the accountability of the domestic SIAs. Take, for instance, the various parliamentary or quasi-parliamentary bodies discussed in chapter 6: the ISCs of

[31] *Liberty v Government Communications Headquarters* [2014] UKIPTrib/13/77/H [47]–[48].

[32] ibid.

[33] Home Office, *Interception of Communications Code of Practice Pursuant to Schedule 7 to the Investigatory Powers Act 2016* (2022) [9.33]–[9.35].

[34] Investigatory Powers Act 2016 (UK), s 9.

New Zealand and the UK, Canada's NSICOP and Australia's PJCIS. These bodies, we have observed, must have and do have access to sensitive information in order to effectively perform the role they are called upon to play in the contemporary national security constitution. Yet in all cases, the access of these bodies to such information is limited by reference to – amongst other things – the origin of the information in question from foreign partners, in accordance with what is sometimes described as the principle of 'originator control' (or the 'control principle'), whereby the entity that 'originates' a piece of intelligence is entitled to determine whether and, if so, under what conditions those with whom it shares that intelligence may disclose it to others.[35]

Canada's NSICOP, for example, is entitled to have access to information that does not fall into one of a limited number of categories. Even where it is entitled to have information, however, the Minister may refuse to provide it if two conditions are met: (i) that it is 'special operational information' as defined in the Security of Information Act; and (ii) that its provision would be 'injurious to national security'.[36] 'Special operational information' means information that 'the Government of Canada is taking measures to safeguard that reveals, or from which may be inferred' one of six particularised things, including (for example) 'the means that the Government of Canada used, uses or intends to use, or is capable of using, to covertly collect or obtain, or to decipher, assess, analyse, process, handle, report, communicate or otherwise deal with information or intelligence, including any vulnerabilities or limitations of those means'.[37] It also includes, however, information or intelligence that is 'similar in nature' to that referred to in any of those six categories if that is 'in relation to, or received from, a foreign entity or terrorist group'.[38] Ministers will therefore in many cases be able to use the fact that information originated from a foreign partner to decline to provide it to NSICOP, even though the Committee would normally be entitled to have that information. It appears, however, from NSICOP's annual reports that no requests to disclose information made by it to a Minister have so far been refused on this ground.

Similar rules apply elsewhere. The PJCIS in Australia must not, its governing statute provides, 'require a person or body to disclose to the Committee operationally sensitive information or information that would or might prejudice Australia's national security or the conduct of Australia's foreign relations'.[39] Operationally sensitive information includes information 'provided by, or by an agency of,

[35] See, eg, the discussion of the Binyam Mohamed case and the violation of the control principle that occurred there, which, the ISC has claimed, 'caused strain in the UK–US intelligence-sharing partnership': ISC (n 5) [58] and [250]. The principle is discussed from a Canadian perspective in Forcese and West (n 28) 472–75.

[36] National Security and Intelligence Committee of Parliamentarians Act (2019) (Canada), s 16(1).

[37] Security of Information Act (Canada), s 8(1).

[38] ibid. A 'foreign entity' includes a 'foreign power' (itself defined to include 'the government of a foreign state'), as well as 'a group or association of foreign powers': ibid, s 2(1).

[39] Intelligence Services Act 2001 (Australia), sch 1, cl 1.

a foreign government where that government does not consent to the public disclosure of the information'.[40] This is not, therefore, an absolute bar but rather one the practical operation of which might reflect the position of the Australian Government as much as that of its foreign partners. The same possibility would seem to arise in the UK, where the Secretary of State might decline to provide information to the ISC where he or she considers that it is 'sensitive information' and 'information which, in the interests of national security, should not be disclosed to the ISC'.[41] Sensitive information is defined to include 'information provided by, or by an agency of, the Government of a country or territory outside the United Kingdom where that Government does not consent to the disclosure of the information'.[42] Finally, the relevant New Zealand rules define 'sensitive information' to include 'information that has been provided to an intelligence and security agency by the Government of any other country or by an agency of such a Government and is information that cannot be disclosed by the intelligence and security agency without the consent of the Government or agency that provided that information' if its disclosure would be likely to have one of a number of consequences, including that it would 'prejudice the entrusting of information to the Government of New Zealand on a basis of confidence' by the Government of any other country or any of its agencies.[43] Where the disclosure of other sorts of sensitive information to the ISC is subject, in effect, to a Prime Ministerial veto – with the disclosure of such information obligatory only where the Prime Minister, who is a member of the Committee, considers that it is 'desirable in the public interest'[44] – this sort of sensitive information cannot be disclosed to the Committee even if the Prime Minister is ostensibly willing to see it disclosed.[45] The result is that the expansion of democratic accountability in each state is limited in important ways by the fact of transnational cooperation of a sort that membership of the Five Eyes alliance makes completely normal and which is, we have seen, regulated inconsistently and often very minimally by domestic law.

C. Transnational Cooperation and Involvement in Mistreatment

Transnational cooperation is, then, entirely standard, even if the extent to which the Commonwealth Five Eyes states seek to regulate it varies, and even if it sometimes works to counter the trend towards a more expansive (and, it is hoped, effective) oversight of those SIAs.

[40] ibid, sch 1, para 1A.
[41] Justice and Security Act 2001 (UK), sch 1, para 4(2) and (3).
[42] ibid, sch 1, para 5(c).
[43] Intelligence and Security Act 2017 (NZ), s 202(2)(d).
[44] ibid, ss 202 and 203(3).
[45] It is not included, that is, in the scope of s 203(3).

Another, more specific concern that arises in an era of pervasive transnational national security cooperation is that, in cooperating with other states, the SIAs will find themselves complicit in activities that they would not themselves be willing to undertake or, at least, to put their name: mistreatment and perhaps even torture. For example, should authorities of a Five Eyes state send information to the authorities of another jurisdiction that an individual residing in that state is believed to be involved in terrorism, knowing or suspecting that the latter state's response will be to detain that person and subject him or her to acts amounting to torture? The question and others like it appear to arise frequently, and most of the states in question – all of them, it would appear, except Australia[46] – have therefore put in place special regimes, both in law and above and beyond it, specifically designed to exclude or minimise the possibility of becoming complicit in the mistreatment of individuals by foreign entities. Before considering these regimes, however, it is useful to note two points. One is that it is, one would hope, likely to be most relevant nowadays to cooperation outside of the context of the Five Eyes alliance. The other, conversely, is that where this sort of complicitly has been alleged (or even demonstrated) in the recent past, it has at times been within that alliance, and in relation in particular to the actions taken by the US following the 9/11 attacks, with the detention and rendition of 'enemy combatants' having now been clearly shown to have involved actions amounting to torture.[47]

In Canada,[48] the Avoiding Complicity in Mistreatment by Foreign Entities Act (2019), which replaces a 2017 Ministerial Direction on the same topic,[49] provides that the Governor in Council must – upon the recommendation of the relevant

[46] This is not to say that the question of complicity in mistreatment has never arisen in Australia: see, eg, Inspector-General of Intelligence and Security, *Inquiry into the actions of Australian government agencies in relation to the arrest and detention overseas of Mr Mamdouh Habib from 2001 to 2005* (2011). The IGIS has said that 'ASIO has implemented guidelines for the communication of information on Australians and foreign nationals to approved foreign authorities. These guidelines impose an internal, risk-based framework for assessing and approving the passage of information, based on such factors as ASIO's previous experience dealing with the authority, how the authority manages information, and the authority's history in relation to human rights issues.' Inspector-General of Intelligence and Security, *2016–2017 Annual Report* (2017) 19.

[47] See Senate Select Committee on Intelligence Committee, *Report of the Senate Select Committee on Intelligence Committee Study of the Central Intelligence Agency's Detention and Interrogation Program together with Foreword by Chairman Feinstein and Additional and Minority Views*, Senate Report 113–288 (2014).

[48] For background, see C Forcese, 'Touching Torture with a Ten-Foot Pole: The Legality of Canada's Approach to National Security Information Sharing with Human Rights-Abusing States' (2014) 52 *Osgoode Hall Law Journal* 263. And see National Security and Intelligence Review Agency, *Review of Departmental Frameworks for Avoiding Complicity in Mistreatment by Foreign Entities* (2019) [16]–[21].

[49] Public Safety Canada, *Ministerial Direction to the Canadian Security Intelligence Service: Avoiding Complicity in Mistreatment by Foreign Entities* (25 September 2017). The Direction, which replaced the original, less restrictive, 2011 Direction on the same topic, was issued under s 6(1) of the CSIS Act (1984) (Canada). The Direction prohibited (at [3]) 'the disclosure of information that would result in a substantial risk of mistreatment of an individual by a foreign entity', 'the making of requests for information that would result in a substantial risk of mistreatment of an individual by a foreign entity' and 'certain uses of information that was likely obtained through the mistreatment of an individual by a foreign entity'.

Minister – issue written directions to a range of persons, including for present purposes the Director of CSIS and the Chief of the CSE, relating to one of three things: 'the disclosure of information to any foreign entity that would result in a substantial risk of mistreatment of an individual'; 'the making of requests to any foreign entity for information that would result in a substantial risk of mistreatment of an individual'; and 'the use of information that is likely to have been obtained through the mistreatment of an individual by a foreign entity'.[50] 'Mistreatment' means 'torture or other cruel, inhuman or degrading treatment or punishment' within the meaning of the United Nations Convention against Torture and Other Cruel, Inhuman or Degrading Treatment or Punishment.[51] No definition of 'substantial risk' is contained in the statute, but CSIS still uses the definition contained in the prior Ministerial Direction, which stated that a 'substantial risk' meant a 'personal, present and foreseeable risk of mistreatment':

> In order to be 'substantial', the risk must be real and must be based on something more than mere theory or speculation. In most cases, the test of a substantial risk of mistreatment will be satisfied when it is more likely than not that there will be mistreatment; however, in some cases, particularly where the risk is of severe harm, the 'substantial risk' standard may be satisfied at a lower level of probability.[52]

Directions (12 of them, 'near identical in language')[53] have been issued to the following effect. If disclosure or a request for information would result in a substantial risk of mistreatment, the Deputy Head (that is, the senior civil servant) must ensure that officials do not disclose the information or make the request, 'unless the officials determine that the risk can be mitigated, such as through the use of caveats or assurances, and appropriate measures are taken to mitigate the risk'.[54] The Departments and Agencies to which the directions were issued must also ensure than information likely to have been obtained through mistreatment of an individual is not used 'in any way that creates a substantial risk of further mistreatment', 'as evidence in any judicial, administrative or other proceeding' or, finally,

> in any way that deprives someone of their rights or freedoms, unless the Deputy Head or, in exceptional circumstances, a senior official designated by the Deputy Head determines that the use of the information is necessary to prevent loss of life or significant personal injury and authorizes the use accordingly.[55]

Those to whom such directions are issued must make them public and provide copies to the NSICOP and the NSIRA.[56] They must then provide an annual

[50] Avoiding Complicity in Mistreatment by Foreign Entities Act, SC 2019, c 13, s 49.1, (Canada), ss 3(1) and (2).
[51] ibid, s 2.
[52] Public Safety Canada (n 49) [7].
[53] National Security and Intelligence Review Agency, *Review of Departmental Implementation of the Avoiding Complicity in Mistreatment by Foreign Entities Act for 2020* (2023) [16].
[54] ibid [17].
[55] ibid [19].
[56] Avoiding Complicity in Mistreatment by Foreign Entities Act (2019) (Canada), ss 5 and 6.

report on the implementation of those directions, a suitably redacted version of which must be published.[57] The Minister must provide a copy of these reports to NSICOP and the NSIRA.[58] Annual reports by CSIS on the Act offer useful insights into its processes, including that where it assesses that a proposed disclosure would create a substantial risk of mistreatment, it can seek 'mitigations' to lower the risk below that threshold, including 'obtaining updated human rights assurances from a foreign agency, placing caveats on information shared with a foreign agency, and using a redacted version of the information'.[59] These exist alongside 'human rights assurances' (outlining 'expectations to foreign agencies that individuals will not be mistreated in any way as a result of CSIS information exchanges with the foreign agency, and that individuals will be treated in a manner consistent with domestic and international law'[60]) and 'human rights caveats' (outlining 'the requirement to ensure that no individual will be mistreated as a result of the shared information, and that the Service expects the recipient foreign agency will respect and adhere to human rights requirements and international law'[61]), which contribute to the same end:

> Caveats and assurances are among the key measures considered by CSIS to mitigate risks of mistreatment stemming from information sharing with foreign entities. CSIS tracks the receipt of assurances received for each individual foreign agency, as well as instances where CSIS may suspect that a foreign agency may not have adhered to such assurances or violated caveats. In instances where CSIS suspects non-compliance by a foreign agency to such caveats or assurances, CSIS raises the issue with the affected entity. While violations of CSIS caveats or assurances provided by a foreign entity are very difficult to confirm or corroborate, the Service does seek updated assurances from foreign entities in instances where uncorroborated reporting may indicate concerns with potential human rights issues, or potential complicity in such violations by the affected foreign agency.[62]

The NSIRA is obliged by its governing act to review annually the implementation of directions given under the Act.[63] One notable finding from its first full such review is that

> even when departments employ similar methodologies and sources of information to inform their determination of whether or not a case involving the same country of concern should be escalated, significant divergences in the evaluation of risk and the required level of approval emerge.[64]

[57] ibid, s 7.
[58] ibid, s 8.
[59] Canadian Security Intelligence Service, *Avoiding Complicity in Mistreatment by Foreign Entities Act: Annual Report to the Minister of Public Safety* (2022) [11].
[60] ibid [12].
[61] ibid [13].
[62] ibid [14].
[63] National Security and Intelligence Review Agency Act (2019) (Canada), s 8(2.2).
[64] NSIRA (n 53) 15.

In the UK, the current equivalent is a document known as 'The Principles',[65] which was introduced in 2019 as the replacement for a document called the 'Consolidated Guidance'.[66] The background here is, in part, allegations of UK involvement in the US programme of extraordinary rendition during the period of the so-called War on Terror, which was the subject of multiple – unsatisfactory – considerations by the Intelligence and Security Committee of Parliament[67] but never by the (oft-promised) judge-led inquiry. The Principles, which apply to the UK's SIAs amongst others, cover both the passing and receipt of intelligence in a variety of circumstances, the key examples of which are when the SIAs are passing intelligence to foreign authorities 'when detention is sought or when personnel know or believe detention will occur as a result of intelligence being passed', or where 'detention is sought and there is a real risk that the foreign authority will unlawfully kill the individual in an extra-judicial killing rather than the individual being taken into custody'.[68] Alongside these, one of two things must be the case: either (i) UK personnel 'know or believe' that one of unlawful killing, torture or extraordinary rendition will result from passing the intelligence; or (ii) there is a real risk of one of these or certain other outcomes.[69] Where the first of these conditions – the knowledge or belief condition – is met, then the UK personnel must not proceed to pass the intelligence.[70] Where the second is met, they should not proceed unless they have consulted others ('senior personnel' and legal advisers) who have concluded that there is no real risk, or it has 'been possible to effectively mitigate the risk to below the threshold of real risk through reliable caveats or assurances which have been reviewed and approved by senior personnel'.[71] If neither of these is possible, the matter must be brought to Ministers for a decision.

Some confusion has arisen regarding what exactly the effect of The Principles is, and in particular whether they permit the passing of intelligence to go ahead notwithstanding that there is a real risk of, for example, an individual's being tortured as a result. When the ISC considered the point, it was told by the then Foreign Secretary that there was an absolute prohibition on this (it was later clarified that this was merely the 'ethical position' of the Secretary himself).[72]

[65] HM Government, *The Principles relating to the detention and interviewing of detainees overseas and the passing and receipt of intelligence relating to detainees* (2019).

[66] For a discussion of the reasons for this, and the some of the specific differences between the two regimes, see PF Scott, 'Law, non-law, and torture: from the consolidated guidance to the principles' [2020] *Public Law* 488.

[67] Intelligence and Security Committee, *Rendition* (Cm 7171, 2007); *Detainee Mistreatment and Rendition: 2001–2010* (HC 2017–19, 1113); and *Detainee Mistreatment and Rendition: Current Issues* (HC 2017–19, 1114).

[68] HM Government (n 65) [6].

[69] ibid.

[70] ibid [11]–[12].

[71] ibid [13]–[16].

[72] Intelligence and Security Committee of Parliament, *International Partnerships* (HC 2023–24, 288) [144].

Though others who gave evidence to the Committee offered an alternative view – one that accorded with the relatively clear implications of the language used by The Principles – they denied that they had ever given such authorisation. This later transpired to be incorrect, with its becoming known that one Minister had authorised action that would result in a real risk of torture, as well as action that would result in a real risk of cruel, inhuman or degrading treatment (on three occasions within a 12-month period) and action presenting a real risk of other unacceptable treatment (on 22 occasions within that same period).[73] Those to whom The Principles apply are required to report non-compliance to the IPC,[74] which also has a general jurisdiction to review compliance with this document.[75] In its reports, the IPC has noted that in cases that have arisen where there is a real risk of torture, unlawful killing or extraordinary rendition that cannot be mitigated, the presumption not to proceed with the relevant action has been insufficiently prominent in communications between the body subject to The Principles and the Minister who makes the final decision,[76] a state of affairs that clearly risks undermining the aim of The Principles. Reflecting that there is at least the possibility that even compliance with The Principles will result in the commission of a crime, MI6 and GCHQ, we know, when bringing a case to a Minister, seek an authorisation under section 7 of the Intelligence Services Act 1994 in order to exclude any civil or criminal liability that might arise from whatever action they ultimately take.[77] Alongside this, the possibility of criminal liability – primary or secondary – for extra-territorial offences is now also addressed by a provision, introduced by the National Security Act 2023, that provides a defence for acts that were necessary for 'the proper exercise of a function of an intelligence service'.[78] A notable aspect of the 2022 report of the IPC on this point was that one body encompassed by The Principles – the National Crime Agency (NCA), rather than any of the SIAs – had 'submitted a "thematic" application when it had assessed a particular country to have had a real risk of torture in relation to certain detainees that could not be mitigated', rather than seeking approval at the level of each individual about whom information was to be shared. This, which

[73] ibid [139]–[142]. 'This is a matter of very serious concern … The authorising of action that carried a real risk of torture is surely so exceptional that it cannot have been merely overlooked or forgotten – yet the full picture was provided only after the Committee pressed for further information.'

[74] HM Government (n 65) [23].

[75] Investigatory Powers Act 2016 (UK), s 269(3C).

[76] Investigatory Powers Commissioner, *Annual Report of the Investigatory Powers Commissioner 2021* (HC 2022–23, 910) [12.5]–[12.6]: 'In cases where there is a real risk of torture, unlawful killing or extraordinary rendition that cannot be mitigated, the effect of the "presumption not to proceed" is that the balance is shifted in favour of refusing the operational proposal. It is therefore crucial that Ministers address their mind to the presumption and are provided with advice to that effect. We have made this clear both to the departments subject to The Principles and to the FCDO and the Home Office, who prepare advice for Ministers on Principles cases.'

[77] Scott (n 66) 502–3.

[78] National Security Act 2023 (UK), s 30, inserting a new s 50A into the Serious Crime Act 2007.

might be taken to indicate a rather loose commitment to the values underlying The Principles, the Commissioner deprecated:

> [O]ur opinion was that sharing in such circumstances needs to be considered on a case-by-case basis by a Minister, who is given advice on why, exceptionally, it is appropriate and lawful to proceed in any given instance. The Minister had approved this application for 12 months of sharing but we recommended that sharing under this thematic authorisation was stopped. The NCA agreed there will not now be any sharing under this authorisation where there is an unmitigated real risk of torture and any such cases will now be put before the Minister for individual consideration.[79]

In New Zealand, where questions about SIA involvement in the CIA rendition regime have also arisen,[80] there exists – as noted in section IV.A – a 'Ministerial Policy Statement', issued in accordance with a requirement found in section 207 of the Intelligence and Security Act 2017, on 'Cooperating with overseas public authorities', which explains that it 'provides policy guidance to, and sets expectations on, GCSB and NZSIS that extend beyond their legal obligations'.[81] Cooperation, it is specified, might be authorised on a case-by-case basis, or so as to allow the provision of intelligence 'to a range of overseas public authorities on an ongoing basis'.[82] All cooperation – whether with Five Eyes partners or others – must be carried out in compliance not only with the law but also the Policy Statement,[83] the latter outlining a number of principles that 'constitute a basis for good decision-making and best practice conduct' and that must be considered 'before, during and after cooperation with overseas public authorities'.[84] Central to this is a risk assessment framework, which starts from an assessment of the record of the relevant country or public authority as regards human rights and international humanitarian law, before considering whether the specific proposed cooperation 'might result in a real risk of significantly contributing to or being complicit in a breach of human rights' – an assessment within which a 'precautionary approach' must be taken.[85] If it is considered at this stage that there is a real risk of a human rights breach as a result of the cooperation that is being proposed, the possibility of mitigating the risk should be considered, 'for example through conditions or restrictions on the cooperation provided, or through assurances

[79] Investigatory Powers Commissioner, *Annual Report of the Investigatory Powers Commissioner 2022* (HC 2023–24, 364) [12.27].

[80] Inspector-General of Intelligence and Security (n 15), concluding – most importantly – at [322] that New Zealand's SIAs 'did not participate in the rendition and detention, or directly in the interrogation of detainees; nor were they complicit in the CIA's unlawful activities'; their failing, rather, 'was one of omission, in not identifying that the CIA programme raised risks for their agencies and for the New Zealand Government, because of their close cooperation (including in Afghanistan) and ongoing intelligence relationships with the US intelligence and security agencies, including the CIA'.

[81] Ministerial Policy Statement, *Cooperating with overseas public authorities* (1 March 2022) [2].

[82] ibid [5].

[83] ibid [17].

[84] ibid [18].

[85] ibid [22].

or caveats on the intelligence exchanged'.[86] If, following this, it remains the case that there is a real risk that the proposed cooperation 'will significantly contribute to, or amount to complicity in, a breach of human rights' then one of two things must happen: (i) either the cooperation must be refused; or (ii) the matter must be referred to the responsible Minister for what the Policy Statement describes merely as 'a decision':

> To inform the Minister's decision-making, the information identified in the steps above must be documented and provided to the Minister, along with a clear statement on the purpose of the proposed cooperation. In circumstances where a decision is put to the Minister, the agencies will notify the Inspector-General of Intelligence and Security.[87]

Clearly implied by this is that – as in the UK – the Minister might authorise a cooperation notwithstanding that there is a real risk of complicity in human rights breaches. This applies, it would seem, only to some forms of cooperation: the Policy Statement further notes that the New Zealand SIAs 'must not request or use intelligence where they know, or assess there is a real risk the intelligence was obtained through a serious human rights breach'.[88] They may nevertheless pass it on to relevant authorities to be used in exceptional circumstances, including 'where the use of the intelligence is necessary to prevent loss of life, significant personal injury or a threat to critical national infrastructure'.[89] So far, the primary concerns that have been expressed about this picture relates to the lack of transparency as to how the policy operates:

> Information should be provided publicly on the criteria on which approved party status is granted, the time period for which a standing ministerial authorisation is approved, whether the time period is adequate if circumstances change and factors that would trigger a review of the status. Such information could be made public. Without such transparency, information sharing with foreign partners is essentially outside the public gaze. This breeds distrust over an activity that may enhance international security.[90]

Some observations on this state of affairs might be offered. As elsewhere, there are important similarities between the regimes applicable in each state. In part, again, this is no doubt a function of the nature of the endeavour: once it is decided that it is necessary to seek to exclude the possibility that transnational national security cooperation will lead to complicity in mistreatment, there are only so many ways one might seek to do so. The functional logic of the task by itself, that is, creates important similarities. Nevertheless, there is more going on here than that. In each case, a large part of the current concern about possible complicity

[86] ibid [23].
[87] ibid [24].
[88] ibid [25].
[89] ibid [27].
[90] T Arnold and M Mahuika, *Taumaru: Protecting Aotearoa New Zealand as a free, open and democratic society* (2023) [10.93].

in mistreatment derives from suggestions of actual complicity in mistreatment, and the most high-profile of those suggestions relate to dealings with the US in the years after 2001. And so, while there are predictable and perhaps uninformative commonalities between the manner in which the task is pursued, the fact that it was felt necessary to pursue it at all is nevertheless telling. Nevertheless, these commonalities have their limits. In the UK and New Zealand, the special procedures are not found in law, though in New Zealand they have a (weak) legal basis of a sort that is not present in the UK. In Canada, a statute governs the procedures, though the substance of the applicable rules is ultimately determined by the executive rather than the legislature. These rules appear to be more restrictive than their equivalents elsewhere, and it is interesting to speculate on the causal connection of form and substance. To put the point another way, it seems unlikely that, if there was parliamentary involvement in the approval of the UK's 'Principles', the ability of Ministers to authorise relevant activities where there was a real risk that it would, for example, result in torture would not have been the subject of critical attention. Perhaps, in fact, document might even have been rewritten to remove that ability. As things stand, however, it may be that these questions – in large part artefacts of a period in which the primary concern of the national security endeavour has been the threat of terrorism – fade away with a shift back to the problem of hostile state activity as the primary focus of the SIAs and, perhaps more importantly, those who construct their legal frameworks and oversee their activities. It is to this point that we now turn.

V. The (Legal) Return to State Threats

I emphasised early in this work that national security constitutionalism has often been treated in a partial fashion in recent decades. National security encompasses a variety of issues, including two that, though no doubt at times related in practice, can and should be distinguished. One of these is counter-terrorism, which has been the primary focus of national security legislation in the Commonwealth Five Eyes states, and most scholarship relating to national security law, in recent decades. Though several of the states at issue have a longer history of domestic terrorism, with which the relevant SIAs have concerned themselves to some degree throughout their existence, and which is explicitly encompassed by many of their statutory mandates, the end of the Cold War, and in particular the 9/11 attacks of 2001, appears to have seen the question of terrorism – and international terrorism in particular – become their primary focus. Though we cannot usually substantiate that inference with budgetary or other operational data, we can certainly see support for it within the activity of the relevant legislatures, which enacted through the 2000s and 2010s a vast range of legislation aimed primarily at the issue of terrorism, and only secondarily, if at all, touching on the national security apparatus of the state more broadly. But as we have seen, especially in chapter 2, this is somewhat exceptional within the longer history of the national security enterprise in these states, for the modern SIAs are creatures of the Cold War, and until the end of the Cold War, the SIAs appear to have focused largely, and at times entirely, upon the threats posed by other states in either direct or indirect form.

It was for this reason that during the Cold War, for example, questions about the protection of official information – against spies or their sympathisers or accomplices – were so prominent but have in many cases become less so in recent decades. It was for this reason too that the Cold War context gave rise, frequently and with much justification, to concerns about the politicisation of the SIAs and their interference in the democratic process; concerns that were then, in ways we have canvassed in chapter 3, reflected in the governing instruments of those SIAs when they were established in law over the course of the Cold War era. In the period after 9/11, these concerns seem often to have diminished, bearing little relation to the nature of what was apprehended to be the dominant threat to national security. Al-Qaeda, that is, did not, it seems, seek to infiltrate Western governments; political parties in the Commonwealth Five Eyes states did not generally possess members who were ideologically sympathetic to the Islamic State or its equivalents elsewhere. In recent years, however, following in particular the collapse of the Islamic State and the emergence and then decline of the phenomenon of 'foreign terrorist fighters', there have been a number of indications that state threats – primarily emanating, it would seem, from Russia and China – have once again become central to the national security enterprise in Canada, Australia, New Zealand and the UK: in two of those states, legislation aimed at addressing the threat has been enacted, and in a third it is in progress. If that is indeed the case – and we should be slow to suggest it is equally so in all of the Commonwealth Five Eyes states, not least because in some of them the contemporary apprehension of threats from hostile states seems to have a longer prehistory, but also because, even if the focus of governments and legislatures shifted in the aftermath of the Cold War, it does not follow that the SIAs themselves stopped paying attention to the question of hostile states – then the dominance of counter-terrorism in the decades after the 9/11 attacks may in the longer term come to be seen as an historical anomaly: an interregnum of sorts.

This is not to say, however, that the apparent return to state threats in recent years involves a simple revival of the specific forms of threat (and legal responses thereto) that were most prominent during the Cold War, being espionage and the protection of official information, and perhaps also sabotage. Rather, the new and renewed concern for the problem of 'state threats' – to which the SIAs of the four states have been seeking, sometimes without any great subtlety, to draw public attention for a number of years – is often expressed nowadays in the language of 'foreign interference' in the domestic political order generally and, in particular, in the democratic process particularly. We see, for example, that when the Director-General of MI5 gave the Agency's 'annual threat update' in 2021, he began with a consideration of 'state threats' before turning to what he acknowledged was 'still the national security threat of greatest concern to the public' – the question of terrorism.[91] Similarly, the equivalent update from the Director-General of ASIO in 2024 explicitly contrasted the level of threat of such foreign interference (which is not formally assessed) with that from terrorism (which is) at that point in time: 'While the terrorism threat level is POSSIBLE, if we had a threat level for espionage and foreign interference it would be at CERTAIN – the highest level on the scale.'[92]

Different accounts of the threat of foreign interference characterise it in slightly different ways, though most seek to distinguish 'foreign interference' (which is held, by governments and SIAs, to be illegitimate) from 'foreign influence' (which is used to describe actions perceived to be legitimate). Foreign interference involves the distortion of the political process by agents of some other state or their proxies, so as to advance directly or indirectly the interests of that other state. At its most blatant, it might, for example, involve paying bribes to a politician to speak out in favour of the interfering state, or to vote against action deemed detrimental to its interests. At the other end of the spectrum – harder, one would think, both to detect and to counter – it might involve agents of a foreign state subjecting groups of voters to pressure to support a particular candidate in an election. As we discuss further in section VI, there is a difficulty here: while a traditional threat from a foreign state – say, the passing of official secrets to a foreign intelligence service – is something that should not happen in any circumstances, and can be dealt with on that basis, foreign interference often involves making happen some act that might be done for a range of reasons, the vast majority of which are wholly legitimate and which might well have happened even without any involvement from a hostile state. In our examples above, politicians are entitled to speak out in favour of foreign states, or vote against actions that might work to harm the interests of those states, and many will do so on their own initiative. Voters might support a particular candidate in an election for an infinite number of reasons. This basic fact has important implications for attempts to address foreign interference, which – we shall see – will often risk coming into contact with the democratic process. For now, it is important to note that what appears most crucially to distinguish foreign interference from foreign influence is that the former takes place clandestinely: as a result, the distinctive element of modern legal responses to the threat of foreign interference is the imposition of requirements that will, if complied with, have the effect of bringing the relevant activity into the open, so that it might be judged (and perhaps discounted) accordingly.

We see examples of allegations or suspicions of foreign interference in each of the Commonwealth states in question, and legislative responses are either already

[91] MI5, 'Director General Ken McCallum gives annual threat update 2021' (14 July 2021).
[92] ASIO, 'Director-General's Annual Threat Assessment 2024' (28 February 2024).

in place or forthcoming in most of them. So, for example, reports in the Australian media suggested that attempts were made by the Government of the People's Republic of China to arrange for a particular candidate to stand for election in the Commonwealth elections of 2019, in an electoral Division in Melbourne with a large number of voters of Chinese heritage.[93] In the lead-up to the 2022 election, ASIO revealed a further example of foreign interference, which subsequent reporting suggested took the form of 'a business figure in Australia with deep ties to China act[ing] as a "puppeteer" to finance potential federal Labor candidates in NSW who would be sympathetic to Beijing'.[94] A few years later, the Director-General, without naming the country involved, discussed extensively ASIO's work to disrupt attempts at foreign interference:

> While some [of those involved] were unwitting, others knew they were working for a foreign intelligence service. We helped the unaware ones extract themselves, and severed the links between the others and the foreign intelligence service. Several individuals should be grateful the espionage and foreign interference laws are not retrospective.[95]

The laws referred to include two key pieces of legislation enacted by the Commonwealth of Australia aimed at the threat of foreign interference. On one hand there is the National Security Legislation Amendment (Espionage and Foreign Interference) Act 2018, which updated and expanded the criminal law in this area, including by creating offences of intentional and reckless foreign interference, and the breadth of which has been criticised in light of early prosecutions brought thereunder.[96] The other statute, the Foreign Influence Transparency Scheme (FITS) Act 2018, introduces the eponymous Scheme with a view to providing, in the Commonwealth's account, 'the public and government decision-makers with visibility of the nature, level and extent of foreign influence on Australia's government and political processes'.[97] The proximate origin of both Acts is a review requested by the Prime Minister of the law in this area – a request that was to involve consideration, specifically, of the desirability of introducing a scheme based upon that found in the US Foreign Agents Registration Act 1938.[98] As with other issues we have considered, then, an endeavour that has since become common to (the majority of) the Commonwealth Five Eyes states

[93] See, eg, A Beech, 'ASIO investigating reports of Chinese plot to install agent in Parliament' *ABC News* (24 November 2019).

[94] A Greene, 'China behind failed attempt to bankroll Labor candidates in federal election' *ABC News* (11 February 2022).

[95] ASIO (n 92).

[96] See, eg, Y Zhuang, 'Australia Wanted to Catch Chinese Spies. Is This Really Whom It Had in Mind?' *New York Times* (17 Marchi 2024), discussing the case of Di Sanh Duong, whose conviction was the first under the National Security Legislation Amendment (Espionage and Foreign Interference) Act 2018.

[97] Australian Government Attorney-General's Department, *Foreign Influence Transparency Scheme – Factsheet 1* (February 2019)

[98] For discussion, see Parliamentary Joint Committee on Intelligence and Security, *Advisory Report on the National Security Legislation Amendment (Espionage and Foreign Interference) Bill 2017* (2018).

originated within the fifth member; having subsequently found its way, under the influence of that fifth member, into the ecosystem of Commonwealth national security constitutionalism, it could then spread easily, and quickly, within it. The Australian Scheme requires those who undertake, or agree to undertake, certain activities on behalf of a 'foreign principal' to register. The activities in question include both parliamentary lobbying and other sorts of activities undertaken in Australia for the 'the purpose of political or governmental influence'.[99] Any activities undertaken by a former Cabinet Minister on behalf of a foreign principal must be registered; so too must activities undertaken by those who have recently held certain designated positions if, 'in undertaking the activity, the person contributes experience, knowledge, skills or contacts gained in the person's former capacity as a designated position holder'.[100] A range of exceptions apply, including – for example – where the activity in question relates to the provision of legal advice.[101]

The key point, then, is the question 'Who is a "foreign principal"?' The definition employed here is relatively wide – though narrower than had originally been proposed – encompassing not only a 'foreign government' but also three other categories: a 'foreign government related entity'; a 'foreign political organisation'; and a 'foreign government related individual'.[102] Each of these is also defined broadly, so that a 'foreign government related entity' includes not only a company of which a foreign government owns a substantial share, but also – for example – one where 'the directors (however described) of the company are accustomed, or under an obligation (whether formal or informal), to act in accordance with the directions, instructions or wishes of the foreign principal'. Similarly, a person is a 'foreign government related individual' if (not being a citizen or permanent resident of Australia) either or both of the following are the case: 'the individual is accustomed, or under an obligation (whether formal or informal), to act in accordance with the directions, instructions or wishes of the foreign principal' and 'the foreign principal is in a position to exercise, in any other way, total or substantial control over the individual'.[103] Government-issued 'transparency notices' can confirm that a body is a 'foreign government related entity' or that a person is a 'foreign government related individual'.[104] The effect of these definitions is to bring within the scope of the Scheme many entities – legal and natural persons – that have no formal connection with a foreign government. Annual reporting required by the Act show that the largest single number of new or renewed registrations – by far – relate to China.[105] No persons seem to have been charged with any of the offences relating to failure to comply with the Scheme since its institution, and

[99] FITS Act 2018 (Australia), s 21.
[100] ibid, ss 22 and 23.
[101] ibid, s 25.
[102] ibid, s 10.
[103] ibid.
[104] ibid, Division 3.
[105] See, eg, Attorney-General's Department, *Annual Report on the Operation of the Foreign Influence Transparency Scheme 1 July 2022 to 30 June 2023* (2023) 6.

the Scheme was heavily criticised by the PJCIS in its mandatory review thereof. The Committee said that

> as currently constructed the FITS Act is largely ineffective, with such meagre results that it would be difficult to justify the ongoing compliance burden and resources without major reform if it is to achieve its key objective – transparency of activities undertaken by Australian people and entities on behalf of foreign principals.[106]

In recommending a range of amendments – including widening in various ways the definition of 'foreign principals' – it noted that efforts elsewhere 'to create similar schemes, including in the United Kingdom and Canada, highlight that there is no "one size fits all" option to providing transparency in this context'.[107]

In the UK, though attention was originally focused on possible Russian influence on the political sphere – it was, the Foreign Secretary said, 'almost certain that Russian actors sought to interfere in the 2019 general election through the online amplification of illicitly acquired and leaked Government documents'[108] – China has ultimately emerged as the primary threat, with (for example) MI5 warning Members of Parliament in 2022 that a particular individual with whom some of them were connected was carrying out what the Home Secretary described as 'political interference activities on behalf of the Chinese Communist Party'.[109] A report by the ISC noted that China's ambition at a global level, 'to become a technological and economic superpower, on which other countries are reliant', posed a national security threat to the UK.[110] Employing the distinction noted above, it concluded that 'China oversteps the boundary and crosses the line from exerting influence – a legitimate course of action – into interference, in the pursuit of its interests and values at the expense of those of the UK'.[111] Reports have also suggested that individuals seeking to stand as Members of Parliament were blocked from doing so after warnings from MI5 that they may be seeking to spy for China.[112] In this context, the ISC's Russia Report had hinted that the introduction of a UK equivalent to the US Foreign Agents Registration Act, 'which would clearly be valuable in countering Russian influence in the UK',[113] should be considered. By the time the UK Government set out to legislate on this matter, it was able to have reflected on 'the value and lessons' not only of the US scheme

[106] Parliamentary Joint Committee on Intelligence and Security, *Review of the Foreign Influence Transparency Scheme Act 2018* (2024) [4.11].

[107] ibid [4.126].

[108] HC Deb (16 July 2020) HCWS384. See generally Intelligence and Security Committee, *Russia* (HC 2019–2021, 632). And, considering that report in wider context, see J Eisler, 'Constitutional Formalities, Power Realities, and Comparative Anglophone Responses to Foreign Campaign Meddling' (2021) 20 *Election Law Journal* 32.

[109] G Corera and J Scott, 'MI5 warning over "Chinese agent" in Parliament' *BBC News* (13 January 2022).

[110] Intelligence and Security Committee, *China* (HC 2022–23, 1605) [1].

[111] ibid 46.

[112] S Swinford and F Hamilton, 'MI5 warned Conservatives that MP hopefuls could be spies' *The Times* (12 September 2023).

[113] ISC (n 110) [115].

but also of that in Australia,[114] with the adoption of such a scheme in one of the Commonwealth Five Eyes states thereby working – even if only in a minor way – to smooth its passage into another.

The resulting statute, the National Security Act 2023, responds to these and related concerns not only by rewriting the criminal law of espionage – much of it quite severely outdated[115] – and expanding it so as to encompass a range of activities identified as illegitimate interference with the democratic process, but also by introducing new mechanisms aimed at the same broad threat.[116] One of these is a civil order backed by criminal sanctions, which applies to the domain of state threats the lessons of counter-terrorism law since 2001. The other is a set of two schemes (or one scheme with two tiers) that require the registration of arrangements for 'foreign activity' and 'foreign influence'.[117] As with the Australian Scheme, the intention is not so much as to prohibit the activity in question as to force it out into the open, so that if – for example – the Chinese Government wishes to pay individuals or organisations to promote its interests within the UK, it must do so openly and transparently, in order that any such promotion may be judged (and, it is likely, discounted) accordingly. The primary scheme – sometimes described as the 'political tier' – is distinguishable from the Australian equivalent largely in terms of its breadth. It applies to 'foreign influence arrangements', being those in which a foreign power (effectively a foreign government, an agency thereof or a political party that is in power) directs a person to carry out 'political influence activities' in the UK.[118] This restriction to 'foreign powers' was not the original formulation of the scheme when introduced into Parliament, with the tier instead defined by reference to the category of 'foreign principals', including not just foreign powers but also foreign companies and unincorporated organisations.[119] Though the narrowing of this tier of the scheme in this way is counterbalanced to some degree by the inclusion alongside it of a separate, 'enhanced' tier, the latter applies only to foreign powers (or legal persons controlled by them) that are designated by the Secretary of State.[120] How widely this element will be used remains to be seen. The overall effect of this part of the 2023 Act should, though, be to 'force those to whom it applies to choose between making their activities open and transparent or, more likely, continuing them notwithstanding that to do so without registration is now unlawful'.[121]

[114] Home Office, *Legislation to Counter State Threats (Hostile State Activity) Government Consultation* (2021) 31.

[115] See Law Commission, *Protection of Official Data: A Consultation Paper* (Law Com CP No 230, 2017); Law Commission, *Protection of Official Data: Report* (Law Com No 395, 2020).

[116] For discussion of the Act in context, see PF Scott, '"State threats", security, and democracy: the National Security Act 2023' (2024) 44 *Legal Studies* 260.

[117] National Security Act 2023 (UK), pt 4.

[118] ibid, ss 69–72.

[119] See the discussion in Scott (n 116).

[120] National Security Act 2023 (UK), ss 65–68.

[121] Scott (n 116).

In Canada too, the issue of foreign interference has been very prominent in recent years but, as elsewhere, certain interventions by the SIAs have implied that the threat was not necessarily treated with sufficient seriousness by those best positioned to address it. In 2018, for example, the Director of CSIS spoke publicly about what he took to be 'the greatest threat to our prosperity and national interest' – 'foreign interference and espionage'.[122] In particular, allegations have been made of Chinese interference in the 2019 and 2021 federal elections in Canada, including in relation to the selection of candidates by the Canadian Liberal Party, with its being suggested in particular that China had sought in the latter election to promote a minority victory by that Party. Both the NSIRA and the NSICOP, which had previously claimed that foreign interference represented 'a significant threat to Canada's society and fundamental institutions',[123] were tasked with carrying out inquiries into aspects of the matter;[124] the Canadian Government initially resisted a full public inquiry, however, instead appointing a 'Special Rapporteur' to 'make expert recommendations on how to further protect our democracy and uphold Canadians' confidence in it'.[125] The interim report of the Special Rapporteur declared:

> Attempts at foreign interference are ubiquitous, especially from the [People's Republic of China]. Successive federal governments have known about it for years and the occurrence of foreign interference has grown in the past several years. It is an increasing threat to our democratic system and must be resisted as effectively as possible. Much has been done to strengthen our capacity to resist, but considerably more remains to be done.[126]

He recommended, however, against holding a public inquiry into the question of foreign interference, on the basis of the limitations that would inevitably apply to such a process and their implications for its ability to satisfy public concern.[127] In

[122] CSIS, 'Remarks by Director David Vigneault at the Economic Club of Canada' (4 December 2018).

[123] See National Security and Intelligence Committee of Parliamentarians, *Annual Report 2019* (2020) ch 2, asserting the need for an approach 'based on a refined calculation of our collective interests and, most importantly, a continued emphasis on Canada's liberal democratic values'. And see also National Security and Intelligence Committee of Parliamentarians, *Special report into the allegations associated with Prime Minister Trudeau's official visit to India in February 2018* (2018) 3–8. Though the Committee's findings on this point are wholly redacted, one of its recommendations was that '[M]embers of the House of Commons and the Senate should be briefed upon being sworn-in and regularly thereafter on the risks of foreign interference and extremism in Canada.'

[124] See National Security and Intelligence Review Agency, *Review of the dissemination of intelligence on People's Republic of China political foreign interference, 2018–2023* (2024).

[125] Prime Minister of Canada, 'Prime Minister announces Independent Special Rapporteur to help protect the integrity of Canada's democracy' (15 March 2023).

[126] Independent Special Rapporteur on Foreign Interference, *First Report* (23 May 2023).

[127] 'A Public Inquiry would delay but not prevent the inevitable grappling that Canadians (as well as media and Parliamentarians without a security clearance) will need to do with the fact that they are not going to see the intelligence, they are not going to see the internal memoranda, and they are not going to hear from the security agencies in any detailed way. This is in many ways unfortunate, but it is necessary to protect our national security, the sources our intelligence agencies rely on, and our obligations to the Five Eyes partners.' ibid 52.

the event, the Special Rapporteur stood down shortly thereafter,[128] with a number of concerns having been raised regarding his appointment (including apparent conflicts of interest)[129] and his work. The first response of the Government had been to propose a non-statutory 'Foreign Influence Transparency Registry',[130] with an annex to the Consultation Paper predictably offering as benchmarks not only the law in the US but also the much more recent schemes introduced in Australia and the UK. Feedback received to the consultation, however, made clear that this alone would be considered insufficient, and in late 2023 the Government of Canada therefore launched a consultation on legislative amendments to the same end of countering foreign interference.[131] By that point, the Government of Canada had bowed to pressure and also instituted a public inquiry of the sort it had originally resisted, under Marie-Josée Hogue, a judge of the Quebec Court of Appeal.[132] Though the question of the appropriate legislative response to the threat of foreign interference is (even) more sensitive than are other questions of national security, not least because it implicates the regulation of the domestic democratic system, it was inevitable that – in keeping with the long-standing pattern we have identified elsewhere in this work – the existence of statutory schemes elsewhere in the Commonwealth Five Eyes states would be used not only to argue for but also to assist in, whether positively or negatively, the design of a Canadian analogue, with a Bill providing for such an analogue eventually introduced in May 2024.[133]

The NZSIS has also spoken openly about the threat not only of espionage but also of foreign interference.[134] Though the New Zealand authorities previously

[128] Letter from David Johnston, Independent Special Rapporteur on Foreign Interference, to Justin Trudeau, Prime Minister of Canada (9 June 2023).

[129] See, eg, P Zimonjic, 'Is David Johnston in a conflict of interest? Experts say only Canadians can decide' *CBC* (26 May 2023). Similar criticisms were made of another assessment that considered the possibility of foreign interference in the 2021 election: M Rosenberg, *Report on the assessment of the 2021 Critical Election Incident Public Protocol* (2023), relating to the Cabinet Directive on the Critical Election Incident Public Protocol, put in place prior to the 2019 election, that 'sets out the ministers' expectations with respect to the general directions and the principles to guide the process for informing the public of an incident that threatens Canada's ability to have a free and fair election during the period that the Caretaker Convention is in effect' and requires an independent report to be completed following each general election. The Rosenberg Report found (ibid 41–43) that there had been 'efforts at foreign interference' in the 2021 election, but not at a level to meet the threshold set out in the Protocol for communication of the matter to the public.

[130] Public Safety Canada, *Enhancing Foreign Influence Transparency: Exploring Measures to Strengthen Canada's Approach – Public and Stakeholder Consultation Paper* (10 March 2023).

[131] Public Safety Canada, *What We Heard Report: Consulting Canadians on the merits of a Foreign Influence Transparency Registry* (2023); and *Enhancing measures to counter foreign interference: Whether to amend the Canadian Security Intelligence Service Act – Public consultation paper* (24 November 2023).

[132] See the originating Order in Council: Public Inquiry into Foreign Interference in Federal Electoral Processes and Democratic Institutions, PC 2023-0882 (7 September 2023).

[133] House Of Commons of Canada, *Bill C-70: An Act respecting countering foreign interference* (6 May 2024).

[134] See, eg, New Zealand Security Intelligence Service, *Annual Report 2022* (2022) 28: 'A small number of states engage in interference activities against New Zealand's national interests. Foreign interference targets our political, academic, media and business sectors, and several of our ethnic communities.'

appeared to prefer to talk only in general terms – not naming specific states – others have once more identified China as the most important threat, and indeed have suggested that New Zealand is 'valuable to China, as well as to other states such as Russia, as a soft underbelly through which to access Five Eyes intelligence',[135] recalling some of the claims quoted in chapter 2 about the fear that Soviet spies once found in New Zealand a more favourable environment in which to operate. And in a threat assessment published in 2023, NZSIS noted that though '[o]nly a small number of states engage in interference against New Zealand … some do so persistently and with the potential for significant harm'.[136] It continued:

> NZSIS has detected interference activity from a number of foreign states. Most notable is the continued targeting of New Zealand's diverse ethnic Chinese communities. We see these activities carried out by groups and individuals linked to the intelligence arm of the People's Republic of China (PRC).[137]

In New Zealand, however, no legislative response to the specific issue of foreign interference has yet been taken or even previewed. Nevertheless, the pattern identified is such that it would be surprising if New Zealand does not come under pressure, internal and perhaps also external, to take steps in this direction in coming years and does not in fact take such steps. The legislative aspect of the (re)turn to state threats, that is, is very likely to recreate many of the dynamics of national security law more generally, with states not only choosing to follow the lead of their counterparts elsewhere but perhaps also – as the 'soft underbelly' comment suggests – being strongly encouraged to do so by those same counterparts. As has been evident from the beginning of the Cold War, close cooperation in the domain of national security might reasonably be taken to rest upon assumptions about the institutions and processes of the cooperating states: no one state will wish to fall too far behind the evolving norm, and the majority may not approve of its doing so. This turn to, or back to, state threats as the most prominent aspect of the national security enterprise – still ongoing but already, it seems, well established – brings us back to the question of the relationship between national security and democratic politics, a question that was a vital part of the Cold War picture but which, we have noted, became secondary in the context of the turn to counter-terrorism since the end of the Cold War and the 9/11 attacks and the predominance of a technocratic understanding of national security. In section VI, therefore, I consider that relationship.

[135] See Canadian Security Intelligence Service, *China and the Age of Strategic Rivalry: Highlights from an Academic Outreach Workshop*, World Watch: Expert Notes (2018) 75–82.
[136] New Zealand Security Intelligence Service, *New Zealand's Security Threat Environment 2023: An assessment by the New Zealand Security Intelligence Service* (2023) 27.
[137] ibid.

VI. National Security and Democracy

A final theme of Commonwealth national security constitutionalism that emerges out of the foregoing – one that, no doubt, would likely be identified in the context of any number of liberal democracies in the contemporary world – is the sometimes fraught relationship between national security and democracy. In each of the states under consideration here, the relationship between the two things was traditionally, as repeatedly noted, an indirect and limited one. That is, the national security enterprise was the exclusive purview of the government of the day; and though that government was itself accountable to the relevant legislative body, directly elected in whole or in part, there was little specific and ongoing accountability to that body as regards the national security endeavour: the government did not provide information on the work of the SIAs to the legislature as a matter of course, and frequently actively refused to do so. Information about what was done entered the public domain only sporadically, usually as a result of some ad hoc review or inquiry, itself prompted by some scandal or other. Those reports, we might note, in the first decades of the Cold War, paid little or no attention to questions of the relationship of the SIAs to the democratic order. This seems to have continued to be the case into the 1970s, at which point democratic principle becomes an explicit part of the context within which key reports unfold and to which attention must be paid. Justice Robert Hope's first report on ASIO, for instance, considers the issue at a number of points, and includes the observation – to modern eyes banal – that there are 'limitations upon what a security organization should do in a democratic society. Aims, even of security, do not justify all means.'[138] In the same period, the terms of reference for the Powles inquiry in New Zealand similarly identified its purpose as being to ensure that the functions of NZSIS conformed with 'both the needs of our country and the character of our society and our democratic form of government'.[139] Democracy at this point seems to have acted most obviously as a (still weak) limit on how the security endeavour might be pursued. The prominence of the concept within the formal and informal literature on national security has continued to grow over time, and nowadays the concept is – within the rhetoric on national security, at least – omnipresent and a source of much hand-wringing: the Australian *Comprehensive Review* of the late 2010s, for example, is anxious to orient the endeavour in relation to fundamental principles and consider what, exactly, in light of the possibly dubious morality (and even legality) of some of what the SIAs do, separates liberal democracies from illiberal and autocratic states.[140]

[138] Royal Commission on Intelligence and Security, *Fourth Report – Volume I*, Parliamentary Paper No 248/1977 (1977) [114].

[139] G Powles, *Security Intelligence Service: Report by Chief Ombudsman*, Appendix to the Journals of the New Zealand House of Representatives (1976) 4.

[140] *Comprehensive Review of the Legal Framework of the National Intelligence Community*, Volume 1: *Recommendations and Executive Summary; Foundations and Principles; Control, Coordination and*

That this prominence is not a purely rhetorical phenomenon is demonstrated by the evolving institutional apparatus surrounding the national security endeavour. As seen in chapter 6, there has been a significant movement away from this historic pattern of minimal legislative involvement, such that all of the states (in which, we recall, the executives are formed out of and accountable to the legislatures) now possess a parliamentary or quasi-parliamentary body responsible for, in the broadest terms, providing oversight of the national security enterprise. These bodies inform and assist the legislature in its work, and so – or this is the theory – bypass the executive and the obstacles it might pose to scrutiny while nevertheless reflecting the sensitivities inherent in the national security context. This is augmented by extra-parliamentary review carried out, whether on an ongoing basis or after the fact, by independent actors of various sorts. That review allows for more direct consideration of operational aspects of the SIAs' work than was originally (and in many cases still is) allowed to the (quasi-) parliamentary bodies, and in its more effective forms not only helps inform the executive as to the propriety and legality of what the SIAs do, but also puts into the public domain information about the powers of the SIAs and the use to which they are put, which itself informs both parliamentary and wider public debates on these issues. There is, in short, an ongoing level of political – democratic – accountability for the work of the SIAs that in the past existed only contingently and sporadically, if at all.

Crucially, it would seem, that process began only late in the Cold War, gathering momentum only after its end, with the majority of innovation in this regard taking place in the 1990s and into the new millennium, as the focus on state threats diminished and terrorism became, in the public and political imagination at least, the dominant threat to national security. The connection between these two phenomena – the cementing of processes of democratic accountability for the national security endeavour and the period of focus upon counter-terrorism, both of them features of the post-Cold War period – is, it seems, as follows. Where the primary threat to national security is considered to be that of terrorism, and so the primary work of the SIAs that of counter-terrorism, we are dealing with a problem the nature of which is in many ways objective, at least at the high level, and not subject to particular contestation within the domestic polity. Though we might disagree as to what the scale of the threat is, and whether some particular group requires to be proscribed, or so on, the methods associated with terrorism are not normally misunderstood. If a bomb detonates in central London or in the central business district of Sydney then that is a threat to national security, which will be understood as such by all relevant actors, and certainly by all those who seek power within the democratic process of the state in question. A technocratic vision of national security might therefore capture what is going on adequately,

Cooperation (2019) ch 7. Another data point regarding this prominence within the discourse is the title of the independent review of New Zealand's 2017 Act: T Arnold and M Mahuika, *Taumaru: Protecting Aotearoa New Zealand as a free, open and democratic society* (2023).

even if – as has sometimes been the case – it involves an implausible separation of foreign policy from the threat of terrorism at home. There is unlikely to be a high-level question of policy to decide, but rather a series of questions of practical reason: how to identify the source of the threat and what steps should be taken in order to address that threat. It is likely – perhaps very likely – that the work of the SIAs to this end will look very similar regardless of which party or parties make up the government of the day, and all that is necessary is to determine how effective they have been, given their resources (material and legal), in dealing with the threat of terrorism. What terrorist acts have they stopped? Which of those that took place could have been stopped? Have they operated in conformity with the law? Given the absence of ideological disagreement on the key issues of what we are seeking to achieve, and what it would mean to succeed or to fail, ex post democratic accountability for the pursuit of the national security endeavour is necessary within this picture, but probably also sufficient.

The approach that has been taken in terms of constitutionalising national security since the 1990s therefore, it seems, reflects an understanding of the nature of the modern national security enterprise that is not always articulated openly or clearly but which is vital to understanding both why it was felt necessary to promote accountability and, more importantly, why it is not (it seems) felt necessary to go beyond that accountability; why, that is, the approach to the democratic oversight of the SIAs and their work is a consciously limited one. Decisions about what (the protection of) national security involves, which of the threats to it to should be prioritised and what steps should be taken to respond to them, are ones best left to experts – the SIAs and their leadership – and the wider democratic order takes an interest only where the decisions in fact made turn out to be wholly unreasonable, the actions taken are executed in an inept or bad-faith fashion, or the tools available are felt by those who must rely on them to be inadequate. In this sense, the national security enterprise is perhaps a forerunner of the broader pattern of modern constitutionalism, whereby a number of tasks are given over to specialist institutions in order to carry out tasks for which particular expertise is required and in relation to which, therefore, direct democratic control is inappropriate if not outright dangerous.[141] This may be a defensible, or even sensible, approach in the context of the post-Cold War domination of the security landscape by the threat of global terrorism. If, however, as seems plausible, we are returning to an era of more open geopolitical competition, in which the states in question are threatened primarily by other,

[141] On which see F Vibert, *The Rise of the Unelected: Democracy and the New Separation of Powers* (Cambridge University Press, 2007) 4, treating unelected bodies as a whole and arguing that they represent a distinct branch of government, one that derives its legitimacy not, as is usually claimed, from their accountability to elected bodies but rather from elsewhere: '[W]hat distinguishes the new branch and provides the basis for its legitimacy is the greater rigour with which it approaches facts, seeks information, weighs the state of empirical knowledge and tries to draw evidence-based conclusions for public policy.' Though Vibert does not consider security bodies, this seems more than capable of encompassing the work of the SIAs – at least in so far as it is focused on terrorism.

hostile, states, then this may no longer be the appropriate way to approach the matter. The technocratic element of the national security enterprise – the extent to which it can plausibly be argued to be an enterprise resting on special expertise and so largely, and justifiably, insulated from the democratic process – is, one might think, therefore likely to diminish, and may already be doing so.

So, for example, we have considered the key moves taken so far by the Commonwealth Five Eyes states to exclude or to otherwise regulate foreign interference by hostile states in their political systems, via a mixture of legal and non-legal mechanisms, and employing both the criminal and civil law. The paradigm of such activity would be where a hostile state takes covert steps to have a sympathiser elected or appointed to some public role, possibly by illicitly providing financial resources to that person, or taking steps to coerce the relevant decision-maker(s) to vote for or appoint that person when they would otherwise have declined to do so. The purpose of this exercise, more likely to be carried out, if at all, in a rather more subtle form, is to promote the interests of the sponsoring state. This might be done directly by its agents, by arguing or voting for its interests, or by their exercising whatever powers they come to possess in a way that promotes those interests. It might also be done rather less directly: it has, for example, been frequently suggested that the purpose of (alleged or apparent) Russian interference is not so much to have the interests of Russia promoted within the relevant political system but rather to sow discord and disagreement, such that the system in question is incapable of putting up a united and energetic front against those interests.[142] Whichever is the case, it appears that this is now considered to be a greater threat than is traditional espionage, on both quantitative and qualitative grounds: the former because it seems unlikely that there will otherwise be sympathisers with, say, the modern Russian or Chinese states in positions of power in the Commonwealth Five Eyes states on the same scale as there once were Soviet sympathisers; the latter because foreign interference operates (or at least is capable of operating) at the systemic level, rather than at that of individuals.

We see, in this brief statement, the outline of the problems the return to an era of state threats, and in particular state threats in the form of 'foreign interference', brings with it. That is, there will be many people within each of the Commonwealth Five Eyes states, including within its formal political order, who wish for their 'home' state to act in a way that is convenient to the interests of some hostile state, without being paid or otherwise influenced by that hostile state. Some of these will be people who have no concern for the national security of the state but prioritise some other good above all else: economic growth perhaps, or simple freedom of commerce. There will, though, be some who think that the interests of their home jurisdiction and its national security are in fact promoted via taking the actions in question: that, perhaps, they can influence currently hostile states to be less so

[142] See, eg, PN Howard et al, 'The IRA, Social Media and Political Polarization in the United States, 2012–2018' *Oxford Internet Institute and Graphika* (2018) 39.

via diplomatic contact and economic exchange. Such views being a legitimate part of the democratic process, what we have is not a dispute about practical reason – how to address a threat to national security that seems to be objectively identifiable, and on which there is effectively no political disagreement – but rather one about what sort of approach to foreign or trade policy or similar would promote national security in the first place. In extreme circumstances, the belief of the SIAs that a particular foreign state represents a threat to the interests of their home state might clash with the conclusions arrived at via the democratic process. But even if there is not such a direct disagreement, it may well be the case that in identifying certain states or certain activities of those states as a threat to national security, or even denying that this is the case, the SIAs run the risk of taking sides within questions on which there is live political dispute. The technocratic approach – the treatment of the object, if not the methods, of the national security endeavour as largely separate from the democratic process – is in this way liable to come under, at the very least, a degree of pressure. It therefore seems likely that, to the extent that this trend continues, we will see in the coming years renewed interest in the way in which the legal regulation of the modern SIAs seeks – as discussed in chapter 3 – to ensure they do not, in carrying out their mandate, promote the interests of some political party or other, or act so as to prevent the expression of lawful political views. We may also anticipate a reaction against democratic oversight of the national security enterprise. It will be argued, that is, that the matter is too important and too contested to be subject to any greater control than is already the case, and perhaps that some of the developments aimed at promoting democratic accountability must be unravelled – de facto if not de jure.

This instinct should be resisted, for a number of reasons. One is that the technocratic vision of national security that has predominated in recent decades, with terrorism front and centre, was always an illusion. National security is not self-defining but always represents a contingent political understanding of what are the interests of the state, and what threatens those interests, at a particular point in time. We see this in the evolving legal frameworks applicable to the various Commonwealth Five Eyes SIAs, which have been altered, sometimes subtly but sometimes substantially, over time to reflect a changing understanding of these issues. The emergence and spread of a concept of economic well-being within the legal regimes governing those SIAs, canvassed in chapter 3, is perhaps the most striking illustration of this phenomenon, bringing as it potentially does within the remits of those SIAs a vast range of activities that were previously excluded from them, but it is by no means the only one. Understanding the concept of national security, and its transposition into law, as inevitably contingent confirms that it must be subject to as many as possible of the same processes of political contestation as would be expected of other areas of policy. The second reason for resisting any attempt to push back the democratic accountability of the SIAs in the renewed era of heightened attention to state threats is the lessons of the first such era. That is, during the Cold War, the SIAs of the various Commonwealth Five Eyes states appear to have lapsed at points into political partiality, treating legitimate political activity (usually on the left) as a threat to national security (usually in the form of subversion) and so as a legitimate target of their attention and interventions. It might be feared – and indeed reasonably feared – that the renewed attention to state threats, in particular in the modern, somewhat amorphous form of what is now usually described as 'foreign interference', will result in a similar outcome, notwithstanding the various statutory inclusions aimed at preventing it. And yet it is not open to the SIAs to simply decline to take seriously the threat of such interference, even if it requires them to investigate those involved within the democratic order. To so decline would be to justify immediately the decision of hostile states to engage in such conduct, and would involve respecting democracy in only the most formal of fashions – standing back and watching the democratic process be hollowed out for fear of being accused of acting in an anti-democratic fashion. The only way, it would seem, of squaring the circle – of reconciling the fact that the democratic system might itself be the mechanism by which a threat to national security is made manifest, and the reasonable fear that the SIAs will in responding to that threat come to use their capacities in a politically partial fashion – would seem to be to double-down on democratic accountability: to have the SIAs know that they must, if necessary, be willing to justify their approach, and their actions, to institutions that are part of that same democratic order. To put the point another way: the SIAs cannot, and should not be expected to, save a society from the consequence of its own decisions.

VII. Conclusion

The Commonwealth Five Eyes states have always had particularly close connections in the domain of national security. Despite a range of remaining differences, many of which are a function of historical happenstance, and despite the fact that there is a clearer and more deliberate divergence in specific areas, we can now identify a model of Commonwealth national security constitutionalism that is common to the four states under consideration. The key point of evidence for the existence of such a model is the very open borrowing that now takes place in this domain: the fact that any attempt to resolve a particular problem in one jurisdiction will be informed by efforts to resolve the same problem in other jurisdictions, leading to similarities that take us beyond even what the common functional logic of the matter, unfolding in the context of shared constitutional fundamentals, might compel. Though not an entirely closed ecosystem, the Commonwealth Five Eyes states are a distinct and discrete one. Amongst the many points that might be made about this model, two are of particular significance for current purposes. One is that the emergence and development of the model is self-reinforcing. As a result of the constitutionalisation of national security in the Commonwealth Five Eyes states, there is now a level of standing national security review that facilitates and accelerates that borrowing and sharing. It is straightforward now, in a way in which it historically was not, for those looking in at a state from elsewhere to identify the legal frameworks applicable to national security and to access high-quality and informed discussion not only of those frameworks in the abstract but also of their operation: the benefits and drawbacks of doing things in one way or another. It is, in that context, hardly surprising that evolutions are taken up more quickly and more fluidly elsewhere than was once the case. And not only is borrowing and sharing facilitated by this state of affairs; it is also often strongly incentivised. Any state that diverges too far from the norm of the Commonwealth Five Eyes states, and in particular any state that falls behind in terms of safeguards and mechanisms of accountability, is likely to be criticised, from within and without, for doing so. Where, conversely, there emerges a new pattern, encompassing multiple of these states, in relation to some practice or process, the most straightforward way for the others to avoid criticism will be to fall in line. The easy availability of comparative material creates an evolutionary and homogenising force, resistance to which will incur ever-increasing political costs.

The other major implication is that it is now accepted that there must be a level of democratic accountability for the work of the SIAs that would once have been unthinkable. All of the states now possess a parliamentary or quasi-parliamentary body tasked with reconciling this imperative with the continued requirement of secrecy for certain matters. The Commonwealth model of national security constitutionalism, however, and in particular its accommodation – most obviously via these institutions, but not solely – of democratic scrutiny, is in many ways the product of a post-Cold War era. The primary threat to national security for most of this era has been terrorism, with that which has an international dimension most politically prominent and the subject of a vast range of legislative interventions in each of the Commonwealth Five Eyes states. The result, I have suggested, has been a (historically anomalous) consensus on the nature and seriousness of the threat, over which there was little political dispute and for which there was effectively no sympathy within the democratic process. Debate was instead about how to respond: what steps were to be taken, what trade-offs made and – very often – what had gone wrong, and why, in attempts to counter that threat. Though the first steps in this direction had been taken before the end of the Cold War, it seems clear that the manner and pace of the development of the model, as well as the frequent separation of the national security endeavour from party politics, owed much to the priority given to terrorism over the sorts of threat that had characterised the Cold War period. If and to the extent that this diagnosis is correct, it becomes evident that the model of Commonwealth national security constitutionalism analysed in this book is likely to come under threat in the coming years. The changing geopolitical environment means that the threat to national security posed by hostile states is likely to surpass not only in fact but also in prominence that posed by terrorism. Legislation to this effect has already been passed in a number of the states at issue and more will follow. The de facto separation of national security from democratic politics of recent decades will very likely be undercut by this trend: what counts as a threat to national security will be contested, while the democratic process itself will be a target of hostile actors and so, in turn, will become the subject of attention from those tasked with protecting national security. It will be tempting in this context to seek to regress back into Cold War norms; to reduce the level of democratic accountability for the state's national security endeavour. That temptation should be resisted.

BIBLIOGRAPHY

Academic Works

Ackerman, B, 'The Rise of World Constitutionalism' (1997) 83 *Virginia Law Review* 771.

Aldrich, RJ, *GCHQ: The Uncensored Story of Britain's Most Secret Intelligence Agency* (Harper Collins, 2011).

Alford, R, 'Bill C-59 and the Former Bill C-22: Compromised Oversight and Continuing Threats to Non-Derogable Rights' (2018) 69 *University of New Brunswick Law Journal* 57.

Andrew, C, *The Defence of the Realm: The Authorized History of MI5* (Allen Lane, 2009).

Barber, NW, *The Principles of Constitutionalism* (Oxford University Press, 2018).

Battersby, J and Ball, R, 'The Phantom Eye: New Zealand and the Five Eyes' (2023) 38 *Intelligence and National Security* 920.

Bignami, F, 'Methodologies of Comparative Constitutional Law: Functional Approach' in R Grote, F Lachenmann and R Wolfrum (eds), *Max Planck Encyclopedia of Comparative Constitutional Law* (Oxford University Press, 2021).

Blackstone, W, *Commentaries on the Laws of England*, vol 1 [1765].

Blaxland, J, *The Protest Years: The Official History of ASIO, 1963–1975* (Allen & Unwin, 2015).

——, *The Secret Cold War: The Official History of ASIO, 1976–1989* (Allen & Unwin, 2016).

Blaxland, J and Birgin, C, *Revealing Secrets: An unofficial history of Australian Signals intelligence & the advent of cyber* (NewSouth Publishing, 2023).

Bochel, H, Defty, A and Kirkpatrick, J, *Watching the Watchers: Parliament and the Intelligence Services* (Palgrave Macmillan, 2014).

Bolto, R, 'Accountability and secrecy in the Australian Intelligence Community: the Parliamentary Joint Committee on Intelligence and Security' (2019) 85 *International Review of Administrative Sciences* 137.

Cain, F, *The Australian Security Intelligence Organization: An Unofficial History* (Frank Cass, 1994).

——, 'Australian Intelligence Organisations and the Law: A Brief History' (2004) 27 *UNSW Law Journal* 296.

Cameron, I, 'Telephone Tapping and the Interception of Communications Act 1985' (1986) 37 *Northern Ireland Legal Quarterly* 126.

Carne, G, 'Guiding Light or Opaque Filter?: The Minister's Guidelines for the Australian Security Intelligence Organisation in Performing its Functions and Exercising its Powers as Relevant to Security' (2022) 43 *Adelaide Law Review* 814.

Carnell, I and Bryan, N, 'Watching the Watchers: How the Inspector-General of Intelligence and Security Helps Safeguard the Rule of Law' (2006) 57 *Admin Review* 34.

Capone, F, Paulussen, C and Mignot-Mahdavi, R (eds), *Returning Foreign Fighters: Responses, Legal Challenges and Ways Forward* (Springer, 2023).

Catterall, P, 'How Imperial was the Committee of Imperial Defence?' (Political Studies Association, 1998).

Clément, D, 'The Royal Commission on Espionage and the Spy Trials of 1946–9: A Case Study in Parliamentary Supremacy' (2000) 11 *Journal of the Canadian Historical Association* 151.

Clode, CM, *The Military Forces of the Crown: Their Administration and Government*, vol 1 (John Murray, 1869).

Cochrane, T, 'Digital Privacy Rights and CLOUD Act Agreements' (2021) 47 *Brooklyn International Law Journal* 1.

Craig, R and Phillipson, G, 'Protecting National Security by Breaking the Law? Prerogative, Statute and the Powers of MI5' (2022) 85 *Modern Law Review* 1274.

Crowder, G, 'The Security Intelligence Service Amendment Act 1977 and the State Power to Intercept Communications' (1978) 9 *Victoria University Wellington Law Review* 145.

Dalla-Pozza, D, 'The Parliamentary Joint Committee on Intelligence and Security: A Point of Increasing Influence in Australian Counter-Terrorism Law Reform?' in R Levy et al (eds), *New Directions for Law in Australia: Essays in Contemporary Law Reform* (ANU Press, 2017) 397.

Daly, P, 'Introduction' in P Daly (ed), *Apex Courts and the Common Law* (University of Toronto Press, 2019) 1.

Dann, P, Riegner, M and Bönnemann, M, 'The Southern Turn in Comparative Constitutional Law' in P Dann, M Riegner and M Bönnemann (eds), *The Global South and Comparative Constitutional Law* (Oxford University Press, 2020) 1.

Darvall, AWLeP and Emmerson, DMcL, 'Eavesdropping: Four Legal Aspects' (1962) 3 *Melbourne University Law Review* 364.

Defty, A, 'Coming in from the cold: bringing the Intelligence and Security Committee into Parliament' (2019) 34 *Intelligence and National Security* 22.

——, 'From committees of parliamentarians to parliamentary committees: comparing intelligence oversight reform in Australia, Canada, New Zealand and the UK' (2020) 35 *Intelligence and National Security* 367.

——, '"Familiar but not intimate": executive oversight of the UK intelligence and security agencies' (2022) 37 *Intelligence and National Security* 57.

de Londras, F, *The Practice and Problems of Transnational Counter-Terrorism* (Cambridge University Press, 2022).

Devanny, J, 'The government has mishandled the appointment of the ISC' *King's College London* (17 July 2020).

Dicey, AV, *Introduction to the Study of the Law of the Constitution*, 8th edn [1885] (Liberty Fund, 1982).

Dixon, R, Ginsburg, T and Kassie Abebe, A (eds), *Comparative Constitutional Law in Africa* (Edward Elgar, 2022).

Dyzenahus, D and Poole, T, 'The Old Commonwealth Model of Constitutionalism' (2023) 1 *Comparative Constitutional Studies* 197.

Edwards, JLlJ, 'The Canadian Security Intelligence Act 1984 – a Canadian appraisal' (1985) 5 *Oxford Journal of Legal Studies* 143.

Edwards, P, *Law, Politics and Intelligence: A life of Robert Hope* (NewSouth Publishing, 2020).

Eisler, J, 'Constitutional Formalities, Power Realities, and Comparative Anglophone Responses to Foreign Campaign Meddling' (2021) 20 *Election Law Journal* 32.

Erdos, D, 'Aversive constitutionalism in the Westminster world: The genesis of the New Zealand Bill of Rights Act (1990)' (2007) 5 *International Journal of Constitutional Law* 343.

Ewing, K, Mahoney, J and Moretta, A, *MI5, the Cold War, and the Rule of Law* (Oxford University Press, 2020).

Fenwick, H, 'The Anti-Terrorism, Crime and Security Act 2001: A Proportionate Response to 11 September?' (2002) 65 *Modern Law Review* 724.

Ferris, J, *Behind the Enigma: The Authorised History of GCHQ, Britain's Secret Cyber-Intelligence Agency* (Bloomsbury, 2020).

Fletcher, C and Coles, A, 'Reflections on the 10th anniversary of the Parliamentary Joint Committee on Human Rights' *Senate Lecture Series* (August 2022).

Forcese, C, 'Touching Torture with a Ten-Foot Pole: The Legality of Canada's Approach to National Security Information Sharing with Human Rights-Abusing States' (2014) 52 *Osgoode Hall Law Journal* 263.

Forcese, C and Roach, K, *False Security: The Radicalization of Canadian Anti-Terrorism* (Irwin Law, 2015).

Forcese, C and West, L, *National Security Law*, 2nd edn (Irwin Law Inc, 2020).

Fowler, DB, 'The Canadian Bill of Rights – A Compromise between Parliamentary and Judicial Supremacy' (1973) 21 *American Journal of Comparative Law* 712.

Galligan, B and Brenton, S (eds), *Constitutional Conventions in Westminster Systems: Controversies, Changes and Challenges* (Cambridge University Press, 2015).

Gardbaum, S, *The New Commonwealth Model of Constitutionalism* (Cambridge University Press, 2013).

Gill, P, 'Symbolic or real? The impact of the Canadian security intelligence review committee, 1984–88' (1989) 4 *Intelligence and National Security* 550.

——, 'Twenty years on: Intelligence and Security Committee and investigating torture in the "war on terror"' (2023) 38 *Intelligence and National Security* 799.

Gillespie, A, 'The Security Intelligence Agencies in New Zealand: evolution, challenges and progress' (2021) 36 *Intelligence and National Security* 676.

Ginsburg, T, Huq, AZ and Versteeg, M, 'The Coming Demise of Liberal Constitutionalism?' (2018) 85 *University of Chicago Law Review* 239.

Goldsworthy, J, 'Is Parliament Sovereign?: Recent Challenges to the Doctrine of Parliamentary Sovereignty' (2005) 3 *New Zealand Journal of Public and International Law* 7.

Goss, R, 'What do Australians Talk About When They Talk About "Parliamentary Sovereignty"?' [2022] *Public Law* 55.

Goodman, MS, *The Official History of the Joint Intelligence Committee*, Volume I: *From the Approach of the Second World War to the Suez Crisis* (Routledge, 2015).

Hall, HD, 'The genesis of the Balfour declaration of 1926' (1962) 1 *Journal of Commonwealth & Comparative Politics* 169.

Hall, WP, *Empire to Commonwealth: Thirty Years of British Imperial History* (Jonathan Cape, 1929).

Hancock, BR, 'The New Zealand Security Intelligence Service' (1973) 2 *Auckland University Law Review* 1.

Hardy, K and Williams, G, 'Special Intelligence Operations and Freedom of the Press' (2016) 41 *Alternative Law Journal* 160.

Hardy, K and Williams, G, 'Executive Oversight of Intelligence Agencies in Australia' in ZK Goldman and SJ Rascoff (eds), *Global Intelligence Oversight: Governing Security in the Twenty-First Century* (Oxford University Press, 2016) 315.

Haynes, JE and Klehr, H, *Venona: Decoding Soviet Espionage in America* (Yale University Press, 1999).

Hickman, T, 'Revisiting Entick v Carrington: Seditious Libel and State Security Laws in Eighteenth-Century England' in A Tomkins and P Scott (eds), *Entick v Carrington: 250 Years of the Rule of Law* (Hart Publishing, 2015) 43.

Hirschl, R, 'The Question of Case Selection in Comparative Constitutional Law' (2005) 53 *American Journal of Comparative Law* 125.

——, 'From comparative constitutional law to comparative constitutional studies' (2013) 11 *International Journal of Constitutional Law* 1.

——, *Comparative Matters: The Renaissance of Comparative Constitutional Law* (Oxford University Press, 2014).

Hogg, P and Bushell, A, 'The Charter Dialogue Between Courts and Legislatures (Or Perhaps the Charter of Rights Isn't Such a Bad Thing After All)' (1997) 35 *Osgoode Hall Law Journal* 75.

Horner, D, *The Spy Catchers: The Official History of ASIO, 1949–1963* (Allen & Unwin (2014).

Hume, D and Williams, G, 'Who's Listening? Intercepting the telephone calls, emails and SMS's of innocent people' (2006) 31 *Alternative Law Journal* 211.

Hunt, M and Duffy, P, 'Goodbye *Entick v Carrington*: The Security Service Act 1996' [1997] *European Human Rights Law Review* 11.

Hutton, M et al, *Erskine May: Parliamentary Practice*, 25th edn (LexisNexis Butterworths, 2019).

Jackson, VC, 'Methodological Challenges in Comparative Constitutional Law' (2010) 28 *Penn State International Law Review* 319.

——, 'Comparative Constitutional Law: Methodologies' in M Rosenfeld and A Sajó (eds), *The Oxford Handbook of Comparative Constitutional Law* (Oxford University Press, 2012) 54.

Jeffrey, K, *MI6: The history of the Secret Intelligence Service, 1909–1949* (Bloomsbury, 2010).

Jenkins, D, 'The handling and disclosure of sensitive intelligence: Closed material procedures and constitutional change in the "Five Eyes" nations' in G Lennon and C Walker (eds), *Routledge Handbook of Law and Terrorism* (Routledge, 2015) 266.

——, 'The First Interception Provision: Section 4 of the Official Secrets Act 1920' (2022) 43 *Journal of Legal History* 352.
——, 'Authorising Crime: The Covert Human Intelligence Sources (Criminal Conduct) Act 2021' (2022) 85 *Modern Law Review* 1218.
——, '"Economic Well-Being" in National Security Law and Practice' (2022) 33 *King's Law Journal* 358.
——, 'Judicial Biography in the National Security Constitution: Lord Diplock and a "Rather Silly Little Secret Racket"' (2024) 87 *Modern Law Review* 624.
——, '"State threats", security, and democracy: the National Security Act 2023' (2024) 44 *Legal Studies* 260.
Sigalet, G, Webber, G and Dixon, R (eds), *Constitutional Dialogue: Rights, Democracy, Institutions* (Cambridge University Press, 2019).
Stevenson, R, 'Reed, Sir Geoffrey Sandford (1892–1970)' *Australian Dictionary of Biography*, vol 16 (Melbourne University Press, 2002).
Stuart, D, *Creating the National Security State: A History of the Law That Transformed America* (Princeton University Press, 2008).
Swinfen, DB, *Imperial Control of Colonial Legislation, 1813–65: A Study of British Policy Towards Colonial Legislative Powers* (Oxford University Press, 1970).
Toohey, B and Pinwill, W, *Oyster: The Story of the Australian Secret Intelligence Service* (Heinemann, 1989).
Tushnet, M, 'Some Reflections on Method in Comparative Constitutional Law' in S Choudhry (ed), *The Migration of Constitutional Ideas* (Cambridge University Press, 2006) 67.
——, 'Saying and Doing in Comparative Constitutional Studies' (2016) 64 *American Journal of Comparative Law* 201.
——, *The New Fourth Branch: Institutions for Protecting Constitutional Democracy* (Cambridge University Press, 2021).
Twomey, A, 'Responsible Government and the Divisibility of the Crown' [2008] *Public Law* 742.
——, *The Veiled Sceptre: Reserve Powers of Heads of State in Westminster Systems* (Cambridge University Press, 2018).
Tyrrel, H, *Human Rights in the UK and the Influence of Foreign Jurisprudence* (Hart Publishing, 2018).
Uitz, R, 'Barber's Pursuit of Positive Constitutionalism in The Principles of Constitutionalism: Towards Exposing Illiberal Constitutional Chicanery' (2021) 24 *Jerusalem Review of Legal Studies* 66.
Vedaschi, A and Lane Scheppele, K (eds), *9/11 and the Rise of Global Anti-Terrorism Law: How the UN Security Council Rules the World* (Cambridge University Press, 2021).
Vibert, F, *The Rise of the Unelected: Democracy and the New Separation of Powers* (Cambridge University Press, 2007).
Vile, MJC, *Constitutionalism & the Separation of Powers*, 2nd edn (Liberty Fund, 1998).
Wade, HWR, 'The Basis of Legal Sovereignty' (1955) 13 *Cambridge Law Journal* 172.
Wadham, J 'The Intelligence Services Act 1994' (1994) 57 *Modern Law Review* 916.
Walker-Munro, B, 'The Richardson Review: Reviving the "Purpose" of Law Enforcement and Intelligence Legislation' (2023) 46 *University of New South Wales Law Journal* 268.
Wallace, W and Phillips, C, 'Reassessing the special relationship' (2009) 85 *International Affairs* 263.
Walsh, PF and Miller, S, 'Rethinking "Five Eyes" Security Intelligence Collection Policies and Practice Post Snowden' (2016) 31 *Intelligence and National Security* 345.
Waluchow, W and Kyritsis, D, 'Constitutionalism' *Stanford Encyclopaedia of Philosophy* (18 May 2023).
Ward, R and Jones, R with Stone, C (eds), *National Security Law, Procedure, and Practice* (Oxford University Press, 2021).
Weller, GR, 'Comparing Western inspectors general of intelligence and security' (1996) 9 *International Journal of Intelligence and Counter Intelligence* 383.
——, 'Change and Development in the New Zealand Security and Intelligence Services' (2001) 21 *Journal of Conflict Studies* 1.
West, L, 'Review and Oversight of National Security in Canada' in S Carvin, T Juneau and C Forcese (eds), *Top Secret Canada: Understanding the Canadian Intelligence and National Security Community* (University of Toronto Press, 2020) 257.

——, 'The perilous prerogative: An argument for legislating defence intelligence in Canada' (2022) 65 *Canadian Public Administration* 585.

——, '"Within or outside Canada": The Charter's application to the extraterritorial activities of the Canadian Security Intelligence Service' (2023) 73 *University of Toronto Law Journal* 1.

West, L and Forcese, C, 'Building Haystacks: Information Retention and Data Exploitation by the Canadian Security Intelligence Service' (2019) 57 *Alberta Law Review* 175.

Whitaker, R and Marcuse, G, *Cold War Canada: The Making of a National Insecurity State, 1945–1957* (University of Toronto Press, 1996).

Wood, FLW, *The New Zealand People at War: Political and External Affairs* (New Zealand Department of Internal Affairs, 1958).

Young, AL, *Democratic Dialogue and the Constitution* (Oxford University Press, 2017).

Zellick, G, 'Spies, Sub Spies, Subversives, Terrorists and the British Government: Free Speech and Other Casualties' (1989–90) 31 *William and Mary Law Review* 773.

Official Publications

Australia

Attorney-General's Department, *Equipping Australia Against Emerging and Evolving Threats: A Discussion Paper to accompany consideration by the Parliamentary Joint Committee on Intelligence and Security of a package of national security ideas comprising proposals for telecommunications interception reform, telecommunications sector security reform and Australian intelligence community legislation reform* (2012).

——, *Report of the Comprehensive Review of the Legal Framework of the National Intelligence Community*, Volume 1: *Recommendations and Executive Summary; Foundations and Principles; Control, Coordination and Cooperation* (2019).

——, *Report of the Comprehensive Review of the Legal Framework of the National Intelligence Community*, Volume 2: *Authorisations, Immunities and Electronic Surveillance* (2019).

——, *Report of the Comprehensive Review of the Legal Framework of the National Intelligence Community*, Volume 3: *Information, Technology, Powers and Oversight* (2019).

——, *Report of the Comprehensive Review of the Legal Framework of the National Intelligence Community*, Volume 4: *Accountability and Transparency; Annexes* (2019).

——, *Annual Report on the Operation of the Foreign Influence Transparency Scheme 1 July 2022 to 30 June 2023* (2023).

Commission of Inquiry into the Australian Secret Intelligence Service, *Report on the Australian Secret Intelligence Service - Public Edition* (1995).

Department of Home Affairs, *Reform of Australia's Electronic Surveillance Framework: Discussion Paper* (2021).

Flood, P, *Report of the Inquiry into the Australian Intelligence Agencies* (2004).

Independent National Security Legislation Monitor, *Report on the impact on journalists of section 35P of the ASIO Act* (2015).

——, *Trust but Verify: A report concerning the Telecommunications and Other Legislation Amendment (Assistance and Access) Act 2018 and related matters* (2020).

Inspector-General of Intelligence and Security, *Inquiry into the actions of Australian government agencies in relation to the arrest and detention overseas of Mr Mamdouh Habib from 2001 to 2005* (2011).

——, *2016–2017 Annual Report* (2017).

——, *2018–2019 Annual Report* (2019).

——, *2020–2021 Annual Report* (2021).

——, *Annual Report 2022–2023* (2023).

Joint Select Committee on the Intelligence Services, *An advisory report on the Intelligence Services Bill 2001, the Intelligence Services (Consequential Provisions) Bill 2001 and certain parts of Cybercrime Bill 2001* (2001).
L'Estrange, M and Merchant, S, *2017 Independent Intelligence Review* (Commonwealth of Australia, 2017).
Parliament of Australia, House of Representatives, *Intelligence Services Bill 2001 – Explanatory Memorandum* (2001).
Parliamentary Joint Committee on Intelligence and Security, *Report of the Inquiry into Potential Reforms of Australia's National Security Legislation* (2013).
——, *Advisory Report on the National Security Legislation Amendment (Espionage and Foreign Interference) Bill 2017* (2018).
——, *Inquiry into the impact of the exercise of law enforcement and intelligence powers on the freedom of the press* (2020).
——, *Advisory Report on the Foreign Intelligence Legislation Amendment Bill 2021* (2021).
——, *Review of the amendments made by the Telecommunications and Other Legislation Amendment (Assistance and Access) Act 2018* (2021).
——, *Inquiry into national security risks affecting the Australian higher education and research sector* (2022).
——, *Review of the Counter-Terrorism (Temporary Exclusion Orders) Act 2019* (2023).
——, *Review of the Foreign Influence Transparency Scheme Act 2018* (2024).
Royal Commission on Espionage, *Report* (1955).
Royal Commission on Intelligence and Security, *First Report*, Parliamentary Paper No 246/1977 (1977).
——, *Second Report*, Parliamentary Paper No 247/1977 (1977).
——, *Third Report: Abridged Findings and Recommendations*, Parliamentary Paper No. 92/1977 (1977).
——, *Fourth Report – Volume I*, Parliamentary Paper No 248/1977 (1977).
——, *Fourth Report – Volume II*, Parliamentary Paper No 249/1977 (1977).
Royal Commission on Australia's Security Intelligence Agencies, *Report on Term of Reference*, Parliamentary Paper No 323/1983 (1983).
——, *Report on the Sheraton Hotel Incident* (February 1984), Parliamentary Paper No 1/1984 (1984).
——, *General Report*, Parliamentary Paper No 231/1985 (1985).
——, *Report on the Australian Security Intelligence Organization*, Parliamentary Paper No 232/1985 (1985).
Senate Legal and Constitutional Legislation Committee, *Inquiry into the Provisions of the Telecommunications (Interception) Legislation Amendment Bill 1999* (2000).

Canada

Canadian Security Intelligence Service, *China and the Age of Strategic Rivalry: Highlights from an Academic Outreach Workshop*, World Watch: Expert Notes (2018).
——, *Avoiding Complicity in Mistreatment by Foreign Entities Act: Annual Report to the Minister of Public Safety* (2022).
——, *Avoiding Complicity in Mistreatment by Foreign Entities Act – Annual Report to the Minister of Public Safety* (2023).
Commission of Inquiry Concerning Certain Activities of the Royal Canadian Mounted Police, *First Report: Security and Information* (October 1979).
——, *Second Report: Volume 1 – Freedom and Security under the Law* (1981).
——, *Second Report: Volume 2 – Freedom and Security under the Law* (1981).
——, *Third Report: Certain RCMP Activities and the Question of Governmental Knowledge* (1981).
Communications Security Establishment, 'Our Story' (nd).
Communications Security Establishment Commissioner, *2018–19 Departmental Results Report* (2019).
Franks, CES, *Parliament and Security Matters* (Canadian Government Publishing Centre, 1980).
Government of Canada, *Our Security, Our Rights: National Security Green Paper*, 2016 (2016).

——, *National Security Consultations What We Learned Report* (2017).
Independent Special Rapporteur on Foreign Interference, *First Report* (23 May 2023).
Interim Committee of Parliamentarians on National Security, *Report* (May 2004–October 2004).
Ministry of the Solicitor General, *On Course: National Security for the 1990s* (1991).
National Security and Intelligence Committee of Parliamentarians, *Special Report on the Prime Minister's Trip to India in February 2018* (2018).
——, *Annual Report 2018* (2019).
——, *Annual Report 2019* (2020).
——, *Special Report on the Collection, Use, Retention and Dissemination of Information on Canadians in the context of the Department of National Defence and the Canadian Armed Forces Defence Intelligence Activities* (2020).
——, *Annual Report 2021* (2022).
——, *Special Report on the Government of Canada's Framework and Activities to Defend its Systems and Networks from Cyber Attack* (2022).
——, *Special Report on the National Security and Intelligence Activities of Global Affairs Canada* (2022).
——, *2022 Annual Report* (2023).
——, *Special Report on the Federal Policing Mandate of the Royal Canadian Mounted Police* (2023).
National Security and Intelligence Review Agency, *Review of Departmental Frameworks for Avoiding Complicity in Mistreatment by Foreign Entities* (2019).
——, *2019 Annual Report* (2020).
——, *2022 Annual Report* (2023).
——, *Review of Departmental Implementation of the Avoiding Complicity in Mistreatment by Foreign Entities Act for 2020* (2023).
——, *Review of the CSE ministerial authorizations and ministerial orders under the CSE Act* (NSIRA Review 08-501-5) (2023).
——, *Review of Government of Canada Institutions' Disclosures of Information Under the Security of Canada Information Disclosure Act in 2022* (2023).
——, *NSIRA Review of CSIS Dataset Regime* (2024).
——, *Review of the dissemination of intelligence on People's Republic of China political foreign interference, 2018–2023* (2024).
Office of the Intelligence Commissioner, *Annual Report 2022* (2023).
——, *2023 Annual Report of the Intelligence Commissioner* (2024).
Public Safety Canada, *Enhancing Foreign Influence Transparency: Exploring Measures to Strengthen Canada's Approach – Public and Stakeholder Consultation Paper* (10 March 2023).
——, *What We Heard Report: Consulting Canadians on the Merits of a Foreign Influence Transparency Registry* (2023).
——, *Enhancing measures to counter foreign interference: Whether to amend the Canadian Security Intelligence Service Act – Public consultation paper* (24 November 2023).
Rosenberg M, *Report on the assessment of the 2021 Critical Election Incident Public Protocol* (2023).
Royal Commission on Security, *Report of the Royal Commission on Security (Abridged)* (1969).
Security Intelligence Review Committee, *Annual Report 1984–85* (1985).
——, *Review of CSIS's use of Data Management and Exploitation Activities*, SIRC Review 2015-02 (2015).
——, *Annual Report 2015–2016: Maintaining Momentum* (2016).
——, *Building for Tomorrow: The Future of Security Intelligence Accountability in Canada – Annual Report 2017–2018* (2018).
Special Committee of the Senate on the Canadian Security Intelligence Service, *Delicate Balance: A Security intelligence Service in a Democratic Society* (1983).
Special Committee on the Review of the CSIS Act and the Security Offences Act, *In Flux But Not in Crisis* (1990).
Taschereau, R and Kellock, RL, *The Report of the Royal Commission Appointed under Order in Council P.C. 411 of February 5, 1946 to Investigate the Facts Relating to and the Circumstances Surrounding the Communication, by Public Officials and Other Persons in Positions of Trust of Secret and Confidential Information to Agents of a Foreign Power* (1946).

New Zealand

Arnold, T and Mahuika, M, *Taumaru: Protecting Aotearoa New Zealand as a Free, Open and Democratic Society, Review of the Intelligence and Security Act 2017* (Ministry of Justice, 2023).

Committee on the Intelligence and Security Agencies Bill, *Intelligence and Security Agencies Bill* (1996).

Cullen, M and Reddy, P, *Intelligence and Security in a Free Society: Report of the First Independent Review of Intelligence and Security in New Zealand* (2016).

Department of the Prime Minister and Cabinet, *Securing our nation's safety: How New Zealand manages its security and intelligence agencies* (2000).

Inspector-General of Intelligence and Security, *Annual Report 1997/98* (1998).

——, *Report on Inquiry into National Control of SIGINT Collection and Reporting by the Government Communications and Security Bureau* (1999).

——, *Report into the release of information by the New Zealand Security Intelligence Service in July and August 2011* (2014).

——, *Lawfulness of NZSIS access to data under the Customs and Excise Act 1996 and the Immigration Act 2009* (2017).

——, *Warrants issued under the Intelligence and Security Act 2017* (2018).

——, *Annual Report for the year 1 July 2018 to 30 June 2019* (2019).

——, *Inquiry into possible New Zealand intelligence and security agencies' engagement with the CIA detention and interrogation programme 2001–2009* (2019).

——, *Warrants issued under the Intelligence and Security Act 2017–2019 update* (2019).

——, *International relations: the Inspector-General's process under s 188 ISA for finalising a public inquiry report* (2020).

——, *Review of an NZSIS Warning – Public Report* (2022).

——, *Annual Report 2022–2023* (2023).

——, *Review of NZSIS Use and Sharing of Vetting Information – Public Report* (2023).

——, *Review of NZSIS counter-terrorism and violent-extremism class warrants – Public Report* (2024).

——, *Inquiry into GCSB's hosting of a foreign capability* (2024).

Intelligence and Security Committee, *Activities of the Intelligence and Security Committee in 2022* (2023).

——, *2021/22 Annual review of the New Zealand Security Intelligence Service* (2023).

Kitteridge, R, *Review of Compliance at the Government Communications Security Bureau* (2013).

New Zealand Government, *Secure Together: New Zealand's National Security Strategy 2023–2028* (2023).

New Zealand Security Intelligence Service, *Annual Report 2022* (2022).

——, *New Zealand's Security Threat Environment 2023: An assessment by the New Zealand Security Intelligence Service* (2023).

Powles, G, *Security Intelligence Service: Report by Chief Ombudsman* (1976).

United Kingdom

Anderson, D, *Report of the Bulk Powers Review* (Cm 9326, 2016).

——, *Independent Review of the Investigatory Powers Act 2016* (2023).

Committee of Privy Councillors appointed to inquire into the interception of Communications, *Report* (Cmnd 283, 1956–57).

HM Government, *Imperial Conference, 1926 – Summary of Proceedings* (Cmd 2768, 1926).

——, *Accountability of the Security Service* (Cm 2197, 1993).

——, *The Principles relating to the detention and interviewing of detainees overseas and the passing and receipt of intelligence relating to detainees* (2019).

—— *Global Britain in a Competitive Age: The Integrated Review of Security, Defence, Development and Foreign Policy* (CP 403, 2021).

Home Office, *Investigatory Powers Bill: Government Response to Pre-Legislative Scrutiny* (Cm 9219, 2016).
——, *Legislation to Counter State Threats (Hostile State Activity)* Government Consultation (2021).
——, *Interception of Communications Code of Practice Pursuant to Schedule 7 to the Investigatory Powers Act 2016* (2022).
Home Secretary, *Interception of Communications in the United Kingdom: A Consultation Paper* (Cm 4368, 1999).
House of Commons Home Affairs Committee, *Accountability of the Security Service* (HC 1992–93, 265).
House of Lords Constitution Committee, *Covert Human Intelligence Sources (Criminal Conduct) Bill* (HL 2019–21, 174).
Intelligence and Security Committee, *Annual Report 1996* (Cm 3574, 1997).
——, *Rendition* (Cm 7171, 2007).
——, *Review of the Intelligence on the London Terrorist Attacks on 7 July 2005* (Cm 7617, 2009).
——, *Annual Report 2010–2011* (Cm 8114, 2011).
——, *Annual Report 2011–2012* (Cm 8403, 2012).
——, *Annual Report 2013–2014* (HC 2014–15, 794).
——, *Women in the UK Intelligence Community* (HC 2014–15, 970).
——, *Privacy and Security: A modern and transparent legal framework* (HC 2014–15, 1075).
——, *UK Lethal Drone Strikes in Syria* (HC 2016–17, 1152).
——, *Detainee Mistreatment and Rendition: 2001–2010* (HC 2017–19, 1113).
——, *Detainee Mistreatment and Rendition: Current Issues* (HC 2017–19, 1114).
——, *Diversity and Inclusion in the UK Intelligence Community* (HC 2017–19, 1297).
——, *Russia* (HC 2019–21, 632).
——, *Extreme Right-Wing Terrorism* (HC 2021–22, 459).
——, *Annual Report 2021–2022* (HC 2022–23, 922).
——, *China* (HC 2022–23, 1605).
——, *Annual Report 2022–2023* (HC 2023–24, 287).
——, *International Partnerships* (HC 2023–24, 288).
Intelligence Services Commissioner, *Report of the Intelligence Services Commissioner for 2014* (HC 2014–15, 225).
Interception of Communications Commissioner, *Report of the Commissioner for 1998* (Cm 4364, 1999).
——, *IOCCO inquiry into the use of Chapter 2 of Part 1 of the Regulation of Investigatory Powers Act (RIPA) to identify journalistic sources* (2015).
Investigatory Powers Commissioner, *Annual Report for 2019* (HC 2019–21, 1039).
——, *Annual Report of the Investigatory Powers Commissioner 2020* (HC 2020–21, 897).
——, *Annual Report of the Investigatory Powers Commissioner 2021* (HC 2022–23, 910).
——, *Annual Report of the Investigatory Powers Commissioner 2022* (HC 2023–24, 364).
Joint Committee on Human Rights, *Legislative Scrutiny: Covert Human Intelligence Sources (Criminal Conduct) Bill: Government Response to the Committee's Tenth Report of Session 2019–21* (HC 2019–21, 1127).
Law Commission, *Protection of Official Data: A Consultation Paper* (Law Com No 230, 2017).
——, *Protection of Official Data: Report* (Law Com No 395, 2020).
Lord Denning, *Lord Denning's Report* (Cmnd 2152, 1963).
Lord Diplock, *The Interception of Communications in Great Britain* (Cmnd 8191, 1981).
Secretary of State for Justice and Lord Chancellor, *The Governance of Britain* (Cm 7170 2007).
Secretary of State for Justice, *Justice and Security Green Paper* (Cm 8194, 2011).

United States

Senate Select Committee on Intelligence Committee, *Report of the Senate Select Committee on Intelligence Committee Study of the Central Intelligence Agency's Detention and Interrogation Program together with Foreword by Chairman Feinstein and Additional and Minority Views*, Senate Report 113–288 (2014).

INDEX

www.ingramcontent.com/pod-product-compliance
Ingram Content Group UK Ltd.
Pitfield, Milton Keynes, MK11 3LW, UK
UKHW020857250525
458758UK00005B/91